Lecture Notes in Computer Science   6462

Commenced Publication in 1973
Founding and Former Series Editors:
Gerhard Goos, Juris Hartmanis, and Jan van Leeuwen

Alejandro Buchmann

Preface

> *"I think there is something wrong with your arithmetic ...*
> *Alex and I are about the same age,*
> *and he and I cannot be getting close to 60."*

Hector Garcia-Molina

Data management has evolved over the years from being strictly associated with database systems, through active databases, to being a topic that has grown beyond the scope of a single field encompassing multiple aspects: distributed systems, event-driven systems, and peer-to-peer and streaming systems. The present collection of works, shedding light on various facets of data management, is dedicated to Prof. Alejandro Buchmann on the occasion of his 60th birthday. His scientific path looks back on more than 30 years of successful academic life and high impact research. With this book we celebrate Prof. Buchmann's vision and achievements.

The works presented here cover many different topics: database systems, event-based systems, distributed systems, peer-to-peer systems, etc. All these are areas in which Prof. Buchmann and his group were active and provided relevant research contributions over the years.

The area of *data management, streams and XML* spans contributions from Theo Härder et al. on XML processing and key concepts implemented in XTC; from M. Tamer Özsu et al. on mining streaming data; from Thomas Kudraß on active database systems; and from Frischbier and Petrov on data intensive cloud applications.

The field of *event processing* is covered through contributions from many leading researchers such as K. Mani Chandy on extending the boundaries of sense-and-respond applications to the Web and the Cloud; from Jean Bacon, Ken Moody et al. on spatio-temporal composite event languages; from Opher Etzion et al. on spatial perspectives in event processing; and from Gero Mühl et al. offering insights on underlying design principles implemented in REBECA.

The fields of *quality of service* and *real-time systems* are represented by contributions from Krithi Ramamritham et al. on safety partition kernel for integrated real-time systems; from Annika Hinze et al. on anonymous mobile service collaboration; and from Dimka Karastoyanova on scientific experiments and services.

The area of *peer-to-peer* concepts and systems contains contributions from Gerhard Weikum offering an overview and in-depth insights on peer-to-peer web search; from Max Lehn et al. on benchmarking peer-to-peer systems; and from Christof Leng et al. on building an SQL query processor for peer-to-peer networks.

The field of *pervasive computing* is covered by interesting contributions from Friedemann Mattern et al. on Internet of Things and RFID; from Bettina Kemme at al. around group communication for mobile devices through SMSs; and from Daniel Jacobi et al. on an approach to declaratively constraining the nodes participating in a sensor network query.

Another active research area of Prof. Buchmann is *performance engineering*, which is represented by a paper introducing the novel QPME 2.0 tool by Samuel Kounev et al. and a workload characterization for event notification middleware from Stefan Appel et al.

We are grateful to all those world-class researchers, colleagues and friends who, with their works, joined us in honoring a truly remarkable figure: as a visionary and a distinguished personality, as a professor and a leading faculty member, as an academic peer and fellow researcher, as supervisor and mentor— Alex Buchmann.

September 2010   Kai Sachs
                                                       Ilia Petrov
                                                    Pablo Guerrero

Joint Celebration of the 60th Birthday of Alejandro P. Buchmann, Sorin A. Huss, and Christoph Walther on November 19th, 2010

Honourable Colleague,
Dear Alex,

Let me first send my congratulations to you as well as to Sorin Huss and Christoph Walther. You jointly celebrate your 60th birthdays this year. I wish you all the best for your future work at TU Darmstadt!

Alex, we have survived many battles and wars in the overlap time of our periods of service in the department's headquarters. In the former period, I was your Deputy Studies, in the latter period, you were one of my Deputies General. I remember well our meetings in your office (yours is more comfortable than mine), where we frequently debated the most urgent challenges of the day. These meetings always took much more time than planned (if they were planned at all). And each time, I left your office a bit smarter than before, and more confident that we would eventually cope with all of the trouble. And we did.

A few months ago, you retired; no, not from your position as professor, but from that treadmill they call "Dekanat". So you made more time for research. By the way, research: your breadth and wealth of research interests, which you pursue together with your research group, are impressing. So is your social network in science and beyond.

You three guys are true institutions of the department (I am tempted to speak of dinosaurs, however, in an absolutely positive sense). You have seen colleagues come and go. Due to your experience and your long time of service in the department, you have become critical nodes of the department's corporate memory network. Your experience has been decisive during many discussions, typically (yet not exclusively) for the better.

I should mention that each of you three guys is equipped with a specific kind of spirit. Your humorous comments, always to the point, made many meetings amongst colleagues really enjoyable for the audience (well, the meeting chair did not always enjoy them, but that's fine). You have always combined passion with reason, spirit with analysis, vision with rationality.

On behalf of the colleagues, the department, and TU Darmstadt, I hope that you three guys continue to have a great time together with all of us and an even longer chain of success stories than ever. Happy Birthday!

September 2010   Karsten Weihe
                                    Dean of the Department of Computer Science,
                                                                TU Darmstadt

Laudation for Alejandro Buchmann

I was delighted to be asked to write a laudation for my colleague Alejandro Buchmann. Not because we are well acquainted or have worked together closely, neither is the case, regrettably, but because he is, for me, a perfect example of a scientist coming from abroad and becoming successfully integrated here without losing his own cultural identity, and in the process enriching our culture and making a lasting contribution to scientific and academic life in this country.

Alejandro Buchmann began his academic career in his native country Mexico, studying not computer science, in those days that was not yet possible in Mexico, but chemistry! He worked briefly as a chemist for Hoechst, but then decided to continue his studies, obtaining his Master of Science degree from the University of Texas in Austin.

But, like other engineers, he soon became fascinated with our blossoming computer science discipline. After successfully completing his doctorate in Austin, Texas, he worked mainly in the field of computer science, which is where his major accomplishments lie. And for TU Darmstadt it was definitely a happy development when he accepted the offer of a C4 professorship there in 1991.

I do not wish, at this point, to go into his numerous academic and scientific achievements and the many honours accorded him. His university colleagues and partners can do a much better job of that. Instead, I would like to draw attention to the way he has used his international network of contacts and his innate capacity for enthusiasm to build and consolidate close ties and cooperation with his home country and other countries across Latin America. We all know that building international ties and cooperation requires a great deal of commitment, and in particular a proper appreciation of the many and sometimes considerable differences between countries in terms of education and training. And who has been able to make better use of such knowledge and understanding for the countries of Latin America than Alejandro Buchmann?

To my regret, I have personally only once had the opportunity to witness him "in action" here: committed, emotional, eminently competent and highly professional! In this role Alejandro Buchmann has become an ambassador for German computer science, and for his achievements in this capacity the German computer science community and its representative body, the Gesellschaft für Informatik (GI), is greatly indebted to him.

Of course, Alejandro Buchmann's work within Germany's computer science community is not confined to this role of "ambassador". As a scientist, he enjoys great national and international renown and respect. This is clearly evidenced by his many activities as the editor, author and reviewer of numerous books and other publications. And despite all of these duties, he has twice been the Dean of the Computer Science Department at TU Darmstadt, a position to which he brought his wonted commitment and competence.

Congratulations on an impressive life's work and my very best birthday wishes!

September 2010   Stefan Jähnichen
                              President of the Gesellschaft für Informatik (GI)

Table of Contents

Key Concepts for Native XML Processing

Theo Härder[1] and Christian Mathis[2]

[1] University of Kaiserslautern, Germany
haerder@cs.uni-kl.de
[2] SAP Germany
christian.mathis@sap.com

Abstract. Over the recent five years, we have designed, implemented, and optimized our prototype system XTC, a native XDBMS providing multi-user read/write transactions and supporting multi-lingual query interfaces (XQuery, XPath, DOM, SAX). We have compared competing concepts in various system layers and iteratively found salient solutions which drastically improved the overall XDBMS performance. XML query processing is critically affected by the smooth interplay of concepts and methods. Here, we focus on the physical level of XML processing: node labeling and mapping options for storage structures; design of suitable index mechanisms; enriched functionality of path processing operators, in particular, for holistic twig joins. In this survey, we outline our experiences gained during the evolution of XTC. We develop "key concepts" to enable fine-grained, effective, and efficient XML processing[1].

1 Motivation

In recent years, XML's standardization and, in particular, its flexibility (e. g., data mapping, cardinality variations, optional or non-existing structures, etc.) evolved as driving factors to attract demanding write/read applications, to enable heterogeneous data stores, and to facilitate data integration. Because business models in practically every industry use large and evolving sets of sparsely populated attributes, XML is more and more adopted by those companies which have even now launched consortia to develop XML schemas adjusted to their particular data modeling needs. As an example, world-leading financial companies defined more than a dozen XML schemata and vocabularies to standardize data processing and to leverage cooperation and data exchange [Projects 08]. For these reasons, XML databases gain increasingly more momentum if data flexibility in various forms is a key requirement of the application and they are, therefore, frequently used in collaborative or even competitive environments [Loeser 09].

Native XDBMSs need tailored XML processing to run complex XQuery read-/write transactions on large XML documents in multi-user mode. For this reason,

---

[1] This work has been partially supported by the German Research Foundation (DFG) and the Rheinland-Pfalz cluster of excellence "Center of Mathematical and Computational Modelling", Germany (see www.cmcm.de).

K. Sachs, I. Petrov, and P. Guerrero (Eds.): Buchmann Festschrift, LNCS 6462, pp. 1–19, 2010.

storage and indexing of dynamic XML documents in flexible formats has to be optimized to best satisfy the needs of specific applications.

Adequate storage and index mechanisms are prerequisites for XDBMSs, which efficiently support not only fine-grained management, but also concurrent and transaction-safe modifications of XML documents. A challenging application is *financial application logging* whose workloads include 10M to 20M inserts in a 24-hour day, with about 500 peak inserts/sec. Because at least a hundred users concurrently run XQuery requests, i. e., *index-based random reads*, to supply data for troubleshooting and auditing tasks, concurrency control has to make sure that short-enough response times do not hinder interactive operations [Projects 08].

During the last five years, we have addressed – by designing, implementing, analyzing, optimizing, and adjusting an XDBMS prototype system called XTC (XML Transactional Coordinator) – all issues indispensable for a full-fledged DBMS. To guarantee broad acceptance for our research, we strive for a *general solution* that is even applicable for a spectrum of XML language models (e. g., XPath, XQuery, SAX, or DOM) in a multi-lingual XDBMS environment. In this survey paper, we report on our experiences gained and, in particular, focus on concepts, functionalities, and mechanisms needed for physical XML processing.

2   Node Labeling

The node labeling scheme is *the key* to fine-grained, effective, and efficient management of XML documents. Initial XML research only focused on navigation and retrieval in static documents where limited functionality of node labels is sufficient. As XML processing has entered the realm of full-fledged, widely-used database products, flexible handling of dynamic XML documents and their fine-grained manipulation in multi-user ACID transactions are indispensable. Hence, labeling must satisfy quite a number of specific criteria.

2.1   Desired Functionality

In the first place, a labeling scheme has to guarantee *uniqueness* and *order preservation* of node labels. Moreover, if two node labels are given, the scheme should directly enable *testing of all (important) XPath axes*: all axes relationships should be determined by computation only, i. e., access to the document (on external storage) is not needed. Dynamic XML documents definitely require *immutable labels* even under heavy updates/insertions to guarantee stable node labels during transaction processing. Furthermore, a given document node label should enable the reconstruction of *all ancestor labels* without accessing the document. Immutability and ancestor label computation have far-reaching consequences to the DBMS-internal processing efficiency: these properties greatly support for a context node *cn* intention locking on the entire path to the root [Haustein 07] and path matching for query processing, e. g., in case of twig queries.

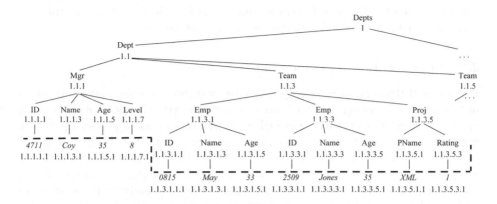

Fig. 1. Document fragment (in the path-oriented storage format, only nodes below the dashed line are physically stored: see Section 3.4)

2.2 DBMS-Adequate Labeling Schemes

Initially, node labeling schemes were not designed to support immutable labels under arbitrary updates or path-matching operations. Therefore, simple and straightforward schemes were proposed such as sequential numbering of nodes. In the sequel, various range-based node labeling schemes were considered the prime candidates for XDBMSs, because their labels directly enabled *testing of all (important) XPath axes*. The advent of prefix-based node labels, however, initiated a *new area* of label design and use [O'Neil 04]. This progress can directly be accredited to the so-called DeweyIDs which facilitate and optimize various XML processing tasks. Each label based on *Dewey Decimal Classification*, e. g., 1.1.3.5.1.1 identifies the value XML for element PName (see Figure 1), directly represents the path from the document's root to the related node and the local order w. r. t. the parent node. Because a DeweyID contains the labels of all ancestor nodes, all DeweyIDs along the path to the document root are delivered for free and are immutable under document updates [Härder 07a]. Some specific variations of the Dewey numbering scheme such as OrdPaths, DeweyIDs, or Dynamic Level Numbering (DLN) are equivalent for all XDBMS tasks and mainly differ only in the way how they provide immutable labels by supporting an overflow technique for dynamically inserted nodes. For these reasons, we also use the generic name *stable path labeling identifiers* (SPLIDs) for them.

While range-based schemes would need for some tasks (such as ancestor label determination or path matching) further index access or similar deviation, i. e., overly expensive look-ups in the disk-based document, only prefix-based node labeling can support all desired labeling properties *without the need of document access* (see Section 2.1). Until today, the missing support of dynamic XML documents is ignored by quite a number of researchers – based on range-based schemes, they still develop solutions which do not meet the state of the art of XML processing anymore. As a strong hint of superiority, the Dewey scheme is nowadays used in all major DBMS products and it definitely embodies the core concept to achieve processing performance [Härder 10].

2.3   Implementation of Node Labels

Because SPLIDs tend to be space-consuming, suitable encoding and compression of them in DB pages is a *must*. Effective encoding of (the divisions of) DeweyIDs at the bit level may be accomplished using Huffman codes [Härder 07a]. It is important that the resulting codes preserve their order when compared at the byte level. Otherwise, each comparison, e. g., as keys in B*-trees or entries in reference lists, requires cumbersome and inefficient decoding and inspection of the bit sequences. Because such comparisons occur extremely frequent, schemes such as *Quaternary String* codes [Li 08] violating this principle may encounter severe performance problems.

When SPLIDs are stored in document sequence, they lend themselves to prefix-compression and achieve impressive compression ratios. Our experiments using a widely known XML document collection [Miklau 09] confirmed that prefix-compression reduced the space consumed for dense and non-dense DeweyIDs orders down to ∼15 – ∼35% and ∼25 – ∼40%, respectively [Härder 07a].

On the other hand, SPLIDs' variable length and prefix compression applied cause some performance problems. Because binary search is not possible on variable-length SPLIDs inside a database page, each node reference implied a search from the beginning of the (B*-tree) page which required on average to reconstruct half of the SPLIDs contained. Although a main-memory operation, performance suffered in case of frequent accesses, e. g., when the query result had to be materialized. Caching of pages with uncompressed SPLIDs relieved such situations. Another performance penalty was decoding of SPLIDs for specific SPLID operations. Therefore, we currently look for solutions enabling direct processing of the most important/frequent operations on the encoded byte representations.

3   Storing Documents

The flexibility of XML gives to the application quite some freedom when modeling or creating XML documents. As a result, existing XML documents are greatly varying in volume and exhibit very different structural complexities. Over time, different XML document processing (XDP) interfaces have been standardized: DOM, SAX, XQuery, and XQuery Update Facility. All of them assume a different model of how XML documents are processed: DOM navigates over individual document nodes, SAX scans over the stored document, XQuery is declarative and internally operates over *sequences* using DOM- and SAX-like operations, and finally XQuery Update modifies the document under a kind of *snapshot semantics*. To serve all these standard interfaces efficiently, an XDBMS first of all needs an appropriate document organization on external storage.

3.1   Desiderata

Because XDBMSs are generic, they should provide adequate performance and functionality for all shapes and volumes of XML documents and for all kinds of XDP models. As a guideline for the design of XML document stores, we have derived a list of eight properties. As the name "desiderata" implies, we do not consider this list normative but, nevertheless, suggest that it is meaningful for many XML applications:

1. *Efficient storage and reconstruction.* Because XML is a format for data interchange, XDBMSs frequently need to receive and emit XML data. Therefore, the document store has to provide fast storage and reconstruction facilities.
2. *Navigational operations.* They are required not only to implement the DOM interface, but also to provide low-level operators for XQuery processing.
3. *Scan and subtree reconstruction.* A SAX parse is typically implemented by a document scan. But also for XQuery evaluation, scans are very important, e. g., for subtree reconstruction during result materialization.
4. *Modifications.* Applications need to update XML data stored in an XDBMS. Therefore, the document store should provide means to modify single nodes, content, and subtrees.
5. *Round-trip property.* The round-trip property guarantees that a document can be reconstructed from the document store without any loss. This is in particular of importance for document-centric XML, for example, when legal contracts need to be stored.
6. *Document and collection support.* Documents might come in single instances of large documents or in large collections of small documents. No matter how, the document store should be able to efficiently manage the XML data.
7. *Succinctness.* A space-efficient document store not only saves external storage cost, but also leads to reduced I/O and logging and, therefore, better XDP performance.
8. *Indexing support.* For query processing, secondary path indexes are of particular importance, because documents and collections often are too large to completely load them into main memory for processing. Therefore, the document store should provide mechanisms that allow for cheap path index construction and maintenance.

3.2   Classification of Approaches

Figure 2 gives a comprehensive overview of the methods and approaches used so far to design XML stores. Obviously, all proposals based on *Shredding* or *BLOB/File* do hardly meet a substantial subset of the desiderata given. Therefore, we exclusively concentrate on the *native approaches*.

Depending on the granule of XML items mapped onto a page, *subtree mappings* can be distinguished from *node mappings*. The first strategy partitions an XML tree into regions or subtrees, which are then mapped to physical pages – thus preserving subtree clusters. In contrast, the second strategy uses individual

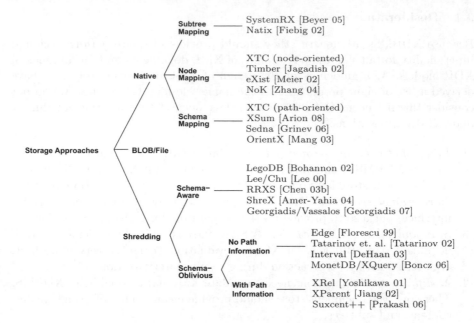

Fig. 2. Classification of related work on XML storage

nodes as the mapping granule, where several nodes in document order are allocated to a page. Hence, node mappings keep clusters w. r. t.document order, but
do not preserve subtree clusters. As indicated in Figure 2, a third solution class
exploits the ad-hoc structure or the schema of a document for the XML store.

Little is known about the performance of subtree mappings. We expect that
navigational operations are efficiently supported, because subtree clustering
makes sure that related nodes are often placed in the same page, thus minimizing I/O. However, we such methods are not aware of document paths, thus
complicating index construction and maintenance. Furthermore, document storage and reconstruction seems to be more complex than in the other approaches,
because pages need to be visited/buffered multiple times [Mathis 09]. Finally,
structure virtualization, which we identified as the best solution (see Section 3.4),
would not be possible.

Node mappings and particular schema mappings satisfy the list of desiderata
to a large extent. For example, the required indexing functionality can be greatly
supported by using the expressive power of SPLIDs together with a path summary. Therefore, we will sketch our XTC implementations as reference solutions
in the following sections.

3.3   Node-Oriented Document Store

Node-oriented methods store each document node explicitly together with its
node label, i. e., its SPLID. Typically, they replace the element/attribute names
of the *plain* (external) format by *VocIDs* to save space and need some *Admin*

metadata to enable variable-length entries. Inner tree nodes, i. e., the "structure", are stored as records containing $< SPLID, VocID, Admin >$, whereas leaf nodes carry the "content" in $< SPLID, Value, Admin >$ records.

In XTC, two kinds of node-oriented mappings are provided. They keep both content and structure: Using the *naive* format, the VocIDs of all element/attribute and content nodes are directly mapped together with their uncompressed SPLIDs to the underlying storage structure (see Figure 1), whereas the *pc* format deviates from the *naive* mapping by applying prefix-compression to all SPLIDs.

All documents are physically represented using a B*-tree as base structure, where the records (tree nodes) are consecutively stored in the *document container* thereby preserving the document order. The *document index* is used to provide direct access via SPLIDs.

As compared to the *plain* format, *naive* as the straightforward internal format typically achieves a storage gain of ~10% to ~30%, although the saving from VocID usage is partially compensated by the need for node labels. Extensive empirical (structure-only) tests using our reference document collection [Miklau 09] identified a further gain of ~27% to ~43% when using *pc* format.

3.4   Path-Oriented Document Store

The structure part of XML documents typically contains huge degrees of redundancy, because each path instance is completely stored in the document. A key observation is that all path instances of the same path class have the same sequence of element/attribute names along the path to the root. Only the node labels among path instances of a path class differ. If we represent the different path classes in a small auxiliary, document-related structure, we can reconstruct the entire path instance starting from some of its nodes.

Using a novel mapping approach, we are able to design the path-oriented storage format called *po* which virtualizes the entire structure part of the document. The reconstruction of a path instance or the entire structure part is achieved by the interplay of three ingredients: SPLIDs, *path synopsis* (PS), and *path class references* (PCRs). A path synopsis is an *unordered* structural summary of all (sub) paths of the document. Each non-content node belongs to a path class which represents all path instances having the same sequence of ancestor labels. To facilitate the use of path classes, we enumerate them with so-called PCRs that serve as a simple and effective path class encoding. PCRs are used as a kind of links from index or document entries to the path class they belong to (see Figure 3).

Because a path synopsis does not need order, maintenance in case of document evolution (creation of new path classes) or shrinking (deleting the last path instance of an existing path class in a document) is very simple. New path classes and related PCRs can be added anywhere and existing, but empty path classes do not jeopardize correctness of path synopsis use. Furthermore, hash-based access to the PCRs guarantees its efficient evaluation. Because providing substantial mapping flexibility, effective lock management support, and also considerable speed-up of query evaluation [Härder 07b], the use of path synopses turned out to be a *key concept* for XTC's processing efficiency.

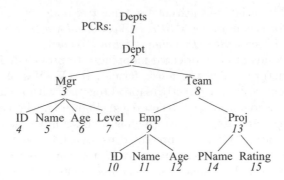

Fig. 3. Path synopsis for our sample document fragment of Figure 1

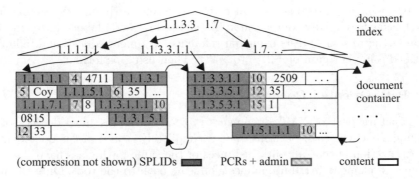

Fig. 4. Stored document fragment of Figure 1 in *po* format

Only the "content part" is physically stored when the *po* format is used (see Figure 1). Reference [Mathis 09] explains the concept of *structure virtualization*, i. e., the *po* mapping, in detail and shows that path reconstruction can be achieved on demand when the SPLID of a node together with its PCR is present. For this reason, leaf records are composed of $< SPLID, Value, PCR, Admin >$ where the SPLIDs are prefix-compressed. All navigational and set-oriented operations can be executed guaranteeing the same semantics as on the node-oriented formats, e. g., *naive* or *pc*. As an example, Figure 4 illustrates the *po* format for the document fragment of Figure 1, where the document index guides a SPLID-based access to the requested node. It further shows that only the content nodes are stored; using the path synopsis, entry $< 1.1.3.1.5.1, 12, 33 >$ stored in the document container tells us that the related path to the value 33 is **/Depts/Dept/Team/Emp/Age** with the ancestor SPLIDs 1, 1.1, 1.1.3, 1.1.3.1, and 1.1.3.1.5.

The *po* format saves considerable storage space and, in turn, I/O. It provides a *naive*-to-*po* gain of ~71% to ~83% [Härder 07b]. Because it also exhibits better mapping and reconstruction times, the *po* format is a substantial performance driver.

Content compression is orthogonal to the storage formats discussed. We have observed [Härder 07b] that, using simple character-based compression schemes, the content size could be considerably reduced in our rather data-centric document collection such that a storage gain of ~22% to ~42% is possible. Even more compression gain could be expected for document-centric XML content.

XTC is designed towards self-tuning and self-administration. By inspecting specific document characteristics, XTC's storage management provides for automatic selection of appropriate mapping formats and adjusted parameters [Schmidt 08].

4   Indexing XML Documents

As in the relational world, secondary indexes are considered non-information-bearing structures. They are used to (substantially) speed up the evaluation of XQuery/XPath statements which need random read requests to locate sets of document nodes on external storage. On the other hand, index maintenance may considerably burden XQuery updates. For this reason, indexing has to be selective and adjusted to the anticipated workload – a permanent tuning task to be taken over in the long run by the XDBMS itself [Schmidt 10].

Because *path and tree patterns* correspond to the XML data model and can accordingly be specified in XQuery/XPath expressions, matching such patterns

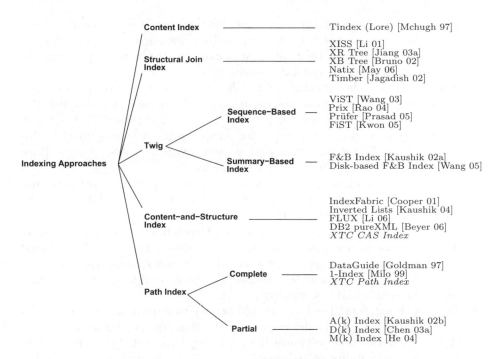

Fig. 5. Classification of related work on XML indexing

in XML documents is a frequently occurring task during query evaluation. Because these pattern may be complex and their optimal evaluation may depend on quite a number of parameters, e. g., XPath axes specified, element selectivities present, shape of the document tree, clustering aspects, etc., the spectrum and the richness of the different proposals concerning XML indexing can be hardly overlooked. Besides the simple *element/attribute indexes*, a variety of *content (value* and *text) indexes, path indexes, adaptive path indexes, content-and-structure indexes* together with those directly tailored to important path processing operations (PPOs), e. g., *twig* or *structural join* evaluation, are studied in the literature (see Figure 5).

Despite this obvious richness of proposals, the problem of XML indexing remains unsolved, because many of the contributions referenced in Figure 5 lack a "system context". They only consider the pure or abstract problem of static XML indexing, but do not deal with dynamic XML aspects or the interplay with other components such as PPO evaluation or concurrency control. For this reason, we try here to emphasize these forgotten issues and, based on our implementation experience, to take a global, system-centric view on XML indexing. The following list of desiderata serves to decide on meaningful index methods.

4.1 Desiderata

An XML indexing scheme should provide for the following six characteristics:

1. *Optional Use*: As in relational systems, indexes should be secondary access paths that are optional (i. e., not required for document storage). This ensures that indexes can be created on demand to trade query performance with maintenance cost and space consumption.
2. *Expressiveness*: The indexing scheme should be able to answer path queries supporting the child (/) and descendant (//) axes, name tests, wildcards (*), as well as one optional content predicate, e. g., `//Emp[Age="33"]`. Queries without content predicates are called *simple paths*, whereas queries with a content predicate, are called *content-and-structure* (CAS) *queries*. Both types frequently occur in XQuery expressions.
3. *Selectivity*: The selectivity of an index, i. e., which paths are actually contained in an index, should be user-defined. Thereby, a set of indexes can be adjusted to document characteristics and query workload.
4. *Updates*: The index should be updateable. Depending on the index selectivity, not all document updates lead to index updates. However, there should exist efficient mechanisms to discovery, when an index needs maintenance.
5. *Applicability*: The test whether an index can be applied for query evaluation should be simple and cost-efficient.
6. *Result Computation*: The index should be able to retrieve all elements on an indexed path, e. g., if an index can answer the above query `//Emp[Age="33"]`, then it should be able to return the matching *Emp* and *Age* nodes. Otherwise, the applicability of the index would be too restricted, w. r. t.further processing algorithms.

4.2   A Minimal Indexing Scheme

Figure 5 gives a comprehensive overview of the more important XML indexing approaches proposed so far. An immediate question is whether or not a (the best) method of each class should be made available in a native XDBMS? Another question concerns the variety of base implementations for the indexes.

When we approach XML indexing from a logical point of view, *element* indexes and *content* indexes are sufficient to evaluate – without scanning or navigating the document – all types of set-oriented requests coming from the PPOs needed for XQuery/XPath processing. An element/attribute index refers to structure nodes, whereas a content index enables direct document access via text values. These access paths use SPLIDs to refer to the indexed nodes, which are located via the document index (see Figure 4). Note here again the beneficial role of SPLIDs to decide on axes relationships, order, etc.

From a performance point of view, the sole existence of both index types would be disastrous, because the processing overhead for complex PPOs could be prohibitive. Furthermore, large parts of the document had to be often accessed in a random node-at-a-time manner, which penalizes performance twice, due to extensive I/Os and unnecessarily large blocking potential to guarantee serializable transactions. Therefore, indexes achieving much more selective document access are mandatory.

In XTC, we voted for minimality of concepts and uniform index implementation. As a minimal basis for physical XML processing, XTC supports two secondary index types:

- *Path index*: This structure can index paths qualified by a simple path predicate p, e. g., `//Mgr/Age` or `//Dept//Emp`. Because SPLIDs carry essential path information, they are utilized together with the path synopsis to directly support path queries. An element index could be obtained by `//*` as a special path index.
- *Content-and-Structure (CAS) index*: As a hybrid index combining content and structure information, it supports the evaluation of CAS queries, e. g., `//Mgr[Age="33"]` or `//Dept//Emp[Name="Jones"]`. Again `//*` delivers a content index as a special form of the CAS index.

All XTC index types are implemented using B-trees or B*-trees. This guarantees effective storage allocation, dynamic reorganization, and logarithmic access cost. With code reuse for the base structures, the indexes distinguish themselves only in the representation of the index keys and index entries, e. g., variable-length reference lists of $< PCR, SPLID >$ entries. Because a text value is associated with a list of $< SPLID, PCR >$ references to the related document nodes, such a combined reference enables together with the path synopsis the reconstruction of the entire path without accessing the document. As a salient performance feature, an index can be defined for *PCR clustering* or *SPLID clustering* (within potentially very long reference lists).

CAS indexes are particularly powerful, because a large share of matching queries can be evaluated solely on the index structure. Only when additional attributes/elements are needed for output, access to the disk-based document is inevitable. This is even true when CAS indexes refer to documents in *po* format, i. e. with virtualized structure part. In a *unique* CAS index, all entries have the same PCR, while in a *homogeneous collective* index, the entries may have varying PCRs, i. e., they may refer to different path classes. For the *heterogeneous collective* CAS index, the index predicate p may be generalized to $p = p_1 \vee ... \vee p_i \vee ... \vee p_n$ where the p_i are simple path predicates. A *generic* CAS index contains all values of a certain type, e. g., $p = //*$.

In [Mathis 09], XTC's indexing mechanisms are matched against the list of desiderata and their performance is evaluated in a systematic way, which confirms that "minimality" of the right concepts and careful index implementation guarantee efficient and cost-effective solutions.

5   Implementing Path Processing Operators

Path expressions occur frequently in XML queries. Special path processing operators (PPOs) for path matching are necessary at the level of any XDBMS's physical algebra. For PPO evaluation, the document itself or secondary index structures can be accessed. We distinguish *navigational*, *join-based*, and *index-based* PPOs:

- The first group of operators is also the most expressive one: every path expression in a query can be evaluated by *navigations* on the document. Compared to join-based and index-based methods, they are, due to random access patterns, often enough the group of operators with the lowest performance. Hence, navigational primitives are a "fallback solution", when specific operators of the other two groups are missing or cannot be applied to evaluate a certain path expression.
- *Join-based operators* stream through the document or over an element index and evaluate path expressions by matching structural relationships among the streamed nodes. Compared to navigational methods, they often provide for better performance. However, their use is restricted to certain XPath axes. The two most prominent representatives for this group are *structural joins* (STJ) and *holistic twig joins* (HTJ). Especially holistic twig joins have gained much attention in the literature and many variations of the original algorithm [Bruno 02] have been proposed (see Figure 6).
- The third group of operators provides access to the XML path indexes presented in the previous section. Typically, *index-scan operators* embody the fastest way to match a path. However, they have yet again a reduced expressiveness compared to join-based operators, because join-based operators can match arbitrary branching path patterns and index-based operators can only match linear paths (without branches).

For PPOs, the situation in the literature is quite similar to what we find for indexing proposals: Many proposals exist, but most of them lack a "system context". They only consider the pure or abstract algorithmic path matching

Algorithms for Holistic Twig Joins	phases	axes			connectors			predicates			output		input	
		descendant	child	optional edges	and	or	not	expressions	filters	pos. predicates	projection	grouping	document/element index	path indexes
PathStack [Bruno 02]	-	+												
PathStack¬ [Jiao 05]	-	+					+							
TwigStack [Bruno 02]	2	+			+								+	
TwigStackList [Lu 04]	2	+	+		+									
TwigStackList¬ [Yu 06]	2	+	+		+		+							
TJFast [Lu 05]	2	+	+		+									+
iTwigJoin [Chen 05]	2	+	+		+									+
TSGeneric+ [Jiang 03b]	2	+			+								+	
Twig²Stack [Chen 06]	1	+		+	+						+	+		
TwigList [Qin 07]	1	+			+						+			
TwigOpt [Fontoura 05]	1	+			+	+					+		+	
Ext. TwigOpt [Mathis 09]	1	+	+	+	+	+	+	+	+	+	+	+	+	+

Fig. 6. Twig algorithms: comparison of functionality

problem, but do not deal with the interplay with other algorithms in the physical algebra or with the requirements imposed by the XQuery language. These points are, however, crucial for efficient query processing. To emphasize these forgotten issues, we will discuss the twig matching algorithm developed for XTC as an example.

5.1   Twig Matching

A twig is a branching path expression. To illustrate the idea, let us assume the following sample query:

```
for $i in doc("departments.xml")//Team
where $i/Emp/Age < 30
return <ratings>{$i//Proj/Rating/text() * 2}</ratings>
```

For each *Team*, the query returns the project ratings multiplied by two if the team has at least one employee of age younger than 30. The structural part of this query can be represented by a twig (also known as branching path expression), with paths `//Team/Emp/Age` and `//Team//Proj/Rating/text()` branching at the `Team` node. Many algorithms have been proposed to simultaneously match these two path expressions against a document (see Figure 6). However, their applicability w. r. t. XQuery is quite restricted: matching the structure is only one half of the work. The other half consists of the evaluation of an existential comparison, an algebraic expression, an implicit group by (by *Team* nodes), projections, and the generation of new XML nodes. Embedding this functionality directly into the twig matching algorithm is performance critical, because

- predicates can be evaluated as early as possible,
- large and complex intermediate results can be avoided, and
- the number of operators in the query execution plan (QEP) can be reduced.

Another often neglected topic is the integration of secondary index structures. The query processor should be able to make use of an existing CAS index, for example on `//Team/Emp/Age`. Therefore, twig matching has to be integrated with path index scans.

5.2   Desiderata for Twig Matching Algorithms

These considerations lead to the following list of desiderata, which served as a catalog of requirements for the twig matching algorithm in XTC:

1. *Axes*: The twig matching algorithm should support the most frequently occurring *child*, *descendant*, and *attribute* axes.
2. *Logical operations*: The algorithm should allow to evaluate structural patterns with logical *and*, *or*, and *not* operations.
3. *Optional subtree patterns*: Due to structural flexibility, subtrees are optional in XML documents. Similar to outer joins in the relational algebra, the algorithm should allow to match optional subtrees. Optional subtree patterns occur frequently in XQuery expressions. An example is given in the above query: the `return` statement generates an empty *rating* node when the path `$i//Proj/Rating/text()` does not match (i. e., this path is optional).
4. *Projections*: The algorithm should allow to return only nodes required as output. Other nodes should only be generated for internal processing, if necessary. In our sample query, only *Rating* nodes are required as output. All other nodes are internal.
5. *Content predicates*: The algorithm should allow to evaluate content predicates during processing. This enables predicate push-down. In our sample query, `Age < 30` could be evaluated directly. Non-matching subtrees will not generate further processing costs.
6. *Positional predicates*: The algorithm should also allow to evaluate positional predicates directly during processing.
7. *Output expressions*: The algorithm should support output expressions, for example, the application of algebraic expressions or the generation of new XML nodes. This option avoids the materialization of complex intermediate results (on which these expressions then would have to be evaluated).

8. *Grouping*: XQuery inherently groups subtrees. In our sample query, all *Age* and *Rating* nodes are implicitly grouped by *Team*. The algorithm should allow to return grouped results (as well as the direct evaluation of aggregate functions on these groups).

9. *One-phase algorithm*: Some twig pattern algorithms first match all subpaths in the twig query (1st phase) and then merge these intermediate result paths (2nd phase). This approach prohibits pipelining (because all subpaths need to be matched first) and may generate large intermediate results. Therefore, the algorithm should match twigs in a single phase.

10. *Index-scan support*: The algorithm should be able to consume XML path and CAS indexes. Otherwise, path indexes could only be applied, when the query exactly matches the index definition (which is rarely the case). Assume a CAS index on `//Team/Emp/Age`. Then, we could directly evaluate the predicate (`Age < 30`) from our sample query on the index and – with the help of the SPLIDs and the path synopsis – reconstruct the *Team* nodes for further processing in the twig algorithm.

On the basis of the well-known TwigOpt algorithm [Fontoura 05], we developed a twig matching algorithm providing all these features exploited in QEPs generated by the XTC system [Mathis 09].

5.3   Implementing the Twig Matching Operator

The Extended TwigOpt algorithm operates on a set of input streams (one for each twig node) and a set of stacks (again, one for each node). The stacks keep the current processing state (parts of twig instances already matched). The performance of this new algorithm is based on the following three observations:

- *Input stream abstraction*: The algorithm can operate on the document and on secondary indexes by abstracting the input streams. Path and CAS indexes introduced in the previous section can – due to the salient concepts *SPLID* and *path synopsis* – reconstruct ancestor nodes on the indexed path to serve as input for twig matching nodes.
- *Skipping*: The algorithm can skip large fractions of the input streams by computing *target nodes*. Target nodes can be derived from the current state kept on the internal stacks. If the nodes of an input stream are indexed (as, for example, the nodes in the document store shown in Section 3), the streams do not have to be processed sequentially. Rather, the relevant nodes can be obtained by index look-ups.
- *Integrated expressions*: Expressions (e.g., projection, grouping, output expressions, etc.) can be evaluated during twig processing based on the current state of the stacks. No materialization of intermediate results is necessary.

Figure 6 compares the functionality of our Extended TwigOpt algorithm with other state-of-the-art approaches. We consider the operator richness provided by Extended TwigOpt as highly desirable, because the higher the expressiveness, the more QEP-relevant operations can be embedded into the twig algorithm. As a consequence, the number of operators can be minimized in a QEP for an XQuery expression.

6 Conclusions

In this survey, we identified the key concepts guiding query processing at the physical system level and outlined their implementation in XTC. We did not find these solutions top-down and in one shot. By observing performance bottlenecks or inappropriate system behavior in early experiments, we could adjust numerous algorithms in XTC. But removing a bottleneck often revealed another one at a higher performance level. Hence, we had to iteratively and repeatedly improve XTC to reach the current system version mature in many aspects. As outlined, we have identified and are still identifying during this maturing process many performance-critical concepts. So far, we have often gained orders of magnitude in component speed-ups and, as a consequence, dramatic overall performance improvements. Future research will address further enhancements in autonomic system behavior [Schmidt 08, Schmidt 10] and energy efficiency by using flash disks and implementing energy-aware algorithms in specific XDBMS components.

References

[Amer-Yahia 04] Amer-Yahia, S., Du, F., Freire, J.: A Comprehensive Solution to the XML-to-Relational Mapping Problem. In: Proc. WIDM, pp. 31–38 (2004)

[Arion 08] Arion, A., Bonifati, A., Manolescu, I., Pugliese, A.: Path Summaries and Path Partitioning in Modern XML Databases. World Wide Web 11(1), 117–151 (2008)

[Beyer 05] Beyer, K., et al.: System RX: One Part relational, One Part XML. In: Proc. SIGMOD, pp. 347–358 (2005)

[Beyer 06] Beyer, K., et al.: DB2 Goes Hybrid: Integrating Native XML and XQuery with Relational Data and SQL. IBM Systems Journal 45(2), 271–298 (2006)

[Bohannon 02] Bohannon, P., Freire, J., Roy, P., Siméon, J.: From XML Schema to Relations: A Cost-Based Approach to XML Storage. In: Proc. ICDE, pp. 64–73 (2002)

[Boncz 06] Boncz, P., Grust, T., van Keulen, M., Manegold, S., Rittinger, J., Teubner, J.: MonetDB/XQuery: A Fast XQuery Processor Powered by a Relational Engine. In: Proc. SIGMOD, pp. 479–490 (2006)

[Bruno 02] Bruno, N., Koudas, N., Srivastava, D.: Holistic Twig Joins: Optimal XML Pattern Matching. In: Proc. SIGMOD, pp. 310–321 (2002)

[Chen 03a] Chen, Q., Lim, A., Ong, K.W.: D(k)-Index: An Adaptive Structural Summary for Graph-Structured Data. In: Proc. SIGMOD, pp. 134–144 (2003)

[Chen 03b] Chen, Y., Davidson, S., Hara, C., Zheng, Y.: RRXS: Redundancy Reducing XML Storage in Relations. In: Proc. VLDB, pp. 189–200 (2003)

[Chen 05] Chen, T., Lu, J., Ling, T.W.: On Boosting Holism in XML Twig Pattern Matching Using Structural Indexing Techniques. In: Proc. SIGMOD, pp. 455–466 (2005)

[Chen 06] Chen, S., Li, H.-G., Tatemura, J., Hsiung, W.-P., Agrawal, D., Selçuk Candan, K.: Twig2Stack: Bottom-Up Processing of Generalized-Tree-Pattern Queries over XML Documents. In: Proc. VLDB, pp. 283–294 (2006)

[Cooper 01] Cooper, B., Sample, N., Franklin, M.J., Hjaltason, G.R., Shadmon, M.: A Fast Index for Semistructured Data. In: Proc. VLDB, pp. 341–350 (2001)

[DeHaan 03] DeHaan, D., Toman, D., Consens, M.P., Özsu, M.T.: A Comprehensive XQuery to SQL Translation using Dynamic Interval Encoding. In: Proc. SIGMOD, pp. 623–634 (2003)

[Fiebig 02] Fiebig, T., et al.: Anatomy of a Native XML Base Management System. VLDB Journal 11(4), 292–314 (2002)

[Florescu 99] Florescu, D., Kossmann, D.: Storing and Querying XML Data using an RDBMS. Bulletin of the Technical Committee on Data Engineering 22(3), 27–34 (1999)

[Fontoura 05] Fontoura, M., Josifovski, V., Shekita, E.J., Yang, B.: Optimizing Cursor Movement in Holistic Twig Joins. In: Proc. CIKM, pp. 784–791 (2005)

[Georgiadis 07] Georgiadis, H., Vassalos, V.: XPath on Steroids: Exploiting Relational Engines for XPath Performance. In: Proc. SIGMOD, pp. 317–328 (2007)

[Goldman 97] Goldman, R., Widom, J.: DataGuides: Enabling Query Formulation and Optimization in Semistructured Databases. In: Proc. VLDB, pp. 436–445 (1997)

[Grinev 06] Grinev, M., Fomichev, A., Kuznetsov, S.: Sedna: A Native XML DBMS. In: Wiedermann, J., Tel, G., Pokorný, J., Bieliková, M., Štuller, J. (eds.) SOFSEM 2006. LNCS, vol. 3831, pp. 272–281. Springer, Heidelberg (2006)

[Härder 07a] Härder, T., Haustein, M.P., Mathis, C., Wagner, M.: Node Labeling Schemes for Dynamic XML Documents Reconsidered. Data & Knowledge Engineering 60(1), 126–149 (2007)

[Härder 07b] Härder, T., Mathis, C., Schmidt, K.: Comparison of Complete and Elementless Native Storage of XML Documents. In: Proc. IDEAS, pp. 102–113 (2007)

[Härder 10] Härder, T., Mathis, C., Bächle, S., Schmidt, K., Weiner, A.M.: Essential Performance Drivers in Native XML DBMSs (keynote paper). In: van Leeuwen, J., Muscholl, A., Peleg, D., Pokorný, J., Rumpe, B. (eds.) SOFSEM 2010. LNCS, vol. 5901, pp. 29–46. Springer, Heidelberg (2010)

[Haustein 07] Haustein, M.P., Härder, T.: An Efficient Infrastructure for Native transactional XML Processing. Data & Knowledge Engineering 61(3), 500–523 (2007)

[He 04] He, H., Yang, J.: Multiresolution Indexing of XML for Frequent Queries. In: Proc. ICDE, pp. 683–692 (2004)

[Jagadish 02] Jagadish, H.V., et al.: TIMBER: A Native XML Database. VLDB Journal 11(4), 274–291 (2002)

[Jiang 02]   Jiang, H., Lu, H., Wang, W., Yu, J.X.: Path Materialization Revis-
                  ited: An Efficient Storage Model for XML Data. Australian Comp.
                  Science Comm. 24(2), 85–94 (2002)
[Jiang 03a]   Jiang, H., Lu, H., Wang, W., Ooi, B.C.: XR-Tree: Indexing XML
                  Data for Efficient Structural Joins. In: Proc. ICDE, 253–264 (2003)
[Jiang 03b]   Jiang, H., Wang, W., Lu, H., Yu, J.X.: Holistic Twig Joins on Indexed
                  XML Documents. In: Proc. VLDB, pp. 273–284 (2003)
[Jiao 05]   Jiao, E., Ling, T.W., Chan, C.Y.: PathStack¬: A Holistic Path Join
                  Algorithm for Path Query with Not-Predicates on XML Data. In:
                  Zhou, L.-z., Ooi, B.-C., Meng, X. (eds.) DASFAA 2005. LNCS,
                  vol. 3453, pp. 113–124. Springer, Heidelberg (2005)
[Kaushik 02a]   Kaushik, R., Bohannon, P., Naughton, J.F., Korth, H.F.: Covering
                  Indexes for Branching Path Queries. In: Proc. SIGMOD, pp. 133–144
                  (2002)
[Kaushik 02b]   Kaushik, R., Shenoy, P., Bohannon, P., Gudes, E.: Exploiting Local
                  Similarity for Indexing Paths in Graph-Structured Data. In: Proc.
                  ICDE, pp. 129–138 (2002)
[Kaushik 04]   Kaushik, R., Krishnamurthy, R., Naughton, J.F., Ramakrishnan, R.:
                  On the Integration of Structure Indexes and Inverted Lists. In: Proc.
                  SIGMOD, pp. 779–790 (2004)
[Kwon 05]   Kwon, J., Rao, P., Moon, B., Lee, S.: FiST: Scalable XML Document
                  Filtering by Sequencing Twig Patterns. In: Proc. VLDB, pp. 217–228
                  (2005)
[Lee 00]   Lee, D., Chu, W.W.: Constraints-Preserving Transformation from
                  XML Document Type Definition to Relational Schema. In: Laender,
                  A.H.F., Liddle, S.W., Storey, V.C. (eds.) ER 2000. LNCS, vol. 1920,
                  pp. 641–654. Springer, Heidelberg (2000)
[Li 01]   Li, Q., Moon, B.: Indexing and Querying XML Data for Regular Path
                  Expressions. In: Proc. VLDB, pp. 361–370 (2001)
[Li 06]   Li, H.-G., Alireza Aghili, S., Agrawal, D., El Abbadi, A.: FLUX:
                  Content and Structure Matching of XPath Queries with Range Pred-
                  icates. In: Amer-Yahia, S., Bellahsène, Z., Hunt, E., Unland, R., Yu,
                  J.X. (eds.) XSym 2006. LNCS, vol. 4156, pp. 61–76. Springer, Hei-
                  delberg (2006)
[Li 08]   Li, C., Ling, T.W., Hu, M.: Efficient Updates in Dynamic XML Data:
                  from Binary String to Quaternary String. VLDB Journal 17(3), 573–
                  601 (2008)
[Loeser 09]   Loeser, H., Nicola, M., Fitzgerald, J.: Index Challenges in Native
                  XML Database systems. In: Proc. BTW. LNI, vol. 144, pp. 508–523
                  (2009)
[Lu 04]   Lu, J., Chen, T., Ling, T.W.: Efficient Processing of XML Twig Pat-
                  terns with Parent Child Edges: a Look-Ahead Approach. In: Proc.
                  CIKM, pp. 533–542 (2004)
[Lu 05]   Lu, J., Chen, T., Ling, T.W.: TJFast: Effective Processing of XML
                  Twig Pattern Matching. In: Proc. WWW, pp. 1118–1119 (2005)
[Mang 03]   Mang, X., Wang, Y., Luo, D., Lu, S., An, J., Chen, Y., Ou, J., Jiang,
                  Y.: OrientX: A Schema-based Native XML Database System. In:
                  Proc. VDLB, pp. 1057–1060 (2003)
[Mathis 09]   Mathis, C.: Storing, Indexing, and Querying XML Documents in Na-
                  tive XML Database Management Systems. Ph. D. Thesis, Verlag Dr.
                  Hut (2009)

[May 06]   May, N., Brantner, M., Böhm 0002, A., Kanne, C.-C., Moerkotte,
                G.: Index vs. Navigation in XPath Evaluation. In: Amer-Yahia, S.,
                Bellahsène, Z., Hunt, E., Unland, R., Yu, J.X. (eds.) XSym 2006.
                LNCS, vol. 4156, pp. 16–30. Springer, Heidelberg (2006)
[Mchugh 97]   Mchugh, J., Abiteboul, S.: Lore: A Database Management System for
                Semistructured Data. In: SIGMOD Record, vol. 26, pp. 54–66 (1997)
[Meier 02]   Meier, W.: eXist: An Open Source Native XML Database. In:
                Chaudhri, A.B., Jeckle, M., Rahm, E., Unland, R. (eds.) NODe WS
                2002. LNCS, vol. 2593, pp. 169–183. Springer, Heidelberg (2003)
[Miklau 09]   Miklau, G.: XML Data Repository (Feburary 2009),
                http://www.cs.washington.edu/research/xmldatasets/
[Milo 99]   Milo, T., Suciu, D.: Index Structures for Path Expressions. In: Beeri,
                C., Bruneman, P. (eds.) ICDT 1999. LNCS, vol. 1540, pp. 277–295.
                Springer, Heidelberg (1998)
[O'Neil 04]   O'Neil, P., O'Neil, E., Pal, S., Cseri, I., Schaller, G., Westbury, N.:
                ORDPATHs: Insert-Friendly XML Node Labels. In: Proc. SIGMOD,
                pp. 903–908 (2004)
[Prakash 06]   Prakash, S., Bhowmick, S.S., Madria, S.: Efficient Recursive XML
                Query Processing Using Relational Database Systems. Data &
                Knowledge Engineering 58(3), 207–242 (2006)
[Prasad 05]   Hima Prasad, K., Sreenivasa Kumar, P.: Efficient Indexing and
                Querying of XML Data Using Modified Prüfer Sequences. In: Proc.
                CIKM, pp. 397–404 (2005)
[Projects 08]   Financial XML Projects.: XML on Wall Street (2008),
                http://lighthouse-partners.com/xml
[Qin 07]   Qin, L., Yu, J.X., Ding, B.: TwigList: Make Twig Pattern Matching
                Fast. In: Proc. DASFAA, pp. 850–862 (2007)
[Rao 04]   Rao, P., Moon, B.: PRIX: Indexing And Querying XML Using Prüfer
                Sequences. In: Proc. ICDE, pp. 288–297 (2004)
[Schmidt 08]   Schmidt, K., Härder, T.: Usage-driven Storage Structures for Native
                XML Databases. In: Proc. IDEAS, pp. 169–178 (2008)
[Schmidt 10]   Schmidt, K., Härder, T.: On the Use of Query-driven XML Auto-
                Indexing. In: Proc. SMDB Workshop, Long Beach, pp. 1–6 (2010)
[Tatarinov 02] Tatarinov, I., et al.: Storing and Querying Ordered XML Using a
                Relational Database System. In: Proc SIGMOD, pp. 204–215 (2002)
[Wang 03]   Wang, H., Park, S., Fan, W., Yu, P.S.: ViST: A Dynamic Index
                Method for Querying XML Data by Tree Structures. In: Proc. SIG-
                MOD, pp. 110–121 (2003)
[Wang 05]   Wang, W., Jiang, H., Wang, H., Lin, X., Lu, H., Li, J.: Efficient
                processing of XML Path Queries Using the Disk-Based F&B Index.
                In: Proc. VLDB, pp. 145–156 (2005)
[Yoshikawa 01] Yoshikawa, M., et al.: XRel: A Path-Based Approach to Storage
                and Retrieval of XML Documents Using Relational Databases. ACM
                Transact. on Internet Technology 1(1), 110–141 (2001)
[Yu 06]   Yu, T., Ling, T.W., Lu, J.: TwigStackList¬: A Holistic Twig Join
                Algorithm for Twig Query with Not-Predicates on XML Data. In:
                Li Lee, M., Tan, K.-L., Wuwongse, V. (eds.) DASFAA 2006. LNCS,
                vol. 3882, pp. 249–263. Springer, Heidelberg (2006)
[Zhang 04]   Zhang, N., Kacholia, V., Tamer Özsu, M.: A Succinct Physical Stor-
                age Scheme for Efficient Evaluation of Path Queries in XML. In:
                Proc. ICDE, pp. 54–63 (2004)

Efficient Decision Tree Re-alignment for Clustering Time-Changing Data Streams

Yingying Tao and M. Tamer Özsu

University of Waterloo
Waterloo, Ontario, Canada
{y3tao,tozsu}@cs.uwaterloo.ca

Abstract. Mining streaming data has been an active research area to address requirements of applications, such as financial marketing, telecommunication, network monitoring, and so on. A popular technique for mining these continuous and fast-arriving data streams is decision trees. The accuracy of decision trees can deteriorate if the distribution of values in the stream changes over time. In this paper, we propose an approach based on decision trees that can detect distribution changes and re-align the decision tree quickly to reflect the change. The technique exploits a set of synopses on the leaf nodes, which are also used to prune the decision tree. Experimental results demonstrate that the proposed approach can detect the distribution changes in real-time with high accuracy, and re-aligning a decision tree can improve its performance in clustering the subsequent data stream tuples.

1 Introduction

Traditional DBMSs are successful in many real-world applications where data are modeled as persistent relations. However, for many recent applications, data arrive in the form of streams of elements, usually with high arrival rates. Techniques for traditional database management and data mining are not suited for dealing with such rapidly changing streams and continuous queries that run on them. Examples of such applications include financial marketing, sensor networks, Internet IP monitoring, and telecommunication [20,23,22,21].

Significant research has been done in mining data streams, with the goal of extracting knowledge from different subsets of one data set and integrating these generated knowledge structures to gain a global model of the whole data set [9]. Clustering is one of the most important data/stream mining techniques. It groups together data with similar behavior. Many applications such as network intrusion detection, marketing investigation, and data analysis require data to be clustered.

2 Motivation

Use of decision trees is one of the most popular clustering techniques. Compared to other clustering techniques such as K-means [12,16], decision tree models are

K. Sachs, I. Petrov, and P. Guerrero (Eds.): Buchmann Festschrift, LNCS 6462, pp. 20–43, 2010.

robust and flexible. There are many decision tree construction algorithms that construct a decision tree using a set of data as training examples, where leaf nodes indicate clusters, and each non-leaf node (called a decision node) specifies the test to be carried out on a single-attribute value. New data can be clustered by following a path from the root to one leaf node.

Most decision tree generation algorithms make the assumption that the training data are random samples drawn from a stationary distribution. However, this assumption does not hold for many real-world data streams. Typically, fast data streams are created by continuous activities over a long period of time, usually months or years. It is natural that the underlying processes generating them can change over time and, thus, the data distribution may show important changes during this period. Examples include applications for monitoring stock prices, network bandwidth usage, foreign currency exchange rates, holiday effect on sales, and so on. This issue is referred to as *data evolution, time-changing data*, or *concept-drifting data* [1,14,17,24].

Distribution changes over data streams has great impact on a decision tree model. A decision tree built previously may not be efficient or accurate when the data evolve. Hence, techniques for detecting distribution changes in data streams and adjusting the existing decision tree to reflect these changes are required.

A naive extension is to rebuild the decision tree from scratch when a distribution change is detected. Since it may take a long time to re-collect training samples for rebuilding a decision tree, this solution is impractical. An alternative solution is to reconstruct the decision tree incrementally, so that the tree can be adaptive to the changes. Some previous approaches adjust an existing decision tree when the distribution of the stream changes by replacing the affected leaf nodes by subtrees to maintain accuracy [11,14,15]. However, this approach may lead to serious inefficiency in clustering.

Consider a simple scenario. An import-export company in the US uses a data stream management system to monitor all its transactions with Canada. The company wants to monitor its transactions and the exchange rate when each transaction is made. Hence, the decision tree should be built using currency exchange rates as the criteria for each decision node in the tree. Assume the data stream starts at a time when the exchange rate is about 1:1.6 US dollars to Canadian dollars. If the US dollar becomes weaker over time, leaf nodes in the original decision tree will be replaced by sub-trees to reflect this change. Over time, the decision tree may have a form similar to the one shown in Figure 1.

Notice the problem here: as the data stream continues, the most recent data will fall in the clusters (leaf nodes) at the lowest level, i.e., the two leaf nodes under decision node "rate >1.2". As the tree gets deeper, clustering becomes increasingly inefficient.

Based on this insight, a new decision tree-based approach is proposed for mining time-changing data streams. The approach can be summarized as follows. The decision tree is continuously monitored and a synopsis is maintained at each leaf node. This synopsis indicates the number of data elements that fall in this cluster in certain time periods. If most of the recent data fall in certain leaf

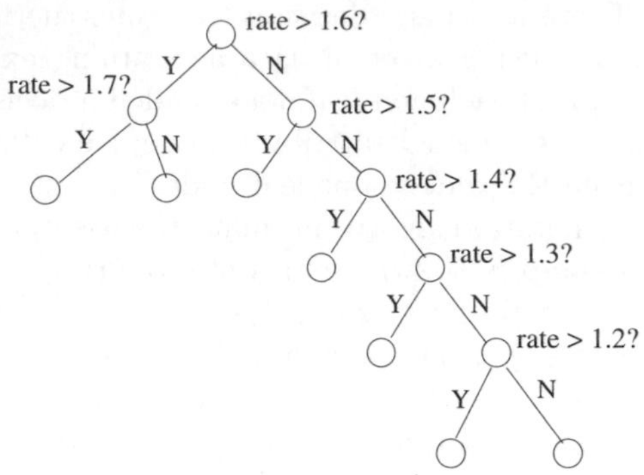

Fig. 1. Example of a decision tree based on exchange rates

nodes (clusters), while other leaf nodes are barely touched, then this could imply a distribution change. Hence, the tree is re-aligned to reflect this change.

This approach is independent of the underlying tree construction method. Re-alignment does not affect the accuracy of a decision tree, since none of the gain functions on the decision nodes is modified, while the efficiency will be increased for concept-drifting data. The overhead introduced in this technique is the time to re-align the tree, and the memory used for keeping synopsis on leaf nodes.

2.1 Summary of Contributions

The contributions of this paper are as follows:

- We propose a new method of detecting distribution changes based solely on timestamps and sliding windows; hence, the change can be detected in real-time with very little overhead.
- We propose a decision tree re-alignment technique that is independent of the underlying decision tree construction method. Our technique adds adaptivity to changes in the existing decision tree, and can considerably improve the performance of the decision tree when distribution changes.
- Our heuristics-based approach provides a novel way for tree-pruning.
- We can improve any two of the three major criteria for decision trees (accuracy, efficiency, and tree-size) with no impact on the third one.

The rest of the paper is organized as follows. In Section 3, we discuss the related work on change detection and clustering time-changing stream. Section 4 discusses our technique for detecting distribution changes in data streams. In Section 5, an algorithm for re-aligning a decision tree is proposed. Section 4 describes an approach for pruning a decision tree effectively. The experimental results are presented in Section 7. We conclude the paper in Section 8.

3   Related Work

The clustering problem can be viewed as partitioning the data into groups. The most similar data are grouped into clusters. There are different algorithms defined for clustering, among which are those that use neural networks, genetic algorithms, nearest neighbor algorithms, and so on. Clustering algorithms for stream data mining can be briefly classified into decision tree based and K-Mean approach.

K-Mean (or K-Median) problem is to find k centers in a set of n points so as to minimize the sum of distances from data points to their closest cluster centers. Charikar et al. propose a K-mean algorithm for the stream clustering problem [4]. This algorithm uses at most k clusters at all times and modifies the clustering solution using a very restricted set of operations. These operations do not allow an existing cluster to be broken up. Charikar and Panigrahy further improve this algorithm by minimizing the sum of cluster diameters [5]. The improved algorithm requires linear space and achieves a constant factor approximation but also increases the number of centers by a constant factor.

Aggarwal et al. introduce a dynamic data stream clustering algorithm using K-means [2]. The idea is to periodically store summary statistics in snapshots. By analyzing these statistics, one can have a quick understanding of current clusters. However, if data are evolving, the model has to be revised off-line by an analyst.

Most K-mean algorithms have large space requirements and involve random access to the input data. Aside from these disadvantages, K-mean approaches also suffer from the well-known problems such as the fixed number of clusters and high computational cost. Compared to K-mean approaches, decision tree-based techniques are more flexible with non-fixed number of clusters; only a small amount of data are required for building a decision tree; and the decision tree can be maintained incrementally. Therefore, decision tree-based clustering approaches are more suitable for mining time-changing data streams.

For stream mining techniques using decision trees, a common solution for detecting and handling time-changing data is to recalculate the gain/loss periodically for a newly arrived data set using the existing classifier. If this gain/loss exceeds a threshold value, it is accepted that the distribution of the data has changed and that the old model no longer fits the new data [7,10]. When a distribution change occurs, one solution is to rebuild the tree. However, rebuilding has a large overhead and for a data stream with a high arrival rate, it may not be feasible.

Domingos et al. study the problem of using decision trees over sliding windows on data streams [6]. They determine the upper bound for the learner's loss in each of the clustering steps by a function in number of data items to be examined. A decision tree-based clustering technique called Very Fast Decision Tree (VFDT) is then proposed using this upper bound determination function. VFDT is I/O bound in that it mines samples in less time than it takes to input them from disk. VFDT does not store any sample (or parts) in main memory so it only uses space proportional to the size of the tree. By seeing each sample only once, VFDT does not require samples from an online stream to be stored. However, VFDT is not sensitive to distribution changes and, hence, does not support time-changing data streams.

Hulten et al. propose the CVFDT algorithm [14] based on VFDT with the ability of detecting distribution changes and re-adjusting the decision tree model for the new distribution. CVFDT reflects the distribution changes in real-time by replacing leaf nodes that seem to be out-of-date with an alternate subtree. Gama et al. point out that CVFDT algorithm cannot deal with numerical attributes and propose an algorithm to extend it [11].

Jin and Agrawal present another approach for constructing a decision tree that can handle numerical attributes [15]. In their approach, the decision tree is also constructed by repeatedly replacing leaf nodes with subtrees. However, as has been discussed in the previous section, both the technique proposed by Jin and Agrawal and the CVFDT algorithm may lead to an inefficient tree for time-varying streams.

4   Detecting Distribution Changes

A data stream S is an unbounded sequence of elements $\langle s, t \rangle$, where s is data, and $t \in T$ is a monotonically increasing timestamp indicating the arrival time of the element. Element s can have different forms, such as a relational tuple, or a set of items, depending on the underlying application that generates S.

4.1   Synopsis Design

Let D_s be a decision tree for clustering data stream S. Let d_j $(j = 1, 2, ..., q)$ be the decision nodes in D_s, and c_i $(i = 1, 2, ..., m)$ be the leaf nodes representing different clusters. Each element in S will be clustered by D_s following a certain path constructed by a set of decision nodes and one leaf node. For each leaf node c_i in D_s, a synopsis is maintained containing the following:

- γ_i - The timestamp of the last element that falls in this node; i.e. when a new element $\langle s_k, t_k \rangle$ is placed in c_i, set $\gamma_i = t_k$.
- η_i - Total number of elements that are within this cluster represented by c_i.
- β_i - The average value of timestamps of all elements that fall in c_i. β_i represents the "time density" of c_i. We will use this value for detecting distribution changes in the data stream.

  Since data streams are unbounded, β_i must be maintained incrementally. Every time a new element $\langle s_k, t_k \rangle$ falls in c_i, β_i is updated as:

$$\beta_i' = \frac{\beta_i * \eta_i + t_k}{\eta_i'} \tag{1}$$

  where β_i' is the new time density and $\eta_i' = \eta_i + 1$ is the updated total number of elements that are in the cluster represented by c_i.

4.2   Change Detection

The algorithm for detecting distribution changes is given in Algorithm 1.

Algorithm 1. Detecting changes in data stream

1: INPUT: Data stream S
2:           Decision tree D_s
3:           Sliding window W
4: OUTPUT: Modified decision tree D'_s

5: **for all** new element $\langle s_k, t_k \rangle$ of S that will fall in leaf node c_j **do**
6:   **if** c_j is replaced by a subtree with leaf nodes c'_j and c''_j **then**
7:      //Set synopsis for c'_j and c''_j
8:      $\gamma'_i = \gamma''_i = t_k$;
9:      $\eta'_i = \eta''_i = 0$;
10:      $\beta'_i = \beta''_i = 0$;
11:      Set c'_j and c''_j to be *unmarked*;
12:   **else**
13:      // Update synopsis
14:      $\gamma_j = t_k$;
15:      $\eta_j + +$;
16:      $\beta_j = \frac{\beta_j * \eta_j + t_k}{\eta_j}$;
17:      **if** $\eta_j > MinClusterSize$ **then**
18:         // Check distribution changes
19:         $distance_j = t_k - \beta_j$;
20:         **if** $distance_j < \gamma$ **then**
21:            **if** the re-alignment mark of c_j is *unmarked* **then**
22:               //Start re-aligning
23:               Mark c_i for re-alignment;
24:               Call Algorithm 2;
25:            **end if**
26:         **else if** the re-alignment mark of c_i is *marked* **then**
27:            Reset c_i to be *unmarked*;
28:         **end if**
29:      **end if**
30:      **for all** $\langle s_i, t_i \rangle$ belongs to leaf node c_i that are moved out of W **do**
31:         //Remove historical data
32:         $\eta_i - -$;
33:         $\beta_i = \frac{\beta_i * \eta_i - t_i}{\eta_i}$;
34:      **end for**
35:   **end if**
36: **end for**

Each time a new element $\langle s_k, t_k \rangle$ falls in a leaf node c_i, the *timestamp distance* of c_i, denoted as $tDist$, is calculated as

$$tDist_i = t_k - \beta_i \qquad (2)$$

This timestamp distance is compared to a threshold value ζ. If $tDist_i < \zeta$, it means that a large portion of newly arrived elements fall in this cluster, which may imply a distribution change. Hence, this leaf node c_i is marked for re-alignment (lines 19-25 in Algorithm 1). Threshold ζ is a predefined value. The larger the ζ, the earlier a change in the stream can be detected. However, the risk for false alarms is also higher, causing more frequent re-alignment, leading to a higher overhead. Issues related to setting ζ will be discussed in Section 7.2.

For a stream that has continued over a long period, historical data can severely affect the accuracy and efficiency of the change detection technique. For example, even when most of the new elements fall in one leaf node c_i, if c_i contains a large number of historical data, its timestamp distance may still be larger than the threshold ζ. Therefore, to reduce the effect of historical data in a cluster, a time-based sliding window W is applied over the data stream S. Window W contains a substream of S that arrives within time $\langle t, t+\Delta \rangle$. Only elements that are within this sliding window are considered in the calculation of β for each leaf node. When a data element $\langle s_k, t_k \rangle$ expires from W as W moves forward, the synopsis for leaf node c_i that $\langle s_k, t_k \rangle$ belongs to is updated. The new β_i' is updated using Equation 1 (lines 30-34).

If a cluster represented by c_i contains only historical data, i.e., none of the elements it contains is within W, then this cluster will have $\eta_i = 0$ and $\beta_i = 0$. Note that, when a new element $\langle s_k, t_k \rangle$ falls in c_i, c_i's synopsis will be updated as $\gamma_i = t_k, \eta_i = 1$, and $\beta_i = t_k$. Since $tDist_i = \beta_i - t_k$ will then be 0, a distribution change will be flagged. This problem is caused by making a decision with very few samples. The problem arises when a leaf node is replaced by a subtree (as will be discussed shortly after), since new leaf nodes contain no elements yet. To solve this problem, a minimum cluster size parameter is introduced to indicate the minimum number of data elements that a cluster must contain to trigger change detection on this cluster.

Once a leaf node c_i is marked, $tDist_i$ may stay below the threshold ζ for a while. After a certain time period, there are two possibilities:

- The total number of elements that fall in c_i is very high, in which case c_i will be replaced by a subtree with one decision node and two leaf nodes c_i' and c_i'' (as in [6,11,15]). We then set $\gamma_i' = \gamma_i'' = t_k, \eta_i' = \eta_i'' = 0, \beta_i' = \beta_i'' = 0$, where t_k is the timestamp of the last element that was placed in c_i before the replacement. Re-alignment flags for c_i' and c_i'' are set to *unmarked* (lines 6-11).
- $dDist_i$ is no longer less than ζ. This may indicate that the distribution change has ended, i.e., the new distribution has stabilized. Hence, the re-alignment flags for c_i is reset to *unmarked* (lines 26-27).

4.3   Determining Windows Size

The size of W in terms of time, denoted as Δ, has great impact on the performance of our change detection technique. Larger window size indicates that more data are collected for detecting changes and, thus, implies a higher accuracy on the results. However, since more "old" data reside in a larger window, a distribution change may not be detected on-time because the historical data dominate in calculating timestamp distances. Hence, some applications, such as network monitoring, may require larger Δ, while other applications, such as time-critical real-time ones, may prefer a smaller Δ. Note that the actual values of the elements are not required to be stored within the window for detecting changes, the time interval of Δ can be very large if needed.

Let α be the minimum accuracy requirement specified by the application, and N be the average number of new samples received during Δ. Then, the clustering result should satisfy:

$$P_r(s \; clustered \; in \; c_j \mid s \; belongs \; to \; c_i) \leq c^{-(1-\alpha)N} \qquad (3)$$

Therefore, a training set can be used to determine the minimum size of Δ based on Equation 3. Similarly, a training set using the minimum efficiency requirement can help to determine the maximum window size. Note that, although these training procedures may not be efficient for an online process, once Δ is established, it usually remains unchanged during the entire lifespan of the stream, unless the accuracy and efficiency specifications are adjusted by the user.

4.4   Complexity Analysis

Algorithm 1 has complexity $O(m)$ for each new data element, where m is the total number of out-dated data elements (i.e., the elements that move out of W) when a new data element arrives. If the arrival rate of the data stream is stable, then each time a new element arrives only one data element will be removed from W. For this case, the complexity of Algorithm 1 is $O(1)$. For a data stream with an unstable arrival rate, m can be greater than 1, indicating that the arrival rate is decelerating, since there are more out-dated data than new data. Hence, although Algorithm 1 may take longer for this case, it remains practical, because when the arrival rate is lower, the clustering process does not require such high efficiency.

5   Decision Tree Re-alignment

The purpose of re-aligning a decision tree D_s is to move more frequently visited leaf nodes higher in the tree. By doing this, the overall efficiency of the clustering process is improved, since most recent elements need to follow shorter paths (i.e., pass fewer decision nodes) to be clustered. For example, for the decision tree shown in Figure 1, recall that most of the recent data elements are in clusters "rate ≤ 1.2" and "$1.2 <$ rate ≤ 1.3 ". Any element that needs to reach either of the clusters must pass five decision nodes (including root). Total number of decision nodes for reaching both leaf nodes is 10. However, if the tree is re-aligned to the form shown in Figure 2, the total number of decision nodes for reaching both of the leaf nodes is three, with one for cluster "rate ≤ 1.2" and two for cluster "$1.2 <$ rate ≤ 1.3". To reach the leaf nodes under decision node "rate > 1.7", six decision nodes need to be passed. However, since these leaf nodes are barely visited after the distribution change, the efficiency of this decision tree improves.

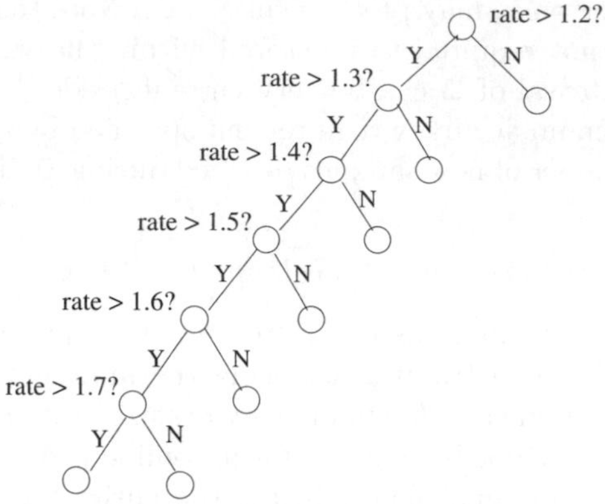

rate > 1.2?

rate > 1.3?

Y   N

rate > 1.4?

Y   N

rate > 1.5?

Y   N

rate > 1.6?

Y   N

rate > 1.7?

Y   N

Y   N

Fig. 2. Re-aligned decision tree

5.1 Assigning Weight to Clusters

The problem of re-aligning D_s can be transformed into a problem similar to the optimal weighted binary search tree construction problem. A weight can be assigned to each leaf node reflecting the number of recent elements in this node. The higher the weight, the more recent elements this leaf node contains; whereas the lower the weight, the more historical elements are within this cluster. An optimal decision tree with the highest weight can then be constructed using dynamic programming. For the applications where efficiency is the major concern, a suboptimal decision tree re-alignment technique can be applied.

Let wht_i be the weight of leaf node c_i $(i = 1, 2, ..., m)$. Initialize $wht_i = 1$. If a leaf node c_i contains only historical data, i.e., all elements within it are outside W, we reduce wht_i by half. Each time W slides through a full length (i.e., every Δ time period) while no new data element arrives in c_i, we continue to reduce its weight wht_i by half. Therefore, the smaller wht_i is, the "older" c_i is. Figure 3 gives an example of how the weight should be adjusted for an out-dated leaf node over time.

Every time c_i is changed from *unmarked* to *marked*, wht_i is incremented by 1. Therefore, whether a leaf node has received recent data can be determined by analyzing the weight attached to it. Based on different applications, a re-alignment strategy can be either eager or lazy. For an eager strategy, every time

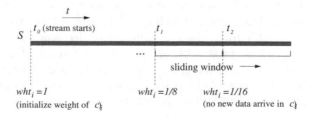

Fig. 3. Example of the weight change of one out-dated leaf node

the weight of one leaf node is increased (which indicates a distribution change), the decision tree is re-aligned. A lazy strategy calls the decision tree re-alignment procedure periodically or after a certain number of leaf nodes are changed from *unmarked* to *marked*.

Notice that wht_i only changes when c_i changes from *unmarked* to *marked*. For any leaf node c_j already *marked*, its weight will not increase every Δ time period and the re-alignment procedure will not be invoked. This is because once a distribution change starts, it may take a while until the new distribution stabilizes. Hence, it takes time for $tDist_j$ to become greater than ζ again, or until c_j is replaced by a subtree, as discussed in Section 4. It is unnecessary for re-aligning the tree before the new distribution stabilizes. If c_j is replaced by a subtree with new leaf nodes c'_j and c''_j, then its weight is reset as $wht'_j = wht''_j = wht_j$, but the re-alignment procedure is not invoked immediately.

5.2   Assigning Weight to Decision Tree

Definition 1. For two decision trees D_s and D'_s with decision nodes d_j, d'_j ($j = 1, 2, ..., q$) and leaf nodes c_i, c'_i ($i = 1, 2, ..., m$), respectively, we say D_s and D'_s are *functionally equivalent* if and only if:

- D'_s is constructed using exactly the same decision nodes and leaf nodes as D_s, i.e., $\{d_1, ..., d_q\} = \{d'_1, ..., d'_q\}$ and $\{c_1, ..., c_m\} = \{c'_1, ..., c'_m\}$, and
- if a data element $\langle s_k, t_k \rangle$ is in S and if it falls into leaf node c_i following D_s, then it will fall into the same leaf node following D'_s.

Functionally equivalent trees have the same number of decision nodes and leaf nodes, and the gain functions on decision nodes are identical. They produce exactly the same results for clustering a data stream. However, the efficiency of these functionally equivalent trees may be different. The goal for tree re-alignment is to find the most efficient tree that is functionally equivalent to the current decision tree D_s. To measure the efficiency of a decision tree, the concept of the *weight* for decision trees is introduced.

Definition 2. Let DEP be the depth of D_s and dep_i be the depth of c_i, i.e., the number of decision nodes an element needs to pass before it reaches c_i. We define the *weight* (WHT) of decision tree D_s as:

$$WHT = \sum_{i=1}^{m}(wht_i \times (DEP - dep_i + 1)) \tag{4}$$

$(DEP - dep_i + 1)$ is the level of leaf node c_i counting bottom-up. For two leaf nodes c_i and c_j with the same weight, if $dep_i < dep_j$ (i.e., c_i is at a higher level than c_j), then $(wht_i \times (DEP - dep_i + 1)) > (wht_j \times (DEP - dep_j + 1))$. Customarily, the level of a node is counted top-down. However, in this case, since the goal is to push leaf nodes with higher weight to a higher level, the level is assigned in reverse.

Given two functionally equivalent trees D_s and D'_s with weights WHT and WHT', respectively, if $WHT > WHT'$, it may imply that leaf nodes with higher weights (i.e., most frequently visited) are aligned at higher levels in D_s than in D'_s. Hence, the goal is to find an equivalent tree of D_s with the highest weight, i.e., the tree D_s^{best} where

$$WHT^{best} = \sum_{i=1}^{m}(wht_i * (DEP - dep_i^{best} + 1)) = max(WHT) \qquad (5)$$

It is possible that two functionally equivalent trees have the same weight. To break the tie, the tree with a lower depth is selected.

5.3   Finding Optimal Weighted Decision Tree

For data streams that do not have very high arrival rates and that do not require frequent re-alignment (i.e., ζ is not set to be very high), dynamic programming can be applied to find optimal weighted binary trees [18,19]. It has been proven that the dynamic programming approach for finding optimal weighted binary tree has time complexity $O(n^2)$, where n is the total number of nodes in D_s. The dynamic programming approach has been shown to admit an implementation running in $O(n \log(n))$ time [19].

However, for high speed data streams and streams whose distributions change frequently, quadratic time complexity may not be practical. In these cases, an approximate algorithm that generates a sub-optimal decision tree using shorter time is required. Thus, we develop an algorithm with $O(m \log(m))$ time, where m is the total number of decision nodes in the tree. The algorithm is described as follows.

Step 1. Calculate the weights of all subtrees in D_s; store the weight of each subtree on its root. Therefore, each decision node in D_s is assigned a weight that indicates the weight of the subtree with root d_i.
Step 2. Select a decision node d_i with highest weight and re-align D_s, so that d_i is the new root of D_s. Update the weights of all subtrees for the re-aligned tree.
Step 3. Repeat step 2 for all the subtrees in D_s, until D_s is completely "sorted".
Step 4. Select d_j from the sorted D_s as the new root, so that the tree is balanced in terms of *weight*. In other words, the weights of the left child and the right child of d_j have minimum difference.
Step 5. Repeat step 4 for all the subtrees in D_s.

Step 1 has $O(m)$ time complexity. The "sorting" process on step 2 and step 3 can achieve $O(m)$ complexity by using the techniques developed by Fredman [8]. However, because the weights of subtrees need to be updated, the total time for steps 2 and 3 is $O(m \log(m))$. Similarly, steps 4 and 5 also have $O(m \log(m))$ time complexity. Therefore, the complexity of this re-alignment algorithm is $O(m \log(m))$. Although this algorithm can only generate a sub-optimal tree, it can be proven that the upper bound of the weight of the resulting sub-optimal tree is $3 \times WHT^{best}$. The proof is omitted.

5.4   Realigning Decision Tree

Let c_i be a leaf node of D_s, and d_j and d'_j be its parent and grandparent nodes. Let c'_i be the direct child of d'_j. That is, c'_i is one level higher than c_i. Starting from the leaf node on the lowest level and going bottom-up, the following heuristic rule is applied to each leaf node c_i $(i = 1, 2, ...m)$ in D_s.

Heuristic HR1: If the weight of c_i is greater than the weight of c'_i, i.e., $wht_i > wht'_i$, then exchange the position of d_j and d'_j in D_s by performing a single rotation.

By applying this heuristic, c_i along with its parent d_j will be moved to a higher level than c'_i and d'_j and, hence, the weight of the new tree is greater than D_s. This heuristic is repeatedly applied until all the leaf nodes are examined.

Note that the resulting decision tree with a higher overall weight than the original tree may be imbalanced. A balanced tree may not be the best solution for many data streams with distribution changes. According to the weight function in Equation 4, the leaf nodes on very low levels should have low weights, indicating that their clusters have not received new data for a long time. Hence, although visiting these leaf nodes may be inefficient, since they are barely visited, the overall efficiency should not be severely affected. Furthermore, the pruning method (introduced in the next section) can be adopted to reduce the tree depth by removing these historical clusters.

The algorithm for assigning weights and eagerly re-aligning the tree is shown in Algorithm 2.

6   Pruning Decision Tree

There are three major criteria for evaluating decision trees: accuracy, efficiency, and tree size. As has been mentioned in Section 2, the proposed approach improves the efficiency of a decision tree for concept-drifting data without affecting its accuracy. A method for effectively reducing the tree size is proposed in this section. This method reduces the tree size by pruning outdated nodes using the proposed synopsis.

Most of the decision tree generation and modification techniques over data streams proposed in literature do not consider the tree size provided that the tree can fit in main memory. Consequently, the most popular solution is to start pruning only when a decision tree is too large to fit in memory. This is not necessarily a good strategy. Since historical data that arrived months or years ago may no longer be useful after the distribution change, clusters containing only out-dated data can be deleted even when memory is sufficient. This early-pruning can result in a reduction in the size and the depth of the tree, leading to lower overall cost for clustering.

Furthermore, scant attention has been paid in literature to the actual pruning algorithm. One common approach is to remove leaf nodes that contain few elements. This approach may not be appropriate for data streams that change over time. For example, assume one leaf node (c_1) has more elements than another (c_2). Based on the common strategy that leaf nodes with fewer elements

---

Algorithm 2. Decision tree re-alignment procedure

1: INPUT: Decision tree D_s
2: OUTPUT: Re-aligned decision tree D'_s

3: **for all** leaf node c_i in D_s **do**
4:     //Initialize weights
5:     $wht_i = 1$;
6:     Call change detection algorithm;
7:     **if** c_i contains only historical data **then**
8:        $wht_i = wht_i/2$;
9:     **else if** the re-alignment mark of c_i is set from *unmarked* to *marked* **then**
10:       $wht_i = wht_i + 1$;
11:       //Start re-aligning D_s
12:       **for all** leaf node c_k in D_s starting from the lowest level **do**
13:          Find its parent d_j and grandparent d'_j;
14:          Find d'_j's direct child c'_k
15:          **if** $wht_k > wht'_k$ **then**
16:             Exchange d_j and d'_j with a single rotation;
17:          **end if**
18:          Move to the leaf node at one level higher;
19:       **end for**
20:    **end if**
21: **end for**

---

should be pruned earlier, c_2 will be removed. However, for a data stream whose distribution changes over time, it is possible that most of the elements in c_1 had arrived long time ago, while new data are falling into c_2. In this case, a better solution is to prune c_1, since it is less important to the current distribution.

Accordingly, two heuristics are proposed for pruning a decision tree using the synopsis presented in Section 4 and the weights introduced in Section 5.

Heuristic HR2: Prune leaf nodes with $\eta \neq 0$ and $tDist$ greater than a certain threshold.

Recall that η is the number of elements that fall in the cluster represented by a leaf node. The greater the $tDist$, the "older" the leaf node is. Hence, by pruning leaf nodes with $tDist$ greater than a certain threshold, historical clusters are deleted from the tree. The appropriate threshold setting is application dependent.

Heuristic HR3: Prune leaf nodes with weight wht less than a certain threshold υ ($0 \leq \upsilon \leq 1$).

The higher υ is, the more leaf nodes will be pruned. For example, if υ is set to $1/2$, then the first time one leaf node is considered out-dated, it will be pruned immediately. If υ is $1/4$, then it takes double the time to make this pruning decision. Hence, when the system resources are limited, υ should be a higher value, whereas if resources are abundant, υ could be smaller.

HR2 can be regarded as an eager pruning strategy, and HR3 is a lazy pruning strategy. For different scenarios, these heuristics can be re-evaluated:

1. every time a new element arrives, when $tDist$ and wht values of all leaf nodes are recalculated, or
2. when the size, depth, or weight for D_s is less than a predefined threshold, or
3. at certain time intervals, or
4. when memory is insufficient.

After several leaf nodes are deleted, the decision nodes connected to them will miss one or both of their children. Usually, a decision tree is a full binary tree; to maintain this property, there are two possible cases:

- **Case 1:** one child of a decision node d_a is deleted after pruning.
  Let the children of d_a be c_a and c'_a (c'_a can be a subtree or a leaf node). Let d'_a be the parent of d_a. Assume c_a needs to be pruned according to HR2 or HR3. If d_a is the root node (i.e. $d'_a = NULL$), then remove d_a and set the root of c'_a to be the new root (illustrated in Figure 4(a)). Otherwise, set the root of c'_a to d'_a, and remove d_a (illustrated in Figure 4(b)).

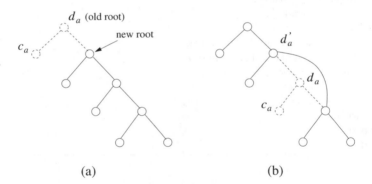

(a)   (b)

Fig. 4. Case 1: one child of d_a is pruned

- **Case 2:** both children of a decision node d_a are deleted after pruning.
  Let the children of d_a be c_a and c'_a. If c_a and c'_a are to be deleted, replace d_a by a new leaf node c_b. Set its synopsis as $\gamma_b = max(\gamma_a, \gamma'_a), \eta_b = 0, \beta_b = 0$. The weight p_b of new leaf c_b is reset to 1.

The total cost of the new decision tree may not be optimal after pruning. However, since the pruning process only modifies historical leaf nodes, recently visited leaf nodes remain at their current levels. Hence, it is not necessary to re-align the tree after pruning.

The full algorithm for pruning a decision tree is given in Algorithm 3. Algorithm 3 has complexity $O(m)$ upon each re-evaluation, where m is the total number of leaf nodes in D_s.

Algorithm 3. Pruning a decision tree

1: INPUT: Decision tree D_s
2: OUTPUT: Modified decision tree D'_s

3: **if** re-evaluation start **then**
4:    **for all** leaf node c_a in D_s **do**
5:       **if** c_a satisfies HR2 or HR3 **then**
6:          //Depend on which heuristic is adopted
7:          //HR1 and HR2 cannot be used at the same time
8:          Find c_a's direct parent d_a;
9:       **end if**
10:      **if** d_a is the root of D_s **then**
11:         Set d_a's another child d'_a as new root;
12:         Remove c_a and d_a;
13:      **else if** d_a's another child is a leaf node c'_a **then**
14:         Create a new leaf node c_b;
15:         $\gamma_b = max(\gamma_a, \gamma'_a)$;
16:         $\eta_b = 0$;
17:         $\beta_b = 0$;
18:         $wht_b = 1$;
19:         Replace d_a with c_b;
20:         Delete c_a and c'_a;
21:      **else**
22:         //d_a's another child is a subtree
23:         Find d_a's another direct child d_b;
24:         Find d_a's direct parent d_c;
25:         Set d_b's direct parent to d_c;
26:         Delete d_a and c_a;
27:      **end if**
28:   **end for**
29: **end if**

---

7   Experiments

To evaluate the performance of the proposed techniques, a series of experiments are performed. All experiments are conducted on a PC with 3GHz Pentium 4 processor and 1GB of RAM, running Windows XP. All algorithms are implemented in C.

The original decision tree for each data stream used in the experiments is generated using the CVFDT algorithm [14]. A decision tree generated by the CVFDT algorithm is adaptive to distribution changes in the stream by replacing leaf nodes with subtrees. In [14], CVFDT is evaluated with categorical attributes only. Hence, the technique presented in [15] is also implemented, so that numerical attributes can be used as classifiers on the decision tree. Both techniques have been discussed in Section 3.

For a decision tree using numerical attributes as classifiers, when one leaf node contains too many data elements and needs to be split, the location of the splitting point is unclear (i.e., the numerical value on the decision node of the new subtree that replaces this leaf node, see Figure 1 for example). In such cases, a gain function is used to find the best splitting point. The gain function is constructed using the Hoeffding bound [13]. In the experiments, for each leaf node, the splitting procedure starts after at least 5,000 data elements fall in it. The α value used to calculate the Hoeffding bound is set to $1 - 10^{-6}$. These two parameters are set exactly the same as in the experiments of [15].

7.1 Change Detection Evaluation

To evaluate the effectiveness of the proposed change detection technique and to obtain comparative results, the proposed technique (denoted as TD in the results) is compared with a distance function-based change detection technique (DF) proposed in [17]. DF detects changes by calculating the distance of the current distribution and the distribution of the newly arrived data. The distance of two distributions can be calculated using different distance measurements; hence, five distance measurement that are used in [17], the Wilcoxon statistic (Wil) [25], the Kolmogorov-Smirnov statistic over initial segments (KS) and over intervals (KSI) [3], and Φ and Ξ statistics [17], are implemented. Their change detection performances are compared with the proposed TD approach.

Six synthetic data streams (denoted as $S_1, ..., S_6$) are used in the experiments. Each stream contains 2,000,000 points with only one numerical attribute for each data element. The distribution changes occur every 20,000 points. Hence, there are 99 true changes in each data stream. S_1 is a data stream whose initial distribution is uniform. The starting distribution of stream S_2 is a mixture of a Standard Normal distribution with some uniform noise. Streams S_3, S_4, S_5 and S_6 contain Normal, Exponential, Binomial, and Poisson distributions, respectively. These are the same data streams used in the experiments of [17].

The arrival speed of this data stream is set to be stable, with one tuple per unit time. This is done to gain control over the size of the sliding window W, since a time-based sliding window will be equal to a count-based one if the speed of the stream is stable. However, note that the proposed techniques do not require the data stream to have an even speed. In these experiments, the time interval Δ of W is set to 500 time units. The minimum cluster size is 100 data elements. Threshold ζ is set as 70 time units. The effect of Δ and ζ settings on the proposed technique is studied in the next section.

If, at the time when a change is reported, the change point (i.e. the first element that belongs to the new distribution) remains in W, or it was contained in W at most Δ time units ago, then this detection is considered to be on-time. Otherwise, it is considered late. The experimental results of the on-time (O) and delayed (D) change detection rate are shown in Table 1.

Table 1. Comparison of change detection techniques

	TD		Wil		KS		KSI		Φ		Ξ	
	O	D	O	D	O	D	O	D	O	D	O	D
S_1	0.42	0.17	0	0.05	0.31	0.30	0.60	0.34	0.92	0.20	0.86	0.19
S_2	0.40	0.09	0	2	0	0.15	0.04	0.32	0.16	0.33	0.13	0.36
S_3	0.46	0.13	0.10	0.27	0.17	0.30	0.16	0.47	0.16	0.38	0.17	0.43
S_4	0.73	0.06	0.12	0.38	0.11	0.38	0.07	0.22	0.07	0.29	0.11	0.46
S_5	0.63	0	0.36	0.42	0.24	0.38	0.17	0.22	0.12	0.32	0.23	0.33
S_6	0.61	0.02	0.36	0.35	0.23	0.30	0.14	0.25	0.14	0.21	0.23	0.22

These results lead to the following observations:

- The distribution changes are usually detected on-time using the proposed technique. For other techniques, the change detections are more likely to be delayed for all test streams except S_1.

  This is because other techniques need to see the "big picture" of the stream data distribution to detect changes, while the proposed technique can quickly locate the clusters (leaf nodes) where changes start without waiting until the new distribution is fully visible.
- The proposed technique performs much better than others for streams S_4, S_5 and S_6. Furthermore, for these streams, most of the distribution changes are detected on-time.

  S_4 has exponential distribution and S_5 and S_6 have discrete distributions. In all three cases, the distribution changes are severe, i.e., the new distribution is considerably different than the old one. These results indicate that the proposed technique performs best for data streams that may have severe distribution changes (such as detecting fraud, instrument failure, and virus attacks).
- For data streams S_1, S_2 and S_3, the proposed technique may not perform better than other techniques on the total number of changes detected (even slightly worse in a few cases). This is because these three streams have relatively slow and smooth distribution changes. For these cases, the efficiency of the proposed technique can only be improved by increasing ζ. However, this increases the chance of false detection, as will be shown in next section.

To evaluate the false detection rate, all six techniques are applied on five streams with 2,000,000 points each and no distribution changes. The results of the total number of false detections on all five streams are shown in Table 2. These results reveal that the proposed technique has a lower false detection rate than most of other techniques.

The experimental results for run time comparison of these techniques is not given. As mentioned in Section 4, the proposed change detection algorithm has a worst case complexity of $O(m)$, where m is the number of out-dated data when new data arrive. Usually m is not a large value unless there is a severe burst in the stream. For data streams with steady arrival rates, the time complexity of

Table 2. Number of false alarms

	TD	Wil	KS	KSI	Φ	Ξ
False alarms	26	40	40	49	18	36

Algorithm 1 is $O(1)$. KS and KSI have $O(log(m_1 + m_2))$ time complexity [17], where m_1 and m_2 are the sizes of a pair of sliding windows. The complexity of computing Wilcoxon is $O(m_1 + m_2)$, and the computation time for Φ_A and Ξ_A is $O([m_1 + m_2]^2)$. Notice that multiple pairs of sliding windows are used in [17] with different sizes; some pairs may have very large window sizes for detecting distribution drifts. Hence, the time complexity of the proposed technique is lower than these techniques.

7.2   Varying Distance Threshold and Sliding Window Interval

To analyze the effect of different Δ and the distance threshold ζ settings on change detection, the proposed approach is applied on data streams $S_1 - S_6$ used in the previous experiments with various settings:

- Keep $\zeta = 70$ time units unchanged, adjust Δ from 300 time units to 800 units by increasing Δ 100 time units each time. Figures 5(a) and 5(b) show the results of the number of changes detected on-time and delayed, respectively.
- Fix Δ to 500 time units, and vary the value of ζ from 30 to 150 time units in increment of 20 units. Figures 6(a) and 6(b) show the results of the number of changes detected on-time and delayed, respectively.

These results lead to the following observations:

- Increasing Δ may result in a reduction in the number of on-time change detections. This is because, as Δ increases, more "old" data are involved in calculating the distance. Hence, it is more difficult to have the distance less than threshold ζ. However, because the definition of "on time" depends on Δ, a larger Δ implies a larger W and, thus, the number of changes detected on-time may increase.
- Larger ζ values may increase the number of changes detected on-time. However, notice that some of the distribution changes detected may be false.
- It is unclear how the number of delayed change detections will vary when adjusting Δ or ζ.

Experiments are also conducted for studying how Δ and ζ can affect the false alarm rate, using the same five stable data streams used in Section 7.1. The results are shown in Table 3 and Table 4. From these results, it can be seen that decreasing Δ or increasing ζ may lead to high false alarm rates.

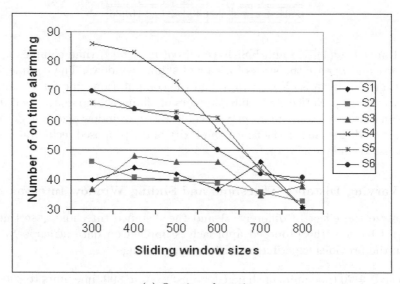

(a) On-time detections

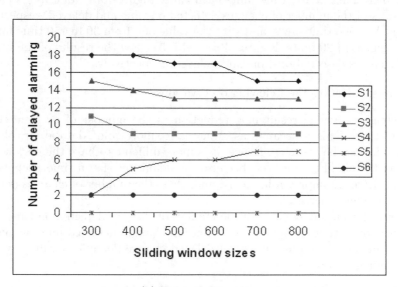

(b) Delayed detections

Fig. 5. Performance of our change detection technique with Δ varied

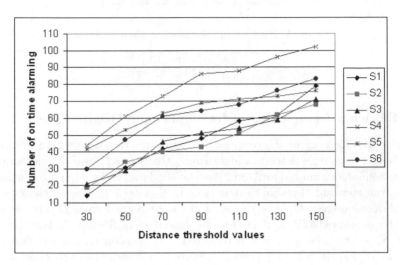

(a) On-time detections

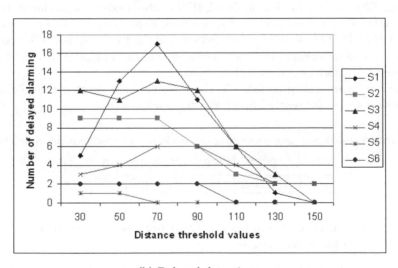

(b) Delayed detections

Fig. 6. Performance of our change detection technique with ζ varied

Table 3. Number of false alarms changing Δ

Δ	300	400	500	600	700	800
False alarms	30	26	26	21	12	10

Table 4. Number of false alarms when ζ varies

ζ	30	50	70	90	110	130	150
False alarms	11	15	26	28	32	43	49

7.3 Efficiency Comparison of Re-aligned and Original Tree

To verify the efficiency of the proposed decision tree re-alignment technique, we apply both the change detection algorithm (Algorithm 1) and the decision tree re-alignment algorithm (Algorithm 2) on the six data streams ($S_1 - S_6$) using the same parameter and threshold settings as in Section 7.1. The efficiency of the original decision trees D_i ($i = 1, ..., 6$) and the re-aligned trees D_i' are measured using the weights WHT_i and WHT_i', as described in Section 5. For each data stream S_i, every time a change is detected, the decision tree is re-aligned and $ratio_j = WHT_i'/WHT_i$ is recorded, where j indicates the j-th change being detected. Notice that although the original tree D_i does not change during processing, each time WHT_i' is calculated, WHT_i also needs to be updated, because the weights attached to some leaf nodes may have changed. The average ratio $Avg(WHT_i'/WHT_i) = \frac{r_1+r_2+...+r_q}{q}$ (where q is the total number of changes detected) is used to estimate the overall efficiency improvement of the decision tree re-alignment algorithm on each data stream.

The results are shown in Table 5. These results indicate that the efficiency of each decision tree is greatly improved after re-alignment.

Table 5. Efficiency improvement of our decision tree re-alignment algorithm

Streams	S_1	S_2	S_3	S_4	S_5	S_6
$Avg(WHT_i'/WHT_i)$	4.67	3.65	7.01	8.69	7.10	4.72

7.4 Performance Comparison of Optimal and Sub-optimal Tree Re-alignment Strategies

In Algorithm 2 for decision tree re-alignment, an approximate algorithm that generates a sub-optimal tree is adopted. This is for the purpose of increasing the efficiency of the decision tree re-alignment process for streams with high arrival rates. However, if the speed of the data stream is not extremely high and the re-alignment process is not triggered frequently, the dynamic programming approach can be applied to generate an optimal tree. To compare the performance of both sub-optimal and optimal re-alignment approaches, we implement the dynamic programming approach for tree re-alignment and apply it on streams

Table 6. Efficiency improvement of using dynamic programming

Streams	S_1	S_2	S_3	S_4	S_5	S_6
$Avg(WHT_i'/WHT_i)$	5.29	4.13	7.66	11.00	8.83	5.56

Table 7. Time of dynamic programming and sub-optimal approach

Streams	S_1	S_2	S_3	S_4	S_5	S_6
Dynamic Programming (time unit)	313	269	370	575	661	396
Sub-optimal (time unit)	14	21	32	27	30	13

$S_1 - S_6$. The performance and time comparison results are shown in Table 6 and Table 7.

From Tables 5 and 6, it is clear that the average performance increment of the optimal decision tree over the sub-optimal tree is 17%. The sub-optimal re-alignment approach is on average 19.92 times faster than dynamic programming.

7.5 Pruning Heuristics Evaluation

A data stream that has only one numerical attribute is generated for evaluating the power of the proposed pruning heuristics. Data arrive at a rate of one element per time unit. The value of the data element grows over time. Hence, the decision tree will grow increasingly deeper as leaf nodes keep splitting and there will be a large number of historical clusters. The pruning procedure is triggered when the height of the decision tree is greater than a threshold (set to 12 in this experiment). Δ is set to 500 time units. For heuristic HR2, the distance threshold is set to 1500 time units. For heuristic HR3, when the weight of one leaf node is less than $1/16$, this leaf node is pruned. Table 8 demonstrates the results of the proposed pruning procedure using HR2 and HR3, respectively.

Table 8. Pruning results using HR2 and HR3

Heuristic	# of nodes before pruning	# of nodes after pruning	tree height after pruning
HR2	35	15	6
HR3	35	21	8

These results demonstrate that the tree size is greatly reduced after pruning. Note that HR2 (eager pruning) usually prunes more nodes than HR3 (lazy pruning). Which heuristics to choose is an application based decision.

7.6 Running on Real Streams

All experiments conducted so far use synthetic data streams. To test the performance of the proposed techniques in practice, a set of experiments is designed using a real data stream.

The data set used in this set of experiment is the TAO stream from the Tropical Atmosphere Ocean (TAO) project. Tao data records the sea surface temperature (SST) from past years. Tao data contains 12218 streams each one of length 962. Since the streams are too short to fit our experiments, we concatenated them in the ascending order of the time when these streams were recorded. This is a reasonable modification because each stream represents the sea surface temperature for a certain period, thus, the concatenation represents a record for a longer period.

The arrival speed of TAO is set to one tuple per time unit. The decision tree is built using temperature values as classifier. Minimum cluster size is 100 data elements. Δ and ζ is set to 500 and 50 time units, respectively.

Experimental results show that 2746 out of the total 3244 distribution changes in TAO stream are detected using the proposed change detection technique, with 2173 on-time and 573 delayed. The average efficiency improvement after applying the decision tree re-alignment technique is 8.68. These results demonstrate that the proposed approach is effective on real data sets.

8   Conclusion

Clustering is one of the most important stream mining tasks. Existing stream clustering techniques either do not support time-changing streams or suffer from decreasing performance when a dynamic stream has continued for a long time. A new decision tree-based technique for detecting distribution changes over dynamic data streams is proposed in this paper. A synopsis is maintained for each leaf node (cluster) in the decision tree. The distribution change is detected by monitoring the timestamps of data in each cluster using its synopsis.

A novel tree re-alignment approach is proposed for re-aligning the decision tree after a distribution change occurs. The frequently visited leaf nodes are moved closer to root after the re-alignment and, thus, the re-aligned tree is more efficient over the current distribution. Two heuristics for pruning a decision tree are designed for reducing the memory consumption.

Experiments verify the feasibility of the proposed approach. According to the results, the proposed change detection technique can report most of the distribution changes in real time. The decision tree re-alignment technique can improve the efficiency by at least a factor of 4. It is also shown that the proposed techniques can be applied to real data streams with good performance.

References

1. Aggarwal, C.: A framework for diagnosing changes in evolving data streams. In: Proc. ACM SIGMOD Int. Conf. on Management of Data, pp. 575–586 (2003)
2. Aggarwal, C., Han, J., Wang, J., Yu, P.: A framework for clustering evolving data streams. In: Proc. 29th Int. Conf. on Very Large Data Bases, pp. 81–92 (2003)
3. Chakravarti, I., Laha, R., Roy, J.: Handbook of Methods of Applied Statistics. John Wiley and Sons, Chichester (1967)
4. Charikar, M., Chen, K., Motwani, R.: Incremental clustering and dynamic information retrieval. In: Proc. ACM Symp. on Theory of Computing, pp. 626–635 (1997)

5. Charikar, M., O'Callaghan, L., Panigrahy, R.: Better streaming algorithms for clustering problems. In: Proc. ACM Symp. on Theory of Computing, pp. 30–39 (2003)
6. Domingos, P., Hulten, G.: Mining high-speed data streams. In: Proc. 6th ACM SIGKDD Int. Conf. on Knowledge Discovery and Data Mining, pp. 71–80 (2000)
7. Fan, W., Huang, Y., Yu, P.: Decision tree evolution using limited number of labeled data items from drifting data streams. In: Proc. 2004 IEEE Int. Conf. on Data Mining, pp. 379–382 (2004)
8. Fredman, M.: Two applications of a probabilistic search technique: Sorting x + y and building balanced search tree. In: Proc. ACM Symp. on Theory of Computing, pp. 240–244 (1975)
9. Gaber, M., Zaslavsky, A., Krishnaswamy, S.: Mining data streams: A review. ACM SIGMOD Record 34(2), 18–26 (2005)
10. Gama, J., Medas, P., Rodrigues, P.: Learning decision trees from dynamic data streams. In: Proc. 2005 ACM Symp. on Applied Computing, pp. 573–577 (2005)
11. Gama, J., Rocha, R., Medas, P.: Accurate decision tree for mining high-speed data streams. In: Proc. 9th ACM SIGKDD Int. Conf. on Knowledge Discovery and Data Mining, pp. 523–528 (2003)
12. Guha, S., Meyerson, A., Mishra, N., Motwani, R.: Clustering data streams: Theory and practice. IEEE Trans. Knowledge and Data Eng. 15(3), 515–528 (2003)
13. Hoeffding, W.: Probability inequalities for sums of bounded random variables. Journal of the American Statistical Association 58, 18–30 (1963)
14. Hulten, G., Spencer, L., Domingos, P.: Mining time-chaning data streams. In: Proc. 7th ACM SIGKDD Int. Conf. on Knowledge Discovery and Data Mining, pp. 97–106 (2001)
15. Jin, R., Aggrawal, G.: Efficient decision tree constructions on streaming data. In: Proc. 9th ACM SIGKDD Int. Conf. on Knowledge Discovery and Data Mining, pp. 571–576 (2003)
16. Kaufman, L., Rousseeuw, P.: Finding groups in data: An introduction to cluster analysis. Addison-Wesley, Reading (1990)
17. Kifer, D., Ben-David, S., Gehrke, J.: Detecting change in data streams. In: Proc. 30th Int. Conf. on Very Large Data Bases, pp. 180–191 (2004)
18. Knuth, D.: Optimum binary search trees. Acta Informatica 1, 14–25 (1971)
19. Knuth, D.: The art of computer programming 3: Sorting and searching. Addison-Wesley, Reading (1973)
20. Babock, B., et al.: Models and issues in data stream systems. In: Proc. 21st ACM SIGACT-SIGMOD-SIGART Symp. Principles of Database Systems, pp. 1–16 (2002)
21. Abadi, D., et al.: The design of the borealis stream processing engine. In: Proc. 2nd Biennial Conf. on Innovative Data Systems Research (2005)
22. Li, J., et al.: Semantics and evaluation techniques for window aggregates in data streams. In: Proc. ACM SIGMOD Int. Conf. on Management of Data, pp. 311–322 (2005)
23. Chen, M., et al.: Path-based failure and evolution management. In: 1st Symposium on Network Systems Design and Implementation, pp. 309–322 (2004)
24. Wang, H., Fan, W., Yu, P.S., Han, J.: Mining concept-drifting data streams using ensemble classifiers. In: Proc. 9th ACM SIGKDD Int. Conf. on Knowledge Discovery and Data Mining, pp. 226–235 (2003)
25. Wilcoxon, F.: Individual comparisons by ranking methods. Biometrics Bulletin 1, 80–83 (1945)

REaltime ACtive Heterogeneous Systems - Where Did We Reach After REACH?

Thomas Kudraß

Fakultät Informatik, Mathematik, Naturwissenschaften
Hochschule für Technik, Wirtschaft und Kultur Leipzig
Postfach 30 11 66
04251 Leipzig
kudrass@imn.htwk-leipzig.de

Abstract. This paper gives a survey of the deployment of ideas from the area of real-time, active and heterogeneous database systems in the years from 1991 to 2010 as they have been embraced by IT industry. During that time the Database and Distributed Systems group (DVS) led by Alejandro Buchmann has made lots of contributions to the development of those ideas by many research projects. After 20 years it is time to conclude insights how far the ideas of the first project REACH are still valid for the development of commercial products and standards. In some cases, industry has taken another direction as it has been expected. In other cases, the DVS research prototypes were forerunners for commercial products that are now well-established.

1 The Early History before REACH

The early research topics of Alejandro Buchmann and his colleagues comprised architectural issues to be resolved when using a database system as an active object in a distributed environment with real-time capabilities. In the end of the 80s years, many of those ideas were discussed in the research community but were still far away from commercial use.

The DOM (Distributed Objects Management) project at GTE Labs addressed the integration of autonomous, heterogeneous database and non-database systems into a distributed computing environment. In [Bu90] the idea of an active object space was sketched to model heterogeneous cooperating information systems. An active object has been defined by its capability to react autonomously and asynchronously to incoming events. Object-oriented models were considered best as common model for federations of heterogeneous systems because of its encapsulation and data abstraction features.

The late 80s years were characterized by the expectations of a soon retirement of the then very popular relational DBMS. Therefore, object-oriented data models were the most favoured to express the behaviour of a system in a heterogeneous environment. There was a variety of ideas how the ideal object model looks like regarding its expressiveness and relationship types. But there was still some hope on an object model standard developed by consortia like the Object Management Group

K. Sachs, I. Petrov, and P. Guerrero (Eds.): Buchmann Festschrift, LNCS 6462, pp. 44–56, 2010.

(OMG) or the Object Database Management Group (ODMG). The notion of active objects was defined with various forms that have appeared in active database systems that were another source of inspiration for DOM.

The research of active databases was mainly influenced by some pioneering projects. Among them HiPAC introduced the event-condition-action (ECA) rule abstraction. One frequently cited HiPAC paper was titled "Rules are Objects Too" [DBM88] that promoted the idea to treat rules as first-class objects. One of the HiPAC ideas was the definition of timing constraints and their assignment to the rules or to a part of it in order to support application scenarios that require reactions within a certain time period. In that way, the real-time feature became the third part of the first Darmstadt research project REACH (REaltime Active Heterogeneous System) that started in 1992. REACH pursued the idea to *really* implement lots of the ideas of HiPAC and DOM to study the real problems in an object-oriented database system that is active, works in a time-constrained manner when executing queries and can be the platform for a mediator in an active object space using rules to control overall consistency or global transactions spanning different components.

The paper is organized as follows: After a retrospective on the early history and the REACH project we look at the development of concepts of system integration, active capabilities and global consistency control driven by IT industry. The paper continues with lessons we have learned from experiences in applying REACH ideas in the development of large information systems. Finally a short outlook on future issues concludes the paper.

2 The REACH Project – REaltime ACtive and Heterogeneous

2.1 Real-Time Databases

The idea to constrain the execution of rules relates to the concept of real-time databases and to the incorporation of the time dimension to specify rules. The ability to process results in a timely and predictable manner will always be more important than fast processing. So real-time databases are able to handle time-sensitive queries, return only temporally valid data, and support priority scheduling. Deadlines are the constraints for soon-to-be replaced data accessed by the transaction [BB95]. Deadlines can be either observant or predictive. The latter approach is a more stable way of dealing with deadlines but requires the capability to predict the transaction behaviour. The response to a missed deadline depends on whether the deadline is hard, firm or soft. A hard deadline has to be met, otherwise it creates serious problems. Transactions passing the deadline must be aborted. Firm deadlines are similar but they measure how important it is to complete the transaction at some point after the transaction arrives. In real-time environments the data quality decreases as time progresses between the time data was acquired and the time it is consumed. This can be expressed by value functions that specify the value of the outcome of the transaction dependent on the elapsed time. Soft deadlines can be applied best, if meeting time constraints is desirable but missing deadlines do not cause serious trouble.

2.2 Active Databases

An active database system monitors situations of interest and triggers an appropriate response in a timely manner when they occur. The desired behaviour is expressed by ECA rules that can be used to specify static or dynamic constraints in a distributed environment. The monitoring component of an active database is responsible for the detection of events and their propagation to a rule engine. An event may trigger the execution of one or more rules. A rule is executed by evaluating the condition and possibly executing the action. We can define a coupling mode between event and condition (EC) and between condition and action (CA) as well. The different coupling modes as they have been introduced in [HLM88] specify the execution of the rule as a single transaction or even as independent transaction (detached) with consequences to the required transaction model for the active system beyond flat transactions. In REACH different rule subclasses that inherit their structure from a RULE superclass were introduced for different domains: access control, consistency enforcement, flow control and application-specific rules [BB+93]. So it was possible to process all rules in a uniform manner.

The event hierarchy of REACH comprised not only changes of the database state as events but also temporal and transaction events. Due to the underlying object paradigm events were related to (active) objects such that method calls and operations on attributes became part of the event hierarchy. By treating transactions as objects, transaction-specific events were subclasses of a method call event. Besides primitive events, composite events were defined using logical operators. Any relative temporal event was defined relative to another event that originated in a committed transaction – contrary to absolute time events that were classified as primitive events. A specific aspect was the event consumption semantics when processing lots of event occurrences together with their parameters. Although events can be considered instantaneous, the time difference between occurrence and detection of an event has to be taken into consideration when implementing an active system with event detection. Events are strictly distinguished from temporal constraints on rules that determine when a rule execution begins and when the execution of a rule must be complete.

2.3 Integrating Heterogeneous Databases

Many large companies use various semi-autonomous and heterogeneous database systems to serve the needs of various application systems. As it has been mentioned above, one important application domain for REACH was the consistency control in heterogeneous database that cooperate together in federations with different degrees of coupling. These federations can be designed in a layered architecture with different abstraction levels [SL90]. The term *interdependent data* was coined to imply that two or more data items stored in different databases are related through a global integrity constraint [SRK92].

The idea of active objects was to set up an object model that represents the local components to be controlled. That could be done on a coarse-grained level by viewing a local component and its interface as an object with methods that represent the behaviour of the whole system. Relational databases could well be integrated into such a system by object-relational mapping techniques that make it possible to define rules on objects that represent relations or single tuples in remote databases.

Many practical problems have to be tackled when dealing with heterogeneous databases. Since the data items to be managed may be distributed throughout a network events on them can also be distributed. In a rather conventional approach all events could be collected and processed by a mediator with active database features as they have been worked out in REACH [KLB96]. One of the unresolved issues was how an event service can deal with distributed events in an open environment without a global clock. Liebig et al. [LCB99] presented algorithms for event composition and consumption that used accuracy interval based timestamping and discussed the problems that result from inaccuracy and message transmission delays.

A global system that interacts with components that have been designed independently has to deal with one main obstacle, the local autonomy of the participant. In general, autonomy can be characterized as the freedom to make decisions. It comprises three different categories: structure, behaviour and communication [Ku97]. Structural autonomy covers all design aspects of a system, e.g. its schema and internal system architecture. The behaviour autonomy describes the capability of a local system to decide independently about the actions it executes. Actions can be executed at different local interfaces (e.g., SQL operation or a local operation call) and change the state of the local database. The behavioural autonomy can be restricted by proscribing local actions or, vice versa, by enforcing actions that are part of a global transaction spanning multiple systems. The communication autonomy describes the freedom of a local system to decide about the information it is willing to provide to the federation. Among them are: status information at run-time of the system, data and schema information, and occurred events.

Even if the schema is public there might by some remaining problems to understand the semantics of the schema elements that is a prerequisite for schema integration algorithms in tightly coupled integration approaches [RB01]. Alternatively, metadata about local systems can be used in a global knowledge base in addition to global integrity rules. In the early REACH prototypes the role of metadata was not completely analyzed but it was worth doing so, because lots of global knowledge could be transferred to a metadata base instead of rules.

3   After REACH: Concepts in Distributed Heterogeneous Systems

3.1   Integration Technologies

Object-Oriented Middleware

When the author left the DVS group at the Technical University of Darmstadt 1997 some new paradigms and trends entered the stage in the IT community. The dominance of relational databases continued, the object-oriented paradigm gained importance as model for middleware in interoperable systems. In such distributed computing infrastructures, DBMSs were considered one kind of component over which distributed applications are built.

As an example, the Common Object Request Broker Architecture (CORBA) was defined as a standard to enable software components written in multiple languages and running on multiple computers to work together [Obj04]. The interface definition language (IDL) of CORBA specifies interfaces that objects will present to the outside world. To use different implementation languages mappings from IDL to specific languages were defined. An Object Request Broker (ORB) is the platform for the cooperating applications to interact. In addition to providing users with a language and platform-neutral remote procedure call specification, CORBA defines a landscape of commonly needed services such as transactions, security, time and events. The CORBA Event Services support the push model, in which a supplier object initiates the transfer of event data to consumer objects, as well as the pull model, in which a consumer of events requests event data from an event supplier. Composite events are not explicitly defined in the standard. The CORBA specification as the brainchild of a committee appeared very complex, ambiguous and hard to implement entirely. Thus, existing ORB implementations were incomplete or inadequate [He08].

There are some other examples of object-oriented middleware that have gained some popularity. Among them is Java RMI (Remote Method Invocation), the Java programming interface that performs the object-oriented equivalent of remote procedure calls. Jini was the more advanced version of RMI with better searching capabilities and mechanism for distributed object applications [Sun99]. A major competitor of CORBA was DCOM (Distributed Component Object Model), a proprietary Microsoft technology for communication among software components distributed across a network. The difficulties of both CORBA and DCOM technologies to work over the internet and on unknown and insecure machines hindered their broad acceptance as middleware standards.

Integration Infrastructures

The integration of heterogeneous systems beyond the communication in a RPC style was addressed in EAI technologies (Enterprise Application Integration) as they become popular in the end of the 1990th years. EAI can be considered a framework to integrate applications within an organization to support business processes that run on different systems, such as supply chain management, or to enable business intelligence applications with complex analytical operations over lots of distributed heterogeneous data [CH+05]. The EAI system can provide a single uniform access interface to different local application (façade) and can ensure that data of different sources is kept consistent. This is also known as EII (Enterprise Information Integration) [HA+05]. An EAI approach avoids point-to-point communication by a centralized infrastructure that has either a hub-and-spoke or a bus topology.

The latter can be implemented using message-oriented-middleware. The advantage of a message-based middleware is the decoupling of the sending, receiving and processing of messages in an asynchronous way. Local applications can preserve more autonomy (cf. 2.3) and the overall system can be more flexible and failure-tolerant. The publish/subscribe model brings message publishers together with message consumers that subscribe messages with certain topics. One of the most widely used technologies providing publish/subscribe capabilities is the Java Message Service (JMS) [Sun02]. Since there are two main use cases for EAI, we can distinguish between mediation and federation scenarios. The mediation scenario resembles the active object style as it has been conceived in [Bu90, KLB96]. Whenever an interesting event occurs in an application (e.g. data change, end of a transaction) a component of the EAI broker is notified, necessary actions (e.g. data propagation) are fired. The federation scenario can be used to shield the user from local interfaces when business intelligence applications on multiple applications have to be executed. Message brokers and enterprise service bus systems (ESB) are typical implementations of the EAI approach.

Data Representation

The coexistence of different data models used by autonomous participants of a distributed information system made it necessary to think about a suitable format for data exchange regardless of the used communication protocol. A canonical data model is considered an independent data model based on a standard data structure. It must be stated that the idea of distributed objects that communicate via method calls has become obsolete due to the same reasons why object-oriented database systems failed to overtake the market. There was no single widely-agreed object model although there have been standards defined by the Object Management Group. The OMG Core Object Model with few basic concepts was just an abstraction usable to define interfaces but required language bindings for every implementation. To exchange information between cooperating systems a data serialization is necessary to represent data independently from their original site. For that purpose, XML (together with XML Schema) was an important milestone. It appears that XML and the use of XML stylesheets has become the standard for this universal business language that has been needed for many years.

Service-Oriented Architecture and Business Process Management

XML is commonly used for interfacing services in a service-oriented architecture (SOA). SOA defines how to integrate disparate applications in a web of autonomous systems with multiple implementation platforms. It can be considered as the further development of EAI technologies. A service in a SOA presents a simple interface in terms of protocols and functionality that abstracts away its underlying complexity. Users can access independent services without knowledge of the service implementation. Web Services can implement a service-oriented architecture. The Web Service Description Language (WSDL) describes the services themselves, while SOAP describes the communication protocol. Alternative light-weight technologies can be used to implement a SOA (e.g. REST).

One main purpose of SOA is to allow users to combine chunks of functionality as they are represented in services to form applications in an agile way (resembling SAP cross-application technologies). Ideally, services can be used to construct executable business processes (also known as workflows) that span different organisations. Standards such as BPMN and WS-BPEL [Obj09] can be used for the definition and execution of business processes with service calls as process steps. So a common language to describe long-running activities over heterogeneous systems is available. The travel reservation example of DOM [BÖ+92] with all dependencies of the activities can be specified in a convenient way using the BPMN notation. WS-BPEL supports business transaction by a compensation-based mechanism (long running transactions). Since we are working in an open environment using the web, closed nested transactions can not be employed. Instead, compensating activities can be executed to undo effects of already finished activities if the overall process has to be cancelled. Fault and compensation handler can be defined as equivalent to contingency transactions of the DOM transaction model [BÖ+92].

3.2 Active Capabilities

Business Rules

Looking back at REACH and the active objects, the question remains: Where are the ECA rules gone? The need for active features is generally accepted. Therefore, so-called business rules have been incorporated into business processes [Ro03]. The idea of business rules is similar to that of triggers, they describe invariants that specify constraints of business aspects, e.g., in a credit application workflow the maximum loan sum that can be given to a bank customer of a certain category. All business rules can be maintained in a central business rules repository that should interact with a workflow engine. Business rules are different from flow logic that is inherent in the business process. The latter can be found in the process specification as there are control flow elements available (such as flow objects in BPMN or structured activities in BPEL). It is a software engineering issue where to place business-related rules. Alternatively, special decision services that encapsulate a more complex logic could be integrated as activity into the business process. Database triggers remain an important part, as they are responsible for local consistency constraints on a (lower) data level. Business Rule Management Systems (BRMS) have been evolved from rule engines, based on declarative definitions of business rules. The rule representation is mapped to a software system for executions. BRMS vendors have been acquired by big middleware companies because of the obvious need to integrate rules into business processes, for example: ILOG + IBM = IBM WebSphere ILOG BRMS [IBM10], Drools + JBoss = JBoss Rules [Jb10]. Thus the business rules approach gains more importance because it is a key to agile processes with flexible rules that are interpreted dynamically and may be changed at run-time of the process without adaptations of services.

Compared to ECA rules, the SQL standard imposes lots of restrictions on database triggers that consider only database operations as event or action. It is interesting to note that there is some more emphasis on the role of events in business process definitions, particularly in BPMN [Obj09]. An event in BPMN is something that happens (rather than an activity which is something that is done). The current BPMN standard provides a rich set of event types. We can classify throwing and catching events that support both scenarios of event-producing and event-consuming processes. An event can trigger a process as Start event, it can represent the result of a process as End event, or it is an Intermediate event that can catch or throw triggers. BPMN supports following event types: Message, Timer (i.e. absolute point in time or period), Error, Cancel (cancellation of a subprocess), Compensation (compensation of an activity), Conditional (triggered by a condition), Link (connections to other process parts), Signal (without specific targets), Terminate (immediate end of all activities without compensation). In BPMN there exists also a "Multiple" event element, which represents a choice between a set of events. An arbitrary number of other events can be connected to the "Multiple" event, which is in fact a complex event. For example, a message event can be combined with a time event to express the wait for a message with a timeout.

Event Processing

Complex Event Processing (CEP) is an approach [Lu02] that incorporates concepts of active databases, middleware and service-oriented architectures. Among them the issue of composite events and their detection is well-known from early active database research [CM94, BB+93]. Applications with lots of occurring events such as network management but also business process management (BPM) have triggered the development of CEP technologies. CEP must interact with BPM since BPM focuses on end-to-end business processes. A complex situation to be dealt with can mostly be considered as a combination of primitive events on a lower abstraction level. A simple example is calculating an average within a certain time frame based on data of the incoming events. A similar scenario is the processing of event streams to identify relevant events within those streams to enable in-time decision making. Typical applications are stock trading, RFID event processing or process monitoring. Composite events were just a part of the event hierarchy in REACH, whereas complex events with a complex detection or calculation algorithm can be considered more business-oriented in CEP. It is still disputed how far BPM is a natural fit for CEP which would motivate the integration of CEP technology into BPM.

A second trend emerged some years ago as a complement to the service-oriented architecture, the event-driven architecture where services can be triggered by incoming events [Ho06]. Sensing devices such as controllers or sensors can detect state changes of objects and create events which can then be processed by an active, i.e. event-driven, system. Such a system typically acts in an open environment characterized by an unpredictable and asynchronous behaviour. An event-driven architecture is characterized by applications and systems which transmit events among loosely coupled software components and services. The pattern recalls the concept of ECA rules with coupling modes to describe their execution. In an event-triggered architecture we can distinguish different components: event generator, event channel and event processing engine. The communication of events is based on the same principles as asynchronous messaging with queues to be processed later by an event processing engine.

3.3 Global Integrity Control in Heterogeneous Systems

Master Data Management

The problem of global data consistency in an organization operating a landscape of heterogeneous information systems has been addressed by the concept of Master Data Management (MDM). It comprises processes and tools to define and manage non-transactional data [WK06]. Among them are customer data or product data which are quite stable and also reference data such as calendars or geographical base data. The need for MDM is caused by mergers and acquisitions or the organizational autonomy of departments of a large corporation. The coarse design approach for MDM is to install a master data hub, a software component that stores the master data and keep it synchronized with the transactional systems [Wo07]. There are several basic styles of architecture used for MDM hubs: In the repository approach, the complete collection of master data is stored in a single database. The applications that use or produce master data have to be modified to use the master data in the hub instead of the local data. The registry approach is the opposite of the repository approach, because none of the master data is stored in the hub. The master data is maintained in the application databases, and the MDM hub contains lists of keys to find all related records in the local databases. The hybrid model, as the name implies, includes features of both the repository and the registry models, whereby the most significant attributes of master data are replicated on the hub so that certain MDM queries can be satisfied directly from the hub database.

Data Quality

The MDM approach is an important technology to implement data quality in a company. The term data quality considers data in an enterprise-wide context, because data is considered a production factor and an asset [WZL01]. The Total Data Quality Management Approach [Wa98] goes far beyond a global integrity control defined by some rules because the data properties that describe quality include not only "classical" database attributes such as completeness but also semantic and time-related aspects that have to be expressed in a knowledge base of a data quality management system.

4   Conclusions: Where Did We Reach?

When we discussed REACH 18 years ago we underestimated some trends that had impact on the next research directions. Although we already identified some problems in that time, their context was narrower and possible solutions for them were more restricted.

Consider viewpoints in architecture. Although process-oriented information systems (such as BPM) and data-oriented information systems (such as MDM or Data Warehouses) should be kept separate in operation, they can be enriched by active functionality as it has been discussed. Database triggers, business rules, complex events or rules in a master data hub base can be processed in a similar way but they are on different abstraction levels. So they have to be implemented in a non-redundant way avoiding cross-effects. The specification of an open distributed system in terms of viewpoints as the RM-ODP model provides, combined with system layers [Ku03] allows us to define the appropriate software architecture with active capabilities.

Rapid growth of events and data. The explosion of data and information driven by the digitalization and the development of the WWW raises new questions about the data quality of digital assets and (possibly event-driven) tools to control the quality. The internet enables lots of people to contribute information to the web as a global database. Web 2.0 media such as blogs or wikis reflect this trend of the active participation of users as information producers. The drawback of this development is a decline of the quality of the published information, it can be erroneous (i.e. with misspellings), incomplete or outdated. Actually the information quality can be maintained only for data that is mission-critical for an organization. Global data integrity has to be defined in different grades, each with a policy that implies the suitable implementation to ensure the necessary degree of consistency.

Unbundling. We can bring back into use the idea of unbundling that has been discussed for REACH [ZK96]. Active functionality, like other key features as access control or transaction management, can be considered a useful but not mandatory component of a database or information system. When required it must be possible to enrich the system by an active component, e.g. a business rule or a CEP engine in a BPM system. The question how far active functionality should be built-in is always a software engineering issue and depends on the application profile. In some cases it makes sense to use database triggers, in other cases log-based or message-based approaches may be superior, for example when managing master data in an environment of loosely-coupled systems.

The same applies to real-time features. In [BL99] some problems have been discussed when combining REACH technologies with different goals and requirements in one system. For example, real-time systems require predictability of resource consumption and execution time. On the other hand, active databases have to react on events and trigger rules dynamically, which makes predictability rather difficult. A second example is the detection delay for complex events in distributed environments, which may have an impact on the temporal consistency of the data. To solve certain trade-offs between conflicting system components, unbundling can be an approach for application-specific solutions.

Services as the new objects. The object paradigm has not gained the broad acceptance as it was expected when we worked out the REACH ideas. Should we replace "object" by "service" – and now define rules as services? First, we should understand why distributed objects and CORBA have failed. On one hand, they provided some abstraction with regard to the implementation platform and language. However, many ORB users did not understand the need to model some abstraction layers atop. Even some component models providing more complex artefacts were not the solution because they were often too specific and also too complex, e.g. Enterprise JavaBeans in the Java Enterprise Edition. Like distributed objects, services provide the same abstraction regarding platform and physical details. They can be design artefacts as well as executable units of work, typically as web services. They allow loose coupling between service provider and service user as it is required in most scenarios that connect multiple parties, even beyond organizational borders. In active systems, a service can be part of an ECA rule or even represent the whole rule.

Autonomy vs. Quality of Service (QoS). A service level agreement (SLA) is a useful concept to describe the necessary quality of service a provider has to guarantee. The requirements on the service agreed herein imply some restrictions on the local autonomy of the system of the service provider. If a service provider has to guarantee a certain response time he has to adapt his system, particularly in multi-tenant applications that are used by independent clients [GK+08]. Besides operational and availability requirements, data quality can be a key component of an SLA if the service deals with many data.

With services as generic concept, it is still necessary to solve the whole bunch of open software architecture issues, for example where to locate consistency constraints, event composition or execution of business rules. The differentiation of services into business services or lower-level infrastructure services allows to distinguish between low-level events (as they are raised by a sensing device) and business-level events (that may be the result of a computation). In [ASB10] QoS is discussed for event-based systems in terms of features they have to provide with an impact on their autonomy.

Convergence of analytics and processes. The separation of concerns in different abstraction layers allows us to decide independently on the best way to implement a multi-tier architecture with active functionality at some level. For example, it would be possible to define a business rule in a business process with a complex event that is interpreted as the result of the aggregation of many simple event occurrences stored in a database. Complex events mark the borderline between analytical and process-centric systems. There are no restrictions what to define as a service. Even CEP is a possible service candidate [AS+10]. In this way it recalls the "Rules are Objects Too" statement [DBM88]. Business process logs can represent the calculation base of complex events as well as the subject of further analytical, not necessarily event-driven, applications that measure the process quality.

5 Outlook

There will be some more progress in the development of hardware with major implications on research in distributed, active and real-time systems.

The growth of event data by enhanced hardware capabilities (e.g., RFID scanners, sensor networks) to monitor the environment in many scenarios, such as traffic control or healthcare systems, results in data streams that are processed in a way different from traditional DBMSs. The term "Internet of Things" refers to the networked interconnection of everyday objects producing billions of parallel and simultaneous events.

Data streams need not be stored persistently. Instead, standing queries or event patterns specify situations an active system has to cope with. As an alternative platform, main-memory databases are faster than disk-optimized databases, which make them attractive for applications where response time is critical. The emergence of solid state disk (SSD) technology that provides higher read performance over current hard disks will also have an impact on future DBMS architectures. Peripheral devices such as disk controllers or sensors can behave like a database becoming ubiquitous smart objects. Those small and mini databases (embedded databases) have to administrate themselves also known as self-managing, self-healing, always-up. They mark a trend that is also important to traditional DBMSs [Gr04].

Combining ideas of active and real-time databases applied in a heterogeneous world as we envisioned it in the REACH project remains a good approach for many today's information systems. However, we have to deal with crucial design issues resulting from the complexity of those systems [BL99]. First it is necessary to understand the interaction between different base technologies before moving the boundaries between them towards the goal of a more generic distributed platform with active and real-time functionality. As we suggested in the paper the future development will offer lots of further research challenges in this area.

Acknowledgment

I am greatly indebted to my scientific advisor, Professor Alejandro Buchmann, for his support and for all his suggestions when I was doing my PhD from 1992-97. Many of the problems and the ideas we discussed in that time appeared in application scenarios and IT trends I encountered later. In many cases, the REACH ideas were a key to understand conceptual and architectural issues of system design.

References

[AS+10]   Achakeyev, D., Seeger, B., Schäfer, D., Schmiegelt, P.: Complex Event Processing as a Service. In: GI-Workshop Database as a Service, HTWK Leipzig (2010), http://fgdb2010.imn.htwk-leipzig.de

[ASB10]   Appel, S., Sachs, K., Buchmann, A.: Quality of Service in Event-based Systems. In: 22nd GI-Workshop on Foundations of Databases (GvD), Bad Helmstedt, Germany (2010)

[BB95]   Branding, H., Buchmann, A.: On Providing Soft and Hard Real-Time Capabilities in an Active DBMS. In: Internat. Workshop on Active and Real-Time Database Systems, Skovde, Sweden (1995)

[BB+93]   Branding, H., Buchmann, A., Kudrass, T., Zimmermann, J.: Rules in an Open System: The REACH Rule System. In: Proc. of the 1st Internat. Workshop on Rules in Database Systems (RIDS), Edinburg, Springer, Heidelberg (1993)

[BL99]   Buchmann, A., Liebig, C.: Distributed, Object-Oriented, Active, Real-Time DBMSs: We Want It All – Do We Need Them (At) All? In: Proc. of the joint 24th IFAC/IFIP Workshop on Real-Time Programming and 3rd Internat. Workshop on Active and Real-Time Database Systems, Saarland, Germany (1999)

[BÖ+92]   Buchmann, A., Özsu, T., Hornick, M., Georgakopoulos, D., Manola, F.: A Transaction Model for Active Distributed Object Systems. In: Elmagarmid, A. (ed.) Database Transaction Models for Advanced Applications. Morgan Kaufmann Publ, San Francisco (1992)

[Bu90]   Buchmann, A.: Modelling Heterogeneous Systems as a Space of Active Objects. In: Proc. of the 4th Internat. Workshop on Persistent Objects, Martha's Vinyard (1990)

[CH+05]   Conrad, S., Hasselbring, W., Koschel, A., Tritsch, R.: Enterprise Application Integration – Grundlagen, Konzepte Entwurfsmuster, Praxisbeispiele. Spektrum Verlag, München (2005)

[CM94]   Chakravarthy, S., Mishra, D.: Snoop: An Expressive Event Specification Language for Active Databases. Data and Knowledge Engineering 14(10) (October 1994)

[DBM88]   Dayal, U., Buchmann, A., McCarthy, D.: Rules are Objects Too: A Knowledge Model for an Active Object-Oriented Database System. In: Proc. of the 2nd Internat. Workshop on Object-Oriented Database Systems, Bad Muenster (1988)

[GK+08]   Gmach, D., Krompass, S., Scholz, A., Wimmer, M., Kemper, A.: Adaptive quality of service management for enterprise services. ACM Transactions on the Web 2(1) (2008)

[Gr04]   Gray, J.: The Next Database Revolution. In: ACM SIGMOD Conference, Paris (2004)

[HA+05]   Halevy, A., Ashish, N., Bitton, D., Carey, M., Draper, D., Pollock, J., Rosenthal, A., Sikka, V.: Enterprise information integration: successes, challenges and controversies. In: ACM SIGMOD Conference, Baltimore (2005)

[He08]   Henning, M.: The rise and fall of CORBA. Communication of the ACM 51(8) (2008)

[HLM88] Hsu, M., Ladin, R., McCarthy, D.: An Execution Model for Active Data Base Management Systems. In: Proc. of the 3rd Internat. Conference on Data and Knowledge Bases, Jerusalem (1988)

[Ho06]   van Hoof, J.: How EDA extends SOA and why it is important. V6.0 (2006), http://soa-eda.blogspot.com

[IBM10] IBM Websphere: What is a BRMS, http://www-01.ibm.com/software/websphere/products/business-rule-management/whatis/ (retrieved on 24-08-2010)

[Jb10]   JBoss Community: Drools 5 – The Business Logic Integration Platform, http://www.jboss.org/drools (retrieved on 24-08-2010)

[KLB96] Kudrass, T., Loew, A., Buchmann, A.: Active Object-Relational Mediators. In: Proc. of the 1st Internat. Conference on Cooperative Information Systems (CoopIS 1996), Brussels (1996)

[Ku97]   Kudrass, T.: Aktive Mechanismen zur Konsistenzsicherung in Förderationen heterogener und autonomer Datenbanken. Dissertation, infix Verlag (1997) (in German)

[Ku03]   Kudrass, T.: Describing Architectures Using RM-ODP. In: Kilov, H., Baclawski, K. (eds.) Practical Foundations of Business System Specifications, pp. 231–245. Kluwer Academic Publishers, Dordrecht (2003)

[LCB99] Liebig, C., Cilia, M., Buchmann, A.: Event Composition in Time-dependent Distributed Systems. In: Proc. of the 4th Internat. Conference on Cooperative Information Systems (CoopIS 1999), Edinburgh, Scotland (1999)

[Lu02]   Luckham, D.: The Power of Events: An Introduction to Complex Event Processing. In: Distributed Enterprise Systems. Addison-Wesley, Reading (2002)

[Obj04] Object Management Group: CORBA Home Page (2004), http://www.corba.org/

[Obj09] Object Management Group BPMN 1.2 – Final Adopted Specification, http://www.omg.org/spec/BPMN/1.2/PDF

[RB01]   Rahm, E., Bernstein, P.: A survey of approaches to automatic schema matching. VLDB Journal 10(4) (2001)

[Ro03]   Ross, R.: Principles of the Business Rule Approach. Addison Wesley, Reading (2003)

[SL90]   Sheth, A., Larson, J.A.: Federated Database Systems for Managing Distributed Heterogeneous and Autonomous Databases. ACM Computing Surveys 22, 3 (1990)

[SRK92] Sheth, A., Rusinkiewicz, M., Karabatis, G.: Using Polytransactions to Manage Interdependent Data. In: Elmagarmid, A. (ed.) Database Transaction Models for Advanced Applications. Morgan Kaufmann Publ., San Francisco (1992)

[Sun02] Sun Microsystems Inc. Java Message Service Specification Final Release 1.1 (2002)

[Sun99] Sun Microsystems Inc.: Jini Architecture Specification – Revision 1.0 (1999)

[Wa98]   Wang, R.: A Product Perspective on Total Data Quality Management. Communications of the ACM 41(2) (1998)

[WK06]   Wolter, R., Haselden, K.: The What, Why, and How of Master Data Management. Microsoft Corp., http://msdn.microsoft.com/en-us/library/bb190163.aspx

[Wo07]   Wolter, R.: Master Data Management (MDM) Hub Architecture. Microsoft Corp., http://msdn.microsoft.com/en-us/library/bb410798.aspx

[WZL01] Wang, R., Ziad, M., Lee, Y.: Data Quality. Kluwer, Dordrecht (2001)

[ZK96]   Zimmermann, J., Kudrass, T.: Advanced Database Systems: From Monoliths to Unbundled Components. In: 8th GI-Workshop on Foundations of Databases (GvD), Friedrichsbrunn, Germany (1996)

Aspects of Data-Intensive Cloud Computing

Sebastian Frischbier and Ilia Petrov

Databases and Distributed Systems Group
Technische Universität Darmstadt, Germany
{frischbier,petrov}@dvs.tu-darmstadt.de

Abstract. The concept of Cloud Computing is by now at the peak of public attention and adoption. Driven by several economic and technological enablers, Cloud Computing is going to change the way we have to design, maintain and optimise large-scale data-intensive software systems in the future. Moving large-scale, data-intensive systems into the Cloud may not always be possible, but would solve many of today's typical problems. In this paper we focus on the opportunities and restrictions of current Cloud solutions regarding the data model of such software systems. We identify the technological issues coming along with this new paradigm and discuss the requirements to be met by Cloud solutions in order to provide a meaningful alternative to on-premise configurations.

1 Introduction

Large-scale, internet-based and data-intensive services have recently become a cornerstone of our daily activities: we buy books on Amazon, sell things on Ebay, stay in contact with friends and colleagues via Facebook, Googlemail or Hotmail, work collaboratively on documents with ThinkFree or GoogleDocs, comment on videos via YouTube, share our snapshots on Flickr or Picasa and plan our journeys with GoogleMaps [1,2,3,4,5,6,7,8,9]. These are just examples to name a few well-known internet-based and data-intensive services we use in our everyday life. All these services are powered by highly scalable applications based upon massive computing infrastructures. Until lately, operating infrastructures to power online-services at this scale involved large up-front investment and running costs for any provider: Whole data centers (or at least sufficient resources within) had to be located, acquired, staffed and operated. The whole technology stack had to be set up and optimised. Even if these resources are not run on-premise but rather as a managed-hosting solution the contracts are usually fixed and not usage-based, shifting the risk of resource planning from the infrastructure provider to the service provider. There has always been the danger of ill-sizing one's infrastructure based on wrong assumptions about the demand to be. Today's Internet is the backbone of global communication, connecting millions of users 24 hours seven days a week. This results in complex patterns of demand that are hard to anticipate and influence. On the one hand this offers the opportunity to attract millions of customers all over the world within hours, sometimes even by a minimum of controlled advertisement. On the other hand, this could backfire as well: unavailable, slow or insecure services get a bad reputation quickly, leading to a drop in demand and a loss of revenue [10]. In recent years there has been an increase in different commercial offerings, all being subsumed under

K. Sachs, I. Petrov, and P. Guerrero (Eds.): Buchmann Festschrift, LNCS 6462, pp. 57–77, 2010.

the keyword Cloud Computing. Due to these solutions offered by Amazon, Google, Microsoft and others, highly-scalable standardized computing power on-demand seems to become a commodity. The promise is to enable nearly everyone to build and operate powerful applications easily without the risks mentioned above. No up-front investment is needed and the risk of ill-sizing is shifted back from the service provider to the infrastructure provider. Thus Cloud Computing seems to be the future architecture to support especially large-scale and data-intensive applications. If the reality of Cloud Computing lives up to its promises we believe this movement to trigger two trends reinforcing each other: on the side of service providers, the financial benefits of Cloud Computing will lead to an overall adoption by companies of all sizes to deliver highly scalable services with as minimal costs as possible. On the user side, the broad supply of online-services raises the bar of expectations regarding usability, availability and reliability of new products even more. Thus companies will have to invest even more into their infrastructure in order to meet their customers' raised expectations. This again may lead to relying even more on Cloud Computing. Alas, on-premise middleware with individual frameworks atop is the dominating architecture for those large-scale, data-intensive applications by now. Especially in the context of Enterprise Computing, extensive middleware solutions are still custom-tailored to the requirements of each application. In turn, the application's functionality and design rely heavily on the properties and requirements of the supporting infrastructure. Although middleware components such as databases, application servers or messaging systems are highly standardized components yet, their individual combination and configuration allows to support highly specialized data-models required by the application logic. To us, this close symbiosis of application and infrastructure is still an obstacle to the broad adoption of Cloud Computing by large enterprises. Switching from traditional middleware to the Cloud has a massive influence on the management of an application's life-cycle. Among the several concerns are matters of design, implementation, testing, deployment, version control, debugging and maintenance. In this paper we focus on the underlying technological issues affecting the architectural decisions at the initial phase of a data-intensive application's life-cycle. We argue that there are certain requirements of data-intensive applications that are hardly meet by today's Cloud Computing. As a result, one still has to build and manage certain infrastructures on-premise in order to meet all requirements. Hence we first introduce the concept of Cloud Computing with its main characteristics, enablers and properties of today's solutions in Sect. 2. The requirements of data-intensive applications are then exemplarily presented in Sect. 3. Afterwards we contrast the mentioned properties of today's Cloud offerings with the requirements regarding data-models of two types of data-intensive applications in Sect. 4. In Sect. 5 we present a selection of academic as well as non-academic research results and sum up our findings in Sect. 6.

2   What Cloud Computing Offers Today

Although being a buzzword widely used in marketing and academia, the definition of Cloud Computing is still somehow blurred. There have been many attempts to define it, leading to multiply defined keywords which may seem contradicting at first [11]. Thus we sum up what we think is the core of Cloud Computing in this section, deducing the taxonomy being used in this paper to avoid any confusion. The section concludes with a discussion of several provider related as well as user related technological issues regarding the paradigm of Cloud Computing.

2.1   What Is Cloud Computing?

To cover the basic principles of Cloud Computing we refer to the definition of Cloud Computing by now being most agreed on. It was introduced by the National Institute of Standards and Technology (NIST) in 2009 [12]:

> Cloud Computing is a model for enabling convenient, on-demand network access to a shared pool of configurable computing resources (e.g., networks, servers, storage, applications and services) that can be rapidly provisioned and released with minimal management effort or service provider interaction.

Hence, the term Cloud Computing does not refer to a single technology or specific product. It rather denotes a generic term covering all solutions that offer computing resources as a commodity. The analogies quite often used are those of power or water supply. Another quite fitting analogy approach was introduced by Thomas Bittman of Gartner in 2009 [13]: transmitted music. The first transmission of music over air started as a very basic service with poor and unreliable quality. Anyway it has been an interesting and quite cheap alternative to the phonographic cylinders used as storage back than. Over time, standardization set in, quality and supply increased. Although these analogies have their weak spots we think it is an interesting idea worth mentioning. Based on their broad definition, Mell and Grance deduce five abstract key characteristics of Cloud Computing all current industrial offerings have in common [12]:

- *On-demand Self Service* In contrast to the provision of resources in on-premise or managed hosting scenarios, no human interaction is necessary to adjust the quantity of resources needed in the Cloud. This is true for provision of additional resources (scale-out) as well as for the release of unused ones (scale-in).
- *Broad Network Access* The service requested is delivered over a standardized network, typically the Internet.
- *Resource Pooling* The resources needed to provide the requested service automatically to the user are drained from a resource pool designed to serve dynamically multiple users (multi-tenancy). Size, location and structure of this resource pool are concealed to the user as well as the identity of the different parties being served by the same physical resource.
- *Rapid Elasticity* The provision of resources from the pool as well as the release of unused resources back to the pool has to be applied rapidly at any quantity and time. This creates the illusion of infinite resources to the user.
- *Measured Service* The performance and usage of resources are monitored and metered automatically in order to optimise the overall usage as well as to provide the information necessary for usage-based billing.

In regard to the parties having access to and control over the resource pool, public, Private and Hybrid Clouds are to be distinguished: Public Clouds are accessible by the general public but are controlled by a single dedicated Cloud provider. In this scenario, the tenants are independent organizations or users sharing the same resources. Private Clouds denote a scenario where Cloud services are only accessible for divisions of a single client's organization. From this point of view, a Private Cloud could be seen as a Public Cloud within a single company. The control over the resource pool is either on-premise or off-premise (managed-hosting solution). Hybrid Clouds combine resources of Private and Public Clouds, hence allowing the quick scale-out of a Private Cloud with resources temporarily drawn from a pool being publicly accessible.

2.2   Comparing Cloud Computing to Related Paradigms

Without first contrasting Cloud Computing to other related paradigms it is hard to point out and evaluate any unique contributions of this new paradigm. Thus we compare the key characteristics of Grid Computing, Utility Computing and Software-as-a-Service (SaaS) with those of Cloud Computing. The concept of Grid Computing emerged in the 1990s to provide an alternative for organisations to obtain computation power hitherto only delivered by supercomputers [14]. As Foster points out in [11] Grid Computing aims at delivering abstracted computational resources drawn from a distributed inter-organizational resource pool. Each participating organisation remains in control of the innate resources being committed to the pool while earning the right to use the Grid as a whole. A multilayered fabric is responsible for abstracting the underlying resources and scheduling the usage accordingly by queuing. Foster introduces a three point checklist to tell Grid and non-Grid infrastructures apart [15] by stating that a Grid (i) coordinates resources that are not subject to centralized control; (ii) is using standard, open, general-purpose protocols and interfaces; (iii) delivers nontrivial qualities of service. Applying these criteria as well as the characteristics mentioned above on Cloud Computing leads to the following conclusion: Grid computing and Cloud computing are not precluding but rather intersecting paradigms as depicted in Fig. 1. Both paradigms aim at delivering abstracted computing resources but differ in their particular approach and subject [11]: (i) Cloud computing aims at serving multiple users at the same time while Grid Computing is intended to deliver functionality at a scale and quality equivalent to supercomputers via a queuing system; (ii) Grids consist of resources owned and operated by different organisations while Clouds are under a single organisation's control; (iii) Cloud services can be obtained by using a standardized interface over a network while Grids require running the Grid fabric software locally. Both Utility Computing and Software-as-a-Service (SaaS) are rather generic terms. Mäkilä et al. define SaaS as a software deployment model, where the software is provisioned over the Internet as a service [16]. Utility Computing is even broader referred to by Ross and Westerman [17]:

> We define utility computing as a collection of technologies and business practices that enables computing to be delivered seamlessly and reliably across multiple computers. Moreover, computing capacity is available as needed and billed according to usage, much like water and electricity are today.

Taking all these top level definitions into account we propose the following categorization of the paradigms being discussed in this section: All concepts mentioned aim at

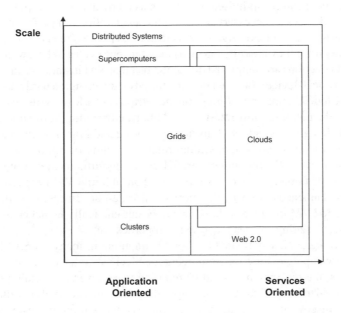

Fig. 1. Relationship of Grid and Cloud Computing as illustrated in [11]

delivering computational functionality as a service. While Utility Computing describes the general approach, the other concepts focus on different ways of realisation. SaaS focuses on delivering application logic while Grid Computing focuses on delivering computational power being equivalent to supercomputers. Thus Cloud Computing embraces these approaches, itself not being restricted to certain functionalities all the while being more palpable than Utility Computing.

2.3   Technological and Economic Enablers

To us, the observed characteristics of Cloud Computing as well as the success of this concept are the result of several economic and technological enablers reinforcing each other. We believe, that understanding these enablers and their connections is crucial to identify the real impact Cloud Computing has on large-scale, data-intensive applications. Thus we start by introducing the five technological and five economic enablers we think are the stepping stones for the success of Cloud Computing so far. Figure 2 illustrates the different enablers and their connection.

Technological Enablers

– *Virtualisation* is the key technology to enable Cloud Computing efficiently on the resource management level as well as on the product feature level. Regarding the resources being operated by the Cloud provider, this approach permits mainly three things: (i) the utilisation of a single physical device is maximised by hosting several virtual machines on it; (ii) the overall utilisation and power consummation of the resource pool can be optimised by running as many instances as possible on as few physical devices as necessary to ensure the availability and performance guaranteed by strict Service Level Agreements (SLA) [11]. The aim is to turn machines automatically off if they are fully idle; (iii) maintenance cycles of hardware and disaster recovery actions are simplified due to the fact that VM instances can be shifted from one physical device to another or be restarted on uncorrupted hardware quickly. Regarding Cloud Computing offerings on the infrastructure level, virtualisation permits the product feature most referred to: Automated scaling. Vertical scaling denotes the resizing of a single VM instance given (e.g. adding and removing RAM or CPU respectively). Horizontal scaling refers to adding or removing additional instances of a given VM running in parallel. By using virtualisation, both types of scaling could be implemented efficiently. Based on an initial VM image, additional instances are launched automatically (horizontal scale-out). In case of vertical scaling, a dedicated VM instance is shut down to be automatically launched again with new parameters setting the desired system properties.

- *Grid Computing* is closely related to Cloud Computing in many aspects. Both are partially overlapping but are far from being identical as we have seen in Sect. 2.2. Nevertheless, the realisation of Grid Computing faces several technological challenges that hold true for Cloud Computing on the infrastructure level as well. Among them are the discovering, scheduling, brokering, assigning, monitoring and load balancing of resources as well as the core communication and authentication in distributed resources [11]. By addressing and overcoming these challenges for Grid Computing, technical solutions emerged that are now used to form the basic fabric on the infrastructure level of Clouds [14].

- *Service-oriented Architecture (SOA)* may be seen as the latest representative of design concepts for distributed systems leading to a paradigm shift in application design in this context. The widespread appliance of this paradigm has laid the general basis for heavily distributed applications in the Cloud [12]: Individual functions are encapsulated as autonomous services being accessible only through an implementation independent interface. The use of shared memory is substituted by message-based communication hence adding transparency of location to the transparency of implementation. New functions can be implemented by combining existing services using message-based interactions. By now there are already several solutions to challenges such as semantic interoperability, state-preservation or parallel computing that have to be solved wile pursuing this design approach. Only applications being based on these principles could benefit from Cloud Computing to the full extent.

- *Rich Internet Applications (RIA)*. For many years, the user experience of web based applications has been far from that of desktop applications. The ever increasing functionality of today's web technology (e.g. client-side processing, asynchronous communication or built-in multimedia support of web browsers) now permits complex web based applications that resemble desktop applications (c.f. ThinkFree or GoogleDocs). Using RIA to deliver the functionality of complex software over the Internet has certain advantages for both user and provider: no software has to be installed and maintained on the user's system because the application is hosted centrally by the provider and accessed by a web browser. Such centrally managed software allows easier maintenance, resource provisioning and usage metering by the provider.

- *Broad network coverage.* To deliver high-volume products and smooth interactions for RIAs over the Internet, the overall coverage of broadband connections is crucial. This holds true not only for a good end user experience but for the interactions between different Cloud services and data centers as well. In recent years there has been a significant increase, not only in the overall coverage of broadband networks all over the world but also in capacity and performance.

Economic Enablers

- *Economy of Scale.* The characteristics of Cloud Computing we have seen so far favour large-scale infrastructures. As Greenberg at al. [18] or Church et al. [19] point out, especially providers of Cloud infrastructure services benefit from economy of scale at multiple cost categories: From one-time investments for land, buildings, power and network infrastructure to frequently returning costs for hardware and running costs for power supply, cooling and maintenance [20]. Especially the rapid decrease of hardware costs intensifies the economies of scale for infrastructures.
- *Multi-tenancy.* Running multiple users on a single resource is not a quite new concept from a technological point of view. Nevertheless, running different external customers in parallel on abstracted resources based on a shared and brokered infrastructure pool with isolated data, performance and application logic embraces certain challenges [21]. Besides the technological issues to ensure such isolation, multi-tenancy has to be accepted by customers.
- *Micropayment.* To exploit a sophisticated willingness to pay a provider has to offer different products in high granularity to different customers. Hence, charging even small quantities effectively with micropayment enables the provider to maximizing both revenue and utilisation. We subsume the emergence of different online payment methods (e.g. PayPal) as well as the increased use of credit card payments under this topic.
- *Open Source Software.* License fees for software have always been a serious matter of expense especially at large-scale data centers. Using open source software today can be an adequate way to decrease the impact of license fees on the revenue dramatically. By now, there are open source substitutes all along the technology stack, starting at the virtualisation layer and ending with the presentation layer (i.e. web browsers). Furthermore, open source software can be altered to suit very specific needs without violating license terms. Although that may be true for other proprietary systems as well, open source systems suit another long-term aspect: By relying on open source software (including open standards) lock-in effects to specific providers are minimised.
- *Standardisation.* Economy of scale and standardisation are closely related: Standardisation fuels economy of scale by making components interchangeable and comparable. In regard to Cloud Computing, standardisation helps to reduce complexity and increase flexibility on all levels of the technology stack (e.g. standardised hardware, application servers or frameworks).

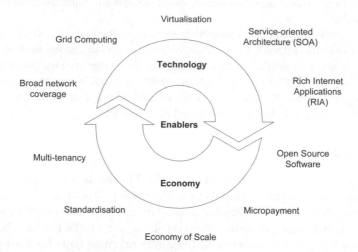

Virtualisation

Grid Computing

Service-oriented
Architecture (SOA)

Technology

Broad network
coverage

Rich Internet
Applications
(RIA)

Enablers

Multi-tenancy

Open Source
Software

Economy

Standardisation

Micropayment

Economy of Scale

Fig. 2. Identified key enablers for Cloud Computing

Having introduced these enablers so far we point out some mutual dependencies between them leading to the characteristics of Cloud Computing as presented in Sect. 2.1:
Virtualisation and Grid Computing form the fabric that enables resource pooling and
rapid elasticity. SOA with its related paradigms reshaped both middleware and application architecture to run on those abstracted distributed resources efficiently as managed
services. Economy of scale, standardisation and open source software make Cloud services cost-effective by rewarding scale, reducing complexity and minimising license fees
as well as lock-in effects. RIA and broad network coverage simplify renting and maintaining computational functionality as on-demand self-services. Micropayment permits
effectively charging the usage of such functionality at fine granularity, making even
highly diversified products lucrative. Multi-tenancy maximizes both utilisation and risk-
reduction by involving different parties. Users benefit from transparent pricing models
based on metered usage and seemingly indefinite resources being provided to them on
an abstraction level being suitable for their own purpose. Hence, further technological
enhancements will be encouraged, fuelling the economic mechanisms mentioned here.

2.4 Resulting Business Models and Pricing

While presenting the characteristics as well as the enablers for Cloud Computing, we
referred to the digital product being delivered only as abstract computing functionality. Substantiating this generic term leads to classifying the different delivery models
of Cloud Computing and their business models. As we have discussed earlier, Clouds
benefit highly from standardisation in order to maximize the economies of scale. Hence
providers of Cloud services tend to standardise as many components of their products
and supporting architecture as possible. Such standardisation is often achieved by adding
an abstraction layer and restricting access to the technology stack beneath it. Therefore,

each delivery model can be defined by two aspects: A core functionality being offered as a service and a ratio of control by user vs. control by provider for the entire technology stack.

- *On-premise*. The whole technology stack is owned and controlled by the user. Until recently this is the typical setting for large-scale data-intensive applications as described in Sect. 1. This scenario could also be used to implement a Private Cloud setting with the technologies discussed in Sect. 2.3.
- *Managed Service Hosting (MSH)*. Entire servers or virtual machines are rented exclusively to a single user. The user can choose the operating system to be used and is in control of layers atop the infrastructure while the provider is responsible for maintenance and operation. The contract period is usually fixed and usage independently. Scale-out could be achieved by additional contracts and is seldom promptly.
- *Infrastructure as a Service (IaaS)*. As in MSH, the product core being delivered is computation power at the infrastructure level for the user to build his own stack upon. Again the user has full control over the layers atop of the infrastructure. In contrast to MSH, the resources being rented by the user are not dedicated servers but virtual machines or equally abstract machine instances based on a shared resource pool. The structure, location and usage of the resource pool are opaque to the user and organised according to the requirements of the provider. This has two advantages: Firstly, scale-in as well as scale-out of instances can be achieved in almost real time according to demand. Secondly, maintenance cycles can be performed by the provider without affecting the availability and performance guaranteed to the user. Pricing is usage-based, generally derived from the number, configuration and usage duration of the active instances.
- *Platform as a Service (PaaS)*. The product core is middleware functionality ranging from databank management systems (DBMS), messaging or load balancing to even more specialized functions to build custom applications upon. The functionality is provided through an abstracted application programming interface (API) making the implementation and detailed configuration of the underlying infrastructure inaccessible to the user. Thus, applications build on PaaS have to take that into account. When the usage for the application upon the platform grows, the provider is responsible for automatically scaling the underlying resources to deliver the quality and performance guaranteed. Pricing is usage-based with the reference value depending on the functionality being consumed.
- *Software as a Service (SaaS)*. The product delivered by SaaS is typically a fully-fledged application. Contrary to PaaS, services at this level mostly aim at end-users by providing high-level user-experience via rich internet applications. As SaaS is the first primarily end-user oriented Cloud business model introduced here, it is quite often identified with Cloud Computing itself by the public. All examples given in Sect. 1 refer to typical SaaS offerings. In addition to the graphical user interface provided by RIAs, advanced functionality can be accessed through APIs quite often to build custom extensions (e.g. as plug-ins for web browsers). Again the provider is responsible for scaling the underlying resources according to the utilisation of the application. Pricing is usage or subscription based (recurring fees).
- *X as a Service (XaaS)*. By restricting the user control even more towards the mere passive use of individual and highly specialised functionalities, new business

models can be derived. We propose here exemplarily the idea of Function as a Service (FaaS) as a special case of SaaS. Unlike SaaS, FaaS focuses on delivering a single functionality through a standardised API only. Examples would be the typical web services: Information about stock exchange prices, appraisal of creditworthiness, weather forecasts or visualisations of GPS coordinates. To us, the further specialisation of SaaS is motivated by the increasing occurrence of smartphone-based applications (apps) over the last two years. Many of these applications are specialised in visualising real-time information being delivered by large-scale online-applications. The throughput of today's mobile connections is still rather limited by way of comparison to broadband networks. In addition, many smartphones still have certain restrictions regarding screen resolution or supported technology. Hence the transmission of core information is often preferred to the use of extensive rich internet applications as in SaaS offerings. In such a scenario, the user would have even less control over the service consumed while the level of abstraction is extremely high. Driven by the trend of highly specialized apps for smartphones we believe the business model of XaaS/FaaS soon to grow out of the status of being a subtype of SaaS.

Although not being a prerequisite, it is often assumed that Cloud services are stacked to leverage the advantages of Cloud Computing at subjacent layers [22,14]. In addition, either IaaS, PaaS, SaaS or XaaS can be implemented as Public or Private Cloud. To us, the attractiveness of the business models mentioned above could be mapped to the Long Tail of users as depicted in Fig. 3. We base our assumption on the following reasoning: Moving from the first to the last business model both standardisation and specialisation

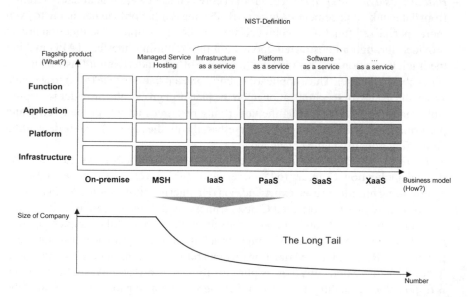

Fig. 3. Different business models of Cloud Computing derived from the level of abstraction and product core

increase. This results in offerings of higher granularity and cost effectiveness. Especially small and middle businesses (SMBs) or start ups may rank cost effectiveness and ease of use over extensive control.

2.5   Current Commercial Solutions for Public Clouds

To cover the range of Cloud solutions available today we present a selection of commercial solutions and their main characteristics in this section.

- *Amazon* offers solutions at all levels of abstraction. Nevertheless the dependencies of most offerings refer to a focus on the IaaS and PaaS levels. Thus we concentrate our brief presentation on representatives from both core and complementary solutions on these levels. With Elastic Cloud Computing (EC2), Amazon offers the archetyp of IaaS Cloud Computing by providing abstract computing facilities in terms of virtual Amazon Machine Images (AMI) [23]. Amazon Simple Storage Solution (S3) resembles a key-value storage solution for large objects that are seldom written but often read. The Relational Database Service allows less complex relational models. CloudFront allows to redirect requests to data stores geographically close to the customer. Other solutions at the IaaS level (i.e. Elastic Load Balancing, Virtual Private Cloud), the PaaS level (i.e. Elastic Block Storage, MapReduce) or as SaaS level (i.e. Cloud Watch, Flexible Payments Service) can be seen as extensions to these core products. For more detail on these solutions as well as use cases we refer to [24,25,26].
- *Google* aims at the layers atop of IaaS with several offerings: With Google App Engine [27], Google provides a PaaS solution to develop, test and host applications written in Java or Python. By developing applications against the Google App Engine API, issues regarding deployment, sandboxing, instantiation, scaling or load balancing are handled by the Google middleware and infrastructure. Google App Engine offers a schemaless datastore with an SQL-like syntax to manipulate tables while not being a traditional relational database. On the downside, there are artificial restrictions to the application's capabilities by the platform as mentioned in [14]. Other offerings such as Google Docs or Google Mail are most prominent rich internet applications with additional API access [28,29,30] as SaaS solutions. Google Docs offers the functionality of viewing and editing documents online by using a rich internet application while Google Mail implements a typical mail client. In addition, there are several experimental offerings that could be assigned to XaaS/FaaS: Google Finance Data API, Google Friend Connect APIs, Gadgets API, Google Geocoding API or the Google Prediction API. All matured offerings mentioned are available with basic functionalities being free of charge. Charging for the Google App Engine is usage-based and derived from the amount of storage and bandwidth as well as the CPU cycles used by the application. Google Docs and Google Mail are also offered subscription-based per user as professional versions.
- *Microsoft* entered the Cloud Computing market with Windows Azure in 2009. The Azure platform can be seen as a mixture of IaaS and PaaS by combining aspects of both [31]. Azure itself contains of offers several Cloud based storage solutions: Windows Azure Storage and Azure SQL. Windows Azure Storage is provided by

the Azure platform itself and consists of Blobs, Tables and Queues as native data models. A Blob stores binary objects up to 50 GB total thus being suitable especially for multimedia objects. Different Blobs are logically combined and managed within a Blob Container. Both Container and single Blob can be associated with metadata in form of key-value-pairs. Tables consist of entities (rows) and associated properties (colums) to support structured data. Queues represent a asynchronous messaging facility. Windows Azure SQL resembles a auto-scalable SQL-server as SaaS solution, claiming to work seamless with on-premise installations of Microsoft SQL Server [32].

– *Salesforce* is an on-demand CRM product that is traditionally regarded as one of the first in the field of Cloud Computing. In the meantime Salesfore supports wide range of applications and supports a robust Cloud platform, powerful application development framework and solid services. It a typical representative of the SaaS group. As underlying technology Salesforce uses Oracle RAC [33] as a relational database. The data model is simple and essentially comprising database tables and indices. Salesforce has a multi-tenant architecture and assigns a tenant to a Salesfore Node. The system has a powerful application development framework and and run-time environment. Applications are developed in Salesforece's own APEX programming language, which supports multi-tenant constructs natively, is dynamic and eases application and data construct generation at run-time.

– *Private Cloud Solutions* are offered by several suppliers. Among them are IBM, Sun Microsystems, Red Hat, Jboss, Oracle and Zimory.

2.6   Technological Issues to Think about

Some of the major issues that distinguish Cloud Computing from other approaches are: scale and simplicity. Under scale we mean: (i) the number of concurrent and potential users and requests per second; (ii) the size of the computing facility (CPUs, aggregate memory, aggregate storage capacity) and the size of the data; (iii) the geographical distribution. Simplicity, on the other hand, is associated with the way the system is used: (a) ease of programming API simplicity; (b) ease of administration and growth; (c) ease of consuming and combining different services. These are not easy to achieve especially under the premise of high performance. Hence most of the vendors and researches mingle Cloud applications (sometimes services) with Cloud infrastructure. Indeed the application requirements influence the way the Cloud infrastructure is designed and vice versa objective facts in the Cloud environment influence hard design choices in the Cloud application architecture. None the less the goal of many Cloud vendors is to provide a general platform on top of which Cloud applications can be developed. Below we discuss some of the issues specific to provider and application separately.

Provider Related

– *Consistency.* The responsibility of enforcing consistency of Cloud data is separated between the infrastructure and the application. In enterprise computing the established approach is expect declarative or implicit consistency such as in ACID transactions. Since at this stage most of the Cloud applications are tightly coupled with their infrastructure the application developers implement application specific consistency mechanisms. Due to issues resulting from scale most of the consistency notions (two phase commit protocol, global atomicity) are inefficient or very difficult to realize. Due to the CAP theorem enforcing consistency (on infrastructural and application level) depends on handling availability and the required network resilience.

- *Availability*. Cloud services/application as well as the Cloud infrastructure are expected to be as available as enterprise applications. There are however several issues that need to be overcome: (i) internet reliability - all Cloud services are available over the internet hence the upper bound to their availability is the internet availability, which is max. 99.9%. The issue can be generalized in terms of network reliability. (ii) hardware fault tolerance since the Cloud utilises commodity hardware the infrastructure has to tolerate high failure rates. For example a recent analysis of the RAM failure rates at Google [34] showed that these lie higher than the currently assumed value. (iii) All these explain why whole data centers can be suddenly detached from the rest of the infrastructure. Methods to address these issues at present are: (a) load balancing; (b) redundancy in terms of (geographical) replication. Careful data placement minimize the response times; having multiple consistent replicas of the data helps to increase the availability (the request can be served on a different site). Careful data placement also helps the Cloud designers to fight latency. While the infrastructure can provide replication mechanisms these only work well if they are suitable to and well instrumented by the application. Latency is another issue that has to be addressed in Cloud applications. (its effect on enterprise applications is not as direct). It can be minimized through careful data placement so that requests can be served close to the user and through extensive caching. Both means to address latency are very application dependent.
- *Predictable Performance + Elasticity*. Since many resource hungry applications are sharing the same set of computing resources in a Cloud Computing facility, it should be guaranteed that there is no resource contention and that applications are isolated form each other and are provided with predicable framework performance. Two factors should be specially emphasized: elasticity and scalability. Elasticity is associated with providing stable and predicable performance as resource demands of applications increase (or decrease) ensuring optimal resource utilisation. If an application grows resources are not only added in terms of new servers, it also means more bandwidth, more storage, better load balancing. Elasticity is related to up- and down-scaling but is more complex in that it involves the Cloud infrastructure as well. Scalability is the relevant term in this context: that data store must be able to execute large requests with low response times and redistribute data an load on the new hardware. Some of the Cloud models (such as IaaS, i.e EC2) rely heavily on virtualization. While virtualization offers significant advantages in handling elasticity and resource sharing the way Disk IO and Network IO are handled. In fact [35,36] report similar results.
- *Multi-Tenancy*. Multi-tenancy is one of the key data storage concepts on the Cloud. It enables user data manageability, common storage and increased performance.

Every user is being seen as a tenant in a multi-tenant store: its data is stored in a common and general schema with other users' data. The data entries for a specific user are automatically annotated with the TenantID. Many Cloud solution derive tenant specific typed tables from the common data storage.

– *Scalable and High Performance Storage.* Due to many technical issues data storage is one of the central issues in Cloud Computing. In Cloud scenario it is one of the key factors for well-performing and scalable Cloud applications/services. While raw storage is needed in enterprise computing, it is an inadequate model for the Cloud. Due to the many possible optimizations and performance gains Cloud storage is almost always bound to a certain data model. Many Cloud providers even report multiple data stores for different data models (nearly relational, key-value stores, unstructured large object stores). For example Large parts of Google's data are stored on GFS which has inherent support for replication. Structured data are stored in BigTable. Facebook's datamodel is graph-based consisting of Fbobj and associations among them. Salesforce's datamodel is essentially relational comprising relational tables and indices. In addition there several different data store types that emerge in Cloud environments. Key Value stores are very widely spread both as storage service and as caching tier. Almost every Cloud provider has a document store or a large object store. Researchers [37] unify those under the term NoSQL databases. Interestingly enough the optimizations and scalability depend indirectly on the application as well. For example both Salesforce and Facbook rely on SQL databases [38,33], however Salesfore can very well partition on tenant level (see multi-tenancy), while Facebook cannot due to the strongly referenced graph nature of their data.

– *Strong and Stable API.* The interface which Cloud frameworks exposes to the Cloud applications should be precisely controlled. In fact many SaaS vendors such as salesforce [33] claim to support internally a single version of their codebase, but emulate older versions. While this allows for a significant maintenance, development and performance gain, it imposes strict requirements on applications and ISVs.

– *Software Licensing.* Software licenses may pose a significant acceptance barrier to the IaaS model. It exposes directly elastic computational resources such as CPUs or storage, while allowing to deploy running images with pre-installed commercial software. Some software vendors require licenses not for present elastic resources, but rather for the physically available hardware resources on the server.

User Related

– *Parallelism.* Commodity hardware, clusters of 10 000 cores and 5 000 computers Cloud systems horizontally scalable with geographical partitioning. To make the best of this horizontal scale computing facility applications should be translatable to parallel jobs that can run onto all these machines in parallel. This is the only way to satisfy the high number of user requests per second against terabytes of data. Yet not every application and not every algorithm implemented in a certain programming language can be translated efficiently into small parallelizable tasks. The task complexity is minimized by employing special-purpose programming languages, especially for data processing ([39]). For example, Google's MapReduce [40] framework and its open source implementation Hadoop by Yahoo [41] provides an excellent utility for Cloud data analysis. Yet complex requests such as ones employing joins cannot be implemented efficiently on MapReduce. Such issues are address by for instance Yahoo's Pig framework in which complex data analysis tasks are expressed in the Pig Latin language and compiled down to MapReduce jobs and deployed on Haddop. Hence not every enterprise application can make optimal use of the Cloud advantages without a complete re-design.

- *Data-Model.* Most of the enterprise applications operate on a relatively well-defined data model. Web- or Cloud applications, alternatively, must be able to handle both structured and unstructured, combine multimedia and semantic metadata, handle text natively. This poses the grand challenge of uniform and efficient handling. Cloud applications have to operate on a general data model delegating all of the heavy-lifting to the infrastructure. (See 2.3.1 and 2.3.1.4). In practice however different Cloud applications rely on different models hence the infrastructure has to support different sores to optimally handle them. For example, Facebook relies on a interconnected graph model comprising FbObjects and Associations, which is heavily metadata driven [38]. Mail attachments will be stored on a large object store, while mail messages will go to a different system. Through heavy use of metadata these pieces of information can be correlated properly. Important is that the infrastructure provides a way to combine services from different stores.

- *Strict ACID-Transactions.* Transactional guarantees are one of the key characteristics of enterprise applications. While ACID transactions represent a very powerful mechanism, it has been proven that they incur a significant performance overhead in highly distributed systems. Many authors argue that [42,43] in the Cloud availability should be traded for consistency. In addition models such as eventual consistency [43] have been proposed. The implications for the applications a manifold: (i) the application developer should custom-build consistency mechanisms; (ii) applications relying on consistency are no suitable for the Cloud. (iii) applications relying on strong consistency guarantees continue to exists on an enterprise facility are exposed a service and are consumed in the Cloud. This however is the least desirable alternative.

- *Security and Encryption.* While the majority of the Cloud providers report major security efforts as part of their infrastructure, security is widely viewed as a major hurdle towards Cloud migration. Enterprise systems with heightened security are designed to operate directly on encrypted data. Such an approach can be adopted in Cloud applications. On the one hand it entails significant restrictions on the applications feature set and design. On the other hand it leverages well with the abundant computing power available within the Cloud.

- *Interoperability.* While the predominant view nowadays is that applications are developed for a certain Cloud provider, this dependence seems too risky and is considered a hurdle for wide Cloud migration [10]. Out of this reason researchers recognize the need to be able to interoperate between Clouds and ideally be able to migrate. Given the experience for distributed computing this task will be very difficult.

3   Requirements of Data-Intensive Applications

The scale is the single most essential property that dominates the discussion of data-intensive applications in enterprise computing and in a Cloud environment. It influences many application characteristics such as basic assumptions, architecture, algorithms as well as features.

3.1   Types of Data-Intensive Applications

While the two general archetypes of data-intensive applications (OLAP and OLTP) are still present they differ from their classical meaning.

OLAP. On-Line Analytical Processing (OLAP) refers to querying mostly historical and multi-dimensional data with the purpose of analyzing it and reporting certain figures. The term is generalized by the terms business intelligence und analytics, although these carry a semantics of their own. In the Cloud most vendors offer approaches and technologies for performing analytics. These analyze terabytes of data calculating statistics or performing aggregate functions. Typical analytical operations such as relational joins are very difficult to implement. Other operators are also difficult to implement [44]. A major advantage and design goal is to be able to process TB of data, and therefore scale on a myriad of small inexpensive machines. This high degree of parallelism and elasticity requires compromises on the algorithmic richness and on the data model part. Nonetheless Cloud providers such as Salesforce do offer a close-to-relational data model and operator set. They have found an elegant way to bring the relational technology to the Cloud. Most of the analytical applications match the Cloud very well. They depend mostly on the cumulative bandwidth with which the data can be read and transferred - bandwidth is present within a Cloud data centre. They depend on the CPU power which is available as well.

OLTP. Although many Cloud applications rely on a batch update mode or expect rare updates there are many cases where frequent updates are rather the rule. Facebook and Salesforce are good example of that. Users of both systems update their enterprise data, profiles, pictures or status frequently. Although updates are a weakness in the Cloud environment both systems seem to handle them very well. The CAP theorem explains the key factor preventing Cloud systems from handling updates. On the one hand to increase the availability (and account for possible hardware failures) Cloud systems replicate data. If updates are to be handled consistently all replicas must be updated before the update operation is acknowledged, which is time consuming and blocks system resources. This cannot be done at the high request rate these systems have to serve. Therefore in the Cloud systems are optimised for availability not consistency [42,43]. In systems such as Facebook or Salesfore consistency is mostly achieved through cache invalidation or partitioning.

3.2   Characteristics Regarding Data

Data partitioning (or data sharding) is the ability to place data into buckets so that every bucket is updated independently of each other. For example, the data of a tenant is a subset of the global tenant table that is updated by a certain set of clients. It is than possible to take that tenants data and place it in a data center in geographical proximity to the client. This is the mode chosen by the architects of Salesfore. Facebook's data on the other hand is very strongly connected. Therefore data partitioning cannot be considered realistic option. Constructing a page on Facebook requires data from different friends of a person. It is difficult to predict the exact geographical distribution of the friends. Even if the system manages to do so there is no guarantee that in future friends from different locations will join. Therefore it is impossible to partition data across Facebook datacenters. Therefore in absence of good partitioning possibilities a pulling friends status from a geographically remote center may slow down the construction of a page. Instead of partitioning [38] Facebook relies on metadata replication, main memory data processing, distributed indexing as well as multiple systems performing specializes data querying.

4   Discussion: Cloud vs. On-Premise

In an on-premise scenario systems with classical three tier architectures are very successfully utilised. Since these are located in the same data centre, latencies are low, throughput is high and the storage high performant. CRM as well as ERP systems are examples of OLTP systems. In a Cloud environment these work well only if the data can be partitioned/sharded properly to increase scalability. In a multi tenant environment it is needed to assign a tenant to a data centre near the client (or the majority of clients). Interestingly enough the tree tier architecture is still preserved within a data centre. Due to the fact that tenants are exclusively allotted to a data centre transactions do not span data centers thus being delayed by high latencies. Text processing on the other hand poses different requirements. In terms of transactions text processing implies long running transactions, where a document can be checked out, processed and checked back in. Thus it minimizes resource contention on shared resources, since no long locks are being held and consistency is being enforced upon check in. Interestingly this mode can be very well combined with versioning; for instance depending on the versioning semantics a new branch or a new version can be created. The check in of a document can trigger a whole set of post-processing operations (such as indexing, analytics ETL etc.) operating on the bulk of the document. Regardless of the rich client presentation requirements this mode of operations is very suitable for the Cloud. Moreover the transparent check-in/check-out operations are performed within the users' private workspace on the Cloud and not on the local machine (as with classical version control systems) thus avoiding possible bandwidth issues.

5   Related Work

By blending economic and technological aspects as well as blurring the line between application and infrastructure, the concept of Cloud Computing is subject to a wide spectrum of academic research. Hence a multitude of academic publications is available. We would like to point out some exemplarily samples we think most suitable for reflecting on the topic of Cloud Computing in its various dimensions.

Armbrust et al. analyse the phenomenon of Cloud Computing by starting from the hardware-level [10,35]. Foster et al. define the key issues of Grid-Computing in [15] and point out the main differences to Cloud Computing in [11]. Yang and Tate give a descriptive review of 58 academic articles regarding Cloud Computing as in 2009 [45]. Han surveys the market acceptance of Cloud Computing in [23]. Greenberg et al. look at possibilities to reduce costs in data centers from a provider related point of view in [18]. Church et al. discuss advantages and drawbacks of geo-diverse, distributed or containerized designs for data centers [19] .

The problem of the concurring requirements consistency, availability and performance in distributed systems is formalized as CAP-Theorem in [46] and further discussed in [43,47,48]. Bining et al. show the first steps towards a benchmark for Cloud solutions in [49]. There are multiple new technologies that are especially developed for Cloud scenarios. Some of the most prominent representatives cover the areas of structured data storage, analytics and caching. Google's BigTable [50] technology is one of the leading structured data stores. Alternative implementations are Yahoo! HBase [51], or Hypertable [52]. Facebook's Cassandra [53] is another distributed storage platform. Amazon S3 is another example of Cloud data store. In terms of analytics some of the dominating frameworks are Google's MapReduce [54] and its open source implementation from Yahoo Hadoop [41]. In addition there are numerous data caching technologies such as Facebook's MemCached [55].

In addition to the publications mentioned above, there is a nearly infinite number of unreviewed industry techreports, whitepapers and presentations available today. Due to the fact that Cloud Computing is mainly an industry-driven topic, we consider some of these to be noted when trying to understand and analyse the phenomena of Cloud Computing. Thus we would like to recommend a few of them [56,57,58,59,60,61].

6   Summary and Conclusions

In the present paper we analyzed different aspect of data intensive Cloud Computing applications and infrastructure. We analyzed requirements and the presented status quo between infrastructural and application requirements, between economic and technical factors. Cloud Computing on the one hand has a wider range of requirements to satisfy compared to enterprise computing, on the other hand many issues due to scale, elasticity and simplicity are still unsolved or implemented in a custom-taylored way. In addition Could Computing as a paradigm inherently offers significant diversity in terms of possible approaches (IaaS, Paas, SaaS, etc.) and possible architectural and design alternatives.

We also reach the conclusion that applications and Cloud infrastructures are tightly coupled and influence each other. In order to achieve high performance and cope with issues resulting from the large scale many Cloud vendors resort to custom solutions. New algorithms and paradigms are developed from scratch (e.g. Google's MapReduce). In this respect data sharding, transactions consistency and isolation are some of the dominating issues. On the other hand many Cloud providers aim at reusing existing approaches and technologies from the field of enterprise computing. One of the issues looming on the horizon is the mechanisms for designing Cloud applications and infrastructures.

To recapitulate data-intensive Cloud Computing is a very fast evolving field offering much room for innovation. New approaches can be expected in the field of transaction processing, access paths, architectures, caching and analytics.

References

1. YouTube: Youtube - broadcast yourself (2010), `http://www.youtube.com/`
2. Yahoo!: Flickr (2010), `http://www.flickr.com`
3. Ebay: ebay - new & used electronics, cars, apparel, collectibles, sporting goods & more at low prices (2010), `http://www.ebay.com`
4. Google: Google picasa (2010), `http://www.google.com/picasa`
5. Microsoft: Microsoft hotmail (2010), `http://www.hotmail.com`
6. Amazon.com: Online shopping for electronics, apparel, computers, books, dvds & more (2010), `http://www.amazon.com`
7. Google: Google documents and spreadsheets (2010), `http://www.google.com/docs/`
8. Facebook: Facebook (2010), `http://www.facebook.com`
9. Google: Google maps (2010), `http://maps.google.com/`
10. Armbrust, M., Fox, A., Griffith, R., Joseph, A., Katz, R., Konwinski, A., Lee, G., Patterson, D., Rabkin, A., Stoica, I., et al.: A view of cloud computing. Communications of the ACM 53(4), 50–58 (2010)
11. Foster, I., Zhao, Y., Raicu, I., Lu, S.: Cloud computing and grid computing 360-degree compared. In: Grid Computing Environments Workshop, 2008. GCE 2008, pp. 1–10 (2008)
12. Mell, P., Grance, T.: The NIST Definition of Cloud Computing. National Institute of Standards and Technology, Information Technology Laboratory (July 2009)
13. Bittman, T.: A better cloud computing analogy (September 2009), `http://blogs.gartner.com/thomas_bittman/2009/98/22/a-better-cloud-computing-analogy/`
14. Giordanelli, R., Mastroianni, C.: The cloud computing paradigm: Characteristics, opportunities and research issues. Technical Report RT-ICAR-CS-10-01, Consiglio Nazionale delle Ricerche Istituto di Calcolo e Reti ad Alte Pestazioni (April 2010)
15. Foster, I.: What is the grid? A three point checklist. GRID Today 1(6), 22–25 (2002)
16. Mäkilä, T., Järvi, A., Rönkkö, M., Nissilä, J.: How to define software-as-a-service - an empirical study of finnish saas providers. In: Tyrväinen, P. (ed.) ICSOB 2010. Lecture Notes in Business Information Processing, vol. 51, pp. 115–124. Springer, Heidelberg (2010)
17. Ross, J.W., Westerman, G.: Preparing for utility computing: The role of it architecture and relationship management. IBM Systems Journal 43(1), 5–19 (2004)
18. Greenberg, A., Hamilton, J., Maltz, D.A., Patel, P.: The cost of a cloud: research problems in data center networks. SIGCOMM Comput. Commun. Rev. 39(1), 68–73 (2009)
19. Church, K., Greenberg, A., Hamilton, J.: On delivering embarrassingly distributed cloud services. Hotnets VII (2008)
20. Patel, C.D., Shah, A.J.: Cost model for planning, development and operation of a data center. Technical report, HP Laboratories Palo Alto (June 2005)
21. Banks, D., Erickson, J., Rhodes, M.: Multi-tenancy in cloud-based collaboration services. Technical Report HPL-2009-17, HP Laboratories (February 2009)
22. Grossman, R.L.: The case for cloud computing. IT Professional 11(2), 23–27 (2009)
23. Han, L.: Market Acceptance of Cloud Computing - An Analysis of Market Structure, Price Models and Service Requirements. Bayreuth Reports on Information Systems Management, p. 42 Universität Bayreuth (April 2009)

24. Varia, J.: Architecting for the cloud: Best practices (January 2010),
    `http://jineshvaria.s3.amazonaws.com/public/`
    `cloudbestpractices-jvaria.pdf`
25. Amazon.com: Amazon web services (2010), `http://aws.amazon.com`
26. Reese, G.: Cloud Application Architectures: Transactional Systems for EC2 and Beyond, 1st edn. O'Reilly, Sebastopol (2009)
27. Google: What is google app engine (2010), `http://code.google.com/intl/en/`
    `appengine/docs/whatisgoogleappengine.html`
28. Google: Google spreadsheets api (2010), `http://code.google.com/intl/en/`
    `apis/spreadsheets/`
29. Google: Google document list api (2010), `http://code.google.com/intl/en/`
    `apis/documents/`
30. Google: Gmail apis and tools (2010), `http://code.google.com/intl/en/apis/`
    `gmail/`
31. Microsoft: Windows Azure (2010),
    `http://www.microsoft.com/windowsazure/windowsazure/`
32. Microsoft: SQL Azure - database as a service (2010), `http://www.microsoft.com/`
    `windowsazure/sqlazure/`
33. Woollen, R.: The internal design of salesforce.com's multi-tenant architecture. In: Proceedings of the 1st ACM symposium on Cloud computing, SoCC 2010, pp. 161–161. ACM, New York (2010)
34. Schroeder, B., Pinheiro, E., Weber, W.D.: Dram errors in the wild: a large-scale field study. In: Proceedings of the eleventh International Joint Conference on Measurement and Modeling of Computer Systems, SIGMETRICS 2009, pp. 193–204. ACM Press, New York (2009)
35. Armbrust, M., Fox, A., Griffith, R., Joseph, A.D., Katz, R.H., Konwinski, A., Lee, G., Patterson, D.A., Rabkin, A., Stoica, I., Zaharia, M.: Above the clouds: A berkeley view of cloud computing. Technical Report UCB/EECS-2009-28, EECS Department, University of California, Berkeley (February 2009)
36. Appel, S.: Analysis and Modeling of Application Behavior in Virtualized Environments. Master's thesis, Technische Universität Darmstadt (2009)
37. Stonebraker, M.: Sql databases v. nosql databases. ACM Commun. 53(4), 10–11 (2010)
38. Sobel, J.: Building facebook: performance at massive scale. In: Proceedings of the 1st ACM symposium on Cloud computing, SoCC 2010, pp. 87–87. ACM, New York (2010)
39. Olston, C., Reed, B., Srivastava, U., Kumar, R., Tomkins, A.: Pig latin: a not-so-foreign language for data processing. In: Proceedings of the 2008 ACM SIGMOD International Conference on Management of Data, SIGMOD 2008, pp. 1099–1110. ACM Press, New York (2008)
40. Dean, J., Ghemawat, S.: Mapreduce: Simplified data processing on large clusters. In: Proceedings of the Sixth Symposium on Operating Systems Design and Implementation, OSDI 2004, pp. 137–150 (December 2004)
41. Yahoo!: The hadoop project (2010), `http://hadoop.apache.org/core/`
42. Brantner, M., Florescu, D., Graf, D., Kossmann, D., Kraska, T.: Building a database on s3. In: Proceedings of the 2008 ACM SIGMOD International Conference on Management of Data, SIGMOD 2008, pp. 251–264. ACM Press, New York (2008)
43. Vogels, B.Y.W.: Eventually consistent. Communications of the ACM 52(1), 40–44 (2009)
44. Stonebraker, M., Abadi, D., DeWitt, D.J., Madden, S., Paulson, E., Pavlo, A., Rasin, A.: Mapreduce and parallel dbmss: friends or foes? ACM Commun. 53(1), 64–71 (2010)
45. Yang, H., Tate, M.: Where are we at with cloud computing? In: Proceedings of the 20th Australasian Conference on Information Systems, ACIS 2009, pp. 807–819 (2009)
46. Gilbert, S., Lynch, N.: Brewer's conjecture and the feasibility of consistent available partition-tolerant web services. ACM SIGACT News 33(2), 51–59 (2002)

47. Finkelstein, S., Brendle, R., Jacobs, D.: Principles for inconsistency. In: Proceedings of the 4th Biennial Conf. on Innovative Data Systems Research (CIDR), Asilomar, CA, USA (2009)
48. Brown, A.B., Patterson, D.A.: Embracing failure: A case for recovery-oriented computing (roc). In: High Performance Transaction Processing Symposium, vol. 10, pp. 3–8 (2001)
49. Binnig, C., Kossmann, D., Kraska, T., Loesing, S.: How is the weather tomorrow? towards a benchmark for the cloud. In: Proceedings of the Second International Workshop on Testing Database Systems (DBTest 2009). ACM, New York (2009)
50. Chang, F., Dean, J., Ghemawat, S., Hsich, W.C., Wallach, D.A., Burrows, M., Chandra, T., Fikes, A., Gruber, R.E.: Bigtable: a distributed storage system for structured data. In: Proceedings of the 7th symposium on Operating Systems Design and Implementation, OSDI 2006, pp. 205–218. USENIX Association, Berkeley (2006)
51. Team, H.D.: Hbase: Bigtable-like structured storage for hadoop hdfs (2007), http://wiki.apache.org/lucene-hadoop/Hbase
52. Hypertable.org: Hypertable (2010), http://hypertable.org/
53. Lakshman, A., Malik, P.: Cassandra: a decentralized structured storage system. SIGOPS Oper. Syst. Rev. 44(2), 35–40 (2010)
54. Dean, J., Ghemawat, S.: Mapreduce: simplified data processing on large clusters. In: Proceedings of the 6th Conference on Symposium on Opearting Systems Design & Implementation, OSDI 2004, pp. 10–10. USENIX Association, Berkeley (2004)
55. Project, M.: What is memcached? (2010), http://memcached.org/
56. Fenn, J., Raskino, M., Gammage, B.: Gartner's hype cycle special report for 2009 (2009)
57. Dubey, A., Mohiuddin, J., Baijal, A.: Emerging Platform Wars in Enterprise Software. Technical report, McKinsey & Company (2008)
58. Dubey, A., Mohiuddin, J., Baijal, A.: Enterprise Software Customer Survey 2008. Customer survey, McKinsey & Company, SandHill Group (2008)
59. Gens, F.: Top 10 predictions: Idc predictions 2010: Recovery and transformation. Survey, IDC (December 2009)
60. Hagiu, A., Yoffie, D.B.: What's your google strategy? Harvard Business Review, 74–81 (April 2009)
61. Thethi, J.P.: Realizing the value proposition of cloud computing. Technical report, Infosys (April 2009)

A Web That Senses and Responds

K. Mani Chandy

California Institute of Technology
Computer Science
Pasadena, CA 91125
mani@cs.caltech.edu

1   Introduction

Sense and Respond Applications

A sense and respond application detects changes in the state of the world relevant to a user and responds proactively on the user's behalf. A response may issue an alert or carry out a sequence of actions. Sense and respond applications (abbreviated to S&R apps) are used in many areas including defense, homeland security, finance, logistics, and manufacturing. Some personal applications, such as location-based services on mobile phones, are S&R apps since they sense a phone's location and respond by offering appropriate services.

Sense and Respond Applications and Event Processing

S&R apps are event-processing applications. Systems that execute S&R apps and event processing apps are similar; the difference is that designs of S&R emphasize the overall behavior of the system from sensing to response and back to sensing whereas event-processing apps emphasize event detection. S&R systems consist of: sensors and other sources of data; agents that detect patterns that indicate significant events; planners that determine the best response to these events; responders or actuators that execute the responses; communication networks for transmitting information between components; and, management layers for controlling the entire application.

Goal of the Paper

The goal of this paper is to suggest that web and cloud computing technologies have matured to the point that they enable a worldwide plug and play S&R web that can grow and change dynamically by the addition and modification of components. An S&R web enables new S&R apps to be developed as easily as web applications are developed today.

Organization of the Paper

The organization of the paper is as follows. In Section 2 we explore the demand for S&R apps for business and personal applications. In Section 3 we propose an architecture for the S&R web and present designs of two, very different, S&R apps based on the proposed architecture.

K. Sachs, I. Petrov, and P. Guerrero (Eds.): Buchmann Festschrift, LNCS 6462, pp. 78–84, 2010.

2   Demand for Sense and Respond Applications

Demand from Business: S&R Apps with Long-Term Contracts

Sense and respond applications are proactive: they monitor the world and respond proactively on behalf of users without (necessarily) waiting for user commands. Proactive applications have long-term contracts with users whereas reactive applications may have short-term contracts. Long- and short-term contracts are illustrated by the following example.

When Professor Buchmann travels from Wiesbaden to the Technische Universität Darmstadt, on August 18 at 10AM he queries a web application to determine traffic conditions along the route; the application's contract is to provide the information when requested, and after the information is delivered the contract terminates. An example of a long-term contract is an application that continuously monitors traffic along the user's commute and alerts the user when alternate routes should be taken; this contract remains in force until the user cancels it. Email and calendar applications also have long-term contracts with users. Your email application continues to manage your email until you delete the application. These applications may be proactive or reactive - they may push alerts to the user or give information to the user only when requested. Applications with long-term contracts serve users better when users give the applications personal information that enables the application to be tailored to the user's specific needs.

Businesses want long-term, personalized contracts with their customers because such contracts allow businesses to serve their customers better and reduce churn. A variety of apps with long-term contracts have become popular and their successes will lead businesses to offer many more S&R apps.

Demand from Individuals

People expect increasingly rapid interactions with systems and with other people. We expect timely information whether we are sharing photographs, getting updates on stocks, receiving alerts about delays in flights, or getting suggestions for alternate routes for commutes. GPS and location-based services are useful to the extent that they provide information when needed. People depend on mobile-phone services to proactively inform them about their world. All these services monitor the state of the world and respond on the user's behalf. The public increasingly expects services that sense and respond for them, and this expectation will drive development of S&R apps.

Technology Trends Driving Sense and Respond Applications

Ubiquitous Sensors

Cars, appliances, the grid, and homes have sensors. Sensors, such as accelerometers are used in car airbags, mobile phones, and computer games. The costs of these devices have dropped as widespread use leads to economies of scale. This, in turn, allows these devices to be used in even more applications such as seismological monitoring. Widespread deployment of sensors drives demand for S&R apps that exploit sensor data in a timely manner.

The mobile phone merits special mention for several reasons: Mobile phones have become necessities in most parts of the world. Mobile phones have built-in sensors such as accelerometers and more phone models can now be connected to external sensors. Alerts are sent to phones and thus phones serve as responders and as sensors. Widespread deployment of GPS devices also drives S&R apps.

Cloud Computing

Cloud computing systems are used in a variety of application domains. Public clouds, such as the Google App Engine and Microsoft's Azure Platform, offer Platforms as a Service (PaaS) that allow web applications to be developed quickly. PaaS systems are not designed specifically for S&R apps; however, they enable the development of a plug and play S&R web, and as a consequence will serve as catalysts for wider deployment of S&R.

Standards and Toolkits

Ubiquity requires standards. Standards and toolkits have made the development of Web applications much easier, and this has led to their widespread deployment. Likewise, standards and toolkits for S&R apps are necessary for developing a ubiquitous, plug-and-play S&R web. Several organizations are developing standards for event schemas, event specifications, and commands to responders. Toolkits, such as the Google Web Toolkit (GWT), for Web applications can be extended to serve as toolkits for S&R apps. Standards and toolkits, particularly in PaaS systems are helping to develop an S&R web.

3 An Architecture for an S&R Web

A ubiquitous, plug-and-play S&R web can be designed using different architectures. Here we propose an architecture appropriate for many, but not all, S&R applications. In this architecture, sensors and other data sources are connected to a cloud computing system that manages the S&R web, accepts data from data sources, detects events, determines optimum responses, and then instructs responders. We explore the use of public PaaS cloud-computing systems such as the Google App Engine (GAE) and Microsoft Azure. Later, we will identify the strengths and weaknesses of the architecture.

The functions of the cloud computing system, acting as a central server, in this architecture include the following. Components such as data sources and responders are registered with the server. Components send periodic heartbeat messages to the server to indicate that they are alive. The server either polls data sources for information or accepts messages pushed to it. Likewise, the server sends commands and alerts to responders. The server stores and manages data from component and accesses this data to enrich information from data sources, detects significant events, and determines optimum responses. PaaS systems, such as GAE and Azure, were not designed specifically for S&R apps; however, they allow S&R server functions to be executed easily.

PaaS systems support Web applications in which clients repeatedly request the server to execute short services. Server functions for managing components in S&R systems are implemented as requests from components for (short) services such as registering new components. A toolkit for implementing S&R apps using a PaaS cloud has a library of functions for managing components. For example, a new sensor is registered with the S&R web merely by invoking a registration function in the library.

PaaS systems were not designed for applications that require intensive computation. In some S&R apps functions for detecting events and computing best responses may require a great deal of computation time; these functions should be executed on a local server outside the PaaS cloud.

Case Study: Responding to Earthquakes

We describe the design of an application that senses shaking from earthquakes and which responds by: (a) alerting people and devices about impending shaking and (b) directs first responders to areas that are most badly damaged. Our goal here is to show how an S&R web can be tailored to develop a specific S&R app such as the earthquake-sensing application.

A sensor is plugged into the system by connecting it to a local computer - the sensor host - through a USB port and then connecting the sensor host to the server by giving the server's address to the host. Responders are plugged into the system in the same way. Sensors and actuators communicate through the Internet to a PaaS system, currently implemented using GAE. Sensors (accelerometers) are placed over a quake-prone region. The sensors continuously monitor movement of the ground and send raw acceleration data to the sensor host, which detects patterns in the raw data that indicate a possible earthquake. When a sensor host detects such a pattern it sends a message, called a pick, to the server. The computational and communication load on the sensor host, when the host is a standard desktop machine, is so low that it is not noticeable. A sensor host may also be a standalone device with enough computational capability to detect patterns in raw accelerometer data. Such devices can communicate by wireless to desktops that send aggregate data from multiple sensors to the server. The advantage of standalone sensor hosts is that they can be placed anywhere with power and wireless connectivity; for instance devices can be placed in places, such as basements and attics, that don't have desktop computers.

A sensor host may send an erroneous pick message due to electronic noise in the sensor or due to the ground shaking from trucks or building construction. The sensor host generates pick messages when it detects low-frequency (less than 10 Hz) waves whereas building construction activity, such as operation of jackhammers, generates waves of higher frequencies. The low-pass filter reduces the rate of erroneous picks. The interval between pick messages from a sensor, even a noisy sensor, is large - at least in the order of tens of minutes. Simple machine-learning algorithms in the server can be used to raise the threshold at which a sensor host identifies picks in the raw data. This reduces the rate at which sensor hosts send messages when there are no earthquakes going on.

Electronic noise in different sensors is uncorrelated. Noise due to ground shaking from trucks and construction is correlated only for sensors in close proximity. Therefore the total rate of pick messages sent to the server from all sensor hosts is small while no earthquake is going on. The rate of pick messages sent to the server is extremely high while an earthquake is going on because most sensors in the earthquake region detect ground shaking. The rate at which a sensor host sends pick messages is throttled so that the total rate of messages to the server does not exceed its capacity. Even so, traffic to the server occurs in intense bursts, and the system is useful only if the server processes bursts of messages. When servers are implemented as public PaaS cloud-computing systems, a concern is that a server may not provide the required capacity when it is most needed.

Sensor registration and deregistration, functionality for monitoring sensor health, and other management functions are common to all S&R apps. Likewise, functionality for alerting clients is generic. We implement a given S&R app, such as the earthquake-sensing application, by tailoring the general S&R framework by specifying: how sensor hosts determine when to send messages and what messages to send, how the server detects events and computes optimum responses, and what responders do when they receive messages from the server. Next, we describe these functions briefly.

The system should react when real earthquakes occur and it should not raise false alarms. Therefore, the server aggregates information from multiple sensors before raising an alarm. The server can be more certain about the existence of an earthquake if it waits for more time and obtains more data to validate its conclusion; however each additional second that the server waits is a second less to react. Thus, a critical challenge in the design of the system is determining when to issue an alert of an earthquake and when to wait for more data.

The earthquake region is gridded, and each sensor belongs to a cell in the grid. The server determines that an entire cell has detected an earthquake when N out of M sensors in the cell send pick messages (alarms) to the server in an interval of duration T where T is determined by the time required for an earthquake wave to propagate across a single cell. The values of N and M are determined by the amount of noise in sensors.

When a sensor sends an alarm, the N value for the appropriate cell is incremented, and the system raises an alarm when this number exceeds a threshold. This computation is fast, and the GAE allows more complex algorithms to be executed rapidly.

PaaS systems, such as the GAE, simplify the development of S&R apps for several reasons. The system is distributed and redundant so that an earthquake doesn't destroy the server. The service provider (Google in this case) acquires and maintains hardware and the underlying software platform. The library of functions for managing components can be repurposed for multiple S&R apps.

Case Study: Rural Health Monitoring in Emerging Economies

Next we consider a very different S&R app that can also be implemented on the same S&R web. The current prototype is also implemented on top of the GAE.

People in remote rural areas in emerging economies may have to travel for hours to reach doctors and hospitals. When a patient feels unwell, a critical decision that the patient must make is to either travel to the remote healthcare facility or use local treatments. Travel to and from a healthcare facility may take several hours and even days, and some rural poor can ill afford such travel. As populations age, the problem becomes acute as increasing numbers of the aged in rural areas have to monitor themselves to make this critical decision.

A prototype system developed at the California Institute of Technology and the medical school of the University of California at Irvine attempts to help deal with this problem by developing an S&R app. The idea is to harness the power of mobile phones (and even computers) that are increasingly used, even in poorer rural areas, in many parts of the world.

The team has built inexpensive auscultation devices (stethoscopes) and EKG devices coupled to mobile phones or laptops. Sensory data is sent to a PaaS cloud computing system (GAE) with additional information about the patient. Healthcare experts monitor the system, and communicate with patients, when necessary.

This application is very different from the earthquake application in many respects. Events are very different - in the case of earthquakes, an event is global in the sense that it impacts everybody in a region, whereas in the medical application, an event is local in the sense that it impacts the patient and perhaps the patient's family and village. Likewise, responses are very different. In the case of earthquakes, responses have to be made in seconds; by contrast, in the medical application responses could take tens of minutes. Though the applications are very different, they are both S&R apps: they sense events and respond to them.

Lessons Learned

Different S&R apps have many functions in common. Sensors and responders are registered with servers. Heartbeat messages are used to check that components are alive. Machine learning is used to calibrate components. The commonality of functions suggests the use of a common framework - an S&R web based on web technologies, web toolkits, and public PaaS cloud computing systems. An S&R web will make the development of S&R apps as easy as the development of web apps is today.

Acknowledgment

A large group of students, research staff members and faculty members at Caltech (the California Institute of Technology) are carrying out the work on earthquakes. The faculty members on the team are Rob Clayton, Tom Heaton, Andreas Krause, and Mani Chandy. The students and research staff in the team make the research possible. Michael Olson's Masters and PhD research is on the S&R web architecture. The design of public PaaS cloud-computing systems for community-based sensing is largely due to him.

The medical application is being developed by a team from the medical school at the University of California at Irvine and at Caltech with the help of doctors at the Christian Medical College, Vellore, India. Dr. George Chandy, M.D., leads the UCI team consisting of several medical school students who study healthcare in emerging economies. The Caltech team includes Dr. Julian Bunn, Karthik Sarma, Jeff Lin, Albert Tana, and Mani Chandy.

Spatial Perspectives in Event Processing

Opher Etzion and Nir Zolotorvesky

IBM Haifa Research Lab, Haifa University,
Haifa, Israel
opher@il.ibm.com, nirz@il.ibm.com

Abstract. The processing of geo-spatial events plays an increasingly important role in constructing enterprise applications that can immediately react to business critical events. In this paper we introduce spatial extensions to the event processing model, starting from the introduction of geo-spatial main concepts, and moving through the life-cycle of event processing application development and discuss spatial event representation, spatial contexts and spatial extensions to event processing patterns. The paper also discusses several use cases from various domains that may benefit from the use of spatial extensions of event processing.

Keywords: Event Processing; Spatial Event Processing; Spatiotemporal Event Processing; Event context; Multi dimensional context, Spatial and spatiotemporal contexts.

1 Introduction

In recent years we have seen substantial growth in the utilization of event processing for a variety of applications, while most product support semantic abstractions that relate to the temporal direction, there are many applications that can be assisted in spatial abstractions. Current Event Processing products have not focused on providing specific primitives that manipulate the geo-spatial aspects, when such processing is required; it is being performed by the regular primitives of the event processing language. However, as both the quantity and complexity of such applications increase, it becomes cost-effective to extend the current models and products to support explicit representation of the geo-spatial aspects of events and extend the processing language to support it.

The contribution of this paper to event processing research and practice is enhancement of the context notion that typically is viewed as temporal (e.g. time window) to include multi dimensional, spatial and spatiotemporal contexts.

1.1 Motivation

Geo-spatial event processing is useful when location based aspects of events are important for business decisions and operations.

Several studies in the GIS community have concentrated on the introduction of a representation model for geo-spatial events. As an example, Worboys introduced a spatial event representation in [17], and a spatio-temporal event representation in [18].

K. Sachs, I. Petrov, and P. Guerrero (Eds.): Buchmann Festschrift, LNCS 6462, pp. 85–107, 2010.
© Springer-Verlag Berlin Heidelberg 2010

However, these models concentrated on the representation of events and not on the processing of events, these models enable reaction to a single event and do not support composition, or pattern matching in event histories.

There were few proposals for methods for handling spatio-temporality using subsets that is tailored to a specific application domain like the data management application presented by Stock in [14], these models do not represent a generic event processing model.

There are a variety of application areas that require the use of location based aspects of event in order to process these events. We introduce a list of such applications to motivate this paper; Section 6 describes some detailed use cases. The various areas are:

- Transportation - infrastructure management, fleet and logistics management.
- Government – with spatial analysis we can analyze revenue collection, economic development, city planning.
- Military/Fire/Emergency Medical Services/Disaster - Military defense can use spatial analysis for intelligence, terrain analysis, mission planning, and facilities management. Public safety personnel can effectively plan for emergency response, determine mitigation priorities, analyze historical events, and predict future events using this spatial CEP system.
- Business - Financial analysts can use this system for targeting their markets by visualizing product and service consumption according to their location.
- Environmental Management - Environmental management can use spatial analysis tools to provide a better understanding of how elements of natural communities interact across a landscape. Spatial analysis tools can be used in ecology labs, planning departments, parks and agencies.
- Natural Resources - Oil and gas exploration, hydrology harnessing, timber management, and mining operations require sound assessment to steer growth into areas that can support it while preventing contamination of rivers or destruction of resources. The delicate balance between industrial development and environmental conservation requires sophisticated modeling and spatial analytical tools.
- Utilities–Power/Electricity/Gas/Telecommunications/Water Management - The process of routing energy/gas/water/ telecommunications is highly dependent on geographic information. From network design to outage management, more than 80 percent of utility data management contains spatial components.

1.2 Structure of This Paper

The paper is structured in the following way: Section 2 provides background, and explains the event processing model extended by the Geo spatial event processing, and provides some introduction to geo-spatial computing; Section 3 describes the representation of the spatial aspects of events; Section 4 describes the notions of spatial context and multi dimensional context; Section 5 discusses spatial event patterns; Section 6 demonstrate the utilization of these concepts using a collection of use cases; Section 7 concluded the paper.

2   Background

There are some variations of event processing concepts and terms, thus in order to provide level setting we shortly introduce the specific model and concepts that are used in this paper in Section 2.1; Section 2.2 provides short background about Geo spatial computing, Section 2.3 discusses Spatio-Temporal reasoning.

2.1   Introduction to Event Processing

Event denotes *something that happens in reality* as defined by Luckham in [8]. While data-item typically denotes the state of some entity, events denote transitions between these states. There is a semantic overload in the term event, since it reflects both the event occurred in reality and its representation in the computer domain (event message or event object). The event processing architecture is called EPN (Event Processing Network); this concept is formally defined in by Sharon & Etzion in [12].

The life-cycle of event processing application is detailed below (some of it in iterative way):

1.   Event schemata are defined.
2.   Event producers devise mechanism to emit events, in push, periodic pull, or on-demand pull. Event producer examples are: instrumented programs, state observers in business process management system and sensors.
3.   The event is published on a channel and routed through an event pipe to one or more event processing agents which – validate, transform, enrich, filter or match patterns and create more events that are in turn published on other channels and routed to more event processing agents.
4.   As mentioned by Adi [1], event processing agents work within a context , a major semantic abstraction which partitions the events according to temporal and semantic partitions (e.g. the context is valid every working day between 9AM – 4PM, and events are partitioned by customer, i.e., the processing of each customer is distinct).
5.   Event processing agents may derive new events and send them to other event processing agents.
6.   At the edge of the event processing network the created events called situation events are routed to event consumers.

Figure 1 shows an EPN example, for a monitored patient in the hospital.

Event producers are:
• Admission office that records admittance and release of patients.
• Blood pressure meter.
• Fever meter.

The agents perform filtering, aggregation, enrichment, transformation and pattern matching, routing channels are designated in r1… r9 and event pipes are designated in p1… p20.

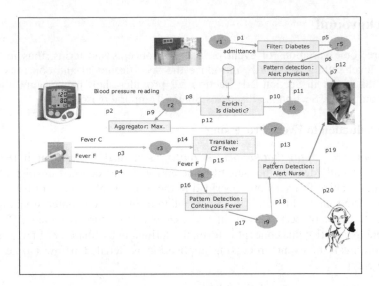

Fig. 1. An example of Event Processing Network

2.2 Geo Spatial Computing

Geo spatial computing or its more familiar name GIS (Geographic Information System) is a discipline that deals with processing spatial information; it is being used by comprehensive collection of applications that cover many aspects of modern life [11].

The first aspect is spatial data storage into digital terms. Data is manipulated for use in a digital environment, and these manipulations often change the data and have profound effects on the results of analysis. Each of these manipulations involves a subtle shift in the representation of spatial entities, and accounting for these modifications and their implications is an important part of GIS.

The second aspect is analyzing, mapping and visualizing GIS results. Visualizing GIS results is vulnerable to the vagaries of the digital environment, and must be consistent with human capacity for perception. Each object in the GIS data model includes attributes which characterize this object. At a small scale, for instance, only a limited number of attributes can be displayed or the map becomes overcrowded (objects are very tight located to each other). At a larger scale, a greater number of attributes can be accommodated. Each of these issues has bearing on how spatial data is analyzed and interpreted. In order to represent geographical space we need to use an appropriate data model. In GIS we generally use three data models: the vector data model, raster data model and object data model. As mentioned by Schuurman [11].

Vector Data Model: The most ubiquitous in GIS, and most closely resembles traditional maps. Vector data models are constructed from points, lines and areas. The point is zero-dimensional primitive; lines are one-dimensional and are constructed by an arc or a chain linking two points. Areas are defined by sets of lines; surfaces are areas that include height or another dimension such as population density that can be used to portray relative elevation. In vector data model polygons are synonyms with areas. Three-dimensional surfaces are, likewise, built from areas.

Raster Data Model: This model divides the world into a sequence of identical, discrete entities, by imposing a regular grid. Frequently the grid is square. Each grid cell in a raster is linked to specific location. Raster data models are distinguished by their conceptual simplicity and ease of implementation. Raster systems are widely used in applications which employ remotely sensed images as satellite imagery is represented using a gridded network.

Raster and Vector data models are also referred to as layer models. Layers refer to the themes or attributes which are registered to the same geographical area under consideration. Layers can be compared with each other to determine a new set   of attributes. One of the most useful functions of GIS has traditionally been the ability to perform map overlay, using the principles of Boolean algebra, to derive new attributes from combination of layers.

Object Data Model: This model is alternative to viewing the world as a series of locationally registered layers; each object represents a single attribute. Rather than focus on location, objects oriented GIS defines phenomena, such as telephone poles or streets as objects. Objects can represent points, lines, areas and three dimensions. Objects are usually represented using vector building blocks such as points, lines and areas. A key difference of object is that object model allows empty space as well as overlapping objects, i.e. multiple objects occupying the same space. This definition was discussed in Schuurman [11].

2.3 Temporal GIS

Temporal GIS [10] is aimed to answer questions such as:

- What location changes have been done in the last T time units?
- How these location changes affected other attributes of related events or the related objects?
- Can we predict future location changes?

Worboy's book [16] discusses changes of spatial properties with time, as Figure 2 shows changes in administrative areas over time.

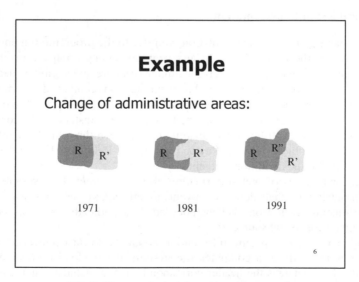

Fig. 2. Change of administrative areas example

- Relevant questions on the spatio-temporal aspect can be:
- What variation has there been in the population density of R' between 1971 and 1991?
- Has the A34 route (road) ever passed through region R'?
- Does the A34 route currently pass through land that has ever belonged to region R'?

These are complex spatial objects that have discrete changes with respect to time.

There is also a problem of storing spatiotemporal data. Simple sequences of snapshots (raster or vector) waste space with redundant information.

A temporal GIS aims to process, manage, and analyze spatial-temporal data. However, the capabilities of any information system largely rely on the design of its data models. According to Date [3], data models present the conceptual core of an information system; they define data object types, relationships, operations, and rules to maintain database integrity. A rigorous data model must anticipate spatiotemporal queries and analytical methods to be performed in the temporal GIS.

The temporal semantics of a spatiotemporal structure depends on the application domain, and determines whether time is discrete or dense; linear, branching or cyclic; and whether metric and topological properties are relevant [18].

Next we move to discuss the spatial aspects of event processing based on this background.

3 Representation of Spatial and Spatiotemporal Events

This Section starts by discussing what events are and how they are defined. We continue our discussion by explaining the logical structure of events in general and the added representation required for added for spatial representation of events.

3.1 General Event Representation

When we speak about event representation we refer to the programming entity that is used to represent the event object. In an event processing application one usually encounters many event objects that have a similar structure and a similar meaning. All events that have same structure, similar meaning and contain the same kind of information are defined to be instances of the same event type. An event type specifies the information that is contained in its event instances. It does this by defining a set of event attributes. We distinguish between three kinds of information carried in an event object: Header, Payload and Event Relations. Figure 3 shows the general structure of the definition element.

The Header consists of meta-information about the event, for example, its type description attributes that describes event identification, composition type and chronology, meta-information also includes attribute indicators such as occurrence time, detection time, event source, etc.

The Payload contains specific information about the event occurrence itself. We can liken this to a file in a computer file system; the payload corresponds to the contents of a file, whereas the header corresponds to file metadata such as its name, time of last access, and so on.

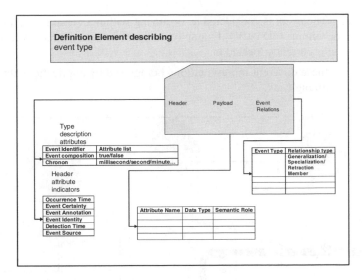

Fig. 3. General structure of the event type definition element

The Event Relation is an optional part; each event type definition may contain references to other event types when there is semantic relationship between them. The event type definition element lists the referenced event types and gives the nature of each relationship. There are four types of relationships: membership, generalization, specialization, and retraction.

3.2 Spatial Event Structure

The first step in processing spatial events is to define the way that the spatial information associated with the event is represented in the event schema.

In the previous paragraph we described the Payload event structure part which consists of a collection of data type attributes. We use this data type attribute to define a new "location" data type which will serve us to define a real-world location associated with the event; it can refer to the location using domain-specific geospatial terms, for example, lines and areas that are defined in a particular geospatial domain.

The Location data type can use one of spatial data models described in chapter 2.2, for example each event can be explicitly represented using a coordinate system; a point might be represented as a latitude/longitude pair or event can be represented by identifier of a spatial object, for example, the name of a building or city.

Spatial representation of events can be one of several spatial Types. Spatial type is a geometric description of the event location. Spatial types are:

- Point - The event is considered as occurring in a specific geometric point in the space, using some coordinate system (2D or 3D). Example: the GPS coordinates of a specific vehicle.
- Line - The event is considered as occurring on a line or polyline. Example: the road (represented by a polyline) that a vehicle is currently driving along.

- Area - The event is considered as occurring within a certain geographical area or volume (2D or 3D).Example: the local authority jurisdiction that a vehicle is currently located in.

Figure 4 shows these different representations being used by applications that monitor traffic on a certain highway.

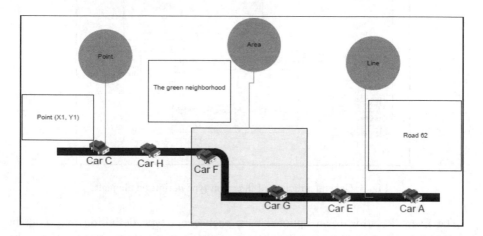

Fig. 4. Traffic monitor example - Car C described as point type, green neighborhood defined by area type and a road specified by line type

Note that the additional attributes denote both content attributes and also other meta-information attributes like temporal attributes that are discussed in Section 3.3.

3.3   The Temporal Dimension

Next we recall the temporal dimension of event representation in order to discuss its relation with the spatial dimension in Section 3.4.

Events may have two major temporal characteristics that determine the semantic of their temporal processing.

- *Detection Time*: The point in time in which the event becomes available for processing through the introduction of the corresponding event message Example: the event flight BA0238 landed in 10:39 this has been reported in 10:40, which is the detection time of this event [5].
- *Occurrence time:* The time-stamp in which the event occurred in the real universe. In many applications the occurrence time is the reference time for the determination of event order, rather than the detection time. In temporal state processing this time dimension has been mentioned as: event time or decision time but was not considered as a major dimension [5].

Next, we discuss how spatiotemporal events are represented.

3.4 Spatiotemporal Events

Temporal GIS should support process-based changes, for example fire spread and storm development. Galton [6] makes the distinction between histories that are functions from a temporal domain to attribute values, or properties of objects, and chronicles that treat dynamic phenomena as collections of happenings. We define a spatiotemporal event as an event that contains both time attributes and spatial attributes. From an ontological perspective, were made several attempts to define spatio-temporal configuration. Grenon and Smith [7] call temporal sequences of object configurations the SNAP ontology, and the event/action/process view, the SPAN ontology. Our spatiotemporal event definition is very close to SPAN ontology that Grenon and Smith proposed.

From a semantic point of view, spatiotemporal events can be viewed as transitions among states, where the transitions are ordered according to the time dimension. There are three types of these events based on the relationships between the spatiotemporal events and the states that created these events.

Mutation Event is an event in which location has not changed relative to the previous state; however some of the attributes change their values.

Movement Event is an event in which only the location attribute has changed its value relative to the pervious state, but other event attributes are not changed.

Mutation Movement event is an event in which both location and content attributes has changed relative to the previous state.

4 Space Related Context

Context as defined by Adi [1] partitions the space of events according to several dimensions – temporal, spatial, state and semantic. It is used as a major abstraction, Each EPA (Event Processing Agent) operates within a specific context, and only events that are associated with a context are evaluated by that agent. The most common context is time window that restricts the activities of an EPA to a certain time interval, however partition can also be semantic, and e.g. the events that related to platinum customers are mapped to a distinct context. For example: if an agent that looks for anti-money laundering suspicion is looking for events related to the same customer during the same week, then the context consists of two dimensions: temporal (the week) and semantic (the customer). Events are partitioned according to the context and each context-instance has its own agents.

The spatial dimension partitions events based on their location. In this Section we discuss the addition of the spatial dimension to the notion of context.

Similar to the definition of temporal context as defined by Etzion [5], we can define spatial context. We call this spatial context Space-Span. In many cases the spatial context is closely associated with a temporal context in which our spatial context is relevant. In order to handle these two contexts we define the notion of complex context which will composite two simple contexts such as temporal and spatial or segmentation and spatial.

In this section we define three types of spatial Contexts that may be relevant when we describe Space-Span.

1. Pure Spatial Context – this context partitions the space of events according to spatial dimension only.
2. Spatiotemporal Context - this context partitions the space of events according to two dimensions – combining spatial and temporal context into one mutated context.
3. Complex Context – complex context is a context that is composed of several one dimensional contexts; example: semantic and temporal contexts or spatial and temporal contexts.

4.1 Fixed Location Context

A Pure Spatial Context limits the events that serve as input to its associated agents to the events that happen within that context with no time constraints. A pure spatial context can be of four types:

1. Fixed Space: at a fixed location.
2. Reference Object based Space: all locations in distance d from a Reference Object.
3. Event based Space: location that starts at event A's location and ends at event B's location.
4. Attribute based Space: all locations of either events or reference objects which have the same attribute value.
5. Computed space: a spatial context that is derived as a function of other locations of either events or reference objects.

4.1.1 Fixed Space
Fixed Space is a space at a fixed location; example: a room; space is defined by room space, rectangle – space is defined by rectangle area and all that happens inside this rectangle is of interest to an event processing agent.

4.1.2 Reference Object Based Space
Reference Object based Space is the collection of all locations from which their distance to a reference object is bounded by a given upper limit. Examples: all locations in distance of 1 mile from road number 2; all locations in distance of 2 miles from the mall; Airport-noise-Area is the area around the airport (E) within a radius of 10KMs. This is sometimes known as buffer, as shown in Figure 5.

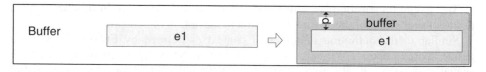

Fig. 5. Buffer representation example

4.1.3 Event Based Space
Event based Space is a space defined by the location of one or more events; example: disease area, space is defined by start event of disease outburst and is defined by all

locations at distance d from the location of this event. Note that we can define space by several events and to calculate distance d from each one of them, creating an area by merging spaces that each event has created.

4.1.4 Attribute Based Space at Fixed Time

Attribute Based Space is a space defined by either reference objects or events that have the same attribute value; it can be based on several attributes values.

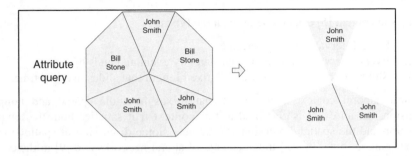

Fig. 6. Attribute query example

A derived spatial context is derived through some function of location of either reference objects or events. The following functions are discussed:

Boundary (L) is a function that returns the boundary of some location, either event's location or reference object's location. A polygon's boundary is a polyline. A polyline's boundary is a multipoint that contains the collection of start and end points of each lines. For point location, the function returns an empty set. Example: The pattern Country-Border occurs when created new polyline event which represents the border of a Country.

Envelope (E1, E2 ...., En) is a function that computes a spatial envelope based on the locations of a collection of events of types E1...En, where all the events have point location. This function follows the convex hull term in computational geometry, which stands for the boundary of the minimal convex set containing a given

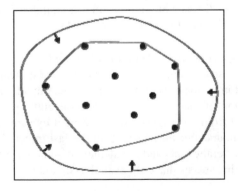

Fig. 7. An envelope

non-empty finite set of points in the plane. Unless the points are collinear, the convex hull is a simple closed polygonal chain. Figure 7 illustrates an envelope; an example can be: The envelope of all locations in which a certain disease has been reported. In this case all events of the type patient complain whose location within this envelope should get specific processing. Note that this context can change in a dynamic way if more relevant instances of these types are emitted.

4.2 Spatiotemporal Context

A temporal context [5] can be one of the three types:

1. Fixed Interval : may be periodic.
2. Event Interval: An interval that starts by event and ends by event.
3. Sliding Interval: An interval with fixed length that slides over the time.

A spatiotemporal context is a context that mixes both the spatial and temporal dimension, i.e. an event is classified to this context if it satisfies both the temporal dimension and the spatial dimension constraints. Some discussion of spatiotemporal contexts can be found in [13] in the context of social networks and [9] in the context of mobile computing.

A Spatiotemporal Context can be of four types:

1. Reference object based Space within a temporal context, all locations in distance d from Reference Object within a temporal context.
2. Event based space within a temporal context, location that starts at event A's location and ends at event B's location within a temporal context.
3. Attribute Base Space within a temporal context – all locations which have same attribute value while this attribute value is checked only in specific time context.
4. Sliding Space over a time interval: space that is being redefined over time.

4.2.1 Reference Object Based Space within a Temporal Context
Reference object based space comprises of all locations in distance d from Reference Object while this space interval is only relevant on specified fixed time interval; example: all locations in distance of 1 mile from road number 2, between 8-10AM; all locations in distance of 2 miles from the mall at 3PM.

4.2.2 Event Based Space within a Temporal Context
Event based space is a space defined by one or more events while this space interval is only relevant within a specified time interval; example: disease area, space is defined by the location of the start event of disease outburst and is defined by all locations at distance d from this event. Time is defined by same start event of disease outburst and lasts 48 hours after the report about the last infected person. Note that we can define space by several events and to calculate distance d from each one of them, creating area by merging spaces that each event has created.

4.2.3   Attribute Based Space within a Temporal Context

Attribute based space is a space defined by events that have same attribute value while this space interval is only relevant on specified fixed time interval; it can be based on several attributes values. *Example: Pollution Area, space is defined by all locations for which the value of the AQI attribute is bigger than 100(AQI >100) while all surveys very done* **Today.**

4.2.4   Sliding Space Over a Time Interval

Time based space is a space whose boundaries change over time. *Example: Flying Aircraft space is defined by area around aircraft at radius 1 mile, while Time interval is starts at takeoff event and ends at landing event, this location is sliding according to the current location of the aircraft.*

4.3   Complex Context

We can use simple operations in order to compound Complex Context.

Complex Context can be of three types:

1. Intersection of contexts: the complex context is the common part of a given one dimensional contexts.
2. Union of Contexts: the complex context is a context which contains all events that satisfy at least one of the given contexts.
3. Symmetric difference of contexts: complex context is the set of events which are classified to one of the contexts, but not in any other of the given contexts.

4.3.1   Intersection of Contexts

This Complex Context is compound from intersection of two or more dimensional contexts. One dimensional context can be of the same type or of different types; Example: Context C1 is fixed interval temporal context (today between 8-10 AM); Context C2 is event based temporal context (from car start moving to car stopped). Context C3 is Reference Object based spatial context (all locations in distance of 1 mile from city center). The complex context denotes all cars that were moving today between 8-10 AM in distance of 1 mile from city center.

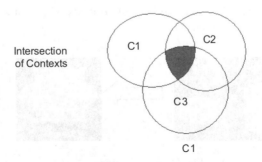

Fig. 8. Intersection of contexts example

Note that the intersection can be an intersection of several contexts with spatial characteristics; the spatial intersection is shown in Figure 9.

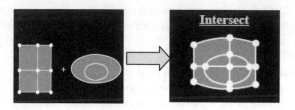

Fig. 9. Spatial intersection

4.3.2 Union of Contexts

This Complex context is compound from union of two or more one dimensional context. One dimensional context can be of the same type or of different types; Example: Context C1 is a fixed temporal context (today between 8-10 AM), Context C2 is an event based temporal context (from car start moving to car stopped) Context C3 is a reference object based spatial context (all locations in distance of 1 mile from city center); The complex context represent all events that happen between 8 and 10 AM today and all the events that relate to a certain car trip and all events that occur in center city.

Union
of Contexts

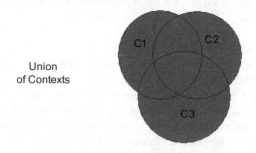

Fig. 10. Union of contexts example

Note that the union can be a union of several contexts with spatial characteristics; the spatial union is shown in Figure 11.

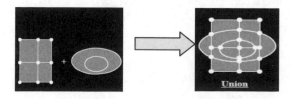

Fig. 11. Spatial unions

4.3.3 Difference of Contexts

This complex context is compound from the difference of two or more one dimensional contexts. One dimensional context can be of the same type or of different types; Example: the context C1 is a fixed temporal context (today between 8-10 AM), the context C2 is an event based temporal context (from car start moving to car stopped), the context C3 is a reference object based spatial context (all locations in distance of 1 mile from city center). The complex context represents all events that happen between 8 and are not related to this specific car trip and do not occur in the center city and (which is the difference between C1 and C2, C3). In a symmetric difference the two other differences are also valid.

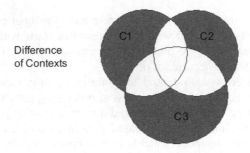

Fig. 12. Difference of Contexts example

Note that the difference can be a difference of several contexts with spatial characteristics; the spatial difference is shown in Figure 13.

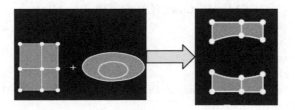

Fig. 13. Spatial Difference

In summary, there are various ways in which spatial context can be applied and be combined with other dimensions, such as the temporal dimension. The extension of the concept of context to include spatial and multidimensional contexts is the major contribution of this paper.

The context determines the events that participate in each EPA processing and next we discuss the event processing patterns that are proposed as an extension to existing event processing patterns.

5 Spatial Oriented Event Processing Patterns

Detecting event processing patterns [12] is a major function of an event processing functionality. A pattern is a predicate on the history of events that may include events from various event types, and has associated policies to tune up its semantics. An event pattern matching is taking one or more event streams as inputs and as output returns a collection of events that satisfy this pattern. Some pattern examples are:

- *AND (e1, e2) where e1.x > e2.y*
- *Sequence (e1, e2, e3)*
- *Not (e1)*

All patterns are associated with contexts that determine the input events. For example, the pattern Not (e1) is associated with the context that starts with the occurrence of event e2 and terminates after 10 minutes later and determines if e1 does not occur within 10 minutes after the occurrence of e2.

The notion of pattern is also central to complex event processing [12].   In this section we discuss initial set of additional event processing patterns that are based on the spatial characteristics of events and extend the set of existing patterns. We discuss distance based patterns and interaction based patterns, which are examples for pure spatial patterns and spatiotemporal patterns with temporal modality.

5.1 Distance Based Patterns

Distance based patterns are used to detect whether the location of an event occurred within a certain distance from referenced object.

The **Min Distance** pattern: the pattern

Min Distance (CP, O, DP, E1... En)

Where:

- CP is a context partition
- O is a reference object;
- DP is a min distance predicate. Examples: > 1KM, = 200 M, ≥ 3KM)
- *E1,...En* are event types
- This pattern is satisfied if ∀ i ∃ e instance of Ei that belongs to the context partition CP, such that the predicate DP (O, e) is satisfied.

The min distance pattern is satisfied when the minimal distance of the entire participant events from a given reference object satisfies the min distance threshold assertion.

To determine whether this pattern is matched or not, you take all the participant events and find out which one occurred closest to the given point. The pattern is satisfied if its distance satisfies a threshold assertion.

Example: The pattern Aircraft-on-Radar occurs when an event "aircraft detected" located in distance of at least 100 KM from the radar location while, when red alert is in effect.

In this example, CP is a temporal context partition that spans between two events: "start of red alert'" and "end of red alert"; O is a radar (in this case it is a transient object, but can also be moving object); DP = ≥100KM; E1.Et are events from type "aircraft detected" which are located at least 100 KM away from radar.

The **Max Distance** pattern: the pattern

Max Distance (CP, O, DP, E1... En)

Where:

- CP is a context partition
- O is a reference object;
- DP is a max distance predicate. Examples: > 1KM, = 200 M, ≤3KM)
- *E1,...En* are event types
- This pattern is satisfied if $\forall$ i $\exists$ e instance of Ei that belongs to the context partition CP, such that the predicate DP (O, e) is satisfied.

The max distance pattern is satisfied when the maximum distance of all the participant events from a given reference object satisfies the max distance threshold assertion.

Max Distance pattern is very similar to Min distance pattern.

The **Average Distance** pattern: the pattern

Average Distance (CP, O, DP, E1... En)

Where:

- CP is a context partition
- O is a reference object;
- DP is an average distance predicate. Examples: 1KM, 200 M
- *E1,...En* are event types
- This pattern is satisfied if $\forall$ i $\exists$ e instance of Ei that belongs to the context partition CP, such that the predicate DP (O, e) is satisfied.

The average distance pattern is satisfied when the average distance of all the participant events from a given point satisfies the average distance threshold assertion.

The **Relative Min Distance** pattern: the pattern

Relative Min Distance (CP, DP, E1, E2)

Where:

- CP is a context partition
- DP is a distance predicate. Examples: > 1KM, = 200 M, ≤ 3KM)
- *E1, E2* are event types
- This pattern is satisfied if $\exists$ e1, e2 instances of E1, E2 respectively which belong to the context partition CP and the predicate DP(e1 , e2) is satisfied.

The relative min distance pattern is satisfied when the minimal distance between any two participant events satisfies the min distance threshold assertion.

To show this in use, we consider a law enforcement application that analyzes burglary reports looking for patterns of similar-looking burglary events. One hypothesis is that there could be a burglar who never commits two crimes in the same neighborhood, to camouflage his tracks. To look for this the application uses a relative min distance pattern to detect when there is a set of similar burglaries always separated by a distance of at least 20 km. Figure 12 illustrates this example.

The **Relative Max Distance** pattern: the pattern

Relative Max Distance (CP, DP, E1, E2)

Where:

- CP is a context partition
- DP is a distance predicate. Examples: $> 1KM$, $= 200\ M$, $\leq 3KM$)
- *E1, E2* are event types
- This pattern is satisfied if $\exists$ e1, e2 instances of E1, E2 respectively which belong to the context partition CP and the predicate DP(e1 , e2) is satisfied.

The relative max distance pattern is satisfied when the maximal distance between any two participant events satisfies the max distance threshold assertion.

Using the burglary story again, the relative max distance pattern can be used to look for lazy burglars who always operate within a single neighborhood. We could, for example, look for a maximal distance of 5 km between similar burglaries.

The **Relative Average Distance** pattern: the pattern

Relative Average Distance (CP, DP, E1, E2)

Where:

- CP is a context partition
- DP is a distance predicate. Examples: $> 1KM$, $= 200\ M$, $\leq 3KM$)
- *E1, E2* are event types
- This pattern is satisfied if $\exists$ e1, e2 instances of E1, E2 respectively which belong to the context partition CP and the predicate DP(e1, e2) is satisfied.

The relative average distance pattern is satisfied when the average distance between any two participant events satisfies the relative average threshold assertion.

This pattern could be useful looking for a burglar who generally stays in a particular neighborhood, but now and then takes a journey further afield.

Figure 12 illustrates these three relative patterns.

Looking at the figure you can see that these partitions satisfy the following patterns:

- The relative max distance pattern with threshold assertion < 5 km is satisfied in the door breaking partition.
- The relative min distance pattern with threshold assertion > 20 km is satisfied in the window breaking partition.

The relative average distance pattern with threshold assertion ≤ 3 km is satisfied in the heavy lifter partition.

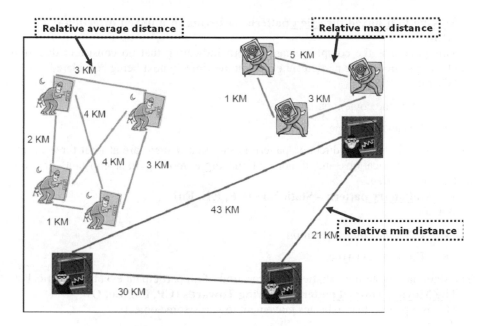

Fig. 14. Example that demonstrate three relative distance patterns

5.2 Spatiotemporal Patterns

Time series consists of a collection of time snapshots. In our context, it is applicable to case where the events are detected in discrete time-points with fixed distance among them. Time series are useful in sensor oriented applications where there is a periodic sensor reading. Within a spatiotemporal context, time series refers to a collection of time points included in the temporal interval for which the sensors reside within the spatial dimension of the context. As with temporal trend patterns we assume that there is just one relevant event type, so all the participant events are instances of this one type. Moreover, the patterns require that the participant events themselves constitute a time series, meaning that they are temporally totally ordered.

Moving in a constant direction pattern – Moving in a constant direction (CP, E1...En)

This pattern is actually a family of patterns, such as moving north, or moving south. For example, the moving south pattern would be satisfied by a vehicle that is transmitting GPS readings of its position while it's traveling from Bologna to Florence.

Where:

- CP is the context partition
- E is an event-type.

The moving in a constant direction pattern is satisfied if there exists a direction from the set {north, south, east, west, northeast, northwest, southeast, southwest} such that for any pair of participant events e1, e2 we have e1 << e2 => e2 lies in that direction relative to e1.

Moving in a mixed direction pattern – Moving in a mixed direction (CP, E1...En)

This pattern is the complementary pattern indicating that no consistent direction can be found among the participant events in the time context being considered.

Where:

- CP is the context partition

- E is an event-type.

The moving in a mixed direction pattern is satisfied if there are at least three events with different locations and if none of the eight moving in a constant direction patterns is satisfied.

The Stationary pattern – Stationary (CP, E1...En)

Where:

- CP is the context partition

- E is an event-type.

The stationary pattern is satisfied if the location of all participant events is identical.

The Moving Toward pattern – Moving Towards (CP, E1...En, O)

This is a pattern that indicates movement towards some object.

Where:

- CP is the context partition

- E is an event-type.

- O is a reference object

The moving toward pattern is satisfied when for any pair of participant events e1, e2 we have $e1 \ll e2 \Rightarrow$ the location of e2 is closer to a reference object O than the location of e1.

Note that this pattern may be true for several objects at the same time.

6   Use Cases

In this section we are showing several examples of event processing applications that can be assisted by the use of spatial abstraction. The examples are from the areas of: utilities grid, insurance, logistics, real estate, low enforcement and healthcare.

6.1 Insurance

Spatial event processing helps insurance companies by giving them the tools to leverage geographic perspective in their management of to exposure to loss while successfully competing in an increasingly demanding marketplace. The use of spatial event processing helps to understand level of risk while making insurance based on location of asset, to see number of claims in the area, see the value of polices in the area of insurance.

Example: When client asks for insurance for his house, an insurance company wants to evaluate risk of making insurance of this house H; company checks the number of insurance claims in the area in order to evaluate policy value.

- Context used: *Reference Object Space within a temporal context - CP.*

- *Reference Object – house H.*

- *Temporal context –year of 2008*

- Pattern (P3) - *Object Distance Pattern* - **MinDistance (CP, H, DP, E1... En)**

- *Events- E1,...En insurance claims event types*

- *DP is a distance Predicate*

- *Pattern P3 is satisfied by finding all locations of the claims events in distance DP from referenced object H within defined context CP.*

The derived event is the collection of all claim events which satisfies the pattern P3. The Insurance company makes decision on the insurance quote based on the cardinality of this event collection.

6.2 Logistics

Spatial event processing offers a better way to handle customer requests or find the best site for company's next warehouse, distribution center, or service department. With a Spatial Analysis, company can blend customer surveys with census data to visualize market penetration, market share, and trade areas. When markets change, spatial analysis can help to plan exit strategies and asset disposal.

Example: A Customer calls our company asks for technical service at his house. The company needs to find the closest service technician and send him to customer. Customer location (events E1) and (Ep1, Ep2, Epn) service technician car locations.

- Context used: *Fixed Space context - CP.*

- Pattern (P4) - - *Events: Distance Pattern* – **Relative Min Distance (CP, DP, E1,Ep1...Epn)**

- *Events- E1 customer location event, (Ep1, Ep2...Epn) service technician car locations.*
- *DP is a distance Predicate*

- *Pattern P4 is satisfied by finding minimum distance DP from customer location to each one of service cars (Ep1, Ep2... .Epn).The smallest DP is nearest service technician location and this technician will be sent to handle customer request.*

6.3 Real Estate

Real estate is all about location, location, location. Spatial event processing offers a variety of location–based solutions designed for all segments of the real estate business such as location–based content management and sophisticated investment analysis. Spatial event processing lets your customer compare multiple properties and their respective proximity to desired amenities such as schools, parks, and shopping centers. It can also gracefully introduce the subject of disclosure by displaying FEMA floodplain data and know toxic sites in an area.

Example: a customer wants to buy an apartment in the center of Manhattan NY. Real Estate agent needs to find all apartments for sale in distance of 1 mile from center Manhattan NY and show them to client.

- Context used: *Reference Object Space - CP.*

- Pattern (P5) - - *Object Distance Pattern* - **MaxDistance (CP, O, DP, E1... En)**

- *Reference Object – center Manhattan NY.*

- *Events- E1,...En sale opportunities event types.*
- *DP is a distance Predicate - 1 mile.*

- *Pattern P5 is satisfied by finding all sale opportunities in not more then 1 mile distance from center Manhattan NY.*

6.4 Healthcare

An effective health care services management use spatial analysis not only to show what resources and needs exist but also where to find them. Health experts also can use spatial event processing in epidemiological and public health monitoring. They can geographically track public health indicators, identify disease clusters, and explore sites of environmental risk.

Example: defining disease spreading direction. (Finding that disease is spreading in same direction as a wind)

- Context used: *Event based Space within a temporal context - CP.*

o *Temporal context – defined by same start event of first disease outburst and lasts till end event of last infected person + 48hours.*

o Pattern (P7) - *Contains Pattern* - **Moving in a constant direction (CP, E1,...En)**

o *Events- E1,...En disease infection event types*

o *Pattern P7 is satisfied by checking if there exists a direction from the set {north, south, east, west, northeast, northwest, southeast, southwest} such that for any pair of participant events e1, e2 we have e1 << e2 => e2 lies in that direction relative to e1.After finding spreading direction we can compare to wind direction.*

7 Conclusion

The paper has introduced spatial and spatio-temporal extensions to event processing aspects; this paper has discussed the notion of spatial events and spatio-temporal events, and discussed spatial and spatio-temporal contexts and patterns. Further work will continue the thinking of new spatio-temporal patterns and how to handle spatio-temporal events.

Future work will deal with collecting more use cases in order to extend the language to include additional spatial patterns and defining the spatial semantics of derived events.

The notions of spatial and spatiotemporal contexts are the major contributions of this paper, applying concepts from GIS into the event processing domain.

As one of the main benefits of event processing is the level of abstractions that enable to use high level languages and express closes functionality in an easy way, the addition of spatial abstractions extends the use of event processing. In our opinion integrating spatial and spatiotemporal processing into event processing languages and tools opens the way for new applications of these technologies and the spatial primitives improve the usability of such applications.

References

1. Adi, A., Biger, A., Botzer, D., Etzion, O., Sommer, Z.: Context Awareness in AMiT. Active Middleware Services, 160–167 (2003)
2. Allen, J.F.: Maintaining Knowledge about Temporal Intervals. ACM Commun. 26(11), 832–843 (1983)
3. Date, C.J.: An Introduction to Database Systems, 6th edn. Addison-Wesley Publishing Company, Reading (1993)
4. Etzion, O.: Towards an Event-Driven Architecture: An Infrastructure for Event Processing Position Paper. RuleML, 1–7 (2005)
5. Etzion, O.: Temporal Perspectives in Event Processing, Technical Report, IBM Haifa Research Lab (2008)
6. Galton, A.: Fields and objects in space, time, and space-time. Spatial Cognition and Computation 4(1), 39–68 (2004)
7. Grenon, P., Smith, B.: SNAP and SPAN: Towards dynamic spatial ontology. Forthcoming in the Journal of Spatial Cognition and Computation (2004)
8. Luckham, D.C.: The Power of Events: An Introduction to Complex Event Processing in Distributed Enterprise Systems. Addison-Wesley, Reading (2002)
9. Padovitz, A., Loke, S.W., Zaslavsky, A.B.: The ECORA framework: A hybrid architecture for context-oriented pervasive computing. Pervasive and Mobile Computing 4(2), 182–215 (2008)
10. Sargent, P.: Spatio-Temporal GIS- JRC Ispra Seminar (1998)
11. Schurman, N.: GIS a short introduction, pp. 12–16, 29-30,53-67. Blackwell Publishing, Oxford (2004)
12. Sharon, G., Etzion, O.: Event Processing Networks – model and implementation. IBM System Journal 47(2), 321–334 (2008)
13. Shevade, B., Sundaram, H., Xie, L.: Exploiting Personal and Social Network Context for Event Annotation. In: ICME 2007, 835–838 (2007)
14. Stock Kristin, M.: Spatio-Temporal Data Management Using Object Lifecycles: A Case Study of the Australian Capital Territory Spatial Data Management System. Journal of Spatial Sciences 51(1), 43–58 (2006)
15. Worboys Mike, F.: Innovations in GIS. Taylor & Francis, Taylor (1994) ISBN 0-7484-141-5
16. Worboys Mike, F.: GIS - A computing perspective. Taylor and Francis, Taylor (1995) ISBN 0-7484-0065-6
17. Worboys, M.F., Hornsby, K.: From objects to events. GEM, the geospatial event model. In: Third International Conference on GIScience (2004)
18. Worboys, M.F.: Event-Oriented Approaches to Geographic Phenomena. International Journal of Geographical Information Systems (2005)

Implementing a Practical Spatio-Temporal Composite Event Language

Ken Moody[1], Jean Bacon[1], David Evans[1], and Scarlet Schwiderski-Grosche[2]

[1] Computer Laboratory, University of Cambridge,
15 JJ Thomson Ave, Cambridge CB3 0FD, UK
{firstname.lastname}@cl.cam.ac.uk
[2] Microsoft Research, 7 JJ Thomson Ave, Cambridge, CB3 0FB, UK
scarlets@microsoft.com

Abstract. An earlier paper introduced *SpaTeC*, a composite event language that enables simultaneous matching of event occurrences over space and time. The driving case study is taken from a paper that describes techniques for monitoring small animals in New Zealand. The semantics of *SpaTeC* is presented in detail with the aid of the case study, but the syntax is essentially mathematical. This paper describes a programming language based on the *SpaTeC* model, illustrating it through a practical application, the analysis of GPS traces of buses serving Cambridge, UK. We describe some of the questions that Stagecoach, the bus operator, wish to have answered, and use these to motivate our extensions to *SpaTeC*. Composite event patterns are essentially those of the earlier paper, with the addition of *primitive patterns*, which enforce restrictions on the space and/or time of event occurrences. Data fields identified during pattern matching can be tested by predicates that further restrict the relevant combinations of primitive events. We show how the language can be used to answer questions posed by Stagecoach and discuss its realisation.

Keywords: Composite event language, mobile systems, spatio-temporal reasoning, session types.

1 Introduction

SpaTeC, a composite event language that enables simultaneous matching of event occurrences over space and time, is described in [1]. *Primitive event* occurrences carry both time and location stamps; the target of the work is to support sensor-based applications in which both clients and the objects monitored can be mobile. The paper defines operators to combine primitive events to form composite event occurrence patterns, specifying their semantics in terms of the time and location stamps of participating primitive event occurrences. A composite event notification service receives primitive (low-level) event occurrences, performs composite event matching against the current set of patterns, and forwards details of composite (higher-level) event occurrences to the relevant subscribers. There was no implementation, and although the paper presented a

K. Sachs, I. Petrov, and P. Guerrero (Eds.): Buchmann Festschrift, LNCS 6462, pp. 108–123, 2010.

detailed mobile event scenario, the data were not easily available for experiment. The present paper describes a new scenario with more challenging features for which data are available, using it to help design a *SpaTeC* programming language that builds on and extends the earlier model. We shall not refer to that paper again, but we assume the reader has access to it and can discover any relevant details from it.

Physical measurements in both time and space are subject to error. We follow the approach established in [2] to take account of local error using interval timestamps, and extend the technique to handle location stamps as well. Time values are essentially one-dimensional, and it makes sense to say that one event took place before another, though if the uncertainty intervals overlap we cannot be sure. For location stamps, the most that we can assert is that two events occurred at different places. Recent work taking account of location, such as [3,4,5], is discussed in the earlier paper.

Operators in *SpaTeC* establish time and location stamps for each composite event occurrence matched, and the semantics of the composite event language depends on the details. Two different semantics are described, which correspond in the time domain to *set-based semantics* and *interval-based semantics* respectively. Which is the more appropriate depends on the specific application; here we adopt interval-based semantics for timestamps, with the corresponding convex-hull semantics for composite event location stamps.

The application scenario described in [1] stems from work carried out in the Department of Biological Sciences at the University of Waikato, New Zealand[1]. King et al. develop effective techniques for predator-control operations on pastoral farmland, where ferrets and other small carnivores are monitored "both for keeping track of the distribution and numbers of native species, and for locating, guiding and auditing control operations against alien species" [6]. Monitoring is done using the so-called Scentinel®, a "smart" tracking tunnel for small mammals that records time, date, weight and a digital photograph of every animal entering it. Identifiers of tagged animals that get close to a Scentinel but do not enter are also recorded. Scentinels represent fixed nodes, radio-tagged animals represent mobile nodes in the system (GPS satellite collars allow continuous monitoring, but they are only suitable for animals weighing 15 or more kg).

Data rich events occur only in the vicinity of Scentinels, hence at fixed locations, though at random times. The present paper uses a complementary scenario, inspired by the needs of one of the Computer Laboratory's current research projects, TIME-EACM [7]. The local Cambridge bus company, Stagecoach, has fitted its buses with GPS transmitters supported by a local company, ACIS, who display anticipated arrival times at bus stops. With the agreement of both Stagecoach and ACIS the data feeds are also sent to the TIME-EACM project. Unlike Scentinel data, bus position data is transmitted at fixed times, but bus locations depend on factors such as traffic congestion. A paper giving a statistical analysis of this bus probe data is forthcoming; see [8]. Stagecoach are interested in the work, and have suggested other questions that we may be able

---

[1] http://www.bio.waikato.ac.nz/research/research1.shtml#zoology

to answer for them. The original *SpaTeC* was designed for applications that require temporal and spatial reasoning. The detailed requirements stemming from the Stagecoach questions have helped us to develop a theoretical design into a practical composite event language.

The rest of this paper is structured as follows: Section 2 gives the background to the GPS tracking support for the Stagecoach bus fleet in Cambridge, and discusses some of the questions of interest to the company. Section 3 presents the syntax and semantics of the *SpaTeC* programming language, motivating the extensions using Stagecoach bus scenarios. We describe our experience using *SpaTeC* to model the bus scenarios in Section 4. In Section 5 we outline some of the considerations when implementing *SpaTeC* in data intensive applications. Section 6 discusses related work. Section 7 concludes the paper.

2   GPS Tracking of Buses

Each bus serving Cambridge UK and surrounding areas that is operated by Stagecoach is equipped with a GPS-based location sensor. Such sensors note the geographical location of the bus and periodically (about once every 30 seconds) report it via wireless communication to a central location. Stagecoach, along with the local County Council and the firm that operates the reporting infrastructure, use these location reports to provide real-time information to passengers via displays at bus stops, web sites, and mobile phones.

Each Stagecoach bus therefore produces a series of location events, each having an associated timestamp. Both the location and the time are subject to uncertainty, the location because of error in the GPS reading and subsequent software processing, and the timestamp because location recording and data transmission are decoupled. Each bus is assigned an offset within a 30 second window at which to transmit. This means that a location report reflects the position of a particular bus some time within the previous 30 seconds. More formally, suppose that the location of bus i is recorded at time t_0 and is reported at time $t_1 = t_0 + \tau_i$. The timestamp of the location will be t_1, whereas the reading was actually taken at t_0. We are guaranteed that $\tau_i < 30$ for each bus i. Further, τ_i will be the same for each report from bus i within some session; the offsets for a given set of buses may then be updated, but this will happen only a small number of times per day. We have no easy way of determining the precise value of τ_i within a particular session. Further details are reported in [8].

Aside from providing information to passengers, Stagecoach is interested in using these location reports to answer questions like the following:

- Does wet weather, as sensed by various environmental detectors, correspond to longer journey times?
- Anecdotes suggest that journey times increase in the build-up to Christmas. Is this true?
- What is the quantitative effect on journey times of road disruptions (accidents, road works, etc.)?
- Are journey times to and from a local hospital longer on Tuesdays, when many outpatient appointments are scheduled?

Answering these questions has a component of historical analysis that amounts to data mining of the GPS traces. However, each question also defines a situation that can be detected as it is happening, so that consequent alerts can be issued. For example, the presence of rain and the lengthening of journey times can cause a "bad weather performance" alert to be issued, possibly triggering operational changes. A language based on *SpaTeC* principles must be able to describe these events.

3   The *SpaTeC* Programming Language

The *SpaTeC* programming language assumes an object-oriented environment. Events that occur in the application to be modelled conform to some type; variables in *SpaTeC* are typed accordingly. Each event occurrence defines an object instance in the corresponding class; attributes of this class can be used within the language.

The language has two parts. The first enables construction of *match expressions*, which are used to define *composite event patterns* that are always present in some phenomenon. The result of each match will be a set of primitive events. A match expression establishes what is, in effect, a session type having receive primitives only [9]. (If the language runtime used has direct support for session types, as can be found for Java and Moose as outlined in [10], the facilities can be used to encode results from match expressions, compare them, move them between modules of code, and so on. We discuss the use of session types further in Section 5.) The second part takes the set of composite events found by a particular match expression and restricts it using *filter predicates*. Zero or more filter predicates are attached to a match expression to form a *phrase*.

Each phrase corresponds to some situation of interest at application level. The purpose of a given phrase is to identify each *composite event occurrence* that identifies a particular instance of that situation. When a specific composite event is detected, its occurrence will depend on a specific set of primitive events. The notification service forwards details of each composite event occurrence to the relevant subscribers, for example by publishing an object instance in a class specific to this type of composite event; its attributes will reflect the associated set of primitive event occurrences.

3.1   Primitive Event Match Expressions

Each match expression has a natural tree structure that represents the event pattern to be identified. Non-leaf nodes in the tree correspond to the operators introduced in Section 3.3. There are two categories of leaf node.

A *primitive event* is a typed data structure that represents the reification of an occurrence. The type of the event is a class (in the object-oriented programming sense) that contains all the information needed to describe a particular event occurrence of that type. In our model, every such class will contain `time` and `location` attributes.

Assume that e is a primitive event type, for example a GPS bus observation. The expression e is a *primitive event match expression* that matches all event instances of type e. Further, the expression

$$e \rightarrow B$$

is a match expression that, each time it matches an event of type e, unifies B with the state carried by that event instance. One can think of B as being a session variable of type e, which in the context of a specific match describes the corresponding matching event occurrence. We shall see shortly how B is scoped and why it is useful.

3.2 Primitive Patterns

Alongside primitive events are *primitive patterns*. These are match expressions that match events not by type, as with primitive events, but by space and time. They can be thought of as matching all possible event types, subject to conditions on their `time` and/or `location` attributes. Examples of patterns are "Tuesday", which contains every event with a timestamp that falls on a Tuesday[2]; and "point x", containing all events at all times having location stamps x.

The rules for matching primitive patterns are as defined in Tables 1 and 2. We also need to specify the `time` and `location` stamps of composite event occurrences matched by expressions that include patterns. First, any composite event expression consisting only of primitive patterns is a *pattern*. When a pattern matches some composite event expression that contains at least one event occurrence, the combined matched expression is given the `time` and `location` stamps of the non-pattern operand. In particular, any combination of primitive patterns can match all possible (composite) event types subject to conditions on the `time` and/or `location` attributes, and the result of matching that composite pattern will leave both `time` and `location` stamps unaltered.

We shall meet examples of the use of patterns in Section 4.

3.3 General Match Expressions

Match expressions are combined to form *composite events* using operators. The event operators for simultaneous reasoning in space and time are listed in Table 1. When we need to reason in only one of space and time, we can use the simpler event operators listed in Table 2. Event patterns pose precise space and time requirements, but sometimes the uncertainty of measurement of the `location` and `time` attributes of primitive event occurrences will mean that we cannot be certain whether there is a match. Notions of *same location* and *same time* must always be interpreted as *within measurement error*, meaning that

---

[2] We are ignoring issues such as time zones and leap years; the motivated reader can imagine a system that begins by following the ISO 8601 standard for writing down times.

Table 1. *SpaTeC* Event Operators for Reasoning in Space **and** Time

Event Operator	Meaning	Description
$E_1 \left\{ \begin{smallmatrix} <> \\ ; \end{smallmatrix} \right\} E_2$	Location overlap, in sequence	The locations of E_1 and E_2 overlap, E_1 happens before E_2
$E_1 \left\{ \begin{smallmatrix} >< \\ ; \end{smallmatrix} \right\} E_2$	Distinct locations, in sequence	E_1 and E_2 occur at distinct locations, E_1 happens before E_2
$E_1 \left\{ \begin{smallmatrix} <> \\ \| \end{smallmatrix} \right\} E_2$	Location overlap, time overlap	The locations of E_1 and E_2 overlap, their timestamps also overlap
$E_1 \left\{ \begin{smallmatrix} >< \\ \| \end{smallmatrix} \right\} E_2$	Distinct locations, time overlap	E_1 and E_2 occur at distinct locations, and their timestamps overlap

Table 2. *SpaTeC* Event Operators for Reasoning in Space **or** Time

Event Operator	Meaning	Description
$E_1 \{<>\} E_2$	Location overlap	The locations of E_1 and E_2 overlap
$E_1 \{><\} E_2$	Distinct locations	E_1 and E_2 occur at distinct locations
$E_1 \{\|\} E_2$	Time overlap	The timestamps of E_1 and E_2 overlap
$E_1 \{;\} E_2$	In sequence	E_1 happens before E_2
$E_1 \{,\} E_2$	Conjunction	Both E_1 and E_2 occur
$E_1 \{|\} E_2$	Disjunction	Either E_1 or E_2 occurs

they are too close to be differentiated. In addition *SpaTeC* supports Boolean operations on match expressions in the obvious way.

This allows the construction of complex composite events that represent occurrences having some spatial and temporal property (such as primitive events happening in sequence, at the same place, etc.) and the restriction of these by spatial and temporal constants.

3.4   Filter Predicates

A stream of composite events is likely to be too broad to describe many phenomena of interest. We therefore introduce *filter predicates* that allow selection of the composite events emerging from a given match expression.

A filter predicate is defined recursively as the conjunction ($\wedge$) or disjunction ($\vee$) of two other filter predicates. Each predicate can be negated ($\neg$). At the lowest level, a filter predicate is a Boolean-valued expression containing elements chosen from the following:

- constants
- attributes from variables that are unified as part of the matching composite event
- simple mathematical operations (by which we mean things like arithmetic operators and exponentiation)
- functions built from the above, such as computing the distance between two points (in whatever space those coordinates lie)
- relational operators $(<, =, >, \leq, \geq)$

The *attributes from variables* component of filter predicates needs a little explanation. The variables are like example B in Section 3.1, and represent the data that characterise matching event instances. This allows predicates to reason over these data, selecting only composite events of interest. For example, consider the event type BUS that, in addition to the standard attributes `time` and `location`, has a vehicle identification attribute VID that indicates to which bus the event pertains. Let e_1 and e_2 represent events of type BUS. The expression

$$(e_1 \to B_1; \quad e_2 \to B_2) \, [(B_1.\texttt{VID}) == (B_2.\texttt{VID})]$$

matches two observations of the same bus, the first taking place before the second. The expression

$$(e_1 \to B_1; \quad e_2 \to B_2) \, [(B_1.\texttt{VID}) == (B_2.\texttt{VID})$$
$$\wedge \; \text{distance} \, (B_1.\texttt{location}, \, B_2.\texttt{location}) \geq 450]$$

matches two observations of the same bus that are at least 450 units apart.

Note that a phrase consists of a match expression and zero or more filter predicates, each of which must be satisfied. Testing a filter predicate requires access to the relevant matched variable attributes; supporting multiple predicates aids specification and offers hints to the optimiser.

4   Using *SpaTeC* to Analyse the Bus GPS Data

In this section we look in more detail at some of the Stagecoach questions, and describe some of the basic requirements for answering them. As a first step we look at two of their interests:

- Anecdotes suggest that journey times increase in the build-up to Christmas. Is this true?
- Are journey times to and from a local hospital longer on Tuesdays, when many outpatient appointments are scheduled?

As we have said in Section 2, we are interested not so much in mining the historical record for answers to these questions as in producing events that correspond to germane situations as they happen. Of course, anecdotal evidence relates to past experience and a first step is statistical analysis of the historical record. If the anecdotal evidence is found to be justified, in general, it is then appropriate to detect patterns in real time; such a pattern may indicate for example that congestion is beginning to build up, so appropriate action can be taken, such as the deployment of extra buses.

Answering these types of question requires selecting bus observations with particular `time` or `location` attributes. The simplest case is that of a single fixed time or place, for example the stop at the local hospital.

4.1   Constant Patterns and Their Uses

Constant patterns are provided as part of the programming environment when defining composite event expressions. To say that a pattern is constant does not mean that its value is necessarily simple; for example, the pattern *Tuesday* is constant, but the value requires careful initialisation. We begin with an example of a point location constant pattern.

To identify observations when a bus is at a particular stop, we have:

$$(e_1 \; \{<>\} \; \text{BusStopX})$$

BusStopX is a primitive pattern with the `location` stamp of BusStopX, which will otherwise match any event. The normal semantics of the $\{<>\}$ operator will cause this expression to match all events of type e_1 whose `location` attributes overlap BusStopX; see Section 3.3. Inevitably buses will not stop precisely at a single fixed location, and we select an uncertainty radius for the primitive pattern *BusStopX* to take account of this.

Suppose that we need to identify, in real time, (composite) events when the journey time from the hospital to the station is less than 6 minutes.[3] e_1 and e_2 are bus observation events. We assume that HospitalStop and StationStop identify the two bus stops.

$$((e_1 \to B_1 \; \{<>\} \; \text{HospitalStop}); \; (e_2 \to B_2 \; \{<>\} \; \text{StationStop}))$$
$$[(B_1.\text{VID} == B_2.\text{VID}) \; \wedge \; (B_2.\text{time} - B_1.\text{time} < 6 * 60)] \quad (1)$$

The composite event $(e_1 \to B_1 \; \{<>\} \; \text{HospitalStop})$ has the timestamp of event e_1, so we can easily check for quick journeys on a Tuesday (unlikely!) by starting with

$$(e_1 \to B_1 \; \{<>\} \; \text{HospitalStop}) \; || \; \text{Tuesday}$$

This works because of the rule for deriving composite event `location` and `time` stamps from primitive patterns (see Section 3.2). The same effect could be obtained using the expression

$$(e_1 \to B_1 \; \left\{ \begin{matrix} <> \\ || \end{matrix} \right\} \; (\text{HospitalStop} \wedge \text{Tuesday}))$$

---

[3] Note that uncertainty in event timestamps means that this can't be detected precisely.

4.2   More Demanding Stagecoach Questions

Detailed statistical study of bus tracking data along two sections of route has allowed us to answer some more complex Stagecoach questions, see [8]. This analysis is time consuming, and by its nature cannot deliver answers in real time. Recall the other two examples given in Section 2:

- Does wet weather, as sensed by various environmental detectors, correspond to longer journey times?
- What is the quantitative effect on journey times of road disruptions (accidents, road works, etc.)?

We have been able to resolve these questions to some extent using historical data, for example looking at the correlation between days when it has rained and longer journey times. However, these can also be detected in real time by writing appropriate *SpaTeC* phrases. For example, suppose that an event of type r occurs when it rains, its `time` and `location` attributes describing the time and place of the rainfall. (r can also be regarded as an event pattern that represents all the points where it is raining.) Starting from *SpaTeC* phrase 1, we can construct the phrase

$$\left(\left((e_1 \to B_1 \; \{<>\} \; \text{HospitalStop}) \; \left\{ \overset{<>}{\parallel} \right\} \; r \right) ; \right.$$

$$\left. \left((e_2 \to B_2 \; \{<>\} \; \text{StationStop}) \; \left\{ \overset{<>}{\parallel} \right\} \; r \right) \right)$$

$$[(B_1.\text{VID} == B_2.\text{VID}) \; \wedge \; (B_2.\text{time} - B_1.\text{time} > 20 * 60)]$$

that detects bus journeys between the hospital and the station, when it is raining at the beginning and end of the journey and the trip takes longer than 20 minutes (we shall also need to ensure that the bus is visiting the station for the first time since it left the hospital).

In addition to the bus tracking data the TIME-EACM project monitors traffic on the nearest main road in real time, and this data can provide early warning of congestion and consequent delay to buses. Equally, the bus GPS data in itself provides evidence of congestion; for example, buses do not make good progress during the morning and evening rush hours, particularly during the school term. We hope to be able to calibrate bus movement behaviours from the historical tracking data, and so develop *SpaTeC* patterns that, if detected, indicate congestion on the roads. A first shot might be to produce an event when the same bus reports 4 successive location observations that overlap pairwise. Even this relatively simple example requires some tedious predicates.

5   *SpaTeC* - Moving towards Deployment

SpaTeC phrases define sets of composite events, and it is the job of the implementation to detect these based on primitive event occurrences. Recall that each phrase consists of an obligatory match expression and optional predicates, which are tested against each matching set of event occurrences. A possible scenario is to implement complex event detection as a service above a publish/subscribe architecture such as Rebeca [11] or Hermes [12]. Clients of the system are publishers, subscribers or both. Event types are defined and managed by the system. Potential publishers advertise their ability to publish event instances. Subscribers subscribe to event types with a subscription filter that represents their particular interests. Notice that publishers and subscribers are mutually anonymous. The system is provided as a distributed broker network. A broker may be publisher-hosting, subscriber-hosting, both or neither; that is, some brokers may merely act as routers. A common optimisation of publish/subscribe is content-based routing (CBR), that allows communication paths to be shared when a published message is transmitted through the network to its subscribers. CBR is typically set up in the event brokers when events are advertised and subscribed to.

Following [13], each composite event detector (CED) subscribes to events and advertises and publishes higher-level composite events. A composite event match expression tree may be split into subtrees that are placed in the distributed system to optimise communication and detection latency.

Each phrase in a *SpaTeC* program is handled independently, meaning that there is no explicit inter-phrase state nor are there references between them. Therefore, a given program may be implemented as a central service or may be distributed as an optimisation.

5.1 Centralised Implementation

We first outline how a centralised implementation works.

1. The text of the phrase is processed by a front-end to check syntax and extract the match expression and predicates. At this stage the match expression is checked to ensure that unified variables are not re-used and are therefore conflict-free. This is done as it would be for any programming language, so it is not discussed further in this paper.
2. Event detectors are built from the phrase's match expression. This is done using finite automata based on those used by Hermes [14, chapter 7]. The automata use initial, ordinary, and generative states but have no need for generative time states, since *SpaTeC* does not deal with time events in the same way. The operators in Tables 1 and 2 that compare location stamps are handled in the same way that Hermes deals with timestamps, with comparisons taking account of the inherent uncertainty.

   The only complication is that when primitive events are matched as part of composite event detection and their instance is unified with a variable, the attributes of that instance must be saved for future evaluation by filter predicates. A naïve approach is to keep a shared dictionary of unified variables, associating with each its class (derived from the type of the corresponding primitive event) and its attributes. The automata contain *unification states* that are inserted as required following matching transitions. These states are responsible for updating the shared dictionary.

3. The filter predicates operate on the output of the automata created in step 2, using the shared dictionary to retrieve any event instance attributes that are needed. This is done through any suitably efficient rule system, meaning that a Prolog or Datalog implementation is feasible.

Following these three steps, event processing begins with CED service nodes evaluating their assigned match expressions.

5.2 Distributed Implementation

In reality a centralised implementation is unlikely to be appealing for the usual reasons, including poor scalability, inflexibility in the context of a heterogeneous communication infrastructure, and unreliability. In addition, it is likely to be inappropriate for multi-organisation systems. A distributed implementation of a *SpaTeC* program follows the pattern of a centralised one. Phrases are parsed and the match expressions and filter predicates extracted. This is likely to remain centralised as the program is presented to the system at only one place, and processing is likely to be done only once. In step 2, the automata are distributed throughout the network in the same manner as are CED subtrees. A shared dictionary is no longer an option for maintaining event instance attributes, but a relevant subset may be included with the composite events produced by the automata at each node. Filter predicates are similarly distributed to the CED service(s) that can, based on the decomposition derived above, subscribe to each required event type. In other words, if the allocation of match expressions means that events of type e are never sent to a particular node, that node need not be sent predicates involving attributes of variables of type e.

In Section 3 we noted that each phrase establishes a session type associated with its match expression. Channels of that session type can be used to communicate attributes of variables to a central site, where the predicates associated with the phrase can be tested. We are planning to build a prototype implementation of *SpaTeC* above Java, with session types provided by SJ [15]. SJ is itself implemented above Polyglot [16,17]. Polyglot has been around for some time, and should help to provide a stable framework.

In practice, for phrases that associate primitive events from widely distributed locations, some of the predicates may test attributes of variables whose locations of occurrence are clustered. It may make sense to move the evaluation of such predicates nearer to the relevant locations. Session types associated with match expressions should support such optimisations, but we shall need to experiment.

6   Related Work

The event-based paradigm emerged during the 1990s when asynchronous notification was seen to be crucial for a wide range of applications. [18] investigates the use of events for building distributed applications based on an object-oriented distributed programming environment. Other applications include sensor-based systems for environmental monitoring and, in general, applications with low latency requirements. For example, in 1999 [19] discusses the need for event-based middleware in Air Traffic Control.

The detection of meaningful patterns of events (so-called composite events) became a subject of research, for example [13]. But early composite event languages supported only temporal reasoning, based on the temporal properties of events; composite event detection was driven by the times of occurrence of constituent events.

In distributed systems, times of occurrence are fundamentally uncertain, because of the way earth-time is measured, the way computers' clocks are set and drift, and because clocks are synchronized intermittently. In [20] event operators *sequence* and *concurrency* are used to determine whether one event happened before another or whether they may have happened "at the same time", that is, their order cannot be established due to the closeness of the timestamps. In 1999, Liebig and others proposed source-specific interval timestamps to capture this uncertainty [2]. A *sequence* is detected if the uncertainty interval of one event precedes that of another. If the uncertainty intervals overlap it cannot be determined which one occurred first. It may be important for the application to be made aware of this, in cases where physical causality is an issue, such as in real-time monitoring for the control and audit of physical systems.

Spatial reasoning, that is, monitoring the spatial properties of events, was not supported in traditional composite event detection. When the nodes in distributed systems are stationary the location of occurrence of node-related events is implicit, and spatial reasoning is "hard-wired" into the system.

Mobile environments were explored in [21,22,23,24,4,25,26] where the focus lies on the adaptation of the publish/subscribe paradigm to different aspects of mobility, such as client mobility or the lack of a system-wide service infrastructure. In general, location is being considered in the design of a publish/subscribe architecture for mobile systems, but not in the underlying event detection capabilities. In [27], Fiege and others consider mobility in publish/subscribe middleware. The Rebeca [11] content-based publish/subscribe middleware is extended in [24] to accommodate mobile clients, achieving location transparent access to the middleware without loss of quality of service. Chen and others define the notion of spatial event and enable a spatial subscription model [3]. In [4], Cugola and Munoz de Cote develop a distributed publish/subscribe middleware where spatial restrictions can be issued by publishers and subscribers. [5] points out that high-level spatial events are necessary to observe physical world events and mentions that traditional composite event systems are not sufficient for this purpose. However, general spatial reasoning with composite events is not supported.

In [28], Römer and Mattern acknowledge the suitability of event-based mechanisms for monitoring physical phenomena and their spatio-temporal properties in sensor networks, and investigate composite event detection for detecting the real-world states associated with such phenomena. In later work they propose spacetime, a four-dimensional vector space where space is represented in three and time in one dimension, to record the time and location of occurrence of an event [29].

Limiting the visibility of events is another important requirement in sensor networks where the lack of an infrastructure and the dynamically changing network topology demand efficient and adaptive event handling. The scoping concept, as introduced in [30], meets this requirement. It represents a fundamental structuring mechanism for event-based systems where components are bundled recursively into higher-level components, so-called scopes, yielding a hierarchical structure. Event notifications are only delivered to subscribers within the same scope. In [31], Jacobi et al. apply the scoping concept to sensor networks.

7   Conclusions

We have defined the *SpaTeC* composite event language that enables simultaneous matching of event occurrences over space and time. We have built on the model for *SpaTeC* presented in [1]. As a source of examples throughout the paper we have used a real application scenario for which data are available; the analysis of the GPS traces of Cambridge buses made available by Stagecoach to the TIME-EACM project.

We have described some questions that Stagecoach wish to have answered, and used them to motivate our extensions to *SpaTeC*. Composite event patterns are essentially those of the earlier paper, with the addition of *primitive patterns*, which enforce restrictions on the space and/or time of event occurrences. Data fields identified during pattern matching can be tested by predicates that further restrict the relevant combinations of primitive events. We have shown how the language can be used to answer some of the questions posed by Stagecoach.

We have described an implementation scenario for *SpaTeC* composite event detection (CED) above a publish/subscribe system. Following [13] we ensure a clean separation between CED services and the event propagation infrastructure; a CED service is a subscriber to low-level events and a publisher of higher-level events. As in [13], processing of composite events arising from a given *SpaTeC* phrase may be distributed to optimise communication and detection latency.

A major concern in this area of work is the measurement uncertainty both for space and time. We have generalised the foundational work of [2], that embodies the fundamental uncertainty in the measurement of earth-time, to a similar uncertainty in location stamps. The `time` and `location` stamps of the composite events detected are an open interval and a convex hull respectively, see [1]. The `time` stamp of a composite event can therefore be represented naturally; describing a general convex hull is not straightforward, and the `location` stamp representation adopted will depend on the semantics of the application.

Future work is to implement *SpaTeC* as a composite event programming language and to carry out experimental evaluation.

Acknowledgements

The paper draws on a number of research projects over the years. We acknowledge the support of the UK Engineering and Physical Sciences Research Council (EPSRC) through grants GR/T28164 (EDSAC21) and EP/C547632 (TIME-EACM). Stagecoach in Cambridge has greatly assisted TIME-EACM by making GPS data feeds from their buses available in real time, and by suggesting some of the scenarios developed in the paper.

We acknowledge the many fruitful interactions with Alejandro Buchmann and the Databases and Distributed Systems Research Group at the Technische Universität, Darmstadt. We are grateful for helpful contributions to the paper from several of our colleagues at the Computer Laboratory, in particular David Eyers and Alan Mycroft. The latter emphasised the relevance of session types. Interaction with Simon Gay by e-mail identified SJ as a potential tool for implementation.

References

1. Schwiderski-Grosche, S., Moody, K.: The SpaTeC composite event language for spatio-temporal reasoning in mobile systems. In: 3rd ACM Intl. Conf. on Distributed Event-Based Systems, DEBS 2009, pp. 1–12. ACM, New York (2009)
2. Liebig, C., Cilia, M., Buchmann, A.: Event composition in time-dependent distributed systems. In: 4th Intl. Conf. on Cooperative Information Systems (CoopIS 1999), pp. 70–78 (September 1999)
3. Chen, X., Chen, Y., Rao, F.: An efficient spatial publish/subscribe system for intelligent location-based services. In: 2nd Intl. Workshop on Distributed Event-Based Systems (DEBS 2003), 1–6 (2003)
4. Cugola, G., de Cote, J.E.M.: On introducing location awareness in publish-subscribe middleware. In: 25th International Conference on Distributed Computing Systems Workshops (ICDCSW 2005), Columbus, OH, USA, June 6-10, pp. 377–382. IEEE Computer Society, Los Alamitos (2005)
5. Bauer, M., Rothermel, K.: An architecture for observing physical world events. In: 11th Intl. Conf. on Parallel and Distributed Systems (ICPADS 2005), pp. 377–383. IEEE Computer Society, Los Alamitos (2005)
6. King, C., McDonald, R., Martin, R., Tempero, G., Holmes, S.: Long-term automated monitoring of the distribution of small carnivores. Wildlife Research 34(2), 140–148 (2007)
7. Bacon, J., Beresford, A., Evans, D., Ingram, D., Trigoni, N., Guitton, A., Skordylis, A.: Time: An open platform for capturing, processing and delivering transport-related data. In: IEEE Consumer Communications and Networking Conference, pp. 687–691. IEEE, Los Alamitos (2008)
8. Bejan, A., Gibbens, R., Evans, D., Beresford, A., Bacon, J., Friday, A.: Statistical modelling and analysis of sparse bus probe data in urban areas. In: 13th IEEE Intelligent Transportation Systems Conference, Madeira, Portugal. IEEE, Los Alamitos (2010)
9. Takeuchi, K., Honda, K., Kubo, M.: An interaction-based language and its typing system. In: Halatsis, C., Philokyprou, G., Maritsas, D., Theodoridis, S. (eds.) PARLE 1994. LNCS, vol. 817, pp. 398–413. Springer, Heidelberg (1994)

10. Honda, K., Yoshida, N., Carbone, M.: Multiparty asynchronous session types. SIG-PLAN Not. 43(1), 273–284 (2008)
11. Mühl, G., Ulbrich, A., Herrmann, K., Weis, T.: Disseminating information to mobile clients using publish-subscribe. IEEE Internet Computing 8(3), 46–53 (2004)
12. Pietzuch, P.R., Bacon, J.M.: Hermes: a distributed event-based middleware architecture. In: 22nd International Conference on Distributed Computing Systems Workshops (ICDCSW 2002), Vienna, Austria, July 2–5, pp. 611–618. IEEE Computer Society, Los Alamitos (2002)
13. Pietzuch, P.R., Shand, B., Bacon, J.: A framework for event composition in distributed systems (Best paper award.). In: Endler, M., Schmidt, D.C. (eds.) Middleware 2003. LNCS, vol. 2672, pp. 62–82. Springer, Heidelberg (2003)
14. Pietzuch, P.R.: Hermes: A scalable event-based middleware. Technical Report UCAM-CL-TR-590, University of Cambridge Computer Laboratory (2004)
15. Hu, R., Yoshida, N., Honda, K.: Session-based distributed programming in Java. In: Vitek, J. (ed.) ECOOP 2008. LNCS, vol. 5142, pp. 516–541. Springer, Heidelberg (2008)
16. Nystrom, N., Clarkson, M.R., Myers, A.C.: Polyglot: An extensible compiler framework for Java. In: Hedin, G. (ed.) CC 2003. LNCS, vol. 2622, pp. 138–152. Springer, Heidelberg (2003)
17. Polyglot, http://www.cs.cornell.edu/projects/polyglot/
18. Bacon, J., Bates, J., Hayton, R., Moody, K.: Using events to build distributed applications. In: 2nd Intl. Workshop on Services in Distributed and Networked Environments, SDNE 1995, Washington, DC, USA, pp. 148–155. IEEE Computer Society, Los Alamitos (1995)
19. Liebig, C., Boesling, B., Buchmann, A.: A notification service for Next-Generation IT systems in air traffic control. In: GI-Workshop: Multicast-Protokolle und Anwendungen, Braunschweig, Germany (May 1999)
20. Schwiderski, S.: Monitoring the behaviour of distributed systems. PhD thesis, University of Cambridge (1996)
21. Meier, R., Cahill, V.: STEAM: event-based middleware for wireless ad hoc networks. In: 22nd International Conference on Distributed Computing Systems Workshops (ICDCSW 2002), Vienna, Austria, July 2-5, pp. 639–644. IEEE Computer Society, Los Alamitos (2002)
22. Huang, Y., Garcia-Molina, H.: Publish/subscribe in a mobile environment. Wireless Networks 10(6), 643–652 (2004)
23. Caporuscio, M., Carzaniga, A., Wolf, A.: Design and evaluation of a support service for mobile, wireless publish/subscribe applications. IEEE Transactions on Software Engineering 29(12), 1059–1071 (2003)
24. Zeidler, A., Fiege, L.: Mobility support with REBECA. In: 23rd International Conference on Distributed Computing Systems Workshops (ICDCSW 2003), Providence, RI, USA, May 19-22, pp. 354–360. IEEE Computer Society, Los Alamitos (2003)
25. Yoneki, E., Bacon, J.: Unified semantics for event correlation over time and space in hybrid network environments. In: Meersman, R., Tari, Z. (eds.) OTM 2005. LNCS, vol. 3760, pp. 366–384. Springer, Heidelberg (2005)
26. Frey, D., Roman, G.C.: Context-aware publish subscribe in mobile ad hoc networks. In: COORDINATION, pp. 37–55 (2007)
27. Fiege, L., Gärtner, F.C., Kasten, O., Zeidler, A.: Supporting mobility in content-based publish/subscribe middleware. In: Endler, M., Schmidt, D.C. (eds.) Middleware 2003. LNCS, vol. 2672, pp. 103–122. Springer, Heidelberg (2003)

28. Römer, K., Mattern, F.: Event-based systems for detecting real-world states with sensor networks: a critical analysis. In: DEST Workshop on Signal Processing in Wireless Sensor Networks at ISSNIP, Melbourne, Australia, pp. 389–395 (December 2004)
29. Römer, K., Mattern, F.: Towards a unified view on space and time in sensor networks. Elsevier Computer Communications 28(13), 1484–1497 (2005)
30. Fiege, L., Mezini, M., Mühl, G., Buchmann, A.P.: Engineering event-based systems with scopes. In: Magnusson, B. (ed.) ECOOP 2002. LNCS, vol. 2374, pp. 309–333. Springer, Heidelberg (2002)
31. Jacobi, D., Guerrero, P.E., Petrov, I., Buchmann, A.: Structuring sensor networks with scopes. In: 3rd IEEE European Conference on Smart Sensing and Context (EuroSSC), IEEE Communications Society, Zurich (2008)

Design and Implementation of the Rebeca Publish/Subscribe Middleware

Helge Parzyjegla[1], Daniel Graff[1], Arnd Schröter[1],
Jan Richling[1], and Gero Mühl[2]

[1] Communication and Operating Systems Group
Berlin Institute of Technology, Germany
[2] Architecture of Application Systems Group
University Rostock, Germany
{parzyjegla,daniel.graff,arnd.schroeter,richling,g_muehl}@acm.org

Abstract. Publish/subscribe is used increasingly often as a communication mechanism in loosely-coupled distributed applications. Research and product development have focused mostly on efficiency issues and neglected methodological support to build concrete middleware implementations so far. In this paper, we present the novel design of the REBECA publish/subscribe middleware that is based on the experience gained with previous versions. As basic design concept, we focus on a modular pipeline architecture that is built around a minimal, but extendable publish/subscribe core. With respect to modularity, we employ the concept of features that are well-defined aspects of a software system's functionality, encapsulated in pluggable modules, and, thereby, facilitate a separation of concerns. We address the composition of features and show how this is realized in REBECA's pipeline architecture with independently working plugins that can influence passing messages in three dedicated stages.

1 Introduction

Publish/subscribe is an appealingly simple, yet powerful and flexible communication style fostering event-driven applications. Application components interact by *publishing* notifications about events occurred and by *subscribing* to notifications of those events they are interested in. The main advantage of event-based interaction using publish/subscribe is the resulting loose coupling of the interacting components: publishers do not necessarily need to know the receivers of their notifications, while subscribers do not necessarily need to know who published a notification. Thus, publishers and subscribers are usually self-contained focusing on their own functionality and the notifications they receive and publish in turn. Such a data-centric approach is especially well suited for dynamic environments in which components need to be seamlessly added, extended, replaced, or removed at runtime.

Publish/subscribe concepts and their variants are known from very different areas of computer science and they can be leveraged on many layers and different scales serving various purposes. Within the area of software engineering,

K. Sachs, I. Petrov, and P. Guerrero (Eds.): Buchmann Festschrift, LNCS 6462, pp. 124–140, 2010.

the observer design pattern [8] is well known. With this pattern, application components are notified when an observed entity's state changes in order to trigger automatic updates of dependent components. Modern operating systems may provide a system-wide message bus [13] that notifies connected applications about system events such as added or removed hardware. Additionally, applications may use the bus as a message-based interprocess communication (IPC) mechanism to exchange data in global or session context in order to talk to each other and coordinate their actions. In distributed environments, applications of the publish/subscribe pattern range from gathering data in sensor networks [9] over real-time data distribution for embedded systems [19] to web service extensions to integrate notifications [20,30] as well as dissemination and processing of complex events in business workflows [14]. Pursuing the shift from centralized systems and data stores towards distributed and networked infrastructures, publish/subscribe is steadily gaining importance as an integrating technology linking autonomous components, intelligent services, and heterogeneous applications.

With publish/subscribe becoming an integral part of sustainable future computer infrastructures, an increasing number of functional and non-functional requirements such as scalability, reliability and security as well as domain-specific extensions and constraints have to be taken into consideration when developing such a system. The sheer quantity of requirements and constraints, even contradictory ones, usually leads to complex system designs and middleware implementations that are not flexibly deployable in those dynamic environments where applications could profit most from loose coupling and publish/subscribe communication. In this paper, we present a modular architecture for publish/subscribe middleware implementations that facilitates the easy composition of single features to a tailor-made, light-weight solution. The approach has been successfully applied to our publish/subscribe system REBECA.

In the following, we give an overview of the REBECA middleware in Sect. 2. Section 3 explains the idea of feature composition that is one of the main concepts of REBECA. Next, we introduce the architecture of REBECA and its main components in Section 4, followed by a description of the features implemented so far in Sect. 5. Section 6 shows how we realized a discrete event simulation based on the actual implementation of REBECA. Finally, we summarize related work in Section 7 and conclude the paper in Section 8.

2   Rebeca Publish/Subscribe Middleware

The REBECA middleware supports event-driven applications built of cooperating components. Components can adopt the roles of publishers or subscribers depending on whether they act as producers or consumers of information or both. To make information available, REBECA offers components an interface to asynchronously publish notifications. Notifications are based on sets of name/value pairs that are either deliberately specified by the producer or, as supported by object-oriented programming languages, derived automatically from the fields (named attributes) of the notification object to publish. To request information, REBECA allows consuming components to issue subscriptions containing notification filters that are Boolean expressions on the content of notifications. Together the subscriptions issued by a component constitute its interest.

Producing and consuming components are connected indirectly with each other by a notification service provided by the REBECA middleware. The notification service, interposed between producers and consumers, is responsible to deliver published notifications to all consumers with matching subscriptions. REBECA implements the notification service by a set of cooperating broker instances distributed in the network and each managing a set of locally connected components. In turn, the brokers are connected via overlay links and exchange published notifications as well as information about issued and revoked subscriptions on behalf of their clients. For this purpose, each broker keeps track of the interests of connected neighbor brokers and local clients by storing their active subscriptions in a content-based routing table. A published notification can, thus, be forwarded stepwise starting at the publisher hosting broker over intermediary brokers to all brokers hosting interested consumers.

The development of the initial version of REBECA started in 1999 and was initiated by Gero Mühl and Ludger Fiege at the Database and Distributed Systems Group of Alejandro P. Buchmann at the Darmstadt University of Technology. REBECA was originally a recursive acronym for *Rebeca Event-Based Electronic Commerce architecture*. The reason to coin this name was that the REBECA middleware was at this time mainly intended to support distributed electronic commerce application such as meta auctions [1]. After this initial development phase, other students and researchers have used the prototypical implementation as a basis to carry out their research. Over the years, REBECA successfully served as a publish/subscribe system to study advanced and efficient routing algorithms [15], to implement visibility and structuring concepts [5], to support mobility of clients and applications [31,17], to consider deployments in actuator/ sensor networks [25], to investigate mechanisms for dynamic reconfiguration [22], adaptability [26], and self-organization [11], to develop fault-tolerant and self-stabilizing networks [10], to derive programming abstractions [29] and to discuss the usage and integration of model-driven architectures [21] as well as to validate stochastic models for performance analysis [27].

Although involving publish/subscribe communication in general, all research approaches followed individual directions that each pose particular constraints to and required specific features from the supporting middleware. As a consequence, REBECA's implementation underwent many metamorphosis and this led from frequent changes in REBECA's implementation over separate development branches and many incompatible program versions to a full-grown maintenance nightmare. Especially, combining extensions and features of different versions usually yielded in rather obscure than desired behavior. Obviously, REBECA would profit tremendously from a much more modular architecture.

3 Feature Composition

Facing the problems described in the previous section, we began with a radical redesign of REBECA, where we focused on the modularity of features to facilitate and ease their composition.

A feature is a well-defined aspect of a software system's functionality. Ideally, it is encapsulated in a separate module fostering separation of concerns. Based on a core system with a basic functionality, a feature-oriented architecture then enables extending the system by simply adding new feature modules. In this way, a general publish/subscribe system could be supplemented and customized, for example, by more efficient routing algorithms, by reconfiguration and self-optimization capabilities as well as fault-tolerance mechanisms. Eventually, the behavior of the system as whole is determined by a composition of the base system and all integrated feature modules.

However, this feature-oriented approach also has its drawbacks. In any non-trivial system, and publish/subscribe systems are inherently complex, it is inevitable that features interact and interfere with each other. There are two types of interactions: desired interactions that are necessary to make dependable features work and undesired interferences that result as cumbersome byproduct through composition. In a publish/subscribe system, for example, optimizing the broker network requires the ability to conduct dynamic reconfigurations of the network topology by replacing network links must be coordinated with an applied fault-tolerance scheme. Otherwise a vanishing network link may be seen as a fault and triggers compensating actions such as activating backup links and brokers.

Nevertheless, a sustainable feature management is indispensable for any complex evolving system. Thus, following a feature-oriented approach, we faced the following questions when redesigning REBECA's architecture:

- How to encapsulate a system feature in a self-containing module to make it pluggable? This is challenging because functional modularity in terms of features and structural modularity in terms of pluggable components are two different and orthogonal concepts.
- How to enable feature modules to interact with each other? As certain features depend on each other, an architectural way has to be provided facilitating the interaction of feature modules.
- How to counter undesired interactions of features? As features may interfere in manifold ways, the system's architecture should make feature interactions explicit and visible in order to ease resolving undesired interferences.
- How to deal with non-functional requirements? Meeting non-functional requirements is challenging because this kind of requirements usually affects the system as whole and, thus, has to be met by all feature implementations. Nevertheless, the architecture should flexibly support the implementation of non-functional properties.

The questions above guided us during REBECA's redesign. As result, we developed a flexible architecture based on plugins presented in the next section.

4   Architecture

In order to address the challenges introduced in the previous section, we decided to consider the functional modularity as primary mean to support fine-grained feature composition. This implies that we consider every feature of our middleware – even those that are usually considered necessary – as subject of feature composition to enable a large degree of configuration freedom even with respect to basic functionality. Therefore, the architecture of REBECA consists of two types of elements: The *extendable broker* forms the functional core of a REBECA system and delivers minimal publish/subscribe functionality together with the possibility to compose features. Such features are implemented as *plugins* that are inserted at run-time into REBECA brokers.

In Sect. 4.1, we describe the architecture of the extendable brokers, followed by an introduction of our plugin concept in Sect. 4.2. Finally, we consider clients and their connection to a REBECA system in Sect. 4.3. Section 5 enumerates a number of features that we implemented as REBECA plugins.

4.1   Extendable Broker

REBECA's new architecture is centered around functional modularity. Therefore, each broker feature, even those that are usually considered basic and necessary, is seen as subject of feature composition to enable a large degree of configuration freedom. Thus, a broker is basically just a container for pluggable components which, in turn, realize the functionality. Following this idea, a broker only supports the basic concepts of message channels and message handling stages into which components can be plugged as described by a configuration.

Looking at the basic functionality of a publish/subscribe broker in more detail, three separate message handling stages can be distinguished as depicted in Fig. 1 that every message has to pass. In the *input stage*, the message is received from a neighboring broker and, for example, needs to be deserialized. Afterwards, the main *processing stage* follows. Here, the routing decision is made whether the message has to be forwarded and, if forwarding is needed, to which neighbors it has to be transmitted. The last stage is the *output stage*, where the message is prepared for transmission, for example, by serializing it again.

The stages have different contexts and scopes: While there are separate input and output channels for each incoming and outgoing connection, there is only one global channel in the main processing stage for all messages. Thus, at the transitions from input to processing stage and from processing to output stage message streams need to be multiplexed and demultiplexed, respectively. Multiplexing is usually done by storing received messages in a queue. Thereafter, they get individually dequeued and handled one by one. Demultiplexing is necessary when the handled message needs to be forwarded to multiple neighbors. To achieve this, the message is usually copied at the end of the processing stage and each message copy is put into the respective output channel to be transmitted separately.

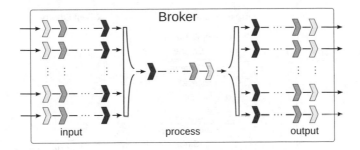

Fig. 1. Pipeline architecture of a broker

Advanced broker functionality which goes beyond simple message forwarding is achieved by manipulating messages and message streams. To implement a new feature, for example, it might be necessary to alter certain messages, defer or delete others, or to create even new ones. To make brokers extendable, REBECA enables feature components to be plugged into the channels of each message handling stage. Thus, these components get the possibility to manipulate messages of interest within the context of their choice, i.e., within the global processing scope or within the scope of a particular connection before or after processing.

When multiple feature components are plugged into the same stage and channel, they are chained to a pipeline. In this case, the effective sequence becomes important in which messages traverse this pipeline. The broker configuration determines which components will be plugged where and in which order. In fact, this configuration constitutes a feature composition and, thereby, defines the behavior of the overall system.

4.2 Plugins

To realize a certain broker feature, message manipulations in all message handling stages may be required, while other features may only need a single intervention. Thus, bundling a feature implementation to a pluggable component of sensible granularity is challenging. REBECA brokers support plugins to extend their features. A REBECA plugin usually consists of two parts: a *broker engine* and a *connection sink*. Figure 2 gives an overview as a Unified Modeling Language (UML) class diagram showing how engines, sinks, and brokers relate to each other.

Broker engines implement the majority of the processing logic to realize a particular functionality. There is only one engine per plugin which encloses and manages all data structures required by a feature. Engines are plugged into the main processing stage of a broker and chained to a processing pipeline. Each engine has a `process` method which takes the message to handle, the neighboring broker it was received from, and an initially empty set of destinations to forward the message to. The engine can then decide whether it wants to leave the message untouched and simply passes it along the message handling chain or whether

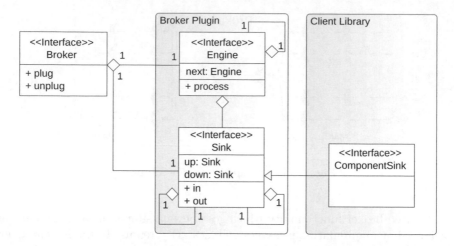

Fig. 2. Class diagram depicting the relationship between broker, engine and sink

it wants to intervene and manipulate the message or its destinations. When intervening the message stream, the engine can completely alter a message's content as well as add or remove neighboring brokers to the set of forwarding destinations. Furthermore, it is also possible to silently drop a message or to insert even new messages into the stream. Thereby, an engine has various means to realize features.

Certain aspects, however, are easier to implement in more specific scopes, for example, serialization and deserialization of messages is usually done within the context of the transmitting connection. Broker engines are, thus, able to create connection sinks that bundle all connection-specific processing logic in one place. Sink instances belonging to the same connection are assembled to a sink chain that messages pass during the input and output stage of a broker. As input and output stages are usually symmetric—for example, if serialization is the processing step right before sending a message, then deserialization should analogously be the next step after receiving it— this leads to a layered design as shown in Fig. 3, where each layer encapsulates a specific functionality. Received messages are, thus, passed upwards the chain using a sink's `in` method, while messages that are to be transmitted are passed down the same chain using the `out` method. Thereby, each sink instance has the possibility to intervene in order to suppress the message, to manipulate or to transform its content, or to insert new ones. Layered architectures are well known from many middleware implementations and have been proven convenient, useful, and flexible.

Ideally, a well designed REBECA plugin implements just one specific feature, works transparently and autonomously, and is independent of other plugins. Transparency means that the plugin's engine and sinks only manipulate those messages needed to realize the feature. Other messages are simply passed along the message handling chains as if the plugin was not present. Autonomy means that the plugin is self-containing and when it needs to intervene into the message

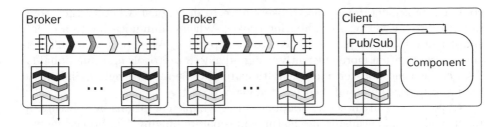

Fig. 3. Interconnection of client and broker using sinks

streams it does not need the help of other plugins. Independence means that it even does not need to be aware of the presence of other plugins. However as features may depend on each other, it is not always possible to build plugins fulfilling all these properties. Thus, plugins need a way to interact with each other. The preferred way is by altering or inserting new messages into the processing chain. Thereby, no further changes are necessary. Beyond that, REBECA does not restrict engines and sinks to implement any additional methods and interfaces they need to coordinate and communicate with other plugins besides the common processing chains. For example, engines and corresponding sinks usually use additional interfaces. Moreover, many connection sinks are even implemented as inner classes of their corresponding broker engines as a convenient way to share common data structures.

An important issue is the functional and non-functional compatibility of different plugins, especially in the case that the properties stated above are not fulfilled. In this case, the plugins depend on each other restricting possible feature compositions. We tackle this problem by enabling plugins to express pre- and postconditions for composition. For instance, a plugin may insert routing control messages into the message stream that contain information needed by other plugins and use some predefined message format. Another plugin may depend on these messages for its functionality. In this case, the first plugin may have a postcondition such as "provides routing control messages version 1.4" while the latter has a precondition "requires routing control messages version 1.2-1.7". This way, possible feature compositions are restricted in order to fulfill these functional requirements. Furthermore, these type of conditions is also used to establish a reasonable order of plugins within the different message handling stages. Beside functional compatibility, non-functional requirements such as safety, security, resource usage or timing may also be important – we plan to address those using techniques of non-functional composability [24].

4.3 Clients

To facilitate and ease the development of publish/subscribe applications, brokers offer clients a simple interface with clearly determined semantics for disseminating notifications and specifying their interests. Although the interface is simple, handling client connections often becomes a burden for brokers and leads to complex implementations since brokers have to distinguish whether they communicate to a client or a neighboring broker. When communicating to a client, simpler interfaces and protocols need to be supported, while brokers usually exchange information more efficiently using advanced protocols and functionality. As a consequence, broker implementations tend to be rather lengthy, difficult to read and understand, and, hence, often error-prone.

REBECA's new architecture simplifies broker implementations by splitting up functionality and encapsulating features in separate plugins, i.e., broker engines and corresponding connection sinks. In order to ease the development of broker engines and clarify their processing logic, the necessity to distinguish between client and broker connections has also been dropped. From a broker's point of view all connections lead to other neighboring brokers, thus, requiring clients to behave like brokers now. In order to still offer the simple client interface as well as to support advanced broker protocols, the concept of pluggable sinks leveraged to modularity extend the broker's functionality is also employed on the client side as shown in Fig. 3.

An application component still uses the traditional publish/subscribe interface for communication. But, however, an additional sink chain provided by the REBECA client library has been transparently plugged into its connection to its hosting broker. There is a corresponding sink instance at the same layer on the client side for every plugged broker engine and sink on the broker side. Thereby, they bundle all logic for client handling already on the client side preventing it from being interwoven into complex broker engine implementations otherwise. Client sinks are developed together with broker plugins, use similar interfaces as broker sinks, and, hence, have the same possibilities to intervene the incoming and outgoing message stream and translate, insert and remove messages. This way, the achieved flexibility enables an easy integration of and a fast adaptation to new broker features while still supporting stable client interfaces with fixed semantics.

Considering performance, however, layered designs have drawbacks. Especially, when broker and clients are running on the same host or even in the same process context, lower layers responsible for message serialization and transport are unnecessary overhead. In this cases, REBECA's modular design and flexible configuration allows to simply omit those layers on the client and broker side that are not required in this particular setup. This way, REBECA efficiently supports client components running locally on the broker as well as remote components connected over network.

5   Feature Plugins

In this section we introduce a number of features that are available for our REBECA middleware. As described earlier, each feature is implemented as plugin that is inserted into a REBECA system.

5.1   Mandatory Features

The concept of feature composition is omnipresent in REBECA in a way that even mandatory functionality is implemented in terms of plugins. Thereby, a broker's core functionality becomes easily exchangeable and can get replaced with custom implementations that may better suit one's needs. In the following, we describe those plugins that are required for a broker to work.

Configuration. The configuration plugin does not manipulate messages. Instead, it contains the information which other plugins need to be added to the broker and where their constituent parts have to be inserted in the processing and sink chain. The configuration itself can be hardcoded within the plugin, read from an external file, or fetched from a network server. The plugin is then responsible for instantiating, initializing, and activating all remaining plugins.

Processing. The processing plugin drives a broker's processing stage. In fact, it connects the processing stage with the input and the output stage and contains the broker's logic for multiplexing and demultiplexing messages. Its engine marks the beginning of the processing chain while its sink instances reside on the topmost layer of the sink chain and, thus, glue the broker stages together. By providing customized implementations, it becomes easily possible to adapt a brokers multiplexing strategy, for example, to support fair strategies, weighted strategies, or strategies based on priorities of connections or messages.

Transport. The functionality of the transport plugin is to deliver messages to connected neighboring brokers and clients. Thus, every connection has exactly one transport sink that is situated at the bottom of the sink chain. Depending on the connection type, however, different transport mechanisms can be used: Communication to neighboring brokers and remote clients is based on TCP and includes message serialization, while the transport plugin for local components may simply pass messages as objects in memory. Furthermore, a transport connector to a discrete event simulation is available as described in Sect. 6.

5.2   Publish/Subscribe Features

A REBECA broker equipped with just mandatory plugins is already able to offer basic publish/subscribe functionality by flooding notifications into the network. However, for more advanced system setups additional features are needed.

Matching and Routing. Content-based routing requires advanced matching capabilities. Instead of flooding notifications to all neighboring brokers, notifications are only directed and forwarded towards interested clients and their hosting brokers. Therefore, the matching plugin administers a routing table, where client interests are stored in form of subscription filters. Based on this table, the decision is made to which neighboring broker or connected client a received notification is finally delivered. Client interests are propagated by subscriptions. When forwarding subscriptions, different strategies can be used that aim at reducing the overhead by exploiting similarities between subscription filters [15]. Plugins are available that support a simple routing, an identity-based routing, and a covering-based routing of subscriptions [16].

Advertising. Advertisements are an additional mean to further reduce the subscription overhead by requiring producing components to announce the kind of notifications they intend to publish. As a consequence, subscriptions need only to be forwarded into the direction of potential publishers. The advertisement plugin, thus, suppresses all subscriptions that would have been unnecessarily send to remaining network regions otherwise. Therefore, the plugin needs to administer an additional advertisement table, where publication announcements are stored in form of advertisement filters. For forwarding advertisements, the same optimizations as for subscriptions can be applied [15]. Advertisement plugins based on a simple routing, an identity-based, and a covering-based routing strategy are available.

Scoping. Scoping [4,6] is a mean to structure the middleware as well as publish/ subscribe applications by delimiting the dissemination of notifications within the broker network. Thereby, scopes enable the creation of visibility domains and hierarchies thereof by which it gets possible to model and reflect organizational structures. A company's publish/subscribe infrastructure, for example, could be organized by division, department, and group, or alternatively by country, region, and city. The scope plugin dynamically assigns publish/subscribe components to scopes based on a given scope specification and available component attributes whereby it is not unusual that components belong to multiple scopes at the same time. Furthermore, when forwarding messages, it enforces that notifications are dropped which are not allowed to pass scope boundaries. For managing scope memberships and announcing available scopes, however, the scope plugin depends on functionality provided by the routing and advertisement plugin, respectively.

5.3   Optional Features

In the following, we describe further features implemented for the REBECA middleware. These features are optional and primarily aim at improving the control over the system as well as to enhance the quality of service.

Management and Monitoring. REBECA's management plugin provides a convenient monitoring and management interface to the broker and instantiated plugins based on the Java Management Extensions (JMX) technology [28]. Regarding a broker's configuration, the management plugin enables the insertion and removal of other plugins at runtime. For every broker plugin a dedicated MBean instance is created which provides access to the plugin's engine. Thereby, it is possible to read properties, change attributes, and query statistics. The management plugin administers all MBeans. Furthermore, various connectors and adapters are available to communicate with the MBeans using protocols such as SNMP, HTTP, or Java RMI.

Encryption. The encryption plugin provides a secure channel for communication. The plugin's sink is inserted into the input and output stage of a broker in order to encrypt and decrypt all outgoing and incoming messages, respectively. A configuration specifies on which connection which encryption algorithm is used. Thereby, it is possible to use strong encryption when communicating to brokers in insecure networks, but switch encryption completely off if clients are connected locally.

Adaptivity. When deploying REBECA in dynamic environments, it is usually desirable for achieving a good system performance, and sometimes even necessary for avoiding certain overload situations, to continuously adapt the middleware to changing network and load conditions. Currently, there are two plugins that autonomously adapt and optimize the broker network and its routing configuration, respectively. The first plugin tries to reorganize the broker network in order to minimize the number of forwarding hops between publishers and subscribers while avoiding expensive overlay links. It is based on the heuristic published in [11]. The second plugin aims at minimizing the number of forwarded messages by edge-wise switching between different routing algorithms. The idea is to always use the most efficient algorithm for the current situation [26].

Fault Tolerance. Since REBECA operates on an acyclic overlay network, the failure of an essential link or broker may lead to the partition of the whole broker network. To improve the fault tolerance, the recovery plugin implements a strategy for reconnecting the network and, thus, adds self-stabilization with respect to the overlay. Based on the assumption that no additional faults occur during the time of repair, it is guaranteed that the subnets get rejoined to a valid broker topology again.

6 Discrete Event Simulation

When developing a new broker feature it is a common task to test and evaluate the implementation under various load, network, and environment conditions. Using deployments of real broker instances is the most realistic way of testing and evaluation which, however, is not always suitable or applicable. Regarding scalability, for example, the size of the testbed is the limiting factor or, considering faults and network conditions, the degree of control necessary to induce specific faults and load situations as well as their reproducibility may not be given. Instead, simulations provide a well established alternative that offers the needed scalability, reproducibility, and fine-grained control.

Publish/subscribe systems are often evaluated using discrete event simulations which model the operation of the whole system as a chronological sequence of events. Events, such as "message arrived at node X" or "message forwarded to node Y", occur at instants in time and are then processed appropriately. Thereby, the system's state is changed and new, causally related events are triggered and scheduled to be processed in future. After an event has been handled, the simulation's time is advanced to the chronological next event which is removed from schedule and subsequently processed. These steps are repeated until no further events are available or a previously specified end time is reached.

REBECA supports discrete event simulations based on the PEERSIM framework [18]. More precisely, REBECA brokers are able to run independently in stand-alone deployments and can alternatively be executed in a simulation environment as well. Due to REBECA's modular architecture and functionality many plugin implementations are reusable without modifications, some need minor adaptations, and only a few have to be replaced to be compatible to simulation setups. Since only absolutely necessary changes were made, implementation and simulation share the same code base—a maximum of simulation validity and accuracy is reached.

Required adaptations include functional as well as non-functional aspects. Regarding functionality, the simulated brokers need a way to communicate with each other. Therefore, a new transport plugin is provided that connects brokers to the simulated network environment. This way, brokers and clients are able to exchange messages.

The non-functional aspects, however, are harder to realize as they mainly affect the style of code execution as well as the simulation's notion of time. As discrete event simulations sequentially process one event after the other, they are usually executed by a single thread without any concurrency. On contrary, additional broker threads may even be harmful when they are used for periodic tasks triggered by the system clock. The reason is that the simulation does not have a continuous time model anymore, provides its own independent and discrete simulation time, and needs explicitly scheduled events to trigger a task. Moreover, as events are just instants in time they do not have a duration. Thus, for modeling a process that takes time (e.g., a broker forwarding a notification) one needs to explicitly schedule at least two events, one for the start and, after an appropriate delay, one for the end. To tackle these issues, plugin implementations (more precisely broker engines) are wrapped in a way that all calls are intercepted that would lead to the instantiation of independent threads. Furthermore, time management is completely done by the wrapper which schedules corresponding simulation events. For processing and manipulating received messages, however, the original plugin implementation is used.

Changing the time and execution model fundamentally affects the whole implementation as it is a non-functional aspects that cannot be decomposed into a separate module or component. Nevertheless, REBECA's modular architecture has proven beneficial for adapting the system to support discrete event simulations. Fine-grained modularity is the primary mean to identify and delimit those portions of code that need to be adapted and reuse the remaining parts.

7   Related Work

In literature, a large number of publish/subscribe systems exist including commercial middleware products as well as research prototypes [23]. As commercial systems are usually closed source, little is known about implementation details and even less about feature management within the software lifecycle. Regarding academic systems, the situation is different but not much better. While implementations are open source and publicly available, they are often designed for a particular research interest with a fine-tuned set of selected features. Thereafter, only a few projects get continuous support and maintenance and even fewer are developed further so that their feature set evolves and grows over time.

REDS [2] is a publish/subscribe system designed for mobile ad hoc networks. It is based on a modular architecture and provides means for integrating custom message formats and filters as well as advanced matching, routing and network management strategies rendering the system quite adaptable and reconfigurable. However, implemented reconfiguration mechanisms primarily aim at adapting its routing overlay structures to the dynamically changing environments and mobile network topologies. Extendability in terms of integrating completely new features was not considered to the same extend.

The PADRES project [3] consists of a distributed, content-based publish/subscribe routing substrate and a whole ecosystem of tools and services designed for workflow and enterprise management solutions [12]. The latter provides features necessary for integration into enterprise infrastructures that have been subsequently added to and build around publish/subscribe messaging. The base broker has a modular architecture that exhibits, similar to our approach, message input and output queues as well as core components. PADRES components are efficient, but seem to be quite coarse and heavy. For example, the full-fledged Java Expert System Shell (JESS) rule engine [7] is used as matching and routing engine. Thus, a fine-grained feature control and composition is rather complex and difficult to realize.

Distributed Feature Composition (DFC) is a versatile architecture used in the telecommunications domain. It facilitates a feature-oriented specification, a modular implementation of features and their dynamic composition to advanced telecommunication services. Customer calls (e.g., telephone calls, Voice-over-Internet-Protocol (VoIP) calls) are processed by dynamically assembling a component chain out of applicable feature boxes from the caller to the callee when routing and establishing a connection. Ideally, each feature box is transparent, autonomous, and independent and implements a specific functional aspect such as blocking calls from particular addresses, suppressing calls at quiet times, forwarding calls to different receivers or recording a voice mail when the line is busy. The overall behavior is then determined by the composition of the feature boxes, i.e., their sequence in the chain.

DFC and REBECA's redesigned architecture are quite similar sharing common concepts and same goals—both emphasize a feature-oriented modularity. Likewise, REBECA provides means to put feature modules into message processing chains, however, REBECA plugins may have up to three hooks in different chains to implement a particular feature. Therefore, these plugins tend to be more dependable and less self-containing than DFC feature boxes.

8 Conclusion

With publish/subscribe systems becoming an integral part of the communication infrastructure in an increasing variety of application domains, the number of requirements posed to a publish/subscribe middleware implementation steadily grows and evolves. Knowing from own experience, it is hardly possible to support all of them at once. Therefore, we centered the new architecture of our middleware REBECA around the concept of functional modularity. This way, it becomes possible to easily build tailor-made, light-weight systems.

In this paper, we introduced the concept of features and presented REBECA's modular architecture facilitating their composition. Based on a minimal functional core, REBECA brokers can be extended by inserting additional plugins implementing specific features. Feature plugins are able to intervene a broker's internal message stream at three different positions and can thereby control the forwarding of messages to neighboring brokers and clients in the network. Messages can be altered, inserted, and removed in order to realize the desired functionality. On the client side, the same mechanism is applied. This way, the development of both broker plugins and client sinks is unified and eased.

REBECA is implemented as prototype together with a variety of plugins to demonstrate the concept of feature composition. Therefore, implemented plugins provide established publish/subscribe functionality such as matching, routing, advertising, and scoping as well as features that aim at improving quality of service, fault tolerance, or the manageability of brokers. Moreover, REBECA can be executed within a simulation environment as well. Due to the modular architecture and functionality, only a few plugins needed to be adapted or replaced to support discrete event simulations.

Future work focuses on equipping REBECA with more autonomy to increase the system's degree of self-organization, self-optimization, and self-stabilization. In this context, it is an open research question how to compose different autonomic algorithms in a way that they do not unintentionally interfere with each other or build up oscillations. Furthermore, we aim at continually improving the integration of REBECA into modern computer infrastructures and application systems. One challenge is to exploit the increasing parallelism provided by current multiprocessor and multi-core architectures while still supporting resource-constrained devices and legacy applications. However, to adequately support these systems, a holistic approach may be needed including new application interfaces and programming abstractions. We are convinced that REBECA's modular architecture will be an invaluable help and ease the development process when tackling these challenges.

References

1. Bornhövd, C., Cilia, M., Liebig, C., Buchmann, A.: An infrastructure for meta-auctions. In: Proceedings of the 2nd International Workshop on Advanced Issues of E-Commerce and Web-Based Information Systems, pp. 21–30. IEEE Computer Society, Los Alamitos (2000)
2. Cugola, G., Picco, G.P.: Reds: A reconfigurable dispatching system. In: Proceedings of the 6th International Workshop on Software Engineering and Middleware (SEM 2006), pp. 9–16. ACM Press, New York (2006)
3. Fidler, E., Jacobsen, H.A., Li, G., Mankovski, S.: The padres distributed publish/-subscribe system. In: Proceedings of the 8th International Conference on Feature Interactions in Telecommunications and Software Systems (ICFI 2005), pp. 12–30. IOS Press, The Netherlands (2005)
4. Fiege, L.: Visibility in Event-Based Systems. Ph.d. thesis, Technische Universität Darmstadt, Darmstadt, Germany (April 2005)
5. Fiege, L., Cilia, M., Mühl, G., Buchmann, A.: Publish/subscribe grows up: Support for management, visibility control, and heterogeneity. IEEE Internet Computing 10(1), 48–55 (2006)
6. Fiege, L., Mezini, M., Mühl, G., Buchmann, A.P.: Engineering event-based systems with scopes. In: Magnusson, B. (ed.) ECOOP 2002. LNCS, vol. 2374, pp. 309–333. Springer, Heidelberg (2002)
7. Friedman-Hill, E.: Jess in Action: Rule-Based Systems in Java. Manning Publications, Greenwich (June 2003)
8. Gamma, E., Helm, R., Johnson, R., Vlissides, J.: Design Patterns: Elements of Reusable Object-Oriented Software. Addison-Wesley, Boston (1995)
9. Intanagonwiwat, C., Govindan, R., Estrin, D.: Directed diffusion: a scalable and robust communication paradigm for sensor networks. In: Proceedings of the 6th Annual International Conference on Mobile Computing and Networking (MobiCom 2000), pp. 56–67. ACM Press, New York (2000)
10. Jaeger, M.A., Mühl, G., Werner, M., Parzyjegla, H.: Reconfiguring self-stabilizing publish/subscribe systems. In: State, R., van der Meer, S., O'Sullivan, D., Pfeifer, T. (eds.) DSOM 2006. LNCS, vol. 4269, pp. 233–238. Springer, Heidelberg (2006)
11. Jaeger, M.A., Parzyjegla, H., Mühl, G., Herrmann, K.: Self-organizing broker topologies for publish/subscribe systems. In: SAC 2007, pp. 543–550. ACM Press, New York (2007)
12. Li, G., Muthusamy, V., Jacobsen, H.A.: A distributed service-oriented architecture for business process execution. ACM Transactions on the Web 4(1), 1–33 (2010)
13. Love, R.: Get on the d-bus. Linux Journal 2005(130), 3 (2005)
14. Luckham, D.C.: The Power of Events: An Introduction to Complex Event Processing in Distributed Enterprise Systems. Addison-Wesley Longman Publishing Co., Boston (2001)
15. Mühl, G., Fiege, L., Gärtner, F.C., Buchmann, A.P.: Evaluating advanced routing algorithms for content-based publish/subscribe systems. In: Proceedings of the 10th IEEE International Symposium on Modeling, Analysis, and Simulation of Computer and Telecommunications Systems (MASCOTS 2002), pp. 167–176. IEEE Computer Society, Los Alamitos (2002)
16. Mühl, G., Fiege, L., Pietzuch, P.R.: Distributed Event-Based Systems. Springer, Heidelberg (2006)
17. Mühl, G., Ulbrich, A., Herrmann, K., Weis, T.: Disseminating information to mobile clients using publish-subscribe. IEEE Internet Computing 8(3), 46–53 (2004)

18. Mark Jelasity, A.M., Jesi, G.P., Voulgaris, S.: PeerSim: A peer-to-peer simulator, http://peersim.sourceforge.net/
19. Object Management Group (OMG): Data distribution service for real-time systems (DDS), version 1.2 (January 2007)
20. Organization for the Advancement of Structured Information Standards (OASIS): Web services notification (WSN), version 1.3. Billerica, MA, USA (October 2006)
21. Parzyjegla, H., Jaeger, M.A., Mühl, G., Weis, T.: Model-driven development and adaptation of autonomous control applications. IEEE Distributed Systems Online 9(11), 1–9 (2008)
22. Parzyjegla, H., Mühl, G., Jaeger, M.A.: Reconfiguring publish/subscribe overlay topologies. In: Proceedings of the 26th IEEE International Conference on Distributed Computing Systems Workshops (ICDCSW 2006), p. 29. IEEE Computer Society, Los Alamitos (2006)
23. Pietzuch, P., Eyers, D., Kounev, S., Shand, B.: Towards a common api for publish/-subscribe. In: Proceedings of the Inaugural Conference on Distributed Event-Based Systems, pp. 152–157. ACM, New York (2007)
24. Richling, J.: Komponierbarkeit eingebetteter Echtzeitsysteme. Ph.D. thesis, Humboldt-Universität zu Berlin, Berlin, Germany (February 2006)
25. Schönherr, J.H., Parzyjegla, H., Mühl, G.: Clustered publish/subscribe in wireless actuator and sensor networks. In: Proceedings of the 6th International Workshop on Middleware for Pervasive and Ad-hoc Computing (MPAC 2008), pp. 60–65. ACM Press, New York (2008)
26. Schröter, A., Graff, D., Mühl, G., Richling, J., Parzyjegla, H.: Self-optimizing hybrid routing in publish/subscribe systems. In: Gonzalez, A., Pfeifer, T. (eds.) DSOM 2009. LNCS, vol. 5841, pp. 111–122. Springer, Heidelberg (2009)
27. Schröter, A., Mühl, G., Kounev, S., Parzyjegla, H., Richling, J.: Stochastic performance analysis and capacity planning of publish/subscribe systems. In: Proceedings of the 4th ACM International Conference on Distributed Event-Based Systems (DEBS 2010), ACM Press, New York (2010)
28. Sun Microsystems, Inc.: Java management extensions (JMX) specification, version 1.4. Santa Clara, CA, USA (November 2006)
29. Ulbrich, A., Mühl, G., Weis, T., Geihs, K.: Programming abstractions for content-based publish/subscribe in object-oriented languages. In: Meersman, R., Tari, Z. (eds.) OTM 2004. LNCS, vol. 3291, pp. 1538–1557. Springer, Heidelberg (2004)
30. World Wide Web Consortium (W3C): Web services eventing (WS-Eventing) (March 2010), http://www.w3.org/TR/ws-eventing/
31. Zeidler, A., Fiege, L.: Mobility support with REBECA. In: Proceedings of the 23rd International Conference on Distributed Computing Systems Workshops (ICDCSW 2003), pp. 354–361. IEEE Computer Society, Los Alamitos (2003)

Anonymous Mobile Service Collaboration: Quality of Service

Annika Hinze[1], Michael Rinck[2], and David Streader[1]

[1] University of Waikato, New Zealand
{hinze,dstr}@cs.waikato.ac.nz
[2] Humboldt Unversity, Berlin, Germany
rinck@informatik.hu-berlin.de

Abstract. Mobile services depend on user context and preferences, and a mobile user's context is constantly changing. Many services are only available locally. The most appropriate service for a user's context is not known in advance and a user may enter or leave a service's range at any time. For a seamless user experience, services need to collaborate. These complex collaborations should be instantaneous yet anonymous – without disclosing user information.

The paper proposes a new service collaboration model using event-based interaction. A prototypical implementation is used to demonstrate functionality, inter-operability, and generality of our solution. The solution guarantees ad-hoc service collaboration while protecting user information.

1 Introduction

Service collaboration in mobile and ubiquitous systems presents challenges for existing service-oriented architectures. Similar services may have limitations on their availability, for example, with respect to the context in which the service is required. Services can thus appear or disappear at any time, calling for the provision of an automatism to select collaboration partners. We refer to this problem as *service selection*. An understanding of quality of service becomes an important issue.

To protect user information, the services should collaborate with each other without revealing their or the user's identity. Therefore anonymity is a central requirement: the services engaged in the interaction should not be mutually aware of each other's identity. We refer to this problem as user *privacy*.

This paper discusses a service infrastructure for collaboration of mobile services that responds to these two challenges. The interaction infrastructure is based on the publish/subscribe paradigm; client and server-side services connect via a (distributed) broker. Its (theoretical) foundations have been discussed in [13].

The following example describes a tourist system that may be achieved through the *collaboration* of:

– a map service, showing the position of the user in some representation of her environment, with pointers to places of interest

K. Sachs, I. Petrov, and P. Guerrero (Eds.): Buchmann Festschrift, LNCS 6462, pp. 141–158, 2010.

- a locator service used to locate the position of the user
- an information service that displays further information about particular locations of interest (e.g., in a city or within a museum)

This simple example of three services (map, location, information service) can already illustrate how service selection is addressed by our quality-of-service extensions to ensure seamless collaboration. If there are two alternative locator services, GPS and RFID, the system selects the one with the better quality for the collaboration context: GPS for outdoor locations and RFID for indoor locations. When the user moves into a building, the services' quality changes. Once the RFID services provide a signal with better quality the broker switches from GPS to RFID.

The map service would not be aware of the switch as it does not know the identity of its provider of location data. Each service registers with a trusted broker and states which types of information it is interested in (e.g., the map being interested in location data). The problem of data privacy is thus addressed by the publish-subscribe infrastructure: The broker then selects the appropriate service (by type and quality) and forwards the data anonymously.

This paper describes a service collaboration infrastructure and an implemented prototype that supports

- anonymous service collaboration using publish/subscribe communication and
- service selection based on QoS data.

The paper discusses alternative architectures for the infrastructure's implementation and introduces our implemented prototype. We demonstrate how the QoS extensions are used to select the appropriate collaboration partners and discuss the data privacy implications. The prototype application was developed for the current revision of our mobile tourist information system TIP [14]. It uses a local broker that enables collaboration between services offered by different providers without the need to access a global service repository. In particular, we discuss how a formal proof of data privacy/anonymity may be achieved.

We commence this paper by analysing the requirements for ensuring quality of service in mobile service collaboration for ad-hoc environments in Section 2. We compare the related approaches for service collaboration with the one proposed in this paper (Section 3). In Section 4, we introduce an extended concept for a mobile service infrastructure that addresses the quality of service requirements. Architecture variations are compared in Section 5. Finally, Section 6 describes the implementation of the architecture. We close with a discussion of formal proofs of anonymity (Section 7) and further extensions of our work.

2   Scenario and Requirements

We start by having a closer look at how mobile service collaboration for ad-hoc environments is different from traditional service collaboration. Existing collaboration techniques [7] assume that services are openly known globally and require negotiated contracts for longer term relations. Conditions in a dynamic mobile environment are fundamentally different. Networks may be available only in small patches, the services are offered locally, and collaboration should be anonymous and immediate (i.e., without negotiation). Traditional architectures are therefore unfit for collaboration between mobile location-based services.

Event-based interaction [9] has mostly been used to initiate service interaction but not for ongoing anonymous service interaction. To help ensure anonymity of services, we suggest that event-based interaction between services should be maintained beyond the initiation of communication.

Let us now revisit the scenario to see how event-based interaction can sustain service collaboration. As in traditional publish/subscribe architectures, each service registers with the broker as publisher or subscriber (a service may have both roles). Interest in data is expressed as interest in data types with possible additional filters. That is, the map service would subscribe to the client's location data, not to any particular location service.

For some services, only data from one out of many services of the same type should be forwarded (e.g., map receiving location information). In standard service-oriented architectures, this service selection is negotiated directly between services. As we aim for service anonymity, this direct negotiation is not an option. Instead we suggest an extension of the traditional publish/subscribe architecture. Its design can be observed in the following situation where the broker has to switch between services.

In our scenario, when the user enters a museum the quality of the GPS-based location service will diminish until no further data is provided. As a consequence, using a standard publish/subscribe approach, the map would 'freeze' as it receives no location updates. Here the anonymity and decoupling supported by publish/subscribe prevents the services from functioning correctly. In our extended architecture, a failing service (e.g., the GPS) will be replaced by an alternative service providing better quality of service (e.g., RFID). If no alternative is available, the subscribing services will be informed by the broker. In our scenario, the map service would be informed that no information about the user location is available (such that an error message can be displayed instead of the 'freezing').

From our scenario description, we derive a number of requirements that must be satisfied to ensure robust service collaboration. The problem domain (situation) is captured in the first three requirements. Services may be:

R1 offered by different providers
R2 offered in restricted locations only
R3 designed for mobility (of users)

The quality of a service can be expressed in terms of *quality of data*: (a) accuracy of data received, and (b) timeliness of data received. The previous example of switching GPS to RFID service was influenced by concerns about accuracy. The notification of the map service that no location data is available is a communication about the timeliness.

R4 service selection based on best quality of data
R5 service liveliness expressed as timeliness of data

In addition to the quality of data, the quality of service a user receives also depends on the *quality of the collaboration infrastructure* used by the services. Consequently to ensure privacy we need to consider more than the quality of an individual service but also the quality of infrastructure:

R6 anonymity of services and user (ensured by infrastructure)
R7 confidence in privacy (supported by formal proof)

Anonymity and privacy are the main concerns of the infrastructure. We aim to find means to prove the anonymity conditions for the general infrastructure not only for given example services. These requirements call for extensions beyond existing approaches.

3   Related Work

The first three requirements have been addressed by a number of architectures for location-based systems, however, the issue of service collaboration has not been a particular focus for concern. Exceptions include, Yau et al. who suggest a subscriber-based means to access location-restricted services in a mobile environment by using a UDDI channel instead of a repository [20]. Another approach uses cloaking to retain privacy when accessing location-based services (using a centralised third party [10] or a P2P approach [5]).

Two event-based approaches in particular, more closely address our requirements. We will compare these approaches to the seven requirements R1–R7 and the TIP3 infrastructure as detailed in [13] (summarized in the next section), see Table 1.

Di Marzo et al. [6] suggested a middleware approach to the problem of reliability of collaborating services. They use metadata to control the behaviour of the middleware, distinguishing functional and non-functional metadata. Policies on the metadata are used to ensure reliability of services. This approach is focussed on the reliability of services and aims to combine services of low quality to achieve a better quality level. The middleware layer in this approach contains

Table 1. Comparison of approaches: ++ approach fully fulfils/supports the requirement, + approach somewhat supports the requirement, o approach partially supports the requirement, – approach does not support the requirement, – – approach explicitly excludes the requirement

	Situation			QoS - data		QoS - infra.	
	R1	R2	R3	R4	R5	R6	R7
Di Marzo et al. [6]	++	++	–	+	+	–	o
Michlmayr et al [18]	++	+	–	++	+	– –	o
TIP3 infrastructure	++	++	++	++	++	++	+

information about which services can and should be connected, though this aspect is not developed in detail. Services are anonymous but a large amount of additional information is required and held in the middleware layer. However, depending on the metadata specification method used, proof of reliability and privacy may be possible. Substantial middleware support is required in this approach, which means that it is not suitable for mobile devices. The approach requires the use of logic reasoners which limits the flexibility of the approach in integrating additional services. The rules followed by the reasoner become complex.

The method proposed by Michlmayr et al [18] supports changing properties of services at runtime. Their approach focuses mainly on the standardization of service requests. Their system is based on the event processing engine Esper, which uses the SQL-like query language EQL to describe service requirements. QoS observation details are not given in the paper. Again, this heavy middleware solution is not particularly suitable for mobile environments. The solution is not anonymous because services can be notified of, or queried for, changes in quality or availability of other (explicitly known) services.

4   Rule-Extended Mobile SOA

The proposed approach is an extension of a simpler prototype described in [13]. A simple anonymous service collaboration has been achieved through publish/subscribe communication managed by a distributed broker network. Our prototype application is the mobile tourist information system TIP [14]. Implementation details of the earlier work can be found in [16]. This simple infrastructure satisfies three requirements: (1) services offered by different providers can collaborate by interacting with a local broker, (2) services offered in restricted locations can collaborate as no global service repository is necessary, and (3) services are anonymous to each other as they are only known to the broker. That initial prototype, however, did not address the quality of the service interaction.

We now discuss an extension of this basic publish/subscribe communication that ensures correct service behaviour. Figure 1 shows the conceptual architecture of a broker in a (mobile) client. The broker contains a message handler for internal communication; publisher and subscribe indexes implement the traditional event-based communication. A cache is used for pre-fetching and caching of location-based information [17].

Service collaboration creates interdependencies between services (e.g., the map depends on location data being available). Because anonymous collaboration has been established by the infrastructure, services can no longer directly communicate with each other and observe service failure. To prevent subsequent inaccuracies in dependent services, these interdependencies between services need to be monitored by the infrastructure. For this, we introduce automatic event monitors (called 'observer' in Figure 1). The event observers adapt to each service's capabilities (protocols, QoS information communicated), and are concerned with service quality and availability. Handling of observed QoS changes is managed by

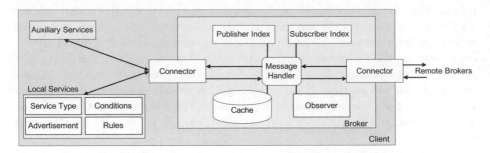

Fig. 1. Conceptual architecture of mobile client with service collaboration via broker

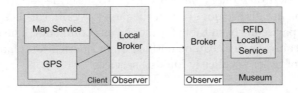

Fig. 2. Architecture for TIP3 infrastructure: Museum example

rules and conditions, which are defined by each service. Rules describe criteria for service selection (e.g, select location service with better location data quality), conditions describe service liveliness constraints (e.g., map needs location data to function). As QoS parameters change, rules and conditions guide automatic switching and service failure handling.

On registration with a broker, each service sends the following information: an advertisement, conditions and rules. An advertisement gives information about the type of data the service offers (i.e. acting as a publisher) and about the type of data to which the service wishes to subscribe (acting as a subscriber). Publishing and subscribing is handled via service type descriptions: The service type allows the broker to identify groups of services with similar functionality (e.g., services providing location data are location services). The advertisement also contains information about quality of service (more about the details in the next section). Information about publishing and subscribing services are stored in the publisher and subscriber index, respectively. Conditions define which information is needed for a service to run correctly. For example, a map service would need the user location to centre the map. Rules define the criteria of how to select services for collaboration. For example, the indoor location system of the museum (RFID) may be identified as offering a better quality of service and should be used instead of the outdoor GPS service. Rules enable services to prioritize between different data types and data qualities.

Auxiliary services are used for compatibility and translations between services. For example, the RFID information for the indoor location service may be translated into GPS-type data. Services and auxiliary services only communicate via the broker. Network communication is implemented between brokers only.

The functionality of the design is now illustrated through an example. Figure 2 shows the conceptual architecture of the museum example. As the user enters the museum; the quality of the GPS service is greatly reduced. We describe two options for how the infrastructure will handle this situation (depending on the available service context):

1. The GPS fails; no other location service is available.

   Since no alternative service is available, the user (and all subscribed services) has to be notified after a timeout that the quality of the service is low.

   The following rules and conditions could have been defined by the services:

Location Service: GPS
Conditions: none
Rules: none
QoS: location data accuracy

Map Service
Condition: Location service available
(single source)
Rule: location data accuracy > threshold
QoS: none

Figure 3 shows a sequence diagram for this case. The beginning shows the setup of the services with the broker: As the mobile device is switched on, the local broker starts and broadcasts a message. Locally starting services directly connect to a given local broker, known through configuration files.

The local broker sends a list of available event data types (known though advertisements). If the service is a publisher, it sends its own advertisement to the broker, which then subscribes the events of this service. If the service is a subscriber, it will evaluate the event types offered in the advertisements and send the local broker a package of rules and conditions under which it will subscribe to certain event type. Services may also subscribe to event types that are not yet offered by publishers; when events of the desired type become available they will be forwarded to the subscriber.

The GPS submits its advertisements, offering to send location data. The broker starts an observer. The map service subscribes for location data; it also submits its rules and conditions as shown above.

The observer receives the rules & conditions and subscribes at the broker for the GPS service to monitor its availability (cf. map condition) and its data accuracy (cf. map rules and GPS QoS). On the first event submitted by the GPS service, the observer checks the quality and advises the broker to forward them to the map. Via the broker, map and GPS are now linked and further events are forwarded automatically as long as the data accuracy does not sink below the threshold.

As the user enters the museum, the GPS service is no longer connected to the satellites. It stops sending location data. The observer waits for a predefined time-span (cf. timeout in condition). It then notifies the broker and the map service.

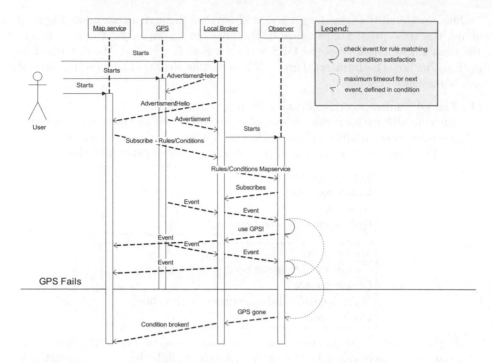

Fig. 3. Sequence diagram: GPS fails and no alternative location service available

2. The GPS fails; alternative service available.

   The museum may be offering its own indoor location service for the exhibits using RFID tags. Figure 4 describes the sequence of switching to the alternative service as the quality of the GPS is reduced and the RFID location service becomes available. Note that the internal timeouts are checked but are of no consequence for this situation. For clarity of presentation timeout arrows have therefore been omitted in this figure. The communication of the observer is also shown in simplified form (omitting communication via the local broker).

   The new service's subscription conditions and rules are similar to the ones of the GPS service:

   > Location Service: RFID
   > Conditions: none
   > Rules: none
   > QoS: location data accuracy

   The starting sequence is the same as in the previous case. Then, as the user moves towards the museum, the RFID service becomes available. That is, the client's local broker and the museum's global broker connect to each other and exchange advertisements. The new broker may then subscribe to data from other brokers (here: the event data from the RFID service).

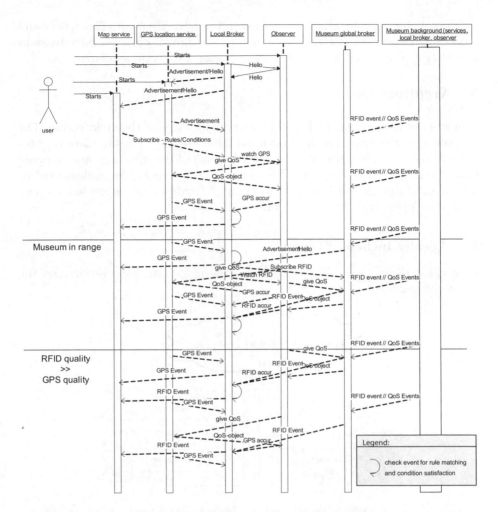

Fig. 4. Sequence diagram: GPS fails, alternative RFID location service available

The service registers but its event data are not forwarded to the map service (yet) as its data accuracy is below the threshold and lower than the accuracy of the already connected GPS (only one location service it to be connected to the map). Then, as the user enters the museum, the GPS quality drops under the threshold. The observer detects the GPS failure and suggests a link to the (now improved) RFID service instead. The broker stops forwarding the GPS data to the map and forwards the RFID data instead.

We thus include QoS metadata in our services, but keep rules and conditions on a low level of single value pairs, as well as the metadata specifications. A proof over these statements is possible, as they can be transformed into prolog statements. The checks for QoS on services are moved into the services themselves. These will be callable via a function delivered with the advertisement. This will ensure a maximum openness of the architecture, as our broker does not have to know how to test certain services. It also helps to keep the services anonymous.

5   Architecture

A number of issues are raised by this example in terms of the architecture. The key feature of the system is the broker and there are three ways to place the broker within our architecture. We now describe each of the variations and compare their suitability for our project. The concept of the broker is implemented as a network of distributed brokers. Brokers may reside on providers' sides, client sides or independently on the network.

5.1   Locally-Included Broker

Each client device has a local broker (see Figure 5). All local services on the client communicate via this broker.

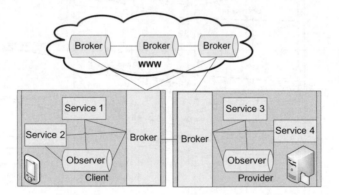

Fig. 5. Locally-included broker architecture

Service providers also have local brokers for their service communication. Brokers are connected via a network that passes service messages (using publish/subscibe).

This architecture allows fast communication between services located on the same device. It provides the greatest possible privacy as each side has a broker acting as a gatekeeper. Switching between services is managed by rules and conditions combined with observation of service quality. This architecture may not be able to cope with an elaborate rule engine performing large calculations.

5.2   Remote Broker

The mobile client connects to the network of brokers via one of the brokers (see Figure 6). The selection of the broker to which a client connects may be done

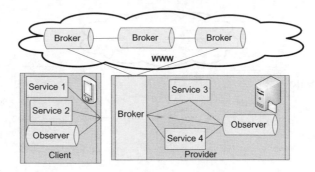

Fig. 6. Remote broker architecture

based on physical location. On the client itself, no broker software is installed. Communication between client and service providers is always directed via the broker network.

This model is appropriate for thin clients. It takes advantage of computational power at the providers' sides and the easy inclusion of provider-based services. However, if the network connection fails, local services can no longer communicate. The local brokers on provider side act as gates, preventing information from being forwarded to the providers' services unless they have permission to access the data. The flow of control, however, is moved towards the providers.

The observer still resides on the client device itself, close to the local services. More than one observer may be used (as shown in the figure) to service the different sides.

5.3   Intelligent Gateway

This variation is a hybrid between the remote broker and the included broker. Each provider has a broker as a gatekeeper for local communication (as in the locally-included broker). Client brokers are split into two parts: each client has a lightweight broker part locally and, in addition, a heavy-weight component residing on the network.

The intelligent gateway has been suggested by Guerrero [11] as a solution for small client devices without dependence on network availability for local communication. Messages are filtered first by simple rules on the lightweight broker. In a second step, heavier rule processing is done on the remote heavy-weight component. Local communication can be maintained even when the network connection fails. The amount of distributed communication increases. This approach leads to a complex distribution model involving several brokers.

5.4   Comparison

All three approaches can deal with different service providers (R1) and restricted service locations (R2). The included broker may not support mobility (R3) well due to restrictions of computing power and space on the mobile devices. The remote broker can work on any mobile device (thick and thin client) as it only

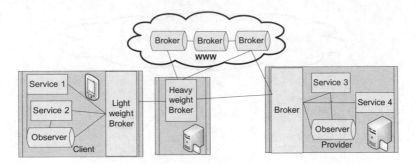

Fig. 7. Intelligent gateway architecture

Table 2. Comparison of architecture variations

	Included Broker	Remote Broker	Intelligent Gateway
R1 Different providers	++	++	++
R2 Restricted locations only	++	++	++
R3 Designed for mobility	– –	++	+
R4 Service selection	ensured by infrastructure		
R5 Service liveliness	ensured by infrastructure		
R6 Anonymity of services and user	++	+	o
R7 Confidence in privacy	++	+ –	– –

requires a very lightweight client software. The quality-of-service requirements (R4+R5) depend on the way the rules and conditions are evaluated.

Anonymity (R6) for the remote broker has to consider the remote connections – if these are untrusted, privacy may be compromised (+). If these are trusted connections, the requirement would be completely met (++) as in the case of the local broker. The intelligent gateway relies on external components for reasoning, which may or may not be trusted components. The same argument applies as for the remote broker: trusted connections and components may ensure privacy. A more detailed discussion of the aspects of privacy is provided in Section 7. As a result of this comparison, we use a remote broker architecture for our prototypical implementation.

For a proof of anonymity/privacy (R7) in the included broker, only the handling of rules needs to be evaluated. No private information is communicated outside the client (++). The main focus for the remote broker would lie in analysing the additional remote communication, which may or may not be compromised (+−). The intelligent gateway has many data transfers, potentially leading to greater difficulties in proving that none of the data may be accessed by an unauthorised source.

6   Prototype Implementation

In this section the prototype architecture is discussed. The implementation does not use existing frameworks (such as JMS) as this would have required substantial

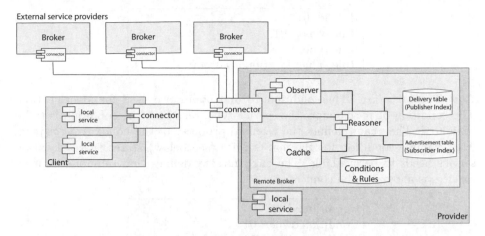

Fig. 8. Prototype implementation: architecture of the TIP remote broker

extensions (e.g., to support multiple connections to multiple providers on the same subject). The service collaboration infrastructure is implemented with a focus on employment for the mobile tourist information system TIP; we therefore used a Java implementation in the prototype (as done for existing TIP services).

The implementation uses the remote broker architecture as described in Section 5.2; here we give more detail about the actual implementation of the broker. The message handler of the earlier version (Figure 1) was extended into a reasoner (handling rules and conditions). All communication uses connectors to encapsulate the network/local traffic. Services and brokers are implemented as Java objects.

Advertisements, rules and conditions, are stored in their respective indexes. Rules and conditions are kept as object lists. Publisher and subscriber indexes are implemented in an SQLite database. The advertisement index is accessed when (1) a new service subscribes and the conditions need to be checked initially, and (2) on timeout if an advertisement needs to be removed and all conditions referring to this service need to be checked again.

Current information about the quality of services is stored in the same database. When the observer detects changes in a service's quality, it notifies the reasoner who will, in turn, change the stored information.

The delivery table is created from the subscriber information, indicating alternative services (cf. map and GPS/RFID services). The observer is set up by the reasoner to monitor the QoS parameters of selected services. The observer is here shown as part of the remote broker; it may also be kept outside the broker next to services or on the client's side.

Rule structure. Rules are implemented as objects with a rule `id` and `owner` for identification. Rule types are currently restricted to comparison between single value types ('<', '>', and '='). The rule `value` determines which event attribute is used. Only subscriber services (e.g., the map) may supply rules and conditions. Example rule for map service (id 01):

```
Rule.id: 01
Rule.owner: 01
Rule.type: >
Rule.value: location.accuracy
```

Condition structure. The condition `id` and `owner` are used for identification. The condition `object` defines the service type, on which the condition is to be evaluated. The `state` defines the required property of the `condition.object`. The example condition for the map service (see below) states that a location service needs to be available. The `cardinality` defines that only one location services is allowed to be connected.

```
Condition.id: 01
Condition.owner: 01
Condition.object: location_service
Condition.state: available
Condition.cardinality: exactly_one
```

Advertisement. The advertisement announces service `id`, `owner` and offered `event type` to the broker. The `QoScheck` value defines a function the broker can use to retrieve a QoS object. For example, for the GPS service, the QoS function is called `check_locationAccuray`. Example advertisement for GPS service (id 02):

```
Advertisement.id: 01
Advertisement.owner: 02
Advertisement.type: location_service
Advertisement.QoScheck:
check_locationAccuracy
```

7 Formal Proof of Privacy of User Information

As stated in Section 1, we assumed that the anonymity of user and services will ensure privacy of user information. In this section, we have a closer look at this assumption and discuss issues in formally proving privacy for an open infrastructure.

As illustrated in Figure 9, the system may be considered on different layers of abstraction. In Section 4 of this chapter, we discussed the conceptual model of the proposed infrastructure (conceptual layer as in Figure 9). Sections 5 and 6 discuss the (implementation) architecture of the infrastructure (cf. architectural layer in Figure 9). The physical layer of a particular mobile device has not been discussed in the chapter.

Each of these three layers is a refinement of the layer above and an abstraction of the layer below. Formal proof of privacy needs to span all three layers. Each proof normally refers to one layer only.[1] Proofs spanning more than one layer require a mapping between the layers.[15,19] This mapping is expressed as a pair of formal refinement/abstraction functions, the correctness of which need formal proof as well.

In our work, we will restrict ourselves to issues of the conceptual and architectural layer, leaving technical issues of the physical device layer unexamined. To do this, we replace this layer with a set of assumptions idealising and abstracting from the physical conditions of various devices.

The infrastructure is designed to be open, i.e., third party services can join the system. However, our view of the overall system only encompassed the infrastructure and services communicating via this infrastructure. We need to acknowledge that there exists an outer world of services and other parties that may interact with the services in the infrastructure or our client device. For the closed world view, a proof of anonymity as argued in this chapter is sufficient for privacy. In an open world environment, anonymity does not ensure privacy: external services may employ statistical methods to aggregate anonymous data in such a way that user identities can be inferred.

For proof of privacy, again we need a set of formalized assumptions that define the extent and nature of the communication between services using the infrastructure and the outside world. For example, services may either freely communicate all their data or give only restrict access within the system.

When analysing the system itself, providing proof of privacy for a closed subset is not sufficient. Most of the available tools for formal analysis and verification only work with closed systems. We attempted such a limited proof in [8]; Baresi now suggested a novel approach to avoid state explosion in complex (closed) systems[3]. Verification of publish/subscribe systems [2] (not their privacy) and service oriented architectures[4] has already been attempted for closed worlds; however, these approaches also encountered problems of state explosion. Proving that the infrastructure preserves privacy for a set number of known services (e.g., the three services used in our example) is not sufficient for an open infrastructure accepting third party services.

Instead one needs to employ symbolic techniques of formal methods: states are not described by enumeration but by variables, which therefore allows for infinite state space. First we need to build both a formal model of our system and a formal statement of the desired properties to be proven (e.g., privacy). Proving properties of a system can give us confidence in its behaviour.

However, we need to remember that a mathematical proof is a formal construction without *inherent* mapping onto the real world. The definition of this mapping, that is, the real world meaning or interpretation of the formal expressions, is left to each reader. This mapping is inevitably informal and inaccuracies may remain hidden in the gap between formality and actuality.

Some attempts have been made to close this gap by defining formal semantics that bring the formal model into closer alignement with real world interpretation. Different layers of abstraction and different desired properties may require different formal semantics.

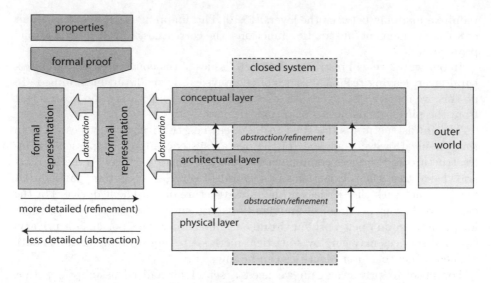

Fig. 9. Layers and issues to consider for proof of privacy

Even using an appropriate semantics, a detailed model of the entire system is likely to be prohibitively large. A standard formal methods technique to address this is to first build a small formal abstract model that specifies the system. In a second step one may then *refine* this model into a more detailed model which, by construction, satisfies the requirements. Many of the standard semantics and refinement tools are often too restrictive for large or complex systems and this necessitates using other approaches, such as building a hierarchy of models where each layer in the hierarchy is formally related to the layers above and below it.

There are no off-the-shelf solutions available but there are many techniques that can be adapted to provide a formal proof of privacy in the infrastructure.

8   Discussion and Conclusion

We introduced a service-oriented architecture for mobile context-aware services using event-based communication. In addition, we described a QoS extension using rules and conditions to ensure quality of the service collaboration (a) in the selection of alterative services and (b) to ensure liveliness of services when dealing with changing availability of collaborating services. The advantage of our approach is that no external information about services is necessary for making coupling decisions. Though the information is anonymized, all QoS decisions are directed by the services. In this way, the collaboration infrastructure is open for all third-party services that adhere to the rule & condition structure.

We implemented a prototype using a remote broker architecture. The prototype was developed and used for our mobile tourist information service TIP. The prototype is useful to show the principle of the proposed service collaboration infrastructure.

We also discussed validation and formal proof of anonymity/privacy for variations architectures. However, complete proof of correctness for a new collaboration method goes beyond the capability of a prototype implementation. For this, a formally verified model for real-time interactions between mobile context-aware services is required. We already developed a set of initial models [12,13] to clarify the modelling challenges: In particular, both the interdependencies between services and the impact of mobility on privacy and user experience cannot be ignored. We also need to investigate issues of distribution. We need to express and prove properties such as: "this device can never get into deadlock (i.e. be unable to make progress towards its current goal)"; "this service will recover if this other service becomes unavailable".

As discussed above, formal methods using enumeration of system states are not suitable for the validation of an open infrastructure: they are restricted to enumerable service instantiations and typically face state explosion. We are therefore currently looking into verification methods using abstraction and process-algebraic approaches.

Acknowledgements

The authors would like to give thanks to Michael Harrison, Newcastle University, for his valuable and constructive feedback on this work.

References

1. Abrial, J.-R.: Modeling in Event-B: System and Software Engineering. Cambridge University Press, Cambridge (2010)
2. Baresi, L., Ghezzi, C., Mottola, L.: Towards fine-grained automated verification of publish-subscribe architectures. In: Najm, E., Pradat-Peyre, J.-F., Donzeau-Gouge, V.V. (eds.) FORTE 2006. LNCS, vol. 4229, pp. 131–135. Springer, Heidelberg (2006)
3. Baresi, L., Ghezzi, C., Mottola, L.: Loupe: Verifying publish-subscribe architectures with a magnifying lens. IEEE Transactions on Software Engineering 99 (2010) (preprint)
4. Baresi, L., Heckel, R., Thöne, S., Varró, D.: Modeling and validation of service-oriented architectures: application vs. style. In: Proceedings of the 9th European Software Engineering Conference, ESEC/FSE-11, pp. 68–77 (2003)
5. Chow, C.-Y., Mokbel, M.F., Liu, X.: A peer-to-peer spatial cloaking algorithm for anonymous location-based service. In: Proceedings of the 14th annual ACM International Symposium on Advances in Geographic Information Systems, GIS 2006, pp. 171–178 (2006)
6. Di Marzo Serugendo, G., Fitzgerald, J., Romanovsky, A., Guelfi, N.: A metadata-based architectural model for dynamically resilient systems. In: SAC 2007, pp. 566–572. ACM, New York (2007)
7. Erl, T.: Service-Oriented Architecture: Concepts, Technology, and Design. Prentice Hall PTR, Upper Saddle River (2005)
8. Eschner, L.: Design and formal model of an event-driven and service-oriented architecture for a mobile tourist information system. Master's thesis, Freie Universität Berlin (July 2008)

9. Eugster, P.T., Felber, P.A., Guerraoui, R., Kermarrec, A.-M.: The many faces of publish/subscribe. ACM Comput. Surv. 35(2), 114–131 (2003)
10. Gruteser, M., Grunwald, D.: Anonymous usage of location-based services through spatial and temporal cloaking. In: Proceedings of the 1st International Conference on Mobile Systems, Applications and Services, MobiSys 2003, pp. 31–42 (2003)
11. Guerrero, P., Sachs, K., Cilia, M., Bornhövd, C., Buchmann, A.: Pushing business data processing towards the periphery. In: IEEE International Conference on Data Engineering, ICDE (2007)
12. Hinze, A., Malik, P., Malik, R.: Interaction design for a mobile context-aware system using discrete event modelling. In: Australasian Computer Science Conference (ACSC 2006), Hobart, TAS, pp. 257–266 (2006)
13. Hinze, A., Michel, Y., Eschner, L.: Event-based communication for location-based service collaboration. In: ADC, vol. 92, pp. 127–136 (2009)
14. Hinze, A., Voisard, A., Buchanan, G.: TIP: Personalizing information delivery in a tourist information system. Journal on Information Technology and Tourism 11(4) (2009)
15. Hoare, C., Jifeng, H.: Unifying Theories of Programming. International Series in Computer Science. Prentice-Hall, Englewood Cliffs (1998)
16. Michel, Y.: Location-aware caching in mobile environments. Master's thesis, Freie Universität Berlin (June 2006)
17. Michel, Y., Hinze, A.: Traditional pre-fetching and caching of limited use for mobile applications. In: Proceedings, Mobile and Ubiquitous Information Systems, pp. 25–38 (2009)
18. Michlmayr, A., Leitner, P., Rosenberg, F., Dustdar, S.: Event Processing in Web Service Runtime Environments. In: Principles and Applications of Distributed Event-based Systems, IGI Global (2010)
19. Reeves, S., Streader, D.: A robust semantics hides fewer errors. In: Cavalcanti, A., Dams, D.R. (eds.) FM 2009. LNCS, vol. 5850, pp. 499–515. Springer, Heidelberg (2009)
20. Yau, S.S., Karim, F., Wang, Y., Wang, B., Gupta, S.K.S.: Reconfigurable context-sensitive middleware for pervasive computing. IEEE Pervasive Computing 1(3), 33–40 (2002)

SParK: Safety Partition Kernel for Integrated Real-Time Systems

S. Ghaisas[1], G. Karmakar[1], D. Shenai[2], S. Tirodkar[2], and K. Ramamritham[2]

[1] Bhabha Atomic Research Centre, Mumbai, India
gkarma@barc.gov.in
[2] Computer Science & Engineering, Indian Institute of Technology, Bombay, India
krithi@cse.iitb.ac.in

Abstract. In safety critical systems, huge manpower and cost goes towards the qualification and certification of software that requires rigorous V&V (Verification & Validation) effort. In practice it has been observed that considerable parts of a safety-critical software do not perform safety-critical tasks (e.g., communication to operator station, hardware diagnostics). Therefore, if the non-critical modules of the class IA/IB systems are partitioned and if the integrity of the partitions is ensured while sharing the same hardware, V&V effort can be minimized while reducing hardware resource needs. We have designed and implemented a Safety Partition Kernel (SParK) to provide such a strictly partitioned operating environment, where partitions reside on top of SParK and are provided with temporal guarantees and spatial isolation from each other. Even though prior art exists for partitioned environments, certain practical issues like handling the effect of blocking due to system calls generated by the Real-Time Operating System (RTOS) running in a partition and handling partition-specific external interrupts while still providing temporal guarantees to each partition, have not been completely addressed. To address this lacuna, we have introduced the concept of a Virtual Interrupt Partition and accounted for the time overheads of servicing interrupts in schedulability analysis of partitions. We have implemented SParK for both Intel x86 as well as for PowerPC architectures; μC-OS II and a customized version of saRTL have been ported as GuestOSs. These have demonstrated the flexibility and practicality of the novel features built into SParK. Applications realized using SParK have shown that SParK is technically capable of serving as a microkernel for Integrated Real-Time Systems.

1 Introduction

An Integrated Real-Time System consists of applications of varying levels of criticality that coexist, sharing the same computational resources in a uniprocessor system. Hence, in order to protect each application from potential interference from others, it becomes very important to guarantee a secure environment for these applications to meet their real-time behavior. A mechanism needs to be provided to partition the applications based on their degree of criticality and

K. Sachs, I. Petrov, and P. Guerrero (Eds.): Buchmann Festschrift, LNCS 6462, pp. 150–174, 2010.
© Springer-Verlag Berlin Heidelberg 2010

functionality. Each partition needs to be spatially isolated from other partitions to ensure reliable memory and device access for every application. Also, temporal guarantees need to be given for every partition to ensure that the CPU time reserved for an application in that partition is not affected by time/space overruns or faulty behavior of other applications.

Safety critical system incur huge manpower and costs for the qualification and certification of software that requires rigorous Verification & Validation (V&V) effort. In practice it has been observed that considerable parts of a safety-critical software do not perform safety-critical tasks (e.g., communication to operator station, hardware diagnostics). For example, in Nuclear Power Plants (NPP), software modules of a class-IA/IB [2] system, even if they do not perform safety-critical/safety-related functions, are raised to the level of class IA/IB criticality because they are part of it [4]. Therefore, if the non-critical modules of the class IA/IB systems are partitioned and if the integrity of the partitions is ensured while sharing the same hardware, the V&V effort will be greatly reduced.

In addition to the clear advantage of reduced V&V effort, an Integrated Real-time system architecture has remarkable advantages from the point of view of maintenance. For example, traditionally, different classes of C&I (Control & Instrumentation) systems, have been developed by different groups of developers even within the same organization, which employ different set of hardware and software, each having its own set of maintenance procedures and hardware inventory requirement. The need for better resource utilization and a uniform set of qualified hardware favors the use of an Integrated Real-time System.

1.1 Our Contributions: The Design, Implementation and Evaluation of SParK

In this paper, we present the concept, design and implementation highlights of a microkernel, SParK (Safety Partition Kernel). SParK provides a strictly partitioned environment where individual partitions can have applications running on their own independent (guest) RTOSs or even without any RTOS.

SParK is essentially a Virtual Machine Monitor (VMM) but, it provides temporal guarantees to each partition, in addition to providing spatial integrity. Although there is significant similarity between current virtualization systems and SParK, strict timeliness requirements in SParK makes it more challenging.

The SParK microkernel uses para-virtualization technique as opposed to full virtualization [12]. This is because full virtualization techniques make it very difficult to ensure time predictability in their operations. Many of the virtualization techniques applied today, like VMware's full virtualization technique, suffer from the fact that the guestOS time lags real time at some instances during their execution. This shortcoming is completely unacceptable for real-time systems.

With para-virtualization, deployment of a new RTOS on the system requires modifications to the source code of the RTOS but, these modifications are mostly at the hardware access layer (HAL) level.

We followed certain guiding principles in design and development:

1. Simplicity in design and implementation, so that V&V is simplified. This dictates the approach to be followed when multiple solution options are available.
2. Keeping the SParK microkernel as light as possible, so that SParK itself can be put to rigorous V&V within a reasonable cost and time.

On partitioned environments, a lot of work has been carried out by researchers during the last decade offering different scheduling strategies for partitions. But, certain practical issues including

1. Handling the effect of blocking due to system calls generated by the GuestOS running in a partition, and
2. Handling the effect of partition-specific external interrupts

and still providing temporal guarantees to each partition have not been completely addressed.

Simple, yet effective, techniques to bridge this lacuna form one of the contributions of this paper: We have introduced the concept of Virtual Interrupt Partition and account for the time of servicing interrupts in schedulability analysis of partitions. Also, we have shown how to take care of blocking. In addition, providing basic clock tick to individual partitions poses challenging implementation issues. We show how our technique of handling timer interrupts addresses the issues effectively.

We have implemented SParK for both Intel x86 as well as for PowerPC architectures; μC/OS-II[19] as well as a customized version of saRTL(stand-alone RT Linux)[14] have been ported as GuestOSs. These have demonstrated the flexibility and practicality of the novel features built into SParK.

Applications used to test and evaluate SParK have shown that SParK is technically capable of serving as a microkernel for Integrated Real-Time Systems. Thus, though our motivation was to utilize the concept of partitioned RTOS in reducing V&V effort, SParK can be used for the development of Integrated Real-Time Systems, e.g., Integrated Modular Avionics (IMA) conforming to ARINC 653[20] that aims at reduction in hardware space, weight and power consumption, yet providing the advantages of a federated architecture.

2   SParK Architecture and Spatial Partitioning

We employ a two level hierarchical architecture (Fig.1). The bottom layer is where SParK resides and provides i) Hardware Initialization, ii) Timer services, iii) Interrupt support, iv) Device driver support, v) Memory Management, vi) Partition scheduling, and vii) Hypercall support. Partitions reside on top of SParK. Individual partitions can have their RTOS, which we term as GuestOS, or it may run single threaded applications without any GuestOS. Scheduling of tasks in the applications running in the partitions is the job of the individual GuestOSes. All GuestOSes get their system clock tick from the SParK Timer service and any hardware access or execution of any privileged instruction is always mediated by SParK.

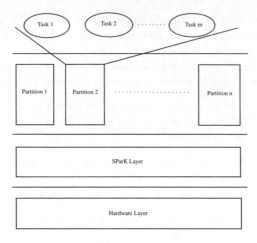

Fig. 1. Basic Architecture of SParK

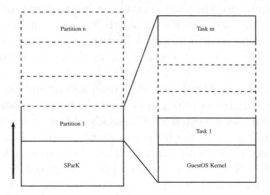

Fig. 2. Spatial Isolation: Memory Layout of SParK System

2.1 Spatial Partitioning

One of the important concepts of SParK is spatial partitioning, the technique
to guarantee spatial isolation between SParK layer and individual partitions, as
well as between any two partitions.

SParK exploits the hardware mediation provided by the Memory Management Unit (MMU) of the target processor. The memory layout of SParK system
is shown in Fig. 2. In Section 6, the implementation issues and challenges in
providing Spatial Partitioning in x86 as well as PowerPC 7447A based hardware
are discussed.

2.2 Communication between Partitions

In integrated real-time systems, there are tasks running in different partitions
to achieve a common goal. Hence, a task running in a partition may need to

communicate with another task running in a different partition. For this purpose, we have implemented Inter-Partition Communication (IPC). The IPC is implemented in such a way that it is in-line with the spatial and temporal requirements of the system. Also it should be flexible enough to be used by variety of heterogeneous operating systems.

In SParK, we have provided a simple IPC interface in accordance with our guiding principles of simplicity in design and implementation. The interface consists of few hypercalls to register a connection, and send/receive the data. The protocol requires the GuestOS (either consumer or producer) to register a connection with SParK using a unique identifier (IPC-UID). The other partition(s) can establish connection with this GuestOS using the same IPC-UID. Once the connection is established, any participating GuestOS can send or receive the data using the IPC interface. Implementation involves copying the sent data from sender to SParK and from SParK to receiver. For IPC, SParK is the only entity that has rights to read/write data from/to the communicating partitions. This ensures spatial isolation between them. Also, the communicating entities are modeled as periodic tasks in a partition, thus taking care of their temporal requirements during the schedulability analysis. Other advantages of this approach are:

- Reduced Complexity : SParK does not need to know the the details of the protocols and the end entities (tasks) involved in the communication. This reduces the design complexity of SParK.
- Flexibility : Flexibility is provided to the GuestOSs to use this minimal communication interface to achieve customized protocols (one-to-one, one-to-many, many-to-one or many-to-many) according to their requirements.

One disadvantage is that this approach involves copying the same data twice, once from sender to SParK and second time from SParK to receiver. This scheme might be inefficient when the data transferred between the sender and receiver is large. So, we have also implemented the shared memory approach to IPC. Out of these two approaches, which one to use can be decided at application design time.

Sharing memory between two partitions without violating the spatial guarantees is a challenging task. This has been solved by reserving a separate memory block exclusively for shared memory IPC. The page tables of both the communicating partitions are manipulated to map one (or more) physical pages from this memory block with exclusive read/write privileges. In this way pages can be shared between two partitions without compromising the safety of the partitions.

3   Temporal Partitioning

Temporal Partitioning ensures that CPU time reserved for a partition would not be affected either by task over-runs or by hazardous events of other applications. In order to achieve the same, SParK employs a two-level hierarchical scheduler structure in which the bottom layer (SParK layer) schedules partitions and the applications in each partition are responsible for locally scheduling their own tasks.

Our work on lower-level scheduling analysis is an extension to the SPIRIT [5] scheduling model, which uses distance-constrained cyclic scheduler in the lower level and fixed-priority scheduler in the higher level.

Assume a system consists of n partitions. Application A_k executes on partition P_k and consists of tasks τ_1, τ_2 ... τ_n. Each task τ_k is invoked periodically with period T_k and has worst case execution time C_k. Also, each invocation of τ_k must be completed before its deadline D_k, where $C_k <= D_k <= T_k$. The notation used for explaining the scheduler is given in Table 1.

Table 1. Notations for Descriptions of SParK Schedulability Analysis

Notation	Description
n	Number of tasks in a partitions
P_k	Partition k
τ_k	Task k
α_k	Partition capacity of partition P_k
η_k	Partition cycle for partition P_k
T_k	Period for task τ_k
C_k	Worst case execution time of task τ_k
D_k	Deadline of task τ_k

For each partition P_k, two values have been defined (α_k, η_k). These partition characteristics represent the scheduling requirement of that partition. The share of the total capacity that partition P_k receives is α_k. The schedulability of the partition is then evaluated with the help of the necessary and sufficient condition of schedulability in [7]. The condition states that task τ_i is schedulable if there exists $t \, \epsilon \, H_i = \{ \, IT_j \mid j = 1, 2, \ldots i \, ; \, I = 1, 2\ldots \lfloor D_i \, / \, T_j \rfloor\} \cup \{D_i\}$, such that

$$W_i(\alpha_k, t) = \sum_{j=1}^{i} \frac{C_j}{\alpha_k} \lceil \frac{t}{T_j} \rceil \leq t \qquad (1)$$

The quantity $W_i(\alpha_k, t)$ represents the worst cumulative demand made on the processor by the tasks with a priority higher than or equal to that of τ_i during the interval [0, t]. The parameter $B_i(\alpha_k)$ is defined now:

$$B_i(\alpha_k) = max_{t \in H_i}\{t - W_i(\alpha_k, t)\} \qquad (2)$$

$$B_0(\alpha_k) = min_{i=1,2,\ldots,n} B_i(\alpha_k) \qquad (3)$$

$B_i(\alpha_k)$ represents the total period in the interval [0,t] that the processor is not running any task with a priority higher than or equal to τ_i. $B_0(\alpha_k)$ is the minimum of $B_i(\alpha_k)$ at all the levels and represents the time for which the partition P_k is idle. $B_0(\alpha_k)$, when scaled with the capacity of the processor that the partition P_k is not using, gives the time for which the partition P_k is idle on the shared processor. Based on this, [5] has shown that

$$\eta_k \leq B_0(\alpha_k)/(1 - \alpha_k) \qquad (4)$$

The quantity η_k represents the cycle time for partition P_k. In other words, the partition must receive an α_k share of the processor capacity at least every η_k time units. Thus now each of the partitions is characterized by a pair of parameters α_k and η_k.

It can be observed that if the partition was executing on a single dedicated processor, the tasks could have finished earlier as the tasks would not have been blocked by the demand on processing capacity by other partitions. In case of shared processing capacity, the execution of any task can be blocked by a partition switch and, η_k in this case, ensures that the consecutive executions of the partition P_k are close enough to satisfy its own processing requirements and at the same time they are spaced out so that the inactivity period of a partition can be used by other partitions.

The pair of characteristics (α_k, η_k) is not unique for a partition. There could be many such pairs for each of the partitions depending on how we calculate the α_k. For any possible combination of (α_k, η_k) pairs for all the partitions in the system, we must ensure that the total allocated capacity of the processor never exceeds 1.

Calculation of α_k: The calculation of α_k has been suggested in [6], but it is based on the execution time (C_i) and the period (T_i) values of the mythical (analysis purpose) slower processor, in which the task set of individual partitions are schedulable. Practicable calculations of α_k needs to be done based on the execution time C_i and the period T_i values of the actual faster processor. Therefore, we suggest that the worst case should be considered because of the following reasons. Firstly, we do not want the processor utilization to go beyond the rate monotonic bound [10]. Thus, we divide the processing capacity of 0.69314 (RM bound) amongst the partitions in proportion to their utilization, i.e.,

$$\alpha_k = \frac{\sum_{i=1}^{n} (C_i/T_i)}{0.69314} \tag{5}$$

Secondly, the above calculation gives us the larger possible value of α_k and because of this larger value, the inactivity period will be governed only by the smallest task period and thus we can get a longer partition cycle. With a longer partition cycle, there will be less partition switching, which is a practical implementation requirement so that less time is wasted in partition switching overhead.

4   Ensuring Temporal Guarantees for Partitions in Spite of Interrupts and Hypercalls

In this section we discuss the issues related to external interrupts and its effect on partition schedulability.

4.1   Interrupts and Schedulability Analysis of Partitions

Accommodating the processing needs of interrupt based devices in a system that guarantees temporal partitioning is challenging. It is necessary that the Interrupt

Service Routine (ISR) execution time needs to be as minimal as possible, because, it is the time that the interrupted task is loosing from its allotted execution time. Also, we have to account for the interrupted time in schedulability analysis.

To minimize the ISR execution time, we split the ISR into two parts, front-end and back-end. Similar solution has been employed in SPRING kernel [1]. The front end is responsible for recognizing the interrupt, clearing the interrupt and saving the information transmitted through the interrupt. The back end is responsible for using the information saved by the front end. When an interrupt occurs only the front end ISR is executed. The back end later executes as a user task. Though this method reduces the ISR's disturbances to the scheduled tasks, a burst of interrupts may still result in missed deadlines of tasks.

Therefore, if we want to run an interrupt based device we have to take care of it in the schedulability analysis of partitions. On the other hand, if we want to run the device in polling mode we have to be sure that the polling is done fast enough so as to ensure reasonable response times and to avoid data losses due to limited buffer space in hardware.

To take care of the external interrupts and accommodating them in schedulability analysis we propose the concept of Virtual Interrupt Partition.

4.2   The Virtual Interrupt Partition

Virtual Interrupt Partition (VIP) is a partition that is solely responsible for handling the interrupts in the system. Temporal partitioning is ensured by assigning some fixed budget to the VIP in the schedulability analysis. For budget assignment, each source of interrupt I_i is modeled as a periodic task τ_i on VIP. The minimum inter-arrival time of interrupt is mapped to the task's period T_i, the execution time of ISR is mapped to the task's execution time C_i and the response deadline is mapped to the task's deadline D_i.

Such an assumption can be justifiably made, because in safety-critical applications, to ensure temporal guarantee, interrupts are made into periodic tasks, when minimum inter-arrival time of interrupts are known or there exists a minimum period, within which a fresh interrupt can be deferred safely till the next period.

Thus, the necessary and sufficient condition of schedulability can be re-stated as: interrupt I_i is schedulable if it runs in a partition with capacity α_{VIP} and there exists a $t \in H_i = \{l * IAT_j \mid j = 1, 2, \ldots, i; \quad l = 1, 2, \ldots, \lfloor D_i/IAT_j \rfloor\} \cup \{D_i\}$, such that

$$W_i(\alpha_{VIP}, t) = \sum_{j=1}^{i} \frac{C_j}{\alpha_{VIP}} \lceil \frac{t}{IAT_j} \rceil \leq t \tag{6}$$

Where $W_i(\alpha_{VIP}, t)$ is worst case response time of the interrupt when all other higher priority interrupts may execute in time $\leq t$. Here, IAT_j is the minimum inter-arrival time of interrupt I_j, D_j is the deadline of interrupt I_j, and C_j is the computation time of interrupt I_j. In the schedulability analysis, VIP is just like any other partition with tasks being interrupt sources modeled as periodic tasks. Using the method discussed in Section 3, α_{VIP} and η_{VIP} are calculated and VIP is included in the cyclic schedule along with other partitions. Whenever an interrupt arrives, it is deferred till VIP is scheduled. When VIP is scheduled, it serves the interrupt.

4.3   Hypercalls and Schedulability of Partitions

When a user task within some partition is to run, the GuestOS in that partition must load the page table corresponding to the task. Similarly it must provide interrupt service routines for various interrupt sources like timer, system call interrupts, etc. that will be used by the partition to carry out its operation. These are some of the privileged operations which can not be directly done by a GuestOS. Hence SParK provides an interface called as *Hypercall* that is used by GuestOS to carry out privileged operations. Since Hypercalls are function calls made between programs running in two different privilege levels and also to functions present in different binary, they are implemented using software interrupts provided by the processor architecture. For maintaining system integrity, SParK executes each Hypercall as a 'critical section'. Since a hypercall is a 'critical section', the timer interrupt occurring while the hypercall is being executed, which would have otherwise lead to partition switch, is kept pending till execution of a hypercall is complete. Without appropriate checks this can violate the temporal guarantees given by SParK to the partitions. Therefore, the blocking cost due to hypercalls needs to be accounted to provide more realistic schedulability analysis of the partition scheduling and establish how the pair (α_k, η_k) is affected.

Let $B_{j(hc)}$ denote the Blocking time for partition switching due to hypercalls (critical section) in task τ_j. The worst-case blocking time for partition switching is the maximum of the execution times of all the hypercalls. This is because, at any given time, the blocking due to hypercall will happen only when the event of partition scheduling occurs during the time interval a GuestOS in a partition is executing a hypercall. Therefore, partition switching can be delayed by the worst-case execution time of the longest hypercall.

The following theorem presents the necessary and sufficient condition of schedulability of a partition under worst-case overhead due to hypercall.

Theorem 1: A partition running a set of n periodic tasks will be schedulable if the following holds.

If there exists a $t \in H_i = \{ IT_j \mid j = 1, 2, \ldots i \; ; \; I = 1, 2 \ldots \lfloor D_i / T_j \rfloor \} \cup \{D_i\}$, such that

$$W_i(\alpha_k, t) = \sum_{j=1}^{i} \frac{C_j + max(B_{j(hc)})}{\alpha_k} \lceil \frac{t}{T_j} \rceil \leq t \tag{7}$$

Where, $\lceil t/T_j \rceil$ represents the number of invocations of task T_j within time t. Each invocation consumes $C_j + max(B_{j(hc)})$ in the worst case, which is then normalized to the share α_k of the running partition P_k.

Proof: Due to blocking caused by current execution of hypercall, the worst case execution time of any task can be elongated further by $max(B_{j(hc)})$, if it is time to switch partition. Therefore, the value of the worst cumulative execution demand $W_i(\alpha_k, t)$ made on the processor by the task with a priority higher than or equal to T_i during the interval [0, t] will be modified as shown in Equation 7. This will reduce the inactivity period $B_i(\alpha_k)$ accordingly, which forms the basis for calculating the partition cycle.

Thus using hypercalls and at the same time taking into account its blocking effect, we maintain system integrity while providing temporal guarantees to the individual partitions.

5   System Clock Management and Virtual Timer Interrupt

A GuestOS in any partition needs regular time ticks to keep track of the real time and to periodically invoke the task scheduler. These time ticks are usually provided by an external hardware timer through interrupts. But in two-level hierarchical system like SParK this hardware timer must be owned solely by SParK. Hence SParK provides the GuestOS with Virtual Timer Interrupts (VTI) to simulate these time ticks.

Different approaches towards implementing VTIs are possible.

1) SParK delivers VTIs to all partitions that have a timer interrupt due, even if those partitions are not currently active/scheduled. This approach leads to far too many context switches and timing overheads.
2) Deliver VTIs only to the currently active partition. But, since the partition may have missed many VTIs during its inactive period, SParK delivers VTIs at a faster rate than that registered by the GuestOS, thus enabling the GuestOS to catch up with the actual time. This catch up phase lasts only till the GuestOS time catches up with actual time. After this VTIs are delivered at expected intervals. Though this method is extensively used in full virtualization based systems [12], it has a major flaw with respect to real-time systems hosting RTOSs. This is because the GuestOS (RTOS) time lags the actual time during the catch up phase, which may affect the scheduling decisions taken by the GuestOS during this phase. Hence this approach can not be used for safety-critical systems.

Given the disadvantages of the two approaches, we now discuss a novel approach implemented in SParK. Each GuestOS registers its timer ISR with SParK through a hypercall. The hypercall accepts the time tick resolution required by the GuestOS. At a given instance, SParK delivers VTIs only to the currently scheduled partition. As a result, the times kept by guest RTOSs lag the actual time. In order to maintain actual time, every GuestOS registers a memory location and this location is updated by SParK before every scheduling instance of the corresponding partition. Thus, it automatically gets its time keeping data structures updated with real time before every scheduled instance.

Whether current partition has a VTI due or not is checked in the hardware timer ISR in SParK. Whenever a partition has a VTI due, SParK manipulates the kernel stack of the partition's GuestOS such that the execution control reaches directly to the registered ISR of the GuestOS. Also, provision is made to transfer control to the code executing before the arrival of hardware timer interrupt upon completion of the GuestOS ISR. This ensures seamless delivery of VTI to the GuestOS, giving it the impression of receiving timer interrupts directly from the timer hardware. This makes porting of the GuestOS easier and also makes the VTI delivery event time predictable.

6   Implementation Highlights: x86 and PowerPC Architectures

It is our design goal to keep the implementation of SParK as simple as possible. To achieve this and to make it easy for any GuestOS to run on top of SParK and to provide temporal and spatial guarantees to partitions, SParK has made innovative use of different features provided by the processor architecture. In this section we list the implementation highlights of SParK for X86 and for PowerPC.

One important issue in space partitioning is to provide three levels of spatial isolation i) between tasks of the same partition, ii) between tasks and GuestOS, iii) between partitions and between SParK & Partitions. We used different techniques to provide the required spatial isolation in PowerPC & x86 hardware because of the variation in hardware MMU (Memory Management Unit) support. However, we made maximum use of features provided by the processor architectures to reduce software overheads and the possibility of software errors, which lead to better system performance and ease of V&V.

6.1   PowerPC 7447A Platform

The main challenge in using the PowerPC was to provide three levels of spatial partitioning using the available hardware support of only two privilege levels [16]. By assigning privilege level 0 to SParK and privilege level 1 to GuestOS & tasks and judicious use of separate page tables for each GuestOS and tasks, the required three levels of spatial partitioning is achieved.

PowerPC architecture has large number of registers. To achieve simple implementation of many of the features, SParK reserves use some of the registers for specific purpose as detailed below.

1. SParK achieves spatial partitioning by maintaining different page tables for each of the GuestOSs.
2. SParK provides necessary support that allows each GuestOS to maintain distinct page tables for each of the user tasks running on top of it and achieve protection of tasks from each other.
3. SParK itself runs in real mode gaining access to the entire memory map. It turns on paging and loads appropriate page table before passing control to the partition.
4. SParK implements hypercall using the software interrupt supported by processor architecture. In order to differentiate it from the system call made by user task within a partition, SParK reserves a register to keep identifier for the call being made.

5. SParK reserves some registers to pass parameters to hypercall.
6. SParK reserves a register to support implementation of critical section within GuestOS. To enter or exit the critical section the GuestOS simply has to write specific values to the register. SParK checks this register before passing any of the interrupts to partition.
7. SParK provides means to each GuestOS to keep backup of values of the registers whose values get altered on occurrence of an interrupt.

6.2   X86 Platform

Spatial partitioning in x86 platform was simplified by the hardware MMU support of four privilege levels [15]. SParK executes at highest privilege level 0, GuestOS kernel at level 2 and the tasks at level 3. The key points are highlighted below.

1. SParK memory management scheme uses segmentation as well as paging. Segmentation provides four execution levels, level 0 (highest privilege) to level 3 (lowest level). SParK executes at the highest privilege level, that is level 0. The GuestOS kernels execute at level 2 and the user tasks at the lowest run level 3.
2. Separate segment tables (GDT) are maintained for every partition, with segment table entries for access to only its own memory block. SParK, on the other hand, has access to the entire physical memory. On top of this, paging is employed, which does a one-to-one mapping between the logical and physical addresses.
3. SParK provides necessary support that allows each GuestOS to maintain distinct page tables for each of the user tasks running on top of it and achieve protection of tasks from each other.
4. In page table of each task, the GuestOS pages are marked as Super User. The tasks running in level 3 cannot access them whereas the GuestOS can access them. (Level 0, 1, 2 are superuser levels and level 3 is user level).
5. SParK implements hypercall using the software interrupt (INT 82) and system call (INT 92).

We have ported third-party RTOS μC/OS-II and a customized version of saRTL (stand alone RTLinux) [14] over SParK as GuestOSs. The ease with which these ports were possible demonstrate the flexibility of the SParK design.

Further we developed a study application using multiple partitions to validate our design and measure the performance parameters. It uses one partition as communication partition (non-safety application) that manages Ethernet as a device (to communicate to the operator) and shared between two other partitions where safety-critical applications run. We have demonstrated how SParK safely handles an illegal operation by a partition, shown the correct functioning of IPC, Inter-Task Communication (ITC) and other system calls. We also measured the performance parameters , such as PST, SDT & WBT as stated below:

1. Scheduling Decision Time (SDT): This is an important parameter, as the scheduler is invoked at every timer tick. So, the scheduler should be efficient. It is the time to for choosing the next partition to be run.
2. Partition Switching Time (PST): It is the time taken to switch between partitions. It constitutes time for saving context of one partition, the scheduling decision making time and the time for restoring context of next partition chosen for scheduling.

   $$PST = SDT + SaveContextTime + RestoreContextTime$$
3. Worst case hyper call blocking time (WBT): This is the worst case execution time for any of the hypercalls. It is the time measured starting from occurrence of software interrupt to the instant when control goes back to instruction following the software interrupt instruction.

Table 2 shows the values of performance parameters measured (averaged over 1000 measurements) for SParK on proprietary PowerPC based CPU board. The processor is clocked at speed 600MHz. The time base register used for measurement of values given below is clocked at 25MHz. Table 3 shows the performance parameters measured (averaged over 1000 measurements)for SParK on desktop Pentium-IV PC.

The wide variation in performance parameters on PowerPC and x86 hardware was mainly because of the following reasons.

- Different Target boards: It was a Pentium-4 3.0 GHz processor in x86, while in PowerPC it was 7447A, 600MHz processor.
- More context-saving time in PowerPC due to large number of registers in use compared to x86.
- x86 has hardware support for context switching. The entire context gets pushed onto the stack in x86, whereas, the same operation is carried out in software for PowerPC.

Our intent behind providing these numbers is to indicate the broad range of system overheads, which are 50 μsecs or less, even for our unoptimized kernel code.

Table 2. Performance Parameters on PowerPC

Parameter	Min	Max
SDT	52 nS	63 nS
PST	519 nS	530 nS
WBT	572 nS	574 nS

Table 3. Performance Parameters on x86

Parameter	Min	Max
SDT	52 nS	63 nS
PST	519 nS	530 nS
WBT	572 nS	574 nS

7 Related Work

Sharing hardware resources between applications with various levels of real-time requirements (hard, firm and soft) is the goal of the Resource Kernel [18]. But, it does not deal with strictly partitioned environments where different applications can employ their own RTOSs having their own scheduling policies as in SParK.

With respect to two-level hierarchical scheduling, Deng and Liu [8] proposed the Open System Environment, which has an EDF scheduler at higher level and the next level scheduling within each real-time application can adopt any scheduling technique, cyclic table driven or priority driven (fixed or dynamic). Kim, et al. [5, 6] discuss a Strongly Partitioned Integrated Real-Time system model in which at higher level, the partitions are scheduled by cyclic partition scheduler and the tasks of a partition are scheduled by the fixed-priority driven local task scheduler of individual partitions. They discuss the schedulability conditions in a partitioned environment, and showed how to find a pair (α_k, η_k) for each partition where η_k is the cycle-time of the partition P_k and α_k is fractional

Table 4. Comparison of SParK with Related Work

Feature	SPIRIT	Open System Environment	DECOS	Integrated Automotive Architecture	SParK	Vx-Works
Partition Scheduler (Bottom Layer)	Cyclic Table-driven (simpler implementation)	EDF (complex implementation with overhead of dynamic calculations)	Time-triggered	Time-triggered	Cyclic Table-driven (simpler implementation)	Cyclic Table-driven
Blocking due to System calls by GuestOS	Not considered	Not considered	Not considered	Not considered	Taken care of in scheduling analysis	Not known
Blocking due to External Interrupt handling	Not considered	Not considered	Not considered	Not considered	Taken care of by VIP Concept	Not known
Device Driver support through front-end and back-end driver technique	Not available	Not available	Not considered	Not considered	Available	Not available
Need for Special hardware	No	No	Yes	Yes	No	No

processor capacity that must be ensured every cycle-time. Lippari & Bini [9], presented a technique to find the best pair (α_k, η_k) that can be assigned to the partition server so that the task group is schedulable, where application(s) in a partition is assigned a server (partition server) that is characterized by a pair (α_k, η_k), with the meaning that the server gets (α_k units of execution every η_k) units of time. But, none of these ([5, 6, 8, 9]) address the issue of handling external interrupts and account for it in partition scheduling analysis.

Obermaisser, et al. [11] discuss an Integrated Automotive Architecture based on multicore Systems-on-Chips (SoC) mainly focused on automotive industry requirement. It calls for special hardware using IP cores interconnected through on-chip network. Schlager and Erkinger discuss the DECOS [13] encapsulation approach, where the integrated architecture consists of multiple nodes that are interlinked by a dedicated communication channel. DECOS runs its kernel at the highest privilege level and the GuestOS kernel (along with user level tasks) at the user privilege level. But, both these approaches ([11, 13]) call for special hardware, where multiple communicating nodes are integrated.

Table 4 gives the comparison of SParK with related work. Even though, for completeness, we have included commercial partitioned RTOS VxWorks[17], since they do not provide much technical details in the open domain, fair comparisons cannot be made. In such cases of non-availability of data, we have stated 'Not known' in the comparison Table 4.

In this paper, we attempted to resolve the practical issues of i) Handling the effect of blocking due to hypercalls (most importantly the system calls generated by the GuestOS in a partition), partition switching and ii) Handling external Interrupts, which to the best of our knowledge, have not been completely addressed by any of the existing systems.

8 Conclusion

SParK provides an environment for integrated real-time systems for safety-critical applications and it accounts for the effect of external interrupts in partition scheduling analysis. It has also been shown as to how blocking is taken care of by SParK. SParK has been ported both into x86 and PowerPC based hardware. Third party RTOS μC/OS-II and a customized version of saRTL [14] have been ported as GuestOSs.

We believe that SParK serves as a unified platform for building Integrated time critical systems which need V&V support. It is built using simple and sound design principles and is analyzable for schedulability. The different hardware platforms and RTOSs that have been deployed with SParK speak to the generality of the design of SParK.

In our ongoing work, we are porting existing applications from Power plant control domain on top of SParK so as to reap the benefits that motivated the development of SParK.

References

[1] Stankovic, J.A., Ramamritham, K.: The Spring Kernel: a new paradigm for real-time operating systems. SIGOPS Oper. Syst. Rev. 23(3), 54–71 (1989)

[2] IEC-61226: Nuclear Power Plants: Instrumentation and Control Systems Important to Safety classification of instrumentation and control functions. Technical Report, International Electrotechnical Commission (2005)

[3] IEC-61513: Nuclear Power Plants: Instrumentation and Control Systems Important to Safety - general requirements for systems. Technical Report, International Electrotechnical Commission (2001)

[4] IEC-60880: Nuclear Power Plants: Instrumentation and Control Systems Important to Safety software aspects for computer based systems performing category a functions. Technical Report, International Electrotechnical Commission (2001)

[5] Daeyoung, K.A., Yann-Hang, L., Mohamed, Y.: Software architecture supporting integrated real-time systems. J. Syst. Softw. 1, 71–86 (2003)

[6] Lee, Y.H., Kim, D., Younis, M., Zhou, J.: Partition Scheduling in APEX Runtime Environment for Embedded Avionics Software. In: Proceedings of the 5th International Conference on Real-Time Computing Systems and Applications, RTCSA 1998. IEEE Computer Society103, Los Alamitos (1998)

[7] Lehoczky, J., Sha, L., Ding, Y.: The rate-monotonic scheduling algorithm: Exact characteristics and average case behavior. In: Proceedings of IEEE Real-Time Systems Symposium, pp. 166–171 (1989)

[8] Deng, Z., Liu, J.W.S., Sun, J.: A scheme for scheduling hard real-time applications in open system environment. In: Proceedings of the 9th Euromicro Workshop on Real-Time Systems (1997)

[9] Lipari, G., Bini, E.: Resource partition among real-time applications. In: Proceedings of the 15th Euromicro Workshop on Real-Time Systems, pp. 151–158 (2003)

[10] Liu, C.L., Layland, J.W.: Scheduling Algorithms for Multiprogramming in a Hard-Real-Time Environment. J. ACM 20, 46–61 (1973)

[11] Obermaisser, R., Salloum, C.E., Huber, B., Kopetz, H.: From a federated to an integrated automotive architecture. IEEE Transactions on Computer-Aided Design of Integrated Circuits and Systems 28(7), 956–965 (2009)

[12] VMware: White paper: Understanding full virtualization, paravirtualization and hardware assist. (2007)

[13] Schlager, M., Erkinger, E.: FBenifits and implications of the DECOS encapsulation approach. Research report 80, Vienna university of technology, Austria (2005)

[14] saRTL (Stand Alone RTLinux), http://www.ocera.org

[15] Intel arch: software developers manual, vol.3. http://www.intel.com/design/processor/manuals/253668.pdf

[16] Programming environments manual: PowerPC architectur, http://e-www.motorola.com/brdata/PDFDB/docs/MPCFPE32B.pdf

[17] VMware: Whitepaper:Safety-Critical Software Development for Integrated Modular Avionics, http://www.windriver.com

[18] Rajkumar, R., Juvva, K., Molano, A., Oikawa, S.: Resource kernels: A resource-centric approach to real-time and multimedia systems. In: Proceedings of the SPIE/ACM Conference on Multimedia Computing and Networking, pp. 150–164 (1998)

[19] Labrosse, J.J.: MicroC/OS-II: The Real-Time Kernel. CMP Books, San Fransisco 94107 (2002)

[20] ARINC: Avoincs Application Software Standard Interface, ARINC Specification 653. Aeronautical Radio Inc., Annapolis, Maryland (1997)

On Scientific Experiments and Flexible Service Compositions

Dimka Karastoyanova

Institute of Architecture of Application Systems,
University of Stuttgart, Germany
dimka.karastoyanova@iaas.uni-stuttgart.de

Abstract. The IT support for scientific experimenting and e-science is currently not at the level of maturity of the support enterprises obtain. Since recently there is a trend of reusing existing enterprise software and related concepts for scientific experiments, scientific workflows and simulation. Most notably these are the workflow technology, which is widely used in business process management (BPM), and integration paradigms like the service oriented architecture (SOA). In this work we give an overview of open issues in the support for scientific experiments and possible approaches to addressing them in a service-based environment. We identify the need for enhancing the BPM practices, technologies and techniques in order to render them applicable in the area of scientific experimenting. We stress on the even greater importance of workflow flexibility and also show why flexibility techniques are crucial when it is about improving the IT support for scientists.

Keywords: Scientific Experiments, Scientific Workflows, Simulation, Workflow, Service Oriented Computing and Architecture, Service Composition, BPEL, Compensation, Aspect-orientation, Flexibility, Adaptability.

1 Introduction

Service orchestration technology gained much attention in research and industry in the last decade. This is due to its high potential for the support of application integration (in both EAI and B2B settings) and flexible and machine-readable business processes. Service orchestration approaches are based on the principles of service orientation and are typically enacted by process-like or workflow-like approaches. A great number of commercial systems exist by all big software vendors providing business solutions, however the support for scientific experimenting is still rudimentary and the commercially available tools do not cover the whole life cycle of scientific experiments. Recently there have been some attempts to combine tools supporting scientists in computations and simulations in service-based applications. Mostly these were prototypical applications that compose several modules or programs that perform some computations using service compositions. These are however only preliminary attempts for proof of concept only and are not satisfying the requirements imposed on scientific calculation.

K. Sachs, I. Petrov, and P. Guerrero (Eds.): Buchmann Festschrift, LNCS 6462, pp. 175–194, 2010.

Obviously, the field of scientific computing is still in need of improvements and in this work an overview will be given of some of the approaches currently under development and in the area of service oriented computing that aim at addressing this need. The objective of these approaches is to improve both the modeling and execution of scientific computations by (re)using features from the conventional workflow technology (as in [5]) and existing scientific workflow systems like Kepler [46], Pegasus [49], Triana [47], Taverna [48] and others.

We use the term scientific experiment to stand for the overall process of performing an experiment including preparation and set-up, experiment execution that may include complex computations, a simulation or a scientific workflow (as defined currently by the e-science community), and post-processing. A scientific workflow is an application that performs some kind of scientific computation or is a simulation and is used to execute a part of the overall experiment. Note that the term scientific workflow does not currently imply that the conventional workflow technology as in [5] and [16] is used. However in this work what we call a scientific workflow may imply a realization in terms of conventional workflow – this however will be disambiguated in this work.

For what concerns scientific experiment modeling the following are the most notable required features:

- domain specific modeling of the overall scientific experiments and of the scientific workflows
- automation of manual steps
- reduced learning curve for scientists
- modeling of multi-scale and multi-physics simulations
- management of large data sets in experiments and simulations stemming from multiple and diverse data sources (e.g. sensors, databases, file systems).

In terms of scientific experiments execution there are features that the existing systems do not completely and adequately enable and these are for example:

- straightforward fault handling
- execution of incomplete or partially modeled experiment models
- automated monitoring of experiments and the constituent workflows and simulations
- parallel execution of multiple instances of scientific experiments.

These are some of the requirements on systems for scientific experimenting which we argue can be addressed in terms of features that can be borrowed from the conventional workflow systems and applied in and enhanced for a service-based environment. For example, scientific experiments can be modeled using conventional standard-based workflow modeling tools extended with domain specific tasks that correspond to particular computational steps or set-up step in an experiment. The major issue in scientific experiments modeling is the complexity of the notations and languages to use and the user-friendliness of the tools and notations. The execution of such experiments needs to be automated in order to shorten experimental runs, while still in control enabled by monitoring facilities. Additionally, to provide scientists with the most suitable support any kind of exceptional situations should be dealt with in an automatic manner, if possible, or the scientists should be given for example a choice when deciding on the way an exception is to be handled.

Since the conventional workflow technology is capable of addressing some of the requirements and due to our expertise in the field, the focus of our work is on extending the conventional workflow technology for scientific experimenting. One very important difference between the two areas is that scientists follow a different life cycle of their processes than the business users. In order to enable support for the life cycle of scientific experiments using conventional workflows we need to enhance the existing meta-models for workflows and the modeling and execution environments appropriately. We devised the so called model-as-you-go approach, in which the flexibility of the workflows (that stand for the scientific experiments) is instrumental.

The rest of this work is structured as follows. Section 2 shortly introduces the basic principles of SOA, the Web service technology and service composition based on the workflow technology. Section 3 presents the observed life cycle of scientific experiments and discusses open issues in terms of both approaches for modeling and execution of such experiments, while the focus is on how the existing service composition approaches can be enhanced to become applicable in the scientific computing area. Since the phases of modeling and execution are continuously alternating and thus resembling the life cycle of agile workflows, in Section 4 we provide a summary and assessment of the approaches for flexibility of service compositions that can be employed for improving the conventional workflow technology for the purposes of scientific experimenting. We close the paper with a summary.

2 SOA, Web Services and Service-Based Workflows

This section provides background information and major assumptions for the presented work. Service oriented Architecture (SOA) is one natural continuation in the evolution of integration technologies [2] and enables the interoperability within and across organizations using basic principles like service abstraction, loose coupling [25], composability, and allows for leveraging of technology and investment. Services are self-contained and self-describing units of functionality exposing stable interfaces in a unified format independent of implementation specifics and interaction formats and protocols. They render a heterogeneous environment homogeneous. Thus services allow for standardized access and identification of functionality/applications and facilitate application integration. Service clients use only the stable interface exposed by the service and hence the client application that uses this service will not break if the implementation of the service itself is changed.

The SOA architectural style specifies three major *roles*: service providers, service consumers and service brokers, and three *operations*. The *operations* defined by SOA are: find, register, and bind and invoke/interact. The find operation is used by service consumers to discover services, while the service providers use the register operation to provide information about their services in the discovery component (the broker). Once a client discovers an appropriate service he binds to the service and starts interacting with it. These operations are realized by the service middleware, the so-called service bus [17, 34] and are made available to the entities playing any of the

SOA roles. The invocation of services is performed by the bus. If the service consumer has not provided the location of the service and the access mechanism, it is up to the bus to discover a service on behalf of the client that meets his requirements.

Web services (WSs) are the only existing standardized implementation of SOA. This technology provides a model for use of (existing) applications, not for programming applications. Web services are about virtualization of applications, which also explains their already huge success in industrial applications and in utility and cloud computing [50]. Services can be implemented in any programming language for any platform, as well as they can be exposed for use via any of the existing interface description languages (IDLs). The novelty in Web services is the notion of binding, which is reflected by the standard language for WS interface description, the Web Service Description Language (WSDL) [3]. Unlike any other existing IDL, WSDL keeps the information about the transport protocol and message encoding separate from the actual interface description (signature). This allows for exposing the same functionality/program/implementation on different endpoints/ports by combining a service interface description with multiple bindings. This improves modularity and facilitates loose coupling between service providers and consumers. The Web Service technology enables composability of technology and specifications. There are many specifications in the WS protocol stack dealing with different concerns of application development and integration. Recently, the need has arisen to virtualize hardware resources in particular in the area of scientific computing and simulation, where the computations are lengthy and resource-consuming due to the nature of the computations and the huge amounts of distributed data used and produced. This need was addressed partly by the Grid, and its name stands for a distributed IT infrastructure for advanced science and engineering applications [20, 21]. Cloud computing and the *aaS delivery models also heavily rely on this.

WS (and Grid services, i.e. WS-Resources [39]) can be combined in more complex applications using some composition approach. The workflow- or process-based approach [5, 16] is the most favored one. The process-based approach to service composition, also known as service orchestration, allows composing services in a very flexible manner by means of improved modularity, separation of concerns and configurability. Processes are created in terms of (i) control logic that specifies the sequencing of tasks and the data they exchange, (ii) the functions/services that implement the tasks and (iii) the human participants in an organization that participate in carrying out the tasks. These entities form the so-called workflow/process dimensions. In (Web) service compositions, due to the fact that services do not involve people or hide their participation, the organizational dimension is not present. The definition of a workflow or process used here is based on those presented in BPM (Business Process Management) literature like [5] and [16]. It is important to note that the workflow technology distinguished between a workflow model and workflow instances. A model can be run multiple times, i.e. multiple workflow instances can be executed simultaneously, which brings significant time savings. To the best of our knowledge, based on our participation in multiple projects together with researchers from the scientific computing community, the definitions of the notion of workflow first differ from group to group in the scientific world, and second stands for only the sequencing of tasks and the data dependencies. According to these definitions workflows do not include the features from the workflow technology, like: interruptible sequences of tasks, modeling of constraints to transitioning from task to task in a global model of the overall computation, modeling parallel execution of independent tasks, forward and backward recovery, fault handling, staff assignment per task. The available scientific workflow infrastructures do not always distinguish among workflow model and workflow instances; moreover, some of them are tailor-made for a concrete scientific domain, which the workflow engines employed in business applications indeed avoid by implementing a generic workflow meta-model suitable for all application domains. In this work we have as a starting point the workflows or processes as defined by the BPM community.

Usually processes are modeled using some graphical notation, however in order to be executed (on a workflow engine/system) they need to be transformed into some executable format. There are many workflow languages and BPEL [1] is the standard language for describing service orchestrations. It contains constructs for control flow and data manipulation, as well as the so-called interaction activities which model the interaction with WSs that implement tasks in a workflow, e.g. book hotel, calculate credit risk, generate a mesh in a FEM computation etc. The interaction activities contain references to the service port type and operation and specifies the input and output data. In BPEL the control flow and the functions (WSs) used are predefined during the modeling of the composition and remain unchanged during the process execution. Processes are executed by process/orchestration/workflow engines and currently these engines make use of the service middleware to invoke services (see Figure 1). The use of Grid infrastructures for involving WS-Resources into BPEL service orchestrations has great potential and will allow for flexible mixing and interchange of WSs and WS-Resources from the point of view of service orchestrations. This should be addressed by research and engineering efforts in this direction.

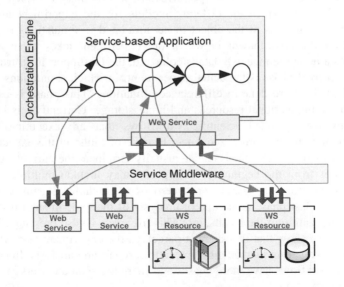

Fig. 1. Interplay among Service Compositions, WSs and Grid Services

BPEL is being extensively used in business applications and all big software vendors have rolled out products with BPEL support. There are preliminary attempts to utilize BPEL for composing scientific computations using existing algorithm and computation implementations [19, 22, 35]. Admittedly, there are many open issues that still have to be considered in the area of applying the SOA paradigm, Web services and Grid services for scientific applications [44, 23]. The major critical issues are in particular the robustness, scalability and availability the infrastructure and resources to maintain the long-running scientific application up and running.

While SOA has great success in improving the support for business applications, techniques from Grid can be utilized to enhance this support further. Some of the reasons for the modern SOA infrastructures to not yet support such features can be explained by the requirements business applications up till now had on technologies. Modern business applications however are much more complex and require most of the features mentioned above.

Indeed, both business and scientific applications miss certain features which the other domain has already implemented. Usually, each industry stays in its own confines and keeps developing its own technology and standards. With the advent of service-orientation, which is employed by both communities, now there is a chance to unify the efforts in developing infrastructures comprising concepts, techniques and implementations from different domains for mutual benefit.

3 Scientific Experiments, Scientific Workflows and Simulation

In general, scientific experiments are performed in several phases. Typically there is a preparation phase, in which the different models for the experiment are prepared (usually these are models of the object to be simulated if simulations is part of the experiment, of the environment in which the experiment takes place and others, dependencies among the models), data is collected, the IT support infrastructure is set up, etc. The second phase is the actual experiment, in which simulations are carried out and calculations are done in different combinations. This phase is usually long and consumes computational resources and huge storage. Currently this is the phase supported by the so-called scientific workflows that are executing the actual computation steps in the correct sequence. In case of faults in the execution and/or incomplete or incorrect data the scientists usually terminate the current experimental run and start it from the beginning. This phase may include multiple runs of the scientific computation (e.g. parameter sweep) or a simulation (again with different parameters). The last phase is the one of analysis of the experimental results, which may need visualization of the results, too. This life cycle is also presented in Figure 2 B, where we also show that the scientist perceives the experiment as a whole and is the only user involved in its modeling, execution, repair and analysis. In contrast, the conventional workflows have more phases and there are separate users in each of the phases (see Figure 2 A).

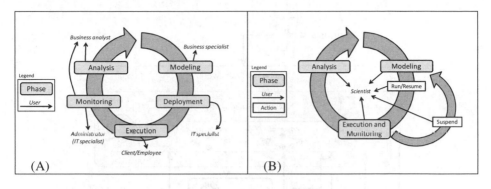

Fig. 2. Life cycle of (A) service compositions/workflows and (B) scientific workflows as perceived by scientist [40]

We argue that the conventional workflow technology can be used to enable the overall lifecycle of scientific experiments and also the scientific workflows that are used for complex computations or simulations during the second phase of the lifecycle of scientific experiments [40]. Thus the advantages the conventional workflow technology provides can be employed and reused for the benefit of scientific experimenting without the need to reinvent the realization and implementation of such features especially for scientific workflows [41]. Since the conventional workflows have been mainly used in business applications, which pose a different set of requirements on the IT support, there is still a need to improve this technology in order to be able to make use of all its advantages for scientific experiments. In particular, the way scientists perceive the experiments needs to be kept the same as with the existing approaches. This requirement solely has important implications on the way the workflow technology has to be enhanced. Essentially, for the scientists the way they carry out their work should not change, to the contrary the support has to be improved and made much more straightforward and user-friendly, while accompanied by improved infrastructure with better performance and flexibility for the users. More details on these requirements on the workflow technology as imposed by the scientific work and the possible ways to address them are given later in this work.

In order to facilitate the presentation next, we present here the architecture of an enhanced workflow management system that is meant to support the features required by scientists [41].

The proposed infrastructure is made available to the users, i.e. the scientists, via a single user interface containing a modeling tool for the overall experiment and its constituent models. It is also responsible for generating all the artifacts needed for the deployment and execution of the experiment. This interactive framework should also contain a facility for monitoring of the experiment and its constituent parts like workflows, services, human participants, the whole infrastructure, its performance, etc. Visualization of the experimental results, in part and completely should be enabled through a set of visualization tools that are to be selected on-the-fly by the scientist. Access to a service registry is also needed for the scientist to choose the services for the computational steps of the experiment. This kind of combination of components in the infrastructure that need to closely interact with each other is novel

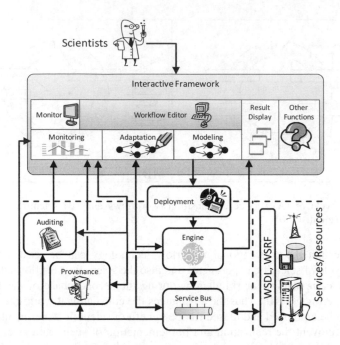

Fig. 3. Architecture of a next generation Infrastructure for Scientific Experiments based on conventional workflows [40, 41]

and is not typical for the workflow management systems for business applications. Different approaches will be needed to engineer this kind of system. This interactive framework used by scientists needs to be coupled to the underlying environment for execution of the experiments, too.

This environment includes a service middleware and a workflow management system that carries out service composition instances. Auditing of execution data and recording of the provenance information are inseparable features of that kind of environments, especially because this data is needed for monitoring, analysis and reproducibility of the experiments.

3.1 Modeling Scientific Experiments

Scientists create their experiments in a step-by-step fashion. Typically, an experiment is not completely modeled when the execution starts. Sometimes the reason for this is missing information or result necessary for a next step in the scientific workflow. Sometimes it is simply a matter of availability of resources, since this information is sometimes also part of the specification of a scientific workflow, because for example the system used requires such a specification. Monitoring of the experimental results is also done before the completion of the experiment specification or the model itself. In conventional workflow systems however, the models are completely specified before being executed, and changes are only sometimes necessary or possible, depending on the modeling language and the supporting infrastructure used.

Sometimes in scientific workflow management systems the overall experiment execution is compiled to a monolithic application, which cannot be split into separate reusable services. This hinders the reusability of computational modules across applications and across scientific domains using similar computations like PDE solvers, FEM implementations for different physical media, etc.

The workflow technology is capable of improving all these features if it is extended appropriately. First of all we argue that conventional workflows can be used to model either the (1) *whole experiment* or (2) only the *scientific computation*, be it a simulation or an experiment. In the former case the workflow will take over the role of controlling the sequencing of steps of the overall experiment, a.k.a. *supervising workflow*, while the actual execution of the experiment will be carried out by reusing the existing monolithic applications. Thus the manual work for set-up and infrastructure provisioning is reduced by virtue of automation; the same is valid for the analysis phase. In the latter, the workflow technology is used to enable a composition of individual computational modules exposed as services. This approach renders the scientific computation a modularized and reusable application allowing the use of existing computations even across scientific domains. A combination of the two approaches is possible too, but complex correlation between the supervising workflow instances and the workflow instances carrying out the computations/simulations also needs to be enforced. A conventional workflow modeling environment needs to enable the modeling of such nested workflows. *Correlation* among many workflows constituting a single scientific experiment is also needed when multi-scale and multi-physics simulations are to be modeled as workflows. More precisely, since these kinds of simulations and their complex interrelationships and data and functional dependencies resemble choreographies of service compositions, the modeling of such choreographies and their correlation is extremely important and a must. This also implies that the execution environment must possess the capability of executing such experiments.

Additional concerns of scientific experiments modeling is the *management of* the huge amounts of *data* scientific experiments deal with. Due to the distributed nature of the conventional workflows and the small amounts of data exchanged with the used services the data is stored in the workflow engine. This is not an option with scientific workflows. Some approaches suggest the use of DBMS directly in the scientific workflows, so that data sets can be stored directly into data bases [51]. Other data sources like sensor networks are also used in scientific experiments for different purposes like populating a simulation with initial data from sensors, or reaction to changes in the environment that is signaled by sensors. Approaches for incorporating sensor data into the workflows are also under development [53]. Note, that whatever the data source, the workflow meta-model needs to reflect these into its constructs, which will inevitably be a part of the extended workflow meta-model for scientific experiments. One such approach for incorporating the management of data is presented in [52], where references to the data sources are allowed as variable values in BPEL processes, so that the data is made available by reference to the workflow engine and hence the experiment and does not need to be transferred to the engine.

One very important requirement on workflows that scientists impose is the ability to *model in a domain-specific* (graphical) *language*; this serves also the purpose of reducing the learning curve for scientists in getting acquainted with the IT infrastructure. While the perceived domain specific modeling is a part of the way the modeling environment is to be engineered, the underlying workflow meta-model must allow for extensions that accommodate the domain-specific constructs. Workflow code generation may be required for this, too. Additionally, interaction between the modeling tool and a registry for scientific computing modules exposed as services is a must. In such a way scientist will be given the possibility to choose a particular service for their workflow from the set of all available ones. Models for such service registries and extensions to the service interface description (functional, non-functional and QoS) will also be required, since the information needed by scientists to choose a service is different than the one typically provided in business scenarios.

During the modeling phase the scientists want to be given the chance to specify the *provenance* data they need to collect. This can be enabled by setting additional parameterization options for the process models in terms of special-purpose auditing and provenance related artifacts in the workflow deployment package.

3.2 Execution of Scientific Experiments

The execution phase of scientific experiments in existing systems does not rely on the concept of workflow instance and therefore the existing infrastructures do not support the simultaneous execution of multiple instances of the same workflow. Typically the scientists simply start manually the next simulation or experiment run, after the first one has been completed. This results in long experiment durations and in a lot of error-prone manual work (in setting-up experimental infrastructure, directories for data, correlating results and simulation runs, etc.) – hence one opportunity for parallel execution is passed by. Note that as another way of enabling parallelism, parallel computing is used in scientific workflows to parallelizing applications on high-performance computing infrastructures and on Grids.

Mostly data management and many manual steps are what existing scientific workflow management systems support. There is no support for the steering workflows, neither there is support for execution of service compositions that represent simulations based on reusable services. The execution of the scientific applications does not always enable the reaction to failures in the environment, in the data quality or errors on behalf of humans.

A very important requirement we derived based on our observations of how scientist perform experiments is that there is a need to *execute partially modeled workflows*. This is not possible with the conventional workflow management systems. This leads to the merging of the modeling and execution phase of workflows and their continuous interleaving, so that scientists can model a part of an experiment as a workflow, start its execution and continue its modeling after the already modeled part has been executed and (the data it produced) analyzed. The implications are manifold and complex:

(i) The *execution* environment needs to start the execution of incomplete model and allow for its continuous step-by-step modeling while the workflow instance is still running in the workflow engine. This feature has not been necessary so far in business workflows and hence has never been dealt with. One way to enable this is to use approaches for adaptation of workflows (described in the next section and) as argued for in [40]. These approaches will also improve the robustness of the scientific experiments, because they can be used to react to changes in the environment like missing services, the need to include additional steps into a workflow and others [26].

(ii) Some of the modeling approaches require special-purpose constructs to be included onto the original workflow model to enable the particular flexibility approach during the execution of the workflow instance. Therefore *modeling for flexibility* needs to be enabled on the level of the workflow meta-model and in the modeling tool.

(iii) The *modeling and execution environment* for scientific experiments must be integrated and perceived by the scientists as a single tool/application so that they do not perceive any distinction in modeling and execution of experiments.

Dealing with *data* while executing processes is a must, as explained in the previous section. Therefore the execution environment must be able to support multiple approaches, regardless of whether they are reflected in workflow modeling constructs or not. For example the engine must be capable of following the references in the model to data or data storage needed for the workflow execution, or distribute the execution close to the data as in [42] where a space-based computing approach for scientific computations has been introduced, or enable the coupling of the infrastructure with data sources of different type.

One additional issue that concerns the execution of scientific workflows that need to reuse existing computations is the granularity of the services to reuse. This is a problem inherent to other domains too, where service orientation has been introduced to infrastructures containing monolithic and complex applications. In our current work we have been experimenting with exposing whole computational modules as services and parts of them; the systems used are DUNE, ChemShell and currently under development is similar work with PANDAS. These applications for FEM simulations are being used and extended in projects of the SimTech Cluster [44]. Most of the work has been on architecting adapters for these applications and implementing them using the Web Service technology. Conventional workflows have been used to supervise the simulations (but not the overall experiment with all its phases) or to implement the simulations themselves.

Supervising workflows have been realized using BPEL and with the existing scientific workflow environment Pegasus [49]. The steering workflow that governs the whole experiment works in cooperation with Pegasus that implements the experimental phase; a demonstration is available at [43].

Auditing of experimental workflows can be enabled by workflow management systems since auditing is instrumental for business applications and their compliance to regulations and law. Still this capability needs to be extended to enable appropriate monitoring and provenance of scientific workflows and experiments for the simple reason that scientists need information about much more details related to the execution of a workflow than businesses.

4 Approaches to Flexibility of Service Compositions

As stated earlier in this work, the approaches for flexibility of conventional workflows are very useful in the area of enabling support for scientific experiments. On the one hand these approaches can be used to enable the model-as-you-go nature of scientific experimenting [40]. On the other hand the robustness of scientific applications can be improved [26]. These approaches can be applied to conventional workflows, which are the basis for our work on the objective to enable a better support for interactive scientific experimenting and simulations. In this section an overview of workflow flexibility approaches is presented and their applicability is assessed.

4.1 Approaches to Flexibility of Service Composition – A Classification

Workflow flexibility has been an area of research for the last decade and lots of approaches have been developed [15, 28, 6 and many others]. Recently with the advent of service-oriented computing and service composition approaches based on the workflow technology, where service compositions are completely automated workflows, the flexibility to react to changes in the environment has been revised for the service-oriented context. Adaptation approaches require support on behalf of the modeling language and of the workflow management system.

Adaptation of service compositions can be performed on the workflow model (design time adaptation) or on the workflow instances (known as ad-hoc adaptation). These changes can be carried out on the control flow and/or data flow of the workflow, or on the business functions implementing steps in the workflows, i.e. the implementations of activities [26]. Approaches for control flow change have been part of our previous work and reported in [29, 32, 4, 9, and 33]. Since service compositions that allow people to be part of the workflow are still a very active research area, the development of flexibility approaches related to the organizational dimension of workflows is still in its early stages and will not be discussed here.

When adapting running workflow instances first it has to be checked if these instances can be modified at all to reflect the new model depending on their current status/position in the execution of the process. The instances that can be modified according to the new model are said to be migrated to this model. This may require changing the internal workflow engine representation of the instances. Additionally, the instances that cannot be migrated may either be terminated or let complete according to the original model. This results into two versions of the same model for a period of time and version management is one of the implied infrastructure features. Instance migration and the supporting infrastructure are not in the scope of this work.

Service composition instances may also incorporate a reaction to changes in the environment, e.g. failing WS, the appearance of a new service with better QoS characteristics, adaptation request due to recommendation of a test run [24], by exchanging a concrete WS implementation that has originally been chosen to perform a task in an instance [30]. An overview of some of the existing approaches is presented in the following.

4.2 Exchanging Concrete Service Implementations during Run Time

Since service compositions reference only port types of services, there must be a mechanism to resolve these port types to concrete service endpoints/ports. The mechanism is called *service binding* (see Figure 4 A). There are several strategies defined in literature [2] for controlling this mechanism called binding strategies. The

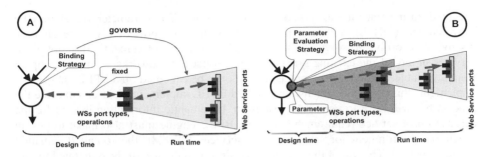

Fig. 4. (A) The role of binding strategies and (B) of parameterization in service compositions [26]

static binding strategy prescribes concrete service ports for each of the tasks in a process during either design time or deployment time; the statically prescribed service ports are used during process execution. Dynamic service binding is a strategy that postulates that the concrete services are to be discovered during process instance execution. It is enabled during both design time and run time. During modeling or deployment time the port types of services that implement a task are specified; these are the functional requirements toward a service. Additionally, the QoS selection criteria, usually provided in terms of WS-Policies, are typically used. During process execution the process engine delegates the discovery and selection of the concrete services for each of the tasks to the service bus, which uses as input these functional and non-functional properties as provided by the process specification. The dynamic binding is an approach used to enable flexibility for each process instance with respect to the functional dimension of service composition.

The mechanism for discovery, selection and invocation of WS is known by the name "find and bind mechanism" and is utilized during the normal execution of service compositions. It can also be used to exchange services that have been bound for use with a service composition, regardless of the strategy used for the original binding, with another port. This may be necessary in order to handle a fault of a service and the inability of the service middleware to discover a new alternative but compliant service. For the discovery of the new service, additional selection criteria must be provided in the process model. There are several ways to do this: (a) to extend the process definition language to allow for specification of such criteria directly in the interaction activity elements; (b) to extend the deployment information by alternative selection policies and use it during execution for the discovery of a substitute for a failed service. The latter approach is much more configurable. Approach (a) has already been defined and implemented [28, 30].

4.3 Parameterized Processes

One approach to make service compositions flexible on the functions dimension is enabled by the so-called parameterized processes [29]. The approach extends BPEL and provides an extension element in the interaction activities to allow for providing or discovering a port type for the service to be bound using a parameter evaluation strategy (see Figure 4 B). Such a strategy is specified during design time but is executed during run time to resolve parameter values. The parameter values may be provided manually by a human participant, or may be provided as a result of a discovery according to service criteria specified in terms of semantic description of services in any of the existing semantic Web services frameworks, or may be copied from a variable. Parameterized processes can only be executed on a BPEL engine that implements this particular extension; standard BPEL implementations can execute the process but will have to ignore the extension. If semantic information is used for the description of service requirements then the BPEL engine must also make use of an execution environment for semantic Web services [29, 28], the so-called semantic service bus [27]. The use of the approach requires also the use of the dynamic binding strategy, since the concrete implementation of the discovered port type for each instance of the task has to be discovered as well (see Figure 4 B). This approach provides a primitive support for control flow change in service composition.

4.4 BPEL^{light}

BPEL^{light} [38] is an extension to BPEL that decouples the process logic from the WSDL descriptions of services and thus enables the use of any kind of service interface descriptions. This approach has been implemented prototypically and described in [33]. The BPEL^{light} specification defines an extension activity, which separates completely the process logic from the descriptions of service interfaces. During process deployment, the service descriptions are simply supplied together with the process logic in a separate artifact. This approach removes the hard-coding to service interfaces into the process models and facilitates the adaptability and reusability of service composition definitions. It is a standard compliant extension of BPEL and can be executed on BPEL compliant engines with appropriate extensions. To enable the use of semantic WSs with BPEL^{light}, the BPEL4SWS specification has also been created. The prototype supports the use of conventional WSs and semantic Web services described in WSMO [33]. Once the service type is discovered based on its semantic description, the discovery of service ports/endpoint is a must. Any other semantic service description framework, like OWL-S and SAWSDL, can also be applied with BPEL4SWS. Through the use of semantics BPEL4SWS improves the discovery of services (port types and ports) through an additional level of abstraction provided by the semantic description of interfaces. This improves further flexibility and reusability of BPEL processes. The approach supports flexibility of the functions dimension of WS compositions and may in some cases enable control flow adaptations similar to the way it is enabled by parameterized processes.

4.5 BPEL'n'Aspects

The BPEL'n'Aspects approach [4] draws on the concepts of the aspect-oriented programming (AOP) paradigm. The approach enables control flow adaptation of running workflow instances. It is a non-intrusive approach, which means that the original process models are kept unchanged, and using the approach only the actual execution of each of the instances of a model are adapted as needed. The analogy used to enable the approach follows the AOP paradigm, which postulates that upon events of a specified type additional functionality, which has not been part of the

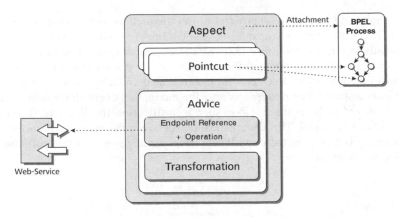

Fig. 5. Aspects in the BPEL'n'Aspects approach [19]

original code, can be executed or weaved into the control flow of the original program. Following this analogy we treat the BPEL processes as the original programs that are executed on BPEL engines; the BPEL engines interpret the BPEL process models and publish navigation events. WSs implement functionalities and can be treated as the functionalities to be weaved in upon a notified navigation event. Similarly the WSs are the advices in AOP terms (see Figure 5). An aspect is specified as a WS-Policy and references the Web Service (advice) that will represent the additional functionality (i.e. inserted activity).

An aspect also specifies upon which event in the process navigation the WS should be executed by means of the so-called pointcut and advice type (before, after and instead). Aspects can also be used to modify the value of variables or transition conditions on links. The aspects/WS-Policies are attached to the workflow models and/or process instances using WS-PolicyAttachment [8] (see Figure 6). This serves the better configurability of the approach and allows for combining any aspect definition with any workflow model.

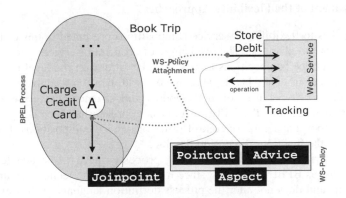

Fig. 6. A BPEL'n'Aspects example [19]

The implementation of the approach follows the architecture presented in Figure 7. A BPEL engine that is capable of publishing navigation events is needed. Additionally, a custom controller [32] (Khalaf & Karastoyanova & Leymann, 2007) implements the functionality of the weaver. It is responsible of including the additional functionality for each process instance as defined by the aspects attached to that process instance. The weaver lets only the navigation events for which there is an aspect deployed to be notified. Upon such a notification the WS referenced in the aspect advice is invoked. This communication (between the process instances and the WSs/advices) is based on the publish/subscribe paradigm and in this particular case uses WS-Notification.

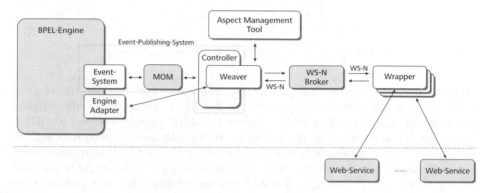

Fig. 7. Architecture of the infrastructure implementing the BPEL'n'Aspects approach [19]

The BPEL'n'Aspects approach improves the modularity and configurability of service compositions, while maintaining the standardization endeavor of the WS technology as a whole, and supports both model evolution and ad-hoc changes in service compositions in a non-intrusive manner. The approach tackles major drawbacks of other flexibility approaches; for further references please consider [28].

4.6 Assessment of the Flexibility Approaches

The approaches to flexibility of service compositions presented in this chapter enable different types of changes. The exchange of concrete services/ports during the execution of service compositions allows for adaptations on the level of functions in processes on per-instance basis. The functions dimension can be modified with respect to the port types used on both models and instances using the approach of process parameterization. The BPEL'n'Aspects approach has been designed with the purpose to support adaptation of control flows of service compositions. It can also be used to render the functions dimension flexible.

In the scenarios where existing running processes need to be adapted, the best approach to use is BPEL'n'Aspects, since it utilizes existing technology and standard specifications and does not alter the process definition language. It however requires extending the execution environment but all the needed extensions leverage existing very well known technologies and concepts like the WS stack and publish/subscribe.

The rest of the approaches are based on changes in the process definition language and hence imply more changes to the execution engine.

We support the same recommendations in the case of scientific experiments, since changes like including or deleting activities/tasks, exchanging failing service implementations and selecting alternative implementations of computational tasks are required for enabling the life cycle of scientific experiments as perceived by scientists.

5 Summary

In this work we presented an overview of current research in the area of supporting scientific experimenting using conventional workflows. The life cycle of scientific experiments and how it compares to the life cycle of conventional workflows has been described. Based on this requirements on the supporting infrastructure for scientific computing have been derived. Some of the requirements can be addressed by existing techniques from conventional workflows, among which are the approaches for (domain-specific) workflow modeling, parallelization of work using the concept of workflow instances, flexibility and others. These still need some extensions to enable a full-fledged support for scientific experimenting, scientific workflows and simulations.

Acknowledgements

The author would like to thank Mirko Sonntag, Katharina Görlach, Michael Reiter, Polina Malets, Rania Khalaf, Ingo Weber, Frank Leymann for the fruitful discussions. Thanks also go to my colleagues at IAAS and many SimTech [44] researchers at the University of Stuttgart.

References[1]

1. OASIS: Web Services Business Process Execution Language Version 2.0. OASIS Standard (2007), http://docs.oasis-open.org/wsbpel/2.0/OS/wsbpel-v2.0-OS.html
2. Weerawarana, S., Curbera, F., Leymann, F., Storey, T., Ferguson, D.F.: Web Services Platform Architecture: SOAP, WSDL, WS-Policy, WS-Addressing, WS-BPEL, WS-Reliable Messaging, and More. Prentice Hall, Englewood Cliffs (2005)
3. W3C: Web Services Description Language (WSDL) Version 2.0 Part 0: Primer (2007), http://www.w3.org/TR/2007/REC-wsdl20-primer-20070626/
4. Karastoyanova, D., Leymann, F.: BPEL'n'Aspects: Adapting Service Orchestration Logic. In: Proceedings of the 7th International Conference on Web Services, ICWS 2009 (2009)
5. Leymann, F., Roller, D.: Production Workflow: Concepts and Techniques. Prentice Hall, Englewood Cliffs (2000)

---

[1] Some of the references are to be considered as additional literature and are not explicitly referenced in the work.

6. Reichert, M., Dadam, P.: Adeptflex – Supporting Dynamic Changes of Workflows Without Losing Control. Journal of Intelligent Information Systems 10(2) (1998)
7. Charfi, A., Mezini, M.: Aspect-Oriented Web Service Composition. In (LJ) Zhang, L.-J., Jeckle, M. (eds.) ECOWS 2004. LNCS, vol. 3250, pp. 168–182. Springer, Heidelberg (2004)
8. W3C: Web Services Policy 1.5 – Attachment. W3C Recommendation (2007), http://www.w3.org/TR/2007/REC-ws-policy-attach-20070904/
9. Wiselka, M.: Erweiterung einer AOP-fähigen BPEL Engine um die Kompensation von eingewobenen Aktivitäten. Diploma Thesis No. 2905, University of Stuttgart (2009)
10. Niemöller, J., Levenshteyn, R., Freiter, E., Vandikas, K., Quinet, R., Fikouras, I.: Aspect Orientation for Composite Services in the Telecommunication Domain. In: Proceedings of 7th International Joint Conference ICSOC-Service Wave (2009)
11. Charfi, A.: Aspect-Oriented Workflow Languages: AO4BPEL and Applications, Fachbereich Informatik, TU Darmstadt, PhD Thesis (2007)
12. Courbis, C., Finkelstein, A.: Towards Aspect Weaving Applications. In: Proceedings of ICSE (2005)
13. Baresi, L., Guinea, S.: Towards Dynamic Monitoring of WS-BPEL Processes. In: Benatallah, B., Casati, F., Traverso, P. (eds.) ICSOC 2005. LNCS, vol. 3826, pp. 269–282. Springer, Heidelberg (2005)
14. Baresi, L., Guinea, S.: A Dynamic and Reactive Approach to the Supervision of BPEL Processes. In: Proceedings of the 1st India Software Engineering Conference, ISEC (2008)
15. van der Aalst, W.M.P., Jablonski, S.: Dealing with workflow change: identification of issues and solutions. International Journal of Computer Systems Science and Engineering 15(5) (2000)
16. van der Aalst, W., van Hee, K.: Workflow Management. Model, Methods and Systems. MIT Press, Cambridge (2002)
17. Chappell, D.: Enterprise Service Bus. O'Reilly Media, Inc., Sebastopol (2004)
18. Czajkowski, K., et al.: From Open Grid Services Infrastructure to WS-Resource Framework: Refactoring & Evolution. Global Grid Forum Draft Recommendation (2004)
19. Emmerich, W., Butchart, B., Chen, L., Wassermann, B., Price, S.: Grid Service Orchestration Using the Business Process Execution Language (BPEL). Journal of Grid Computing 3, 283–304 (2005)
20. Foster, I.: What is the Grid? - a three point checklist. GRIDtoday 1 (2002), http://www.Gridtoday.com/02/0722/100136.html
21. Foster, I., Kesselman, C.: The Grid 2: Blueprint for a New Computing Infrastructure. Morgan Kaufmann Publishers, San Francisco (2004)
22. Fox, G.C., Gannon, D.: Workflow in Grid Systems. Concurrency and Computation: Practice and Experience 18, 1009–1019 (2006)
23. Gannon, D.: A Service Architecture for eScience Grid Gateways. In: Grid Computing, High-Performance and Distributed Applications, GADA 2007 (2007)
24. Gehlert, A., Hielscher, J., Danylevych, O., Karastoyanova, D.: Online Testing, Requirements Engineering and Service Faults as Drivers for Adapting Service Compositions. In: Proceedings of MONA+ at ServiceWave (2008)
25. Kaye, D.: Loosely Coupled: The Missing Pieces of Web services. RDS Press (2003)
26. Karastoyanova, D., Leymann, F.: Making scientific applications on the grid reliable through flexibility approaches borrowed from service compositions. In: Antonopoulos, et al. (eds.) Handbook of research on P2P and grid systems for service-oriented computing: Models, methodologies and applications, Information Science Publishing, United Kingdom (2009)

27. Karastoyanova, D., Van Lessen, T., Nitzsche, J., Wetzstein, B., Wutke, D., Leymann, F.: Semantic Service Bus: Architecture and Implementation of a Next Generation Middleware. In: Proceedings of the 2nd International Workshop on Services Engineering (SEIW) 2007, in conjunction with ICDE (2007)
28. Karastoyanova, D.: Enhancing Flexibility and Reusability of Web Service Flows through Parameterization. PhD Thesis. TU-Darmstadt, Shaker Verlag (2006)
29. Karastoyanova, D., et al.: Parameterized BPEL Processes: Concepts and Implementation. In: Dustdar, S., Fiadeiro, J.L., Sheth, A.P. (eds.) BPM 2006. LNCS, vol. 4102, pp. 471–476. Springer, Heidelberg (2006)
30. Karastoyanova, D., Houspanossian, A., Cilia, M., Leymann, F., Buchmann, A.: Extending BPEL for Run Time Adaptability. In: Proceeding of EDOC (2005)
31. Keller, A., Badonnel, R.: Automating the Provisioning of Application Services with the BPEL4WS Workflow Language. In: Sahai, A., Wu, F. (eds.) DSOM 2004. LNCS, vol. 3278, pp. 15–27. Springer, Heidelberg (2004)
32. Khalaf, R., Karastoyanova, D., Leymann, F.: Pluggable Framework for Enabling the Execution of Extended BPEL Behavior. In: Proceedings of the 3rd ICSOC International Workshop on Engineering Service-Oriented Application: Analysis, Design and Composition (WESOA 2007). Springer, Heidelberg (2007)
33. van Lessen, T., Nitzsche, J., Dimitrov, M., Konstantinov, M., Karastoyanova, D., Cekov, L.: An Execution Engine for Semantic Business Process. In: 2nd International Workshop on Business Oriented Aspects concerning Semantics and Methodologies in Service-oriented Computing (SeMSoC), in conjunction with ICSOC (2007)
34. Leymann, F.: The (Service) Bus: Services Penetrate Everyday Life. In: Benatallah, B., Casati, F., Traverso, P. (eds.) ICSOC 2005. LNCS, vol. 3826, pp. 12–20. Springer, Heidelberg (2005)
35. Leymann, F.: Choreography for the Grid: towards fitting BPEL to the Resource Framework: Research Articles. Journal of Concurrency and Computation: Practice & Experience 18, 1201–1217 (2006)
36. Leymann, F., Roller, D.: Production Workflow: Concepts and Techniques. Prentice Hall PTR, Englewood Cliffs (1999)
37. Mietzner, R., Karastoyanova, D., Leymann, F.: Business Grid: Combining Web services and the Grid. In: Jensen, K., van der Aalst, W.M.P. (eds.) Transactions on Petri Nets. LNCS, vol. 5460, pp. 136–151. Springer, Heidelberg (2009)
38. Nitzsche, J., van Lessen, T., Karastoyanova, D., Leymann, F.: BPEL light. In: Alonso, G., Dadam, P., Rosemann, M. (eds.) BPM 2007. LNCS, vol. 4714, pp. 214–229. Springer, Heidelberg (2007)
39. OASIS Web services Resource Framework (WSRF) TC (2008),
    http://www.oasis-open.org/committees/documents.php?
    wg_abbrev=wsrf
40. Sonntag, M., Karastoyanova, D.: Next Generation Interactive Scientific Experimenting Based On The Workflow Technology. In: 21st IASTED International Conference on Modelling and Simulation (2010)
41. Sonntag, M., Karastoyanova, D., Leymann, F.: The Missing Features of Workflow Systems for Scientific Computations. In: Proceedings of the 3rd Grid Workflow Workshop, GWW (2010)
42. Sonntag, M., Görlach, K., Karastoyanova, D., Leymann, F., Reiter, M.: Process Space-based Scientific Workflow Enactment. International Journal of Business Process Integration and Management (IJBPIM) Special Issue on Scientific Workflows 5(1), 32–44 (2010)

43. Sonntag, M.: BPEL4Pegasus Demonstration Video (2010),
    http://www.iaas.uni-stuttgart.de/institut/mitarbeiter/
    sonntag/indexE.php#videos
44. SimTech Cluster of Excellence at the University of Stuttgart:
    http://www.simtech.uni-stuttgart.de/
45. Ludaescher, B., et al.: Scientific workflows: Business as usual? In: Dayal, U., Eder, J.,
    Koehler, J., Reijers, H.A. (eds.) Business Process Management. LNCS, vol. 5701, pp. 31–
    47. Springer, Heidelberg (2009)
46. Altintas, I., et al.: Kepler: An extensible system for design and execution of scientific
    workflows. In: Proc. International Conf. on Scientific and Statistical Database
    Management (2004)
47. Churches, D., et al.: Programming scientific and distributed workflow with Triana
    services. In: Concurrency and Computation: Practice and Experience. Special Issue on
    Scientific Workflows (2005)
48. Oinn, T., et al.: Taverna: Lessons in creating a workflow environment for the life sciences.
    Concurrency and Computation: Practice and Experience 18(10), 1067–110 (2006)
    doi:10.1002/cpe.993
49. Deelman, E., et al.: Pegasus: Mapping scientific workflows onto the grid. In: Proc. of 2nd
    European AcrossGrids Conf., pp. 11–20. Springer, Heidelberg (2004)
50. Mietzner, R., Leymann, F.: Towards Provisioning the Cloud: On the Usage of Multi-
    Granularity Flows and Services to Realize a Unified Provisioning Infrastructure for SaaS
    Applications. In: Proceedings of the International Congress on Services, SERVICES
    (2008)
51. Reimann, P.: Optimization of BPEL/SQL Flows in Federated Database Systems, Diploma
    Thesis No. 2744 (2008)
52. Wieland, M., Görlach, K., Schumm, D., Leymann, F.: Towards Reference Passing in Web
    Service and Workflow-based Applications. In: Proceedings of the 13th IEEE Enterprise
    Distributed Object Conference, EDOC 2009 (2009)
53. Benzing, A., Koldehofe, B., Rothermel, K.: Distributed Diagnostic Simulations for the
    Smart Grid. Accepted Poster at the 1st International Conference on Energy-Efficient
    Computing and Networking: E-Energy (2010)

Peer-to-Peer Web Search:
Euphoria, Achievements, Disillusionment,
and Future Opportunities

Gerhard Weikum

Max-Planck Institute for Informatics
Saarbruecken, Germany
weikum@mpi-inf.mpg.de

Abstract. The peer-to-peer (P2P) computing paradigm has been very successful like file sharing in Internet-wide communities (e.g., Gnutella, BitTorrent) or IP telephony (e.g., Skype). P2P systems promise perfect scalability from few peers to many millions, and resilience to failures, dynamic variability, and even misbehaving peers with egoistic or even malicious behavior. None of these salient properties requires any global planning, administration, or control; so P2P systems are completely self-organizing.

Web search seems to be a perfect match for P2P architectures. The Web has naturally distributed data, spread across the entire Internet, as opposed to artificially hosting all content by a centralized search engine. For user-provided contents in Web 2.0 communities, consideration of the content ownership, the autonomy of users, and the individualized control of privacy would also suggest decentralized solutions with many peers. Using the combined power and knowledge of millions of users and their computers could offer a more informative and pluralistic view of the world's information. A P2P search engine could benefit from the intellectual input – bookmarks, queries, clicks – of a large user community, without undue risks about privacy or censorship, because users can gather logs on their own computers and control further sharing and aggregation by their individual policies. These potential benefits have motivated a wealth of exciting research on algorithms and systems for P2P Web search. This paper gives a brief overview on the last decade's research achievements along these lines.

Despite all these intriguing promises and notwithstanding the impressive success of simpler file-sharing applications, P2P approaches to Web search or Web 2.0 services did not make a significant impact on the practical deployment side. The wave of P2P euphoria in academic research was followed by a phase of disillusionment about the lack of business models and user incentives. This paper discusses these shortcomings, and points out new opportunities for the P2P paradigm to play a more successful role in future Web applications.

1 Promises and Euphoria

Peer-to-peer (P2P) systems [38] aim to provide *scalable* and *self-organizing* ways of loosely coupling thousands or millions of computers in order to jointly achieve some global functionality. In the last decade, very successful systems of this kind have been built. Most notably, these include file-sharing networks such as Gnutella or BitTorrent,

K. Sachs, I. Petrov, and P. Guerrero (Eds.): Buchmann Festschrift, LNCS 6462, pp. 195–208, 2010.

and IP telephony like Skype and other collaborative messaging services. They organize peers in so-called *overlay networks* on top of the standard Internet infrastructure, and use various forms of *epidemic dissemination ("bounded flooding")* and distributed data structures like *distributed hash tables (DHTs)*. The basic functionality that underlies many of these systems is the distributed and dynamic maintenance of a dictionary with efficient support for exact-match key lookups. A key property of P2P systems is that there should be "no centralized anything": data, computation, control, and administration should be *fully decentralized* and preserve the autonomy of the participating peers. The latter implies high dynamics, as peers may join or leave the network without prior notice.

Web search is not a "naturally born" P2P application, as it requires much richer functionality than exact-match lookups. Keyword queries over Web contents combine multiple dimensions of a very-high-dimensional data space in an ad hoc manner so that standard multi-dimensional data structures are not applicable, and they require ranking of query results based on statistics about local and global keyword frequencies. Thus, P2P Web search cannot be implemented as a straightforward application of a P2P file-sharing network. On the other hand, it is extremely intriguing to build Web search in a P2P manner for various reasons:

- **Naturally distributed contents.** First, the producers and owners of Web pages are widely distributed and autonomous. Thus, the standard approach of crawling the Web and collecting all pages in a central site for a global index and centralized search engine is actually unnatural, but has advantages regarding system management and commercial services (e.g., query-specific advertisements and the monitoring of click-through rates).
- **User behavior at individual and community level.** Second, user queries and clicks can be locally observed on the user's computer for personalized search with the user staying in control (e.g., for physical deletion of logged activities), whereas a centralized collection of all this user information may be perceived as a potential privacy risk. On the other hand, whenever users are willing to release specific parts of their personal information, possibly in aggregated or anonymized form, this data could be a great asset in exploiting community behavior – bookmarks, tags, clicks, etc. – at massive scale without committing to a large centralized provider.
- **Computing power and energy.** Third, when a P2P network succeeds in attracting millions of peers, the total computing power would vastly exceed the performance capacity of the data centers of today's major search engines and could facilitate advanced forms of natural-language processing or machine learning for deeper analysis and enhanced indexing of Web contents. Moreover, although the energy-efficiency of many small computers is clearly worse than that of a high-end-engineered data center, the fact that many small computers across the world are continuously running with substantial idle times could still potentially yield enormous energy savings and reduce environmental damage.
- **Pluralism and political dimension.** Finally, but perhaps even more importantly, a P2P Web search engine could also facilitate pluralism in informating users about

Internet contents, which is crucial in order to preclude the formation of information-resource monopolies, the biased visibility of content from economically powerful sources, and politically motivated censorship.

Motivated by these compelling expectations, there was a euphoric wave of research projects on P2P search in the last decade. Many of them focused on algorithmic building blocks, but quite a few actually built full-fledged systems (e.g., [7,12,19,28,31,35], see also [38] for further literature) that could, in principle, be deployed at Internet scale. In recent years, it was also recognized that *Web 2.0 communities*, with their user-provided and richly interlinked contents, would be a natural fit for P2P approaches. For example, one could combine Web search with recommendations derived from social networks in the modern cyber-world. However, despite this intriguing potential, today's Web and Web 2.0 solutions are more centralized than ever: Web search is firmly in the hands of three "mega-providers", and the market for social-network providers has also evolved towards a very small number of big commercial players.

This paper reviews the research achievements on P2P Web search, and discusses why the P2P paradigm did nonetheless not have any significant impact on Web solutions and business practice. On the optimistic side, the paper also speculates on future opportunities for the P2P paradigm.

2 Technical Problems

Approaches to P2P Web search are reminiscent of earlier work on *distributed information retrieval (IR)*, most notably, various kinds of metasearch engines where queries are routed to judiciously chosen search providers [9,15,25]. However, the P2P setting is much more challenging regarding the enormous *scale* of the underlying data sources, the *dynamics* of the system, and the *autonomy* of the individual peers.

We assume that every peer has a powerful local search engine, with its own crawler (or other means of content organization such as photo albums), indexer, and query processor. Such a peer can compile its own content from thematically focused crawls or by organizing user's personal data, and make this content available in a P2P overlay network. This entails the issue of how to best connect a peer with other peers, using either a *structured overlay*, e.g., based on DHTs, or *unstructured overlay*, e.g., with epidemic dissemination in bounded neighborhoods. Search requests issued by a peer can first be executed locally, on the peer's locally indexed content. When the recall of the local search result is unsatisfactory, the query can be forwarded to a small set of other peers that are expected to provide thematically relevant, high-quality and previously unseen results. Deciding on this set of target peers is the *query routing* problem in a P2P search network, also known as "collection selection" in IR terminology. Subsequently, the actual search on the chosen target peers requires efficient algorithms for *distributed top-k query processing*. Search results are then returned by different peers and need to be meaningfully merged, which entails specific problems for *result ranking*. Both query routing and result ranking can build on various forms of *distributed statistics*, computed in a decentralized way and aggregated and disseminated in a scalable P2P manner (using compact synopses such as Bloom filters or hash sketches and leveraging a DHT infrastructure).

3   Achievements

3.1   Self-organizing Overlay Networks

Peer-to-peer overlay networks should have various good properties, that are algorithmically guaranteed at least with high probability. These include the *efficiency* of basic operations like searching for a key or inserting a new key-value pair, all of which should have worst-case run-times that are logarithmic in the network size. The desiderata also include *resilience to peer failures*, and smoothly coping with the potentially *high dynamics of load, data, and network structure*, including the so-called "churn" problem that arises when many peers join or leave the P2P system. All this should be *scalable*, so that with a growing number of peers the same performance and availability levels can be guaranteed at every scale and with near-perfect load balancing, and it should be *self-organizing*, meaning that the system never needs to resort to external intervention by a human administrator.

Structured overlays based on *distributed hash tables (DHTs)* are the best known approaches to satisfy these requirements; the *Chord* and *Pastry* systems fall into this category [39,36]. Their principle is to hash searchable keys onto peer identifiers organized as a ring or other suitable topology. Then any peer can initiate a search request, and small routing tables of logarithmic size at every peer are sufficient to reach the key (or find out that it does not exist in the overall network) in a logarithmic number of message-forwarding steps. In case of peer failures or churn, the overlay network is self-repairing by adjusting the routing tables. The load across peers is always kept balanced (except for unavoidable minor fluctuations). For faster average access time and high availability in the presence of transient failures, data items can be easily replicated onto multiple peers. The hash-based organization ensures that failure probabilities are independent among the replica holders of an item, and the replication mechanism can be seamlessly integrated with the DHT self-maintenance.

Building simple *Web search and IR functionality* on top of a DHT is relatively straightforward. Every term that can be used in a keyword query is treated as a key for the DHT. This can include words, word stems, but also bi-grams (two successive words), variable-length phrases like names of people, organizations, locations, songs, etc. The data item associated with such a key can be either a set of Web pages or other forms of documents, or it can be an inverted list for the given term, that is, a list of pointers to the documents that contain the term. In the former case, the documents are spread across all peers of the network; in the latter case, only the inverted lists are spread and the documents themselves can stay at their "native" location, usually the peer of the data owner. Both cases are easily supported by the DHT infrastructure. However, queries with multiple terms entail advanced query processing with multiple DHT operations with various degrees of freedom for query optimization. Moreover, this approach by itself does not support any statistics-based ranking of search results. While some form of scores can be easily stored in the entries of an inverted list, their interpretation and aggregation over multiple lists is a separate issue (see below) and not directly supported by the DHT.

Unstructured overlays are an alternative to the DHT-based architectures. Typically, peers are connected into a *random graph* with $O(\log n)$- or even $O(1)$-bounded degrees (i.e., incident edges per node). Instead of truly random graphs (in the Erdös-Renyi sense), some randomized form of graph construction may be used, and nodes are dynamically re-wired to cope with failures and churn. Ideally, the overlay would form a so-called expander graph, for which the diameter, and thus maximum number of message hops, is guaranteed to be logarithmic in the network size (with high probability). [24] has shown how to achieve this objective in a fully self-organizing manner. To obtain an overlay network with short diameter and high connectivity, any initial topology can be turned into a regular random graph (with the same constant degree for every node) by repeatedly performing a very inexpensive, purely local Pointer-Push&Pull operation that involves only two neighboring peers, with the peers chosen by random walks. With this method, the network provably converges to an expander graph asymptotically almost surely. Moreover, the method can easily maintain this property as the network itself evolves, simply by continuously running in the background. While this an example of an overlay with mathematically provable properties, there are alternative approaches with similar flavor that are practically superior. For example, the *BubbleStorm* method [41] uses randomly wired, regular multi-graphs where multi-edge degrees reflect the corresponing link bandwidths of the underyling physical network. This approach combines the advantages of random graphs with practical considerations of real network properties.

Searching keys in an unstructured overlay of this kind is bound to be either speculative – hoping that the keys are found in the local neighborhood – or exhaustive – potentially asking every peer in the network. More technically, bounded forms of *"epidemic flooding"*, or equivalently random walks, are used to prompt the peers in an increasingly enlarged neighborhood of the search request's origin. Therefore, worst-case execution times for queries are poor. However, the randomized nature of the search and the small diameter of the network can be harnessed to derive probabilistic guarantees for finding keys within a small number of hops with high probability. With data items replicated at random peers, the probability of unsuccessfully terminating a search for an actually existing key drops even further and is often neglibly small. With these properties, unstructured overlays are an attractive alternative to DHTs for supporting Web search and other IR tasks. It is straightforward to implement inverted-lists-driven algorithms in this setting, but also more complex operations such as partial-match search or similarity-based approximate search (e.g., tolerating mis-spellings) fit nicely with the principles of unstructured overlays. In this regard, unstructured overlays are more versatile than DHTs.

3.2   Query Routing

In unstructured overlays and also in structured overlays where peer autonomy dictates that the full content of searchable data items stays with the owner, search can usually never be exhaustive. DHT-based inverted lists and epidemic exploration should provide directives for contacting good peers that could answer a user query, but would typically limit this selection to a subset of the possible answers. This is the query routing problem, or peer selection problem. A practically viable query routing strategy needs to consider the similarity of peers in terms of their thematic profiles, the overlap of their contents, the potential relevance of a target peers collection for the given query, and also the costs of network communication and peer-specific processing loads.

Traditionally, the most important measure for assessing the benefit of a candidate target peer for a given query is the estimated relevance of the peer's overall content for the query. This standard IR measure can be estimated frequency statistics over the query's keywords (terms in IR jargon). In conventional, document-oriented, IR, these would be term frequencies (tf) within a document and the so-called inverse document frequencies (idf), the reciprocal of the global number of documents that contain a given term. In P2P IR, the estimation is based on the overall content of a peer as a whole. Instead of tf we consider the *document frequency (df)* of a peer, the total number of documents that contain the term and are in the peers collection; and instead of idf we consider the *inverse collection frequency (icf)*, which is the reciprocal of the total number of peers that contain (at least one document with) the term. These basic measures are combined into a relevance or query-specific quality score for each candidate peer. There are various models for the combined scores; among the most cited and best performing models are CORI [9], based on probabilistic IR, and statistical language models adapted to the setting of P2P collection selection [23]. The Decision-Theoretic Framework (DTF) [32] provides a unified model for incorporating quality measures of this kind as well as various kinds of cost measures. All these models are also applicable to Web 2.0 settings, especially so-called "social tagging" communities, where the concept of user annotations (tags) would take the role of terms.

Selecting peers solely by query relevance, like CORI routing, potentially wastes resources when executing a query on multiple peers with highly overlapping contents. To counter this problem, methods for estimating the overlap of two peers' contents have been developed. These estimates are then factored into an *overlap-aware query routing* [27] method by using a weighted combination of peer quality and overlap (or novelty) as ranking and decision criterion.

Query routing decisions are typically made at query run-time, when the query is issued at some peer. But the above methods involve directory lookups, statistical computations, and multi-hop messages; so it is desirable to pre-compute preferred routing targets and amortize this information over many queries. A technique for doing this is to encode a similarity-based pre-computed binary relation among peers into a *Semantic Overlay Network (SON)* [11,40]. The routing strategy would then select target peers only or preferably from the SON neighbors of the query initiator.

3.3 Distributed Top-k Query Processing

Search engines execute multi-keyword queries by aggregating pre-computed partial scores for individual keywords and computing the *top-k* results with the highest total scores (with typical k being 10 for end-user consumption, but potentially in the hundreds for search-result diversification, clustering, visualization, etc.).

For centralized systems, the algorithm of choice for processing such top-k aggregation queries is the family of threshold algorithms, also known as Fagin's TA [13]. This method operates on pre-computed index lists, one for each keyword (searchable term). Each list consists of entries that capture a score for a document or data item, and the entries are sorted in descending order of scores. TA scans the lists to which a given query refers and incrementally aggregates the scores that are seen for result candidates. Additionally, TA can look up values for promising candidates at the cost of random access to the relevant index entries. In distributed settings, however, the index lists usually reside on different peers, and the fine-grained nature of the TA algorithm then incurs high communication costs. Notwithstanding some interesting work on distributed extensions of TA [3], the cost of many small messages makes TA less attractive for P2P querying and rather suggests alternatives that operate with fewer (but larger) messages for data exchange.

A fundamental alternative to the TA paradigm is to convert the top-k query into a set of range queries with educated guesses (e.g., driven by pre-computed statistics such as histograms) for the range parameters, thus producing result candidates for subsequent aggregation and priority-queue-based ranking. For distributed settings, this approach has led to the TPUT and KLEE algorithms, which define the state of the art. TPUT [10] operates on m distributed lists in three phases: the first phase retrieves the best k candidates from each list and aggregates them; the second phase then generates range queries on all lists to retrieve all further candidates whose local values exceed or equal $1/m$ of the rank-k partially aggregated value from the first phase; the third phase performs random lookups to complete the aggregation for all retrieved candidates and safely determine the top-k result items.

The KLEE family of algorithms [26] (see also [47] for related parallel work) generalizes and improves the TPUT approach by adding statistics for predicting scores of candidates after the first phase of initial retrieval. To this end, index lists are enhanced by score-distribution histograms and a set of Bloom filters that capture the items whose scores fall into specific score intervals. Histograms and Bloom filters are very compact data structures that can be piggybacked on the result transfer of the first-phase candidate fetching, at very small extra cost. The query coordinator that is responsible for aggregating partial scores thus obtains valuable additional information about candidates that allows speculative completion of scores. In particular, the additional knowledge can be harnessed for deriving a higher threshold for the second phase's range queries and saving substantial execution and communication costs in this most expensive step. As Bloom filters are hash-based and potentially lossy, this approach leads to an approximation algorithm, but the potential error is typically negligible and can be explicitly tuned to the application needs. The KLEE family goes even one step further in its explicit control of quality/cost tradeoffs, and optionally allows omitting the final random-lookup phase and other optimizations. For large numbers of input lists and peers with highly varying performance characteristics, it is often desirable to structure the overall execution into a flexible execution tree of aggregation operators. Then, database query optimization algorithms, based on dynamic programming, can be used to compute a cost-optimal or near-optimal form of operator tree [30].

3.4 Search Result Ranking

When a query returns results that have been obtained from different peers, the scores that the peers assign to them are usually not comparable. The reason is that different peers may use different statistics, for example, for estimating the idf value of a term which is crucial for weighting the importance of different query terms, or they may even use completely different IR models. This situation leads to the problem of *result merging*. It is addressed by re-normalizing scores from different peers to make results meaningfully comparable. A variety of such methods exist in the literature, some using only the peer-specific scores and some aggregated measures about peers (e.g., the total number of documents per peer), some using sampling-based techniques, and some using approaches that first reconstruct the necessary global statistics (e.g., global document frequencies for each term) for optimal re-normalization of scores.

Web search ranking usually considers also the query-independent authority of pages as derived from link analysis, and a P2P network is a natural habitat for such *"social ratings" of authority or trust*. Link analysis algorithms such as PageRank [8] are centralized algorithms with very high memory demand. Executing them in a distributed manner would allow scaling up to even larger link graphs, by utilizing the aggregated memory of a P2P system. Various decentralized methods have been developed to this end, including a general solution to the spectral analysis of graphs and matrices, which underlies the PageRank computation.

Most of these methods assume that the underlying Web graph can be nicely partitioned among peers (e.g. [22]). In contrast, a P2P system with autonomous peers faces a situation where the Web pages and links that are known to the individual peers are not necessarily disjoint. The JXP algorithm [34] computes global authority measures such as PageRank in a decentralized P2P manner, when the Web graph is spread across autonomous peers and the peers' local graph fragments overlap arbitrarily, and peers are (a priori) unaware of other peers' fragments. With JXP, each peer computes the authority scores of the pages that it has in its local index, by locally running the standard PageRank algorithm. A page may be known and indexed by multiple peers, and these may have different scores for that same page. A peer gradually increases its knowledge about the rest of the network by meeting with other, randomly chosen, peers and exchanging information, and then recomputes the PageRank scores for its pages of interest. The local computations are very space-efficient (as they require only the local graph and the authority-score vector), and fast (as they operate on much smaller graph fragments than a server-side global PageRank computation). The scores computed by JXP provably converge to the same values that would be obtained by a centralized PageRank computation on the full Web graph.

These kinds of algorithms are also interesting for analyzing authority and reputation measures in large-scale social networks (e.g. [16]). For example, in a bookmark-sharing and social-tagging environment such as librarything.com, every user may manage her own collections (such as books), friendship lists, and friends information on her own computer or at least by means of a personalized agent governed by the user's individual policy (e.g., for visibility by other parties and for revoking information). Finding the highest-authority data items, such as books, and the most influential or most trusted users require extended forms of link analyses (over typed graphs with different kinds of entities as nodes). Then, a decentralized peer-to-peer algorithm would again be the method of choice.

3.5 Distributed Statistics

P2P search engines require statistics about data and load at both local and global levels. For example, query routing needs estimates of candidate peers' content features, their content overlap, the local and global correlations among different keywords in the query, and so on. It has turned out that this issue of distributed statistics management is a very important, overriding research topic by itself. It entails the gathering of distributed statistics, the efficient estimation of a wide variety of interesting measures, with tunable accuracy, and the dissemination of the results to peers that are in need of such statistics.

There are at least three major alternatives for going about these issues:

- *aggregation trees* that build on the topology of the overlay network for statistical computations (e.g., [45,46]),
- *gossiping algorithms* that spread partially aggregated data (e.g., partial sums) through the network, with eventual convergence to the full result (e.g., [20,41]), and
- *distributed synopses* that combine compact, often hash-based, approximations of local statistics into globally aggregated synopses (e.g., [33]).

All three approaches have strengths, but also limitations. Algorithms based on aggregation trees scale very well but typically depend on specifics of the overlay network and have limited adaptivity to high network dynamics. Gossiping algorithms are best suited for unstructured overlays; they may be wasteful on network resources when run in structured overlays. Synopses-based methods are based on probabilistic summaries like Bloom filters, hash sketches, etc. They are very elegant, but strictly bounding estimation errors in a distributed setting is not an easy issue. Both gossiping and synopses may give probabilistic results only, that is, approximate results that are correct with probability converging to one; this is usually acceptable in a large-scale, highly dynamic system.

As a concrete example for combining synopses-based statistical estimation with a DHT overlay, consider the estimation of global document frequencies in a P2P system, an IR measure that counts for each term the number of *distinct* documents that contain this term. Because of the overlap in the contents of different peers, this counting is not straightforward at all. An analogy is the species-counting problem for bird watchers: each bird watcher reports a total number of birds and her estimate of the number of distinct species that she saw. When aggregating over all bird watchers, one cannot simply sum up the observations, as several bird watchers may have seen the same flock passing by. The solution builds local Flajolet-Martin hash sketches [14], for each term on each peer, then distributes them based on the DHT's hash function, and finally aggregates the hash sketches that different peers send for the same term by a simple bit-wise union. The correctness of this approach falls out directly from the distributivity of the hash-sketch construction [6]. Similar ideas have led to approaches for capturing important correlations among search terms in large-scale P2P networks [5].

There is a wealth of efficient and scalable P2P algorithms for similar statistical tasks, within each of the three paradigms outlined above.

4 Disillusionment and Lessons Learned

The last decade's intensive research on P2P Web search has contributed many good building blocks for distributed data management in general. These are not only suitable for P2P search, but also applicable to Grid environments or Cloud computing. Examples are distributed link analyses, statistical computations, and further analytics on Web-scale datasets. In fact, the services of major Internet, Web, and Web 2.0 providers would not be possible without such scalable algorithms. However, these algorithms run inside centralized data centers: large distributed systems with hundred thousands of computers but very different from a P2P system. Overall, the P2P paradigm has not been successful in influencing practical solutions for Web search, recommendations, and analytics. None of the research prototypes made it into notable business stories, and commercial endeavors with P2P flavor did not catch on either. There are several technical and non-technical reasons for this disillusioning observation about the poor impact of P2P research: 1) manageability issues, 2) the business model, 3) misbehaving users, and 4) privacy concerns.

Manageability: The promise of self-organizing large-scale systems has not been fulfilled yet. Although the abstract arguments about self-healing and self-optimizing P2P systems are valid in principle, nobody seems to have found a practical way yet of fully realizing this potential. Components break all the time, software is buggy or corrupted by attacks, and consistently good performance with quality-of-service guarantees needs a lot of human planning and continuous care by system administrators. The manageability of centralized data centers is still much bettter and the service guarantees are much stronger and tangible than what has been achieved so far with P2P architectures where individual peers may exhibit unpredictable and arbitrary wild behavior. For simple applications like file-sharing, this is not a P2P showstopper, but for richer functionality like Web search and higher standards of user expectations about service quality, this is a serious impediment.

Business model: Every system paradigm, technology, or service that strives for impact on millions of users needs a business model, with a good balance of financing the steady-state costs of the system or service and low pricing or even free service to attract a large user community. Web search engines have gone through this before, and their business model today is clearly the income from clicks on advertisements. This model cannot be easily copied by P2P search engines for various reasons: first, the ads market is already controlled by big stakeholders, and second, it is not easy at all to intelligently place fresh ads, based on a real-time auction with many commercial advertisers, on "just the right computer" at "just the right time" in a huge and totally decentralized P2P network. Refining the second point, it is also tremendously difficult to monitor user activities in a P2P fashion and ensure that all clicks on ads are properly tracked for accounting, while eliminating clickthrough fraud. It has taken the search engine industry major investments to establish their currently successful systems. This cannot be easily mimicked by totally decentralized approach. One may wonder why and how other P2P applications have managed to become widely deployed. A speculative answer lies in the "no centralized anything" paradigm, which includes *no centralized accounting*, de facto meaning that services are free, and *no centralized legislation*. The former applies to Skype, which has attracted so many users because it is free, and the latter applies to file-sharing where a large fraction of the contents presumably is pirate copies of software, music, and movies.

Misbehaving users: Clickthrough fraud and content piracy are specific forms of misbehaving users. In P2P Web search, abnormal behavior would span a wide range from content spamming and manipulating of search results or rankings all the way to sabotaging the entire system. It is a huge challenge to counter such anomalies and attacks in a fully decentralized way. As a concrete case in point, reconsider the distributed link analysis over Web graphs or social-network graphs spread across thousands or millions of autonomous peers. Algorithms for this purpose must rely on message passing between peers, which implies the risk of cheating peers. For example, when replying to a request about locally computed PageRank values or social-authority scores, a peer may lie and return incorrect values to manipulate the prestige scores of the user or her contents. Such misbehavior cannot be easily countered. Although the research literature contains ideas and approaches to this end, there are also lower-bound theorems on the communication complexity of cheating-resilient link analysis over autonomous peers [37]. Unfortunately, these results are not exactly encouraging, as they imply that every approach with certain desirable properties needs a large number of messages and a very long time for the computation to converge to the correct outcome. This is a big showstopper unless fundamentally new approaches can be found.

Privacy concerns: More than ever, there is growing concern that centralized search engines collect enormous amounts of personal data about users' queries, clicks, reading news, joining user groups, etc. The same holds for the providers of Web 2.0 social networks. Even without any bad intentions on the side of those providers, there may be bugs, system-management accidents, or attacks or internal sabotage that could unduly release or abuse privacy-critical information. Ideally, a totally decentralized system like a P2P architecture would be much less susceptible to these kinds of risks. The argument is that every individual peer bears only a small risk because it has few data and few connections to neighboring peers. Moreover, as peers are autonomous, every user could perfectly control to what extent her data is shared with others and used for aggregation, recommendation, etc. In reality, however, it is very unclear if the masses of users really want to be bothered with fine-grained policy decisions about sharing-versus-privacy issues, possibly on a daily basis. In addition, it is unclear if the P2P software is indeed in no way corrupted. It is a grand challenge to enforce the privacy policies of millions of users in a humongous distributed system with ever-changing structure. Thus, although privacy has been an early argument in favor of the P2P approach, it still seems to be a point where P2P solutions are much weaker than centralized ones.

5   Future Opportunities

The bottom line of this paper is that research on P2P Web search has contributed technically very interesting results, but has failed to become practically deployed at large scale. Nevertheless, algorithmic building blocks are useful assets for other forms of distributed computing, including the current wave of big-data analytics on Cloud platforms. Perhaps, Web search is simply not a good application for P2P paradigm, despite

the intriguing arguments that we gave in the beginning and that led to the initial euphoria about this topic. We leave further discussion of this debatable point to the readers.
Instead, we conclude the paper with some speculation about potential killer applications
for P2P search in other settings.

First, there is a megatrend towards Web services on smart phones. This requires
location-aware search and recommendation (see, e.g., [29] and references given there).
Obviously, nearby devices could be an asset here. Also, the privacy concerns about
tracking users day and night at very precise resolutions may become super-critical, and
could trigger another wave of P2P euphoria (if business models can be worked out).

Second, instead of explicitly initiated search, many users may prefer being alerted
when something interesting happens that matches their search profiles. This calls for
publish-subscribe services, where conceptually queries are continuously running. As
such services have higher resource consumption than traditional simple search, P2P approaches may become more attractive from a cost/performance point of view [42,43,48].

Third, in a similar vein, queries themselves seem to become much more complex,
for example, by searching for entities (celebrities, diseases, drugs, etc.) and their relationships (e.g., side-effects of drugs) rather than keywords to be matched by Web
pages. Also, now that the Web exists for almost two decades, there is huge value in the
history of digital-born content, so that advanced users (e.g., sociologists, journalists,
business or media analysts, etc.) are interested in "time-travel" access to Web archives
and also in "longitudinal" analytics of the data, e.g., to analyze the people, places, and
organizations related to a politician along the time dimension. The amount of data and
the complexity of the workload exceeds the capacity of today's data centers and could
perhaps justify moving towards distributed, P2P-style architectures [1].

Fourth and last, the "Web of (Structured) Data" is finally growing at a high rate.
For example, governments and other public organizations are publishing an enormous
amount of data about their services and activities, using the RDF data model and following the principles of Linked Open Data. News providers and the entertainment industry
also seem to pursue this direction of more structured data on the Web. This will lead
to a vastly distributed set of data-centric hosts, and it is questionable whether crawling
stays a viable option of handling this data. Instead, we may well see a revival of P2P approaches to managing this richly interlinked data in a fully decentralized manner (see,
e.g., [17,18,44]).

References

1. Anand, A., Bedathur, S.J., Berberich, K., Schenkel, R., Tryfonopoulos, C.: EverLast: a distributed architecture for preserving the web. In: JCDL 2009, pp. 331–340 (2009)
2. Baeza-Yates, R.A., Castillo, C., Junqueira, F., Plachouras, V., Silvestri, F.: Challenges on
Distributed Web Retrieval. In: ICDE 2007, pp. 6–20 (2007)
3. Balke, W.-T., Nejdl, W., Siberski, W., Thaden, U.: Progressive Distributed Top k Retrieval in
Peer-to-Peer Networks. In: ICDE 2005, pp. 174–185 (2005)
4. Barroso, L.A., Dean, J., Hlzle, U.: Web Search for a Planet: The Google Cluster Architecture.
IEEE Micro 23(2), 22–28 (2003)
5. Bender, M., Ntarmos, N., Triantafillou, P., Weikum, G., Zimmer, C.: Discovering and exploiting keyword and attribute-value co-occurrences to improve P2P routing indices. In: CIKM
2006, pp. 172–181 (2006)

6. Bender, M., Michel, S., Triantafillou, P., Weikum, G.: Global Document Frequency Estimation in Peer-to-Peer Web Search. In: WebDB (2006)
7. Bender, M., Michel, S., Parreira, J.X., Crecelius, T.: P2P Web Search: Make It Light, Make It Fly. In: CIDR 2007, pp. 164–168 (2007)
8. Borodin, A., Roberts, G.O., Rosenthal, J.S., Tsaparas, P.: Link analysis ranking: algorithms, theory, and experiments. ACM Trans. Internet Techn. 5(1), 231–297 (2005)
9. Callan, J.P., Lu, Z., Bruce Croft, W.: Searching Distributed Collections with Inference Networks. SIGIR, 21–28 (1995)
10. Cao, P., Wang, Z.: Efficient top-K query calculation in distributed networks. In: PODC 2004, pp. 206–215 (2004)
11. Crespo, A., Garcia-Molina, H.: Semantic Overlay Networks for P2P Systems. In: Moro, G., Bergamaschi, S., Aberer, K. (eds.) AP2PC 2004. LNCS (LNAI), vol. 3601, pp. 1–13. Springer, Heidelberg (2005)
12. Cuenca-Acuna, F.M., Peery, C., Martin, R.P., Nguyen, T.D.: PlanetP: Using Gossiping to Build Content Addressable Peer-to-Peer Information Sharing Communities. In: HPDC 2003, pp. 236–249 (2003)
13. Fagin, R., Lotem, A., Naor, M.: Optimal aggregation algorithms for middleware. J. Comput. Syst. Sci. 66(4), 614–656 (2003)
14. Flajolet, P., Nigel Martin, G.: Probabilistic Counting Algorithms for Data Base Applications. J. Comput. Syst. Sci. 31(2), 182–209 (1985)
15. Gravano, L., Garcia-Molina, H., Tomasic, A.: GlOSS: Text-Source Discovery over the Internet. ACM Trans. Database Syst. 24(2), 229–264 (1999)
16. Guha, R.V., Kumar, R., Raghavan, P., Tomkins, A.: Propagation of trust and distrust. In: WWW 2004, pp. 403–412 (2004)
17. Harth, A., Hose, K., Karnstedt, M., Polleres, A., Sattler, K.-U., Umbrich, J.: Data summaries for on-demand queries over linked data. In: WWW 2010, pp. 411–420 (2010)
18. Hartig, O., Bizer, C., Freytag, J.C.: Executing SPARQL Queries over the Web of Linked Data
19. Kalnis, P., Ng, W.S., Ooi, B.C., Tan, K.-L.: Answering similarity queries in peer-to-peer networks. Inf. Syst. 31(1), 57–72 (2006)
20. Jelasity, M., Voulgaris, S., Guerraoui, R., Kermarrec, A.-M., van Steen, M.: Gossip-based peer sampling. ACM Trans. Comput. Syst. 25(3) (2007)
21. Kempe, D., Dobra, A., Gehrke, J.: Gossip-Based Computation of Aggregate Information. In: FOCS 2003, pp. 482–491 (2003)
22. Kempe, D., McSherry, F.: A decentralized algorithm for spectral analysis. In: STOC 2004, pp. 561–568 (2004)
23. Lu, J., Callan, J.P.: Content-based retrieval in hybrid peer-to-peer networks. In: CIKM 2003, pp. 199–206 (2003)
24. Mahlmann, P., Schindelhauer, C.: Distributed random digraph transformations for peer-to-peer networks. In: SPAA 2006, pp. 308–317 (2006)
25. Meng, W., Yu, C.T., Liu, K.-L.: Building efficient and effective metasearch engines. ACM Comput. Surv. 34(1), 48–89 (2002)
26. Michel, S., Triantafillou, P., Weikum, G.: KLEE: A Framework for Distributed Top-k Query Algorithms. In: VLDB 2005, pp. 637–648 (2005)
27. Michel, S., Bender, M., Triantafillou, P., Weikum, G.: IQN Routing: Integrating Quality and Novelty in P2P Querying and Ranking. In: Ioannidis, Y., Scholl, M.H., Schmidt, J.W., Matthes, F., Hatzopoulos, M., Böhm, K., Kemper, A., Grust, T., Böhm, C. (eds.) EDBT 2006. LNCS, vol. 3896, pp. 149–166. Springer, Heidelberg (2006)
28. Mislove, A., Gummadi, K.P., Druschel, P.: Exploiting Social Networks for Internet Search. HotNets (2006)
29. Mokbel, M.F. (ed.): Special Issue on Spatial and Spatial-temporal Databases. IEEE Data Eng. Bull. 33(2) (March 2010)

30. Neumann, T., Bender, M., Michel, S., Schenkel, R., Triantafillou, P., Weikum, G.: Distributed top-k aggregation queries at large. Distributed and Parallel Databases 26(1), 3–27 (2009)
31. Nguyen, L.T., Yee, W.G., Frieder, O.: Adaptive distributed indexing for structured peer-to-peer networks. In: CIKM 2008, pp. 1241–1250 (2008)
32. Nottelmann, H., Fuhr, N.: Comparing Different Architectures for Query Routing in Peer-to-Peer Networks. In: Lalmas, M., MacFarlane, A., Rüger, S.M., Tombros, A., Tsikrika, T., Yavlinsky, A. (eds.) ECIR 2006. LNCS, vol. 3936, pp. 253–264. Springer, Heidelberg (2006)
33. Ntarmos, N., Triantafillou, P., Weikum, G.: Distributed hash sketches: Scalable, efficient, and accurate cardinality estimation for distributed multisets. ACM Trans. Comput. Syst. 27(1) (2009)
34. Parreira, J.X., Castillo, C., Donato, D., Michel, S., Weikum, G.: The Juxtaposed approximate PageRank method for robust PageRank approximation in a peer-to-peer web search network. VLDB J. 17(2), 291–313 (2008)
35. Podnar, I., Rajman, M., Luu, T., Klemm, F., Aberer, K.: Scalable Peer-to-Peer Web Retrieval with Highly Discriminative Keys. In: ICDE 2007, pp. 1096–1105 (2007)
36. Rowstron, A.I.T., Druschel, P.: Pastry: Scalable, Decentralized Object Location, and Routing for Large-Scale Peer-to-Peer Systems. In: Guerraoui, R. (ed.) Middleware 2001. LNCS, vol. 2218, pp. 329–350. Springer, Heidelberg (2001)
37. Sozio, M., Parreira, J.X., Crecelius, T., Weikum, G.: Good Guys vs. Bad Guys: Countering Cheating in Peer-to-Peer Authority Computations over Social Networks. In: WebDB (2008)
38. Steinmetz, R., Wehrle, K.: Peer-to-Peer Systems and Applications. Springer, Heidelberg (2005)
39. Stoica, I., Morris, R., Karger, D.R., Frans Kaashoek, M., Balakrishnan, H.: Chord: A scalable peer-to-peer lookup service for internet applications. In: SIGCOMM 2001, pp. 149–160 (2001)
40. Tang, C., Xu, Z., Dwarkadas, S.: Peer-to-peer information retrieval using self-organizing semantic overlay networks. In: SIGCOMM 2003, pp. 175–186 (2003)
41. Terpstra, W.W., Kangasharju, J., Leng, C., Buchmann, A.P.: Bubblestorm: resilient, probabilistic, and exhaustive peer-to-peer search. In: SIGCOMM 2007, pp. 49–60 (2007)
42. Terpstra, W.W., Behnel, S., Fiege, L., Zeidler, A., Buchmann, A.P.: A peer-to-peer approach to content-based publish/subscribe. In: DEBS 2003 (2003)
43. Tryfonopoulos, C., Koubarakis, M., Drougas, Y.: Information filtering and query indexing for an information retrieval model. ACM Trans. Inf. Syst. 27(2) (2009)
44. Tummarello, G., Cyganiak, R., Catasta, M., Danielczyk, S., Delbru, R., Decker, S.: Sig.ma: live views on the web of data. In: WWW 2010, pp. 1301–1304 (2010)
45. van Renesse, R., Birman, K.P., Vogels, W.: Astrolabe: A robust and scalable technology for distributed system monitoring, management, and data mining. ACM Trans. Comput. Syst. 21(2), 164–206 (2003)
46. Yalagandula, P., Dahlin, M.: A scalable distributed information management system. In: SIGCOMM 2004, pp. 379–390 (2004)
47. Yu, H., Li, H.-G., Wu, P., Agrawal, D., El Abbadi, A.: Efficient Processing of Distributed Top-k Queries. In: Andersen, K.V., Debenham, J., Wagner, R. (eds.) DEXA 2005. LNCS, vol. 3588, pp. 65–74. Springer, Heidelberg (2005)
48. Zimmer, C., Tryfonopoulos, C., Weikum, G.: Exploiting correlated keywords to improve approximate information filtering. In: SIGIR 2008, pp. 323–330 (2008)

Designing Benchmarks for P2P Systems

Max Lehn[1], Tonio Triebel[2], Christian Gross[3], Dominik Stingl[3],
Karsten Saller[4], Wolfgang Effelsberg[2], Alexandra Kovacevic[3],
and Ralf Steinmetz[3]

[1] Databases and Distributed Systems,
Technische Universität Darmstadt, Germany
mlehn@dvs.tu-darmstadt.de
[2] Praktische Informatik IV,
Universität Mannheim, Germany
{triebel,effelsberg}@pi4.informatik.uni-mannheim.de
[3] KOM – Multimedia Communications Lab,
Technische Universität Darmstadt, Germany
{gross,stingl,sandra,steinmetz}@kom.tu-darmstadt.de
[4] Real-Time Systems Lab,
Technische Universität Darmstadt, Germany
karsten.saller@kom.tu-darmstadt.de

Abstract. In this paper we discuss requirements for peer-to-peer (P2P)
benchmarking, and we present two exemplary approaches to benchmarks
for Distributed Hashtables (DHT) and P2P gaming overlays. We point
out the characteristics of benchmarks for P2P systems, focusing on the
challenges compared to conventional benchmarks. The two benchmarks
for very different types of P2P systems are designed applying a common
methodology. This includes the definition of the system under test (SUT)
and particularly its interfaces, the workloads and metrics. A set of common P2P quality metrics helps to achieve a comprehensive selection of
workloads and metrics for each scenario.

1 Introduction

In the past decade, peer-to-peer (P2P) systems have become an active research
area. Originally used for file sharing applications such as Napster, P2P networks
are nowadays used for various tasks like video streaming, voice communication,
and gaming. It turned out that the different fields of applications require different types of P2P overlays. When new overlays are proposed, each group of
researchers evaluates their system based on their individual tools and methodology, counteracting a fair comparability. Hence our goal is to develop benchmarks
for P2P systems so that an unbiased comparison of different solutions can be
achieved. Due to the fact that P2P networks are tailored for different purposes,
the network architectures vary significantly. Thus it is not possible to create one
single benchmark that is capable to evaluate every kind of P2P network. Rather
it is necessary to define classes of P2P networks. Within such a class the systems

K. Sachs, I. Petrov, and P. Guerrero (Eds.): Buchmann Festschrift, LNCS 6462, pp. 209–229, 2010.

can be compared. The main challenge therefore is to understand the functionalities and interfaces of the systems that are evaluated. Based on this knowledge the classes can be defined and meaningful benchmarks can be built.

In this paper, we present exemplary benchmarking approaches for two different classes of P2P overlays. The first class are search overlays, tested using a synthetic workload on top of a minimalistic DHT interface (Section 3). DHTs are designed for large-scale applications, thus the scenario focuses on scalability (Section 4). The second class are information dissemination overlays (IDO), tested with a gaming application scenario. Unlike the DHT scenario, gaming focuses less on high scales, but rather on timing constraints which are set by a fast-paced game.

In contrast to standard benchmarks of computing systems, P2P-benchmarks have to define relevant properties of the underlay network to be reproducible. We thus propose a generic underlay model, based on commonly accepted studies on Internet node connectivity and capabilities (Section 2.4).

2 Benchmarking

The purpose of a benchmark is to quantify the performance of a system or of one of its components according to a set of quality aspects.

A useful benchmark generally should fulfill a set of basic requirements, as identified in previous work [28], [18]:

- It must be based on a workload representative of real-world applications.
- It must exercise all critical services provided by platforms.
- It must not be tuned/optimized for a specific product, i.e. it must provide a level playing field for performance comparisons.
- It must generate reproducible results.
- It must not have any inherent scalability limitations.

In the remainder of this section, we define the important terms for benchmarking and specify the quality aspects that are used for the evaluation. At the end of the section we consider issues that are specific to P2P-benchmarks and describe the underlying network model, we utilize for our benchmarks.

2.1 Terminology

System Under Test (SUT): The term System Under Test denotes the system that shall be tested or benchmarked. This system consists of several interacting components and summarizes a set of services that are offered by the service interface to a further component.

Scenario: The benchmark scenario defines the environment in which the benchmark takes place. It describes the expected functionality of the SUT and what interfaces the SUT has to provide.

Workload: The entirety of operations that are performed by the users on the SUT interface are called the *workload*. The workload specified by a benchmark can be *synthetic*, i.e., generated according to an abstracted application model. On the other hand there are *application level* workloads that are generated by real applications. A benchmark's workload is typically parametrized to be able to scale with the SUT's capabilities.

There are two common scaling dimensions in benchmarks for distributed systems (e.g., SPECjms2007 [28]), namely *horizontal* and *vertical*. Horizontal scaling affects the number of users in the system while vertical scaling affects the load generated by each user. A benchmarking system typically provides a *workload generator* component which simulates the users' behavior. The workload generator takes workload parameters as an input and operates on the SUT interface.

Metrics: To evaluate the performance of a system, it is necessary to have a set of *metrics*. Exemplary metrics are average response times, throughput, CPU consumption, or failure rates. The component that measures the system's performance according to the metrics is called *monitor*.

We differentiate between *macro metrics* and *micro metrics*. Macro metrics measure the system on its application interface level, e.g., response times of queries on a DHT. Micro metrics measure internal system aspects, e.g., routing table completeness, which help to understand *why* a system behaves a certain way. Comparing different systems using micro metrics may however be difficult due to the differences in their internal structure.

Test Procedures: In benchmarking, there are generally two basic test procedures, the *static test* and the *variation test*. The static test provides a predefined, fixed workload. Certain metrics are calculated from the system's behavior and directly account for the benchmark results. The variation test increases the load over time to push the SUT to its limits. Those limits are defined by certain QoS criteria, which are derived from system metrics (e.g., response time has to be less or equal to 2 seconds). The load is typically derived from one scalar load parameter. The benchmark result is the highest load value under which the system meets the given QoS criteria.

2.2   P2P Quality Aspects

There are certain key quality aspects that each P2P system can be evaluated for. Our benchmarks target at the quality aspects that were identified by the QuaP2P research group [3, 20].

Validity, *meaning that the system responses are complete and correct.* All responses of a P2P system must match the expected responses. The term "expected" in this context means that the results obtained from the system are logically correct and complete. The system response varies depending on the type of systems being investigated. For instance, in context of search overlays the system response is the query result obtained after injecting a query request into the overlay.

Efficiency, *defined as the ratio of performance and costs.* Performance is the ability of a system to deal with its workload to a certain degree of quality. Usually this refers to the number of operations that the system can handle in a certain amount of time or the time the system needs to perform a set of operations. The term cost means how many resources are spent while the system is dealing with a given workload.

Fairness, *meaning that both the costs for operating the system and the availability of services are distributed over the participating entities (peers) such that a given fairness criteria holds.* There can be various types of fairness criteria, depending on the system type and requirements. Typical examples are uniform distribution, capacity or resource proportional distribution, and contribution proportional distribution.

Scalability, *the quantitative adaptability of the P2P system to a changing number of entities (peers or services) in the system, while preserving validity, efficiency, and fairness.* In contrast to client/server systems where resources have to be added manually in case that the system load exceeds a given threshold, P2P systems automatically scale as new joining peers share their resources with the system. Thus, scalability in the area of P2P systems is the quantitative adaptability of the system in case of a changing number of entities (peers or services), while preserving the quality aspects validity, efficiency, and fairness.

Robustness, *the persistence of a P2P system when crucial parts of a system fail.* The definition of robustness is similar to the common understanding of fault-tolerance. Robustness is, however, broader since it examines multiple failures or the failures of the participants identified to have a crucial role in the system, while fault-tolerance is a system persistence under single parts failures. Robust systems have no single points of failure, repair themselves, and failures are not propagated through the system.

Stability, *the persistence of the P2P system under system perturbations such as intensive or frequent use of system functions.* Under heavy load or load hotspots, a stable system has to maintain its functionality. In contrast to robustness, the stability definition only refers to intended system operations and does not include failures of parts of the system.

2.3   P2P Benchmarking Specifics

P2P benchmarks have certain characteristics that distinguish them from most other benchmarks. Usually, it is assumed that the SUT is self-contained, i.e., the whole system from the lower ('physical') hardware layers up to the software layers providing the SUT interface are part of the SUT. In contrast to that, the 'physical world' of P2P systems is the Internet. The Internet, however, cannot be assumed as a part of the SUT. This would contradict the requirement of reproducibility for benchmarks, since the Internet is growing every day and thus does not represent a fixed reference. While physical underlay networks can only be reproduced in small scales, it is infeasible to build a real underlay network according to the specifications provided by the benchmark. The practical approach is to simulate (or emulate) the underlay network and to run the SUT instances in the simulation. The simulator has to fulfill certain requirements (e.g., concerning simulation granularity) which must be specified in order to reproduce the simulation environment for further benchmarks, enabling comparability of results. Since it is feasible to either implement a given network specification in a simulator or to use existing simulation tools which provide the specific underlay model, the reproducibility requirement can be fulfilled. As a result, the underlying network has to be excluded from the SUT and instead specified as a part of the benchmark scenario. The following subsection describes our proposed network model.

2.4 Underlay Model Specification

In this section, we give a brief overview about current techniques to abstract and model the network with its characteristics. Subsequently, we present the chosen solution integrated in our simulation environment and detail the connection type of the hosts to the Internet within the underlay model.

Dealing with the representation of the underlay, there exist several approaches to model the underlay which may address one or several aspects of real networks like the network topology, geographical locations, delay, jitter, or packet loss. On the one hand, current models generate network topologies based on mathematical functions (e.g., Positive-Feedback-Preference-Model [34]) or topology generators like Inet-3.0 [33], where each connection between two elements exhibits its own delay and loss probability. On the other hand, some models just focus on the estimation of delays and loss probabilities of an entire communication path between two hosts, while the details of the path in between are not considered. The latter models can utilize a lookup table to estimate the delay between two communicating hosts, as proposed by Gummadi et al. [14], or following the approach of global network positioning as introduced by [24].

Regarding the utilised underlay model for our simulations, we adopt the proposed model from Kaune et al. [17] which avoids static delays and splits the calculation of the delay between two hosts up in two different parts, as depicted in Figure 1. The static part of the delay returns the minimum delay between any two hosts based on their distance to each other in the n-dimensional space. For calculating the distance between the hosts, the embedding within the space is realized using global network positioning [24]. The data for creating the positioning and for the calculation of the delay relies on the measured data of the Macroscopic Topology Project from CAIDA [1]. The dynamic part of the delay consists of the jitter for the connection between two hosts. Out of the provided data from the PingER project [4], different jitter distributions based on the geographical positions of the hosts are derived. During a simulation, a value for the jitter between two hosts is randomly chosen from the respective distribution.

Besides the realistic and accurate calculation of delay, the model of the underlying network should also take the connection type of a host to the Internet into consideration. Thus, the utilized network model for our simulations also consists of hosts with different access types, which vary regarding their available

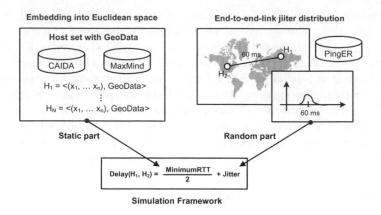

Fig. 1. The calculation of delay [17]

Table 1. OECD broadband statistics from 2009

Internet connection type	Number of subscribed connections	Average upload speed (kbit/s)	Average download speed (kbit/s)
Cable modem	81.253.021	2.269	25.474
DSL[1]	168.964.115	3.055	14.404
FTTH[2]	31.589.868	51.692	76.792

bandwidth. This feature allows for simulations focusing on the heterogeneity of hosts. As an proposal for the distribution of utilized access types, Table 1 depicts an overview about the worldwide broadband access during 2009 obtained from the OECD Broadband Portal [2]. The report lists three different broadband connection types comprising the number of subscriptions and the average upload and download speed. The presented distribution of the different connections can be used as basis for a detailed model of the simulated access types specifying their characteristics and utilization. By offering the developed model, its reuse for other simulations can be facilitated and allows for obtaining comparable results.

3   Scenario 1: Distributed Hashtable

In this section we define a basic benchmark for Distributed Hashtables (DHT) which fulfills the interface presented in Section 3.1. Our benchmark addresses two main goals. Firstly, it enables the comparability of existing DHT implementations under different workloads. Based on this comparison, it is possible to determine which DHTs are suitable for a specific application scenario stating specific workload characteristics. Secondly, by pushing DHT implementations to their performance limits, their strengths and weaknesses become visible.

3.1   SUT Interface

In our scenario we focus on distributed hashtables, supporting the two basic methods `put(key, data, lifetime)` and `get(key) -> data` for storing and retrieving a data item associated with a key. The `get` function asynchronously returns the result. It is expected to always deliver a result. If no item for the requested key is found, it returns an empty data item. In most applications the key is calculated by hashing the data item using a hash function such as MD5 or SHA-1. Each data item is stored with a maximum lifetime after which it is deleted, enabling a simple garbage collection mechanism.

3.2   Workload

For the workload generation, we assume a Wikipedia-inspired document model. We model documents with a given maximum lifetime, which are stored into the DHT and retrieved afterwards. All documents that are stored in the DHT are also stored in a global document database which is not part of the SUT. Since this benchmark is designed for simulated or emulated environments, we assume that this database can be maintained as part of the global knowledge of the simulator. The database is used for selecting documents to be queried as well as for validating results obtained from the DHT. The following parameters are considered for our model:

Number of Peers, Online Time, Persistent storage on peers. An important parameter is the number of peers. The peer's online times are determined by the churn model which is described by their online time distribution. In our workload model we assume a non-persistent storage in case that a peer goes offline, which means that its stored data is deleted.

Document Size, Popularity, Lifetime. The second parameter set is related to the documents to be stored in the DHT. We model the document size and the popularity of documents based on distribution functions derived from Wikipedia article statistics. In order to avoid a constantly growing number of documents, we introduce a document lifetime after which an article is considered to be outdated and deleted from the DHT.

Peer Activity. The third set is related to the peer activity, specifying how often a peer executes a certain type of action. We define three basic operations: creating a new document, requesting an existing document, and updating a document. Hence, it is necessary to specify an execution probability per peer for each of these operations. In addition, the time between successive operations needs to be modeled based on peer activity statistics taken from Wikipedia measurements. A grace period between the creation or update of a document before a read or update request for the same document allows the DHT to properly store the documents. The delete operation is not part of the peer activity as the deletion of articles is done automatically by the DHT in case that an article's time-to-life counter has expired.

Global Document Database. We introduce a *Global Document Database* which maintains information about all documents stored in the DHT. For each document this information comprises the document id, the document lifetime, the document store timestamp, and a hash value of the document's content. This information is needed in order to verify whether the correct version of requested document is returned by the DHT. The document database offers methods for creating, updating, and requesting a document.

Per Peer Workload Generation. The workload generation algorithm which is run by each peer works as follows. Initially an activity index is defined per peer drawn from a global activity index distribution $X_{activity}$. The activity index defines the expected value of inter-arrival times between two successive actions performed by the peer. The peer action algorithm is shown in Listing 1.

```
- select action to be performed (add, modify, read)
    based on propability
- if action = add:
  - create article from global article database
  - put article to DHT
- if action = read:
  - count read action
  - get article ID to be read from global article
      database
  - get article from DHT
  - if retrieve succeeds:
    - verify document content using hash value
    - if correct: count correct response
    - else: count incorrect response
  - else:
    - count incorrect response
- if action = update:
  - perform read action
  - if read succeeds:
    - create new version of the document from the
        global document database
    - put article to DHT
```

Listing 1. Per Peer Workload Algorithm

Load Variation Schemes. In the following different load variation schemes of the workload within the DHT scenario are explained. Each scheme covers a specific situation in a DHT lifetime each assuming a different churn behavior of the peers (times without any churn, exponential churn phase, and massive join or leave).

Scheme 0: Without Churn. Peers join the network according to join function $F_{join}(t)$ until the specified number of peers n is reached. After a silent

Table 2. Workload parameters for the DHT scenario

Variable	Description	Unit	Levels
n	Number of peers in stable state (after the join process)		$[1..\infty]$
$F_{join}(t)$	Function describing the number of peers over time during the join process		$e^{\lambda t}$
t_{silent}	Duration of the graceful phase after initial join phase	s	$[0..\infty]$
X_{time}	Peer Online Time Distribution	s	$\mathrm{Exp}(\lambda)$
$X_{activity}$	Peer Activity Distribution	s	$\mathrm{Zipf}(s)$
$p_{create},$ $p_{update},$ p_{read}	Execution probability for the actions create, update, or read		$[0,1],$ $p_{create}+p_{update}+p_{read}=1$
$X_{popularity}$	Document Popularity Distribution		$\mathrm{Zipf}(s),\ \mathrm{Exp}(\lambda)$
X_{size}	Document Size Distribution	bytes	$\mathrm{Zipf}(s),\ \mathrm{Exp}(\lambda)$
$t_{liftime}$	Document Lifetime	s	$1..\infty$
$b_{persist}$	Whether peers persist their documents while offline		$\{0,1\}$
$r_{massleave},$ $r_{masscrash}$	Ratio of leaving/crashing peers in case of a massive leave/crash		$[0,1]$
$t_{massleave},$ $t_{masscrash}$	Time after the silent period after which a massive leave/crash occurs	s	$[0..\infty]$
$r_{massjoin}$	Ratio of joining peers in case of a massive join		$[0,1]$
$t_{massjoin}$	Time after the silent period after which a massive join occurs	s	$[0..\infty]$
$t_{flashcrowd}$	Time after which the flash crowd starts	s	$[0..\infty]$
$d_{flashcrowd}$	The duration of the flash crowd	s	$[0..\infty]$
$r_{flashcrowd}$	Ratio of increased requests per peers in case of a flash crowd	s	$[0..\infty]$
$F_{request}(t)$	Function describing the variation of the inter-arrival time of per-peer actions over time.		$m * t + a$

period of t_{silent} seconds where no further join or leave of peers occurs the workload is deployed on the system. (Figure 2a)

Scheme 1: Exponential Churn. After a join phase as in Scheme 0, there is a silent period of t_{silent} seconds after which the system should be in stable state. Then, an exponential churn phase with exponentially distributed session times of the peers together with the workload is deployed on the system. (Figure 2b)

Scheme 2: Massive Leave/Crash. The third scheme covers the extreme situation of a massive leave or crash of peers. As in Scheme 1, peers join, and

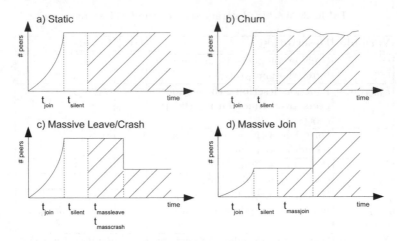

Fig. 2. DHT scenario schemes

the workload starts after a silent period. Then, after $t_{massleave}$ $(t_{masscrash})$ seconds, a massive leave (crash) with $r_{massleave}$ $(r_{masscrash})$ of leaving (crashing) peers occurs. (Figure 2c)

Scheme 3: Massive Join. Scheme 3 is similar to Scheme 2 but with joining instead of leaving or crashing peers. (Figure 2d)

Scheme 4: Flash Crowd Behavior. In this scheme, a large amount of the peers requests a specific content in a short amount of time. Based on Scheme 1, after $t_{flashcrowd}$ seconds, the flash crowd phase begins. The request frequency per peer is increased by a factor of $r_{flashcrowd}$ with a duration of $d_{flashcrowd}$ seconds.

Scheme 5: Linearly Increasing Number of Peers. Peers join according to a linear join function $F_{join}(t)$, increasing their number as long as system remains stable. The workload is deployed instantly at the beginning of the benchmark.

Scheme 6: Linearly Increasing Number of Requests. Based on Sscheme 1, the workload is deployed on the peers with a decreasing inter-arrival time as defined by the request increasing function $F_{request}(t)$.

3.3   Metrics

This section combines the load variation schemes with appropriate metrics (Table 3) to provide benchmarks for the P2P quality aspects as described in Section 2.2.

Robustness. For testing robustness, we use Scheme 2 with massively crashing peers. After $r_{masscrash}$ of the peers have crashed, the system either becomes stable again after t_r seconds or it remains unstable where the remaining peers are unable to reorganize the DHT topology. t_r is the time the system takes to return to a certain minimum acceptable QoS level. In case of our

Table 3. Metrics for the DHT scenario

Variable	Metric	Unit	Description
t_q	Average query response time	s	The time that passes between the insertion of query into the system and its response averaged over time.
q	Number of queries		The total number of all executed queries within the measurement interval.
r_+	Number of correct responses		The total number of correct responses within the measurement interval. A response is considered to be correct if and only if the right document in the latest version is returned.
r_-	Number of negative responses		The total number of incorrect responses within the measurement interval. Both invalid responses and missing responses are counted as incorrect.
S	Success ratio		The ratio of successfully executed query requests. $S = \frac{r_+}{q}$.
$\bar{S}$	Fail ratio		The ratio of failed query requests. $\bar{S} = \frac{r_-}{q}$.
t_r	Recovery time	s	The time needed by the quality metric of a system to return back to a defined QoS level after a massive perturbation of the system.
l_i	The average load on peer i	$\frac{bytes}{s}$	The bandwidth usage on peer i within the measurement interval averaged over time.
L_i	The average relative load on peer i		The bandwidth usage on peer i in relative to its maximum capacity within the measurement interval averaged over time.
μ_l	The average load on the overall system	$\frac{bytes}{s}$	The average bandwidth usage of all peers. $\mu_l = \frac{1}{n} \sum l_i$
μ_L	The average relative load on the overall system		The average relative bandwidth usage of all peers. $\mu_L = \frac{1}{n} \sum L_i$

DHT scenario the QoS level is defined by the query time t_q and the success ratio S. For instance, the average query time should always be below 2 seconds and the query success ratio should be above a threshold of 0.95 ($t_q < 2 \wedge S > 0.95$).

Efficiency. The efficiency of the system is measured using Scheme 1 where peers join and leave the system according to an exponential churn model. Furthermore, a typical workload is applied on the DHT. Efficiency is defined as the quotient of performance and costs. In case of a DHT, the performance is the average query response time t_q. Costs are defined as the average load μ_l on the system for solving the query requests. In order to calculate how efficient the system is the average query time is divided by the average system load.

Validity. In order to benchmark the validity of the results returned by the DHT we again consider a typical churn influenced environment as described in Scheme 1 and measure the success ratio S.

Fairness. Benchmarking fairness is done by applying Scheme 1 and measuring the average load l_i on each peer. For the purpose of simplification in our DHT scenario the distribution of load is considered to be fair if the load is distributed equally over all peers. More sophisticated definitions of fairness can be taken into account, e.g., a capacity-proportional definition of fairness where load has to be distributed according to the capacities of the peers. To calculate the degree of fairness the standard deviation of the relative load over all peers is calculated as $\sigma_L = \frac{1}{n-1} \sum (L_i - \mu_L)^2$.

Stability. To test the stability of a DHT, we use Scheme 1 with an increasing exponential churn factor. The stability is measured by the maximum churn level under which the query reponse times t_q and success ratio S fulfill the required QoS levels.

Scalability. The scalability of a DHT is tested by increasing the workload on the system vertically (number of request) or horizontally (number of peers) according to Schemes 5 and 6 respectively. In both cases we measure the maximum scale up to which the query response times t_q and success ratio S fulfill the required QoS levels.

4   Scenario 2: Massively Multiplayer Online Game

The area of P2P Massively Multiplayer Online Games (P2P MMOG) is much more complex and less standardized than the field of DHTs. Several groups have been doing research in P2P MMOGs in the last ten years, focusing on various aspects. Those can be categorized to six main issues [13]:

Interest Management. In an MMOG, every player has his own personal view on the game world, depending on his current state, most importantly his location. That view defines what parts of the world he can see and what events he can perceive. Interest management (IM) decides which information is necessary for each player to build his personal view of the world. The *area* *of interest* (AOI), typically centered at the player's position and bounded by his *vision range* (VR), defines the region within which the player needs to receive game event information.

Game Event Dissemination. The game event dissemination system has to ensure that each player receives all relevant game events within his AOI. Real-time games require low latencies in the event dissemination to keep the players' views as fresh as possible. Since the AOI is bound to game world positions, the dissemination systems are typically based on game world proximity. The task can thus also be formulated as a spatial publish/subscribe model.

NPC Host Allocation. Many games have the concept of so-called *non-player characters* (NPC) which are game entities controlled by scripts and/or artificial intelligence and which interact with the human players in the game. Since there is no central server the program controlling an NPC has to run on some peer. The assignment of NPC routines and states to peers and, if necessary, their relocation to alternative peers is part of the NPC Host Allocation.

Game State Persistence. Any object in the game world that is not directly associated to a player has to be kept persistent and consistent. The object state must be replicated to one or more peers in the network, and leaving peers must transfer their objects to others. An important requirement specific to games is that operations on game objects must not induce high latencies since the game cannot be paused until the operation is complete.

Cheating Mitigation. P2P games require special mechanisms for cheating prevention and reaction. There is no central server with a full view on the whole game world, thus the cheating mitigation algorithms must work in a decentralized manner without access to the complete game state.

Incentive Mechanisms. A P2P system lives from the resources provided by the participants. Those resources include network bandwidth, CPU cycles, and storage capacity. Incentive mechanisms make sure that every participant has to provide a certain amount of resources and prohibit free-riders.

In our scenario we concentrate on the first two aspects, Interest Management and Game Event Dissemination. While NPC Host Allocation and particularly Game State Persistence are topics for a future benchmark, the performance of cheating mitigation mechanisms is hardly quantifiable. Incentive mechanisms are a general topic on P2P systems, and P2P MMOG do not make special demands on these mechanisms. Therefore, they can be analyzed in separate scenarios.

4.1   SUT Interface

A typical MMOG information dissemination overlay (IDO) integrates the two issues Interest Management and Game Event Dissemination. As introduced above, Interest Management in an MMOG is based on an AOI defined by the vision range. The two systems VON [15] and pSense [29] act as references for our scenario. Both VON and pSense interpret the vision range as a (more or less constant) radius and the AOI as a circle on the 2D plane of the game world.

The overlay network topology is constructed locally by each player (i.e., each peer) using the AOI radius and the relative positions of surrounding players in the game world. Thus, an important aspect of MMOG IDOs is their awareness of player positions in the game world.

It is the purpose of the IDO to disseminate the game events generated by each player to all other players in whose AOI he currently is. Those events include first and foremost the player's movements (or, more generally, his position), but also other game-specific activities such as firing a missile. Since the IDO is aware of game world positions but should still be generic, it is necessary to split the disseminated information into position updates, which have semantics known by the IDO, and game-specific data that is opaque to the IDO. Besides the dissemination to the whole set of interested nodes, it should be possible to send messages to single nodes.

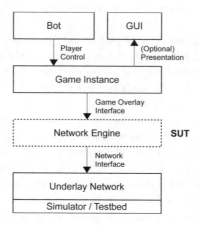

Fig. 3. The abstract game architecture

The core of our architecture (Fig. 3) consists of the *game instance* containing the local game logic and the *network engine* managing the network communication. From the benchmarking point of view, the network engine implements the SUT and the game instance applies the workload.

Based on the given requirements, our API connecting the local game logic and the network component comprises the following concepts:

- The network engine regularly pulls the local player's state (particularly its current game world coordinates) from the game instance and disseminates them. Depending on the particular IDO, the position information is also used to build the overlay topology. The pull and dissemination frequency is chosen by the network engine so that it can adapt the generated update traffic when necessary (e.g., in case of congestion).
- Neighboring players within the AOI and their positions are pushed by the network engine to the game instance whenever new information is available.

- Game actions other than player movements are pushed by the game instance to the network engine at a time when they occur, to be disseminated or to be sent to a single player. Those messages do not have a semantic meaning to the network engine; they have to be delivered reliably and without modification.

4.2 Workload

A synthetic workload appears infeasible for a gaming scenario. Games have a relatively complex and unstandardized network functionality which makes it difficult to collect measurements to derive representative workloads. While there are plenty of studies analyzing and modeling the network traffic generated by (massively) multiplayer games (e.g., [6], [7], [30]), there are only a few trying to characterize player behavior on a game activity level, such as [31].

Network traffic models of online games, since they deal with the traffic *below* the game's network component, do not contain enough information to model the workload *on top of* that component. And player behavior models or traces from real matches cannot realistically represent the game workload on the various network implementations. This is because of the high degree of interactivity, which introduces feedback loops making the player's behavior depend on the network's properties (such as message delay).

For the given reasons, we propose a workload generation process that directly originates from the game mechanics specifying the player's capabilities. For the purpose of reproducible workload generation, all players are controlled by autonomous players (*bots*) which are designed just with the goal of successfully playing the game. With this approach we can model the whole degree of interactivity which, of course, is also influenced by the SUT properties.

Gameplay Scenario. Planet $\pi4$ [32], the game designed as a workload reference, is a spaceship first-person shooter (FPS). The game scenario consists of n players. Each player is assigned to one of m teams within which they cooperate and compete with the other teams. The game world is a 3D space in which the spaceships can freely move in all directions.

Certain strategic *points of interest* (POI) are randomly scattered within a bounded region of the game world. Specifically, a POI is a base that can be captured by the teams. For each base that a team possesses, it gains game points and/or other rewards such as weapons and energy. Once captured, a team has to defend a base by keeping players from other teams out of the base's range. To capture a base it is necessary to stay within the range of the particular base with at least one player and to prevent any other teams' players to enter that range. The bases are placed on fixed solid bodies in the space, comparable to asteroids in an asteroid field. Those also serve as obstacles in the otherwise free space.

The POIs have two important aspects concerning workload generation:

- The distribution of players in the game world is influenced by the POI. Particularly, attractive POIs will generate hotspots in player density, while spaces between the POI are expected to have low densities.

– The borders of the region containing the POI are natural borders of the effective game world without the need for artificial boundaries. Although players could move far beyond the borders, there is no incentive to do so. Limiting the effective size of the game world is necessary to be able to control the average player density.

High maximum spaceship velocities together with the hotspots allow for a high workload scalability. Thereby, the overlay implementations (SUTs) can be stressed enough to find their effective limitations.

Workload Parameters. The game scenario described above provides several parameters that can be utilized to adjust the workload.

Players and teams. Each player corresponds to a peer in the network. So the number of players (n) in the game equals the number of peers. The players are divided into m (almost) equally sized teams.

POI (bases). The bases that have to be captured by the teams cause hotspots in the player density. The hotspot magnitudes can be controlled by adjusting the values (i.e. the benefit for the possessing team) of each base separately. Each base has a range in which it can be captured and a time it takes to capture it.

Gameplay region. The gameplay region is the region within which the bases are located, thus in which the gameplay happens. Together with the total number of players, its size influences the average player density. The height of the region may be set relatively small to obtain a flat, thus pseudo-2D, game world. Pseudo-2D mode is used for gaming overlays that are only designed for a 2D world.

Ships' capabilities. The game activities (moving, shooting) are heavily influenced by the corresponding capabilities of the players' spaceships. A very important factor is the maximum velocity. All position changes affect the players' AOI and thus require certain updates in the gaming overlay. The ship's maximum forward velocity limits the rate of AOI changes. (We assume that the forward velocity is the highest velocity component and thus the most important.) Additionally, the ship's inertia limit the maximum acceleration in any direction. Missile fire events have to be delivered reliably, forming a different category than position update messages. Their rate is limited by the maximum missile firing frequency.

4.3 Metrics

Metrics are used as the performance criteria for the evaluation and have a major impact on the result of the benchmark. The goal is to choose a complete and non-redundant set of metrics with a low variability [16]. Completeness can be considered as covering the relevant quality aspects *validity, efficiency, fairness, stability, robustness, and scalability* (see Section 2.2).

In the P2P gaming scenario the central services are interest management and event dissemination. Also, we are aiming to benchmark different P2P gaming overlays. Thus, a set of macro metrics must be defined. A concrete list of metrics can be derived based on the quality aspects:

Validity. The validity of an IDO is determined by the list of AOI members. Such a list is maintained by the interest management service. Thus we define the metric for validity as correctness of the AOI member list. A first approach is to use the ratio of correct entries. An improvement can be achieved by weighting wrong entries with their importance, e.g., the distance to the player's avatar, since players mainly interact with other players or objects in their vicinity. Schmieg et al. proposed to use a position quality metric [29].

Efficiency. The efficiency of a system is defined as the ratio of performance and costs. For realtime games the performance is reflected by the responsiveness. The costs are the bandwidth that is consumed to achieve the performance. In order to calculate the efficiency quotient the responsiveness must be expressed by a responsiveness index. High latencies of events are represented by a low index, low latencies correspond to a high value.

Fairness. The fairness metric depends on a given fairness criteria. In the case of pure P2P IDOs without any incentive strategies (like pSense and VON) the distribution of load can considered as fair if the load is distributed equally to all peers.

Stability. A gaming overlay is considered stable if it reacts in a valid and responsive way under stress. If either validity or responsiveness decreases to a certain amount, the system becomes unstable. Stress is a result of high player density, velocities, and interaction rates (e.g., shooting). In order to quantify the stability, QoS criteria for validity and responsiveness must be defined. The stability index is then derived from the maximum stress parameters under which the system remains stable.

Robustness. The robustness of a gaming overlay is determined by the coherence of the virtual world. Thus, the main robustness criteria is the probability of partitions when a large fraction of the peers fails.

Scalability. Like the stability, the scalability is a second level metric. It is used to measure how a systems validity, efficiency, fairness, and robustness perform with an increasing/decreasing number of participants. For each quality aspect a threshold must be defined. The scalability metric can be formulated as maximum/minimum number of participants a system can handle without exceeding a given quality threshold.

5 Related Work

There is a wide range of benchmarks in the area of computing, starting with classic CPU benchmarks such as Dhrystone or Linpack. Other popular examples are Futuremark's 3DMark [9] for 3D graphic rendering and BAPCo SYSmark [8] for business applications. Recognized database benchmarks are defined by the Transaction Processing Performance Council (TPC) [12].

Further relevant benchmarks in the area of distributed systems are provided by the Standard Performance Evaluation Corporation (SPEC) [11], for instance

SPECjms2007 [27, 10] for message-oriented middleware systems. The SPECjms 2007 benchmark describes a supermarket supply chain application scenario. It consists of company headquarters, distribution centers, supermarkets, and suppliers communicating through the message-oriented middleware. Continuing work presents performance evaluation methods for event-based systems in general [19] and particularly for publish/subscribe systems [26].

In the area of P2P there are only a few benchmarking approaches yet. General ideas for a P2P benchmarking platform and an analysis of existing tools for P2P network simulation have been presented by Kovačević et al. [22]. A concrete benchmarking scenario for structured overlays in the context of Network Virtual Environments [21] focuses on lookup and routing latencies as well as the overlay message distribution.

Carlo Nocentini et al. present a performance evaluation of implementations of the JXTA rendezvous protocol [25]. JXTA specifies a set of protocols for P2P communication of which the rendezvous protocol provides a DHT mechanism. The paper specifies the metrics lookup time, memory load, CPU load, and dropped query percentage, as well as the parameters query rate, presence of negative queries, and type of peer disconnections (gentle or abrupt). The authors omit the specification of underlay network properties; the evaluation tests are run in a local area network whose properties are not comparable with the Internet.

A comprehensive benchmark for P2P web search engines was proposed by Thomas Neumann et al. [23]. The benchmark suggests the freely available Wikipedia content as the benchmark's document corpus. The queries, are taken from Google's Zeitgeist archive. The result quality metrics are recall and precision; efficiency is measured as query response time and network resource consumption. In contrast to most others, this work includes concrete performance properties of the network and the nodes' local disk IO. However, the network property model is simplistic, assuming a fixed latency and maximum transfer rate between all nodes, and thus not taking any kind of heterogeneity into account.

P2PTester [5] is a project aiming to provide a tool for measuring large-scale P2P data management systems. The project focus is on the applicability to various kinds of systems using a modular measurement architecture. P2PTester could be a useful tool for conducting benchmarks which particularly need to measure the connectivity traffic. The presented version of P2PTester, however, only considers a real network deployment where reproducible and Internet-like network properties are hard to achieve.

6   Conclusion and Future Work

In this paper we have discussed general requirements for P2P benchmarks, and we have presented benchmarking approaches for two very different scenarios. While the DHT scenario has a relatively clear scope and well-known functionality, the gaming scenario includes several aspects that have to be identified first and analyzed separately. Despite the wide spectrum of functionalities covered by the two exemplary scenarios, we we have shown that a common methodology can be applied.

In each scenario definition we start with a description the SUT including and the general context, its functionalities, and interfaces. Based on the SUT interface, the workload is specified, including the relevant parameters that can be used to scale the workload. Metrics then have to be defined to quantify the system behavior. Those metrics are assigned to the common P2P quality aspects which provide a general-purpose categorization of the performance criteria.

Particularly for P2P benchmarks we provide an underlay model specification that reflects the important network aspects for P2P systems derived from Internet measurements. This model can be adapted for various kinds of benchmarks for P2P, or more generally, Internet-scale distributed systems.

This work is supposed to be the starting point for a larger number of Benchmarks for various types of P2P systems. The variety of P2P solutions for different purposes should become much more tangible once there is set of system classes with clearly defined functionalities and interfaces. This categorization plus the opportunity to compare the performance of alternative solutions, significantly simplifies engineering approaches for P2P applications using existing and new solutions.

It is, however, still a long way to go towards a standardization of P2P system components that are comparable trough common interfaces. With this work we have made a first step in defining a common benchmarking methodology which can be applied for any kind of P2P system.

References

1. CAIDA - Macroscopic Topology Measurements,
   http://www.caida.org/projects/macroscopic
2. OECD Broadband statistics, http://oecd.org/sti/ict/broadband
3. QuaP2P Project Website, http://www.quap2p.tu-darmstadt.de
4. The PingER Project, http://www-iepm.slac.stanford.edu/pinger
5. Butnaru, B., Dragan, F., Gardarin, G., Manolescu, I., Nguyen, B., Pop, R., Preda, N., Yeh, L.: P2PTester: a tool for measuring P2P platform performance. In: ICDE 2007. IEEE 23rd International Conference on Data Engineering, Istanbul, pp. 1501–1502 (2007)
6. Chambers, C., Feng, W.-C., Sahu, S., Saha, D.: Measurement-based characterization of a collection of on-line games. In: 5th ACM SIGCOMM conference on Internet Measurement. USENIX Association, New York (2005)
7. Chen, K.-T., Huang, P., Huang, C.-Y., Lei, C.-L.: Game traffic analysis: An MMORPG perspective. Computer Networks 50(16), 3002–3023 (2006)
8. BAPCo consortium. SYSmark 2007 Preview,
   http://www.bapco.com/products/sysmark2007preview/
9. Futuremark Corporation. 3DMark Vantage,
   http://www.futuremark.com/benchmarks/3dmarkvantage/
10. Standard Performance Evaluation Corporation. SPECjms (2007),
    http://www.spec.org/jms2007/
11. Standard Performance Evaluation Corporation. SPEC's Benchmarks and Published Results, http://www.spec.org/benchmarks.html

12. Transaction Processing Performance Council. TPC Benchmarks,
    http://tpc.org/information/benchmarks.asp
13. Fan, L., Trinder, P., Taylor, H.: Design Issues for Peer-to-Peer Massively Multi-
    player Online Games. In: MMVE 2009 (2009)
14. Gummadi, K.P., Saroiu, S., Gribble, S.D.: King: Estimating latency between arbi-
    trary Internet end hosts. In: 2nd ACM SIGCOMM Workshop on Internet Measur-
    ment, pp. 5–18. ACM, New York (2002)
15. Hu, S.-Y., Liao, G.-M.: VON: A Scalable Peer-to-Peer Network for Virtual Envi-
    ronments. IEEE Network 20(4), 22–31 (2006)
16. Jain, R.: The Art of Computer Systems Performance Analysis. John Wiley & Sons,
    Chichester (1991)
17. Kaune, S., Pussep, K., Leng, C., Kovacevic, A., Tyson, G., Steinmetz, R.: Mod-
    elling the internet delay space based on geographical locations. In: 17th Euromicro
    International Conference on Parallel, Distributed, and Network-Based Processing
    (PDP 2009), pp. 301–310 (2009)
18. Kounev, S.: Performance Engineering of Distributed Component-Based Systems
    - Benchmarking, Modeling and Performance Prediction. Shaker Verlag, Aachen
    (2005)
19. Kounev, S., Sachs, K.: Benchmarking and Performance Modeling of Event-Based
    Systems. It - Information Technology 51, 262–269 (2009)
20. Kovacevic, A.: Peer-To-Peer Location-Based Search: Engineering a Novel Peer-To-
    Peer Overlay Network. PhD thesis, Technische Universität Darmstadt (2009)
21. Kovacevic, A., Graffi, K., Kaune, S., Leng, C., Steinmetz, R.: Towards Bench-
    marking of Structured Peer-to-Peer Overlays for Network Virtual Environments.
    In: 14th IEEE International Conference on Parallel and Distributed Systems, pp.
    799–804. IEEE, Los Alamitos (2008)
22. Kovacevic, A., Kaune, S., Liebau, N., Steinmetz, R., Mukherjee, P.: Benchmark-
    ing Platform for Peer-to-Peer Systems (Benchmarking Plattform für Peer-to-Peer
    Systeme). It - Information Technology 49(5), 312–319 (2007)
23. Neumann, T., Bender, M., Michel, S., Weikum, G.: A Reproducible Benchmark
    for P2P Retrieval. In: International Workshop on Performance and Evaluation of
    Data Management Systems. ACM, New York (2006)
24. Eugene Ng, T.S., Zhang, H.: Towards global network positioning. In: 1st ACM
    SIGCOMM Workshop on Internet Measurement, pp. 25–29. ACM Press, New York
    (2001)
25. Nocentini, C., Crescenzi, P., Lanzi, L.: Performance Evaluation of a Chord-based
    JXTA Implementation. In: First International Conference on Advances in P2P
    Systems, pp. 7–12. IEEE, Los Alamitos (2009)
26. Sachs, K., Appel, S., Kounev, S., Buchmann, A.: Benchmarking Publish/Subscribe-
    based Messaging Systems. In: Yoshikawa, M., Meng, X., Yumoto, T., Ma, Q.,
    Sun, L., Watanabe, C. (eds.) Database Systems for Advanced Applications. LNCS,
    vol. 6193, pp. 203–214. Springer, Heidelberg (2010)
27. Sachs, K., Kounev, S., Bacon, J., Buchmann, A.: Performance evaluation of
    message-oriented middleware using the SPECjms2007 benchmark. Performance
    Evaluation 66(8), 410–434 (2009)
28. Sachs, K., Kounev, S., Carter, M., Buchmann, A.: Designing a workload scenario
    for benchmarking message-oriented middleware. In: SPEC Benchmark Workshop
    (2007)
29. Schmieg, A., Stieler, M., Jeckel, S., Kabus, P., Kemme, B., Buchmann, A.: pSense -
    Maintaining a Dynamic Localized Peer-to-Peer Structure for Position Based Mul-

ticast in Games. In: IEEE International Conference on Peer-to-Peer Computing (2008)

30. Svoboda, P., Karner, W., Rupp, M.: Traffic Analysis and Modeling for World of Warcraft. In: IEEE International Conference on Communications, pp. 1612–1617 (2007)

31. Tan, S.A., Lau, W., Loh, A.: Networked Game Mobility Model for First-Person-Shooter Games. In: 4th ACM SIGCOMM workshop on Network and system support for games, p. 9. ACM, New York (2005)

32. Triebel, T., Guthier, B., Süselbeck, R., Schiele, G., Effelsberg, W.: Peer-to-Peer Infrastructures for Games. In: 18th International Workshop on Network and Operating Systems Support for Digital Audio and Video, NOSSDAV 2008, pp. 123–124 (2008)

33. Winick, J., Jamin, S.: Inet-3.0: Internet topology generator. Technical report, University of Michigan (2002)

34. Zhou, S.: Characterising and modelling the internet topology – the rich-club phenomenon and the pfp model. BT Technology Journal 24(3), 108–115 (2006)

Distributed SQL Queries with BubbleStorm

Christof Leng and Wesley W. Terpstra

Databases and Distributed Systems, Technische Universität Darmstadt, Germany
{cleng,terpstra}@dvs.tu-darmstadt.de

Abstract. Current peer-to-peer (p2p) systems place the burden of application-level query execution on the application developer. Not only do
application developers lack the expertise to implement good distributed
algorithms, but this approach also limits the ability of overlay architects
to apply future optimizations. The analogous problem for data management was solved by the introduction of SQL, a high-level query language
for application development and amenable to optimization.

This paper attempts to bridge the gap between current access-oriented
p2p systems and relational database management systems (DBMS). We
outline how to implement every relational operator needed for SQL
queries in the BubbleStorm peer-to-peer overlay. The components of
BubbleStorm map surprisingly well to components in a traditional DBMS.

1 Introduction

Due to its advantages SQL became the most widely used query language for
structured data. It combines a powerful set of query operations with a relatively clean abstraction of system internals. The abstraction benefits both the
user and the DBMS developer. A user can easily learn and use SQL without
understanding how the DBMS executes his queries. The DBMS developer on
the other hand has the freedom to optimize the execution of the query in many
different ways. This combination leads to an easy to learn yet performant query
language. Beyond that SQL offers flexibility for both sides. The user can introduce new queries or change existing ones at any time. The DBMS developer can
integrate new optimizations without breaking existing applications. The advantages of SQL have made it almost ubiquitous in computing. Many standalone
applications like Firefox use SQL internally to manage their data and countless
hobby programmers use MySQL and the like for their web projects.

In contrast to the SQL success story, things in peer-to-peer look quite bleak.
The best-known interface for peer-to-peer search overlays is *key-based routing*
(KBR) [5]. It provides an abstraction that works more or less with all *distributed
hash tables* (DHT), but is not much more than a hash table interface. This
limits users to simple key-value lookups or forces them to build tailor-made
algorithms for their more sophisticated problems on top of that primitive. The
execution plan of such a query is thus moved from the realm of the system
architect to the responsibility of the user. Obviously this contradicts the idea of
an abstraction like SQL. Now the user needs to have the expertise to implement
search algorithms and the system architect can not optimize the execution easily.

K. Sachs, I. Petrov, and P. Guerrero (Eds.): Buchmann Festschrift, LNCS 6462, pp. 230–241, 2010.
© Springer-Verlag Berlin Heidelberg 2010

With key-value lookup as the only means of access, DHTs resemble indexes in traditional database systems. Indexes are an important tool for database performance tuning, but with ever increasing hard disk throughput and nearly constant random access times, their relevance is decreasing. Instead, scanning the table directly is often more efficient than using the index. The rise of solid state disks with their super fast random access might change the rules here, but there won't be such a thing for the Internet. The latency of Internet connections is dictated by the physical distance between the communication partners and the speed of light. On the other hand according to Gilder's Law [4] the bandwidth doubles or even triples each year. Or as David Clark once put it "There is an old network saying: bandwidth problems can be cured with money. Latency problems are harder because the speed of light is fixed - you can't bribe God."

Therefore, a more powerful abstraction for peer-to-peer search overlays should be based on a technology that is able to benefit from continuing bandwidth growth. Such an abstraction might be based on the established SQL standard. This would enable developers to build upon their database programming experience for peer-to-peer application development resulting in an easier learning curve. In this paper we present how to implement distributed SQL queries with the BubbleStorm [12] peer-to-peer search overlay. Its rendezvous approach makes BubbleStorm a perfect fit for this kind of abstraction because it resembles a table scan in a traditional database system.

We cover all major aspects of SQL queries like selection, projection, and aggregation. A focus of this paper is the discussion of join algorithms applicable in BubbleStorm. Furthermore query execution planning for the peer-to-peer environment is discussed. The data definition language (DDL) for schema modifications and the data manipulation language (DML) for inserts and updates are beyond the scope of this paper.

2   Related Work

Distributed search is probably the most prominent research topic in peer-to-peer networking. Most publications focus on algorithms for more efficient or more powerful search and relatively few propose abstractions or query languages for those algorithms. Of those, key-based routing [5] is the most well-established approach. Unfortunately, it is so low-level that it should be used to build application-level query languages rather than direct application development. Also, it focuses on DHTs which are limited to indexing functions and cannot be scanned efficiently.

A few projects have considered SQL as a query language for their peer-to-peer system. All of them have in common that they keep local databases that are shared with other users instead of a global database that is distributed over the network. Thus, when a user goes offline, he takes his data with him. Furthermore, a user with a large amount of data might become overloaded with requests and will be unable to answer all of them reliably.

PeerDB [9] was one of the earliest attempts at accessing distributed data with SQL queries. In the tradition of multi-database systems they assume no general schema and apply a schema matching algorithm that relies on human interaction. The underlying naïve flooding-based overlay is clearly not scalable.

Minerva [3] is a peer-to-peer database based on DHTs. The DHT is used to index the local databases of the participating peers. To execute a query, one looks up the most promising peers for the relevant query terms in the DHT and then queries them directly. The distributed index might become prohibitively expensive if the number of terms and users grows. Like PeerDB, queries that combine data from multiple nodes like joins are not considered.

Astrolabe [14] is a peer-to-peer information dissemination system that allows queries to be formulated in SQL. As an information dissemination system it does not support storing data in the network but queries the current state of online nodes. Astrolabe is organized hierarchically and thus relatively static. Sacrificing one of the major advantages of SQL, it only allows predefined queries because it pre-aggregates information in its hierarchy.

3   BubbleStorm Overview

BubbleStorm [12] is a rendezvous-based peer-to-peer search overlay. A rendezvous search system is a distributed system that ensures that a query meets all data that is available in the system. Meeting means that the query is executed on at least one node that has a copy of the data item in its local dataset. This is typically achieved by replicating both data and queries onto $O(\sqrt{n})$ nodes. The benefit of a rendezvous system is that any selection operator that can be executed locally can be executed in the distributed search overlay.

Designed for highly dynamic, failure-prone and open-membership scenarios BubbleStorm does not guarantee an unobtainable 100% search success, but instead gives a tunable probabilistic success guarantee. Replicating query and data to $\sqrt{\lambda n}$ nodes guarantees a search success probability of $p = 1 - e^{-\lambda}$. Thus, the application developer can pick the right traffic vs. recall tradeoff for his application by setting λ.

This probabilistic approach is implemented by a random graph topology which gives BubbleStorm extreme resilience against node failures [12]. Every node can pick its own degree and will keep this number of neighbours. Since the load of a node in BubbleStorm scales linearly with its degree, this ensures load balance in heterogeneous environments.

The actual replication of data and queries in the overlay is implemented with a binary-tree-based algorithm called bubblecast. Being a tree, bubblecast reaches x nodes within $\log x$ hops. The intersection of a given query and data bubble is called the rendezvous (Figure 1). The nodes in the rendezvous (there could be several) can test this data item for the searcher's query.

To compute the global parameters for bubblecast and topology maintenance BubbleStorm monitors a number of system statistics like the network size. To do this it uses a gossip-based measurement protocol [13] that computes system-wide sums, maxima, and averages and provides the results to all nodes in the system.

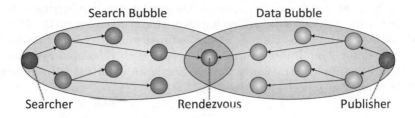

Fig. 1. Intersection of two bubbles in BubbleStorm

4 SQL Query Optimization

Our proposal for executing SQL queries closely follows the approach used in modern DBMS systems. To understand it, a short review of standard SQL query processing is in order. For a more complete understanding, the interested reader is referred to [7].

Architecturally, the system goes through the steps shown in Figure 2(a). First, the SQL query is parsed into an expression involving relational operators. Then, various result-preserving rearrangements of these operators, called query plans, are considered by the optimizer. The plan generator creates the rearrangements and the cost estimator determines how expensive they would be. Finally, the chosen query plan is fed into the interpreter which executes the query.

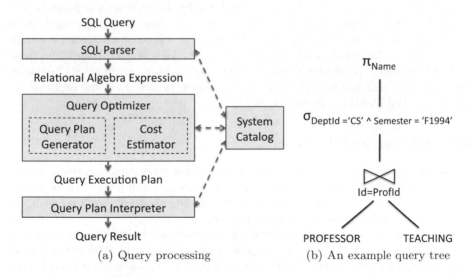

(a) Query processing   (b) An example query tree

Fig. 2. DBMS query execution (taken from [7])

The SQL Parser needed for a BubbleStorm DBMS is unchanged from a traditional DBMS system. It produces relational expressions like those in Figure 2(b).

The plan generator also remains more-or-less unchanged, considering only left-deep plans using a dynamic programming algorithm [7]. Where the BubbleStorm DBMS differs is the plan interpreter, cost estimator, and system catalog. Section 5 will detail how BubbleStorm can execute each relational operator and derive a cost estimator for each technique. Section 6 details how to implement a DBMS catalog in a peer-to-peer setting.

5   Plan Execution in BubbleStorm

Before discussing how we choose an optimized query plan, we first turn our attention to how we execute a given plan in BubbleStorm. Armed with this understanding, we will be able to estimate the cost of a plan and thus choose an acceptable strategy.

To execute a query plan in a peer-to-peer network, we pay several different costs. First, there is the time required for participating peers to locally execute the query, which we ask a traditional DBMS to estimate. As every operation includes this classically estimated cost, we elide them from discussion to keep things simple. A real implementation should include the local execution cost in its estimates during query optimization. We will henceforth focus on the bandwidth costs.

Depending on the execution plan, the bandwidth costs may be paid by the executing peer (we call this local bandwidth cost) or by intermediate peers in the network (we call this network bandwidth cost). Query plans can trade between a very selective, but large query (imposing a large network bandwidth cost) or a smaller, simple query (requiring more local bandwidth to filter the results). The correct trade-off between these local/network costs depends on the application and resources of the executing peer. In our cost analysis, we assign a simple weighting: $\mathscr{L}$ for local bandwidth cost and $\mathscr{N}$ for network bandwidth cost. When discussing bandwidth costs, message headers play an important constant-wise role. We will use h to designate their length, typically on the order of 100 bytes in a BubbleStorm implementation.

5.1   Selection and Projection

As discussed in Section 3, BubbleStorm provides a rendezvous search interface. This lends itself naturally to the execution of selection and projection on a base table. Since both selection and projection may be executed simultaneously, we consider a combined select/project operator.

To execute the operator, we define two intersecting bubble types. One bubble type consists of the rows (or tuples) in the base table. The other bubble type contains a particular select/project operator. To be concrete, each bubble of the first type contains a tuple insertion statement like, "`INSERT INTO tableA VALUES (4, 5, 6);`". These insert statements are individually replicated onto several of the participating peers. Each bubble of the second type contains a select statement like, "`SELECT project-clause FROM tableA WHERE select-clause;`", which is executed by several participating peers.

Each peer locally stores the tuples it receives in a traditional database. Upon receipt of a projection/selection operator, it uses this database to execute the operator and then forwards the results to the originator of the query. BubbleStorm ensures that every tuple and every operator meet on some peer with a user-specified probability, $p = 1 - e^{-\lambda}$. Therefore, the query originator receives p of the requested tuples. Unfortunately, each matching tuple might be received multiple times (on average, λ times).

The cost to execute this operator has several parts. First there is the cost of shipping the query to the n executing peers. If the selection/projection-operator has length q, then the originator as the root of the bubblecast tree pays $2(h+q)$ traffic to send the query to two peers, but the network pays $2(h+q)m$ by replicating the query to $m \approx \sqrt{\lambda n}$ peers for the rest of the tree. This includes the cost of sending and receiving the query.

Finally, there is the cost to download the result-set. Suppose the result table R has r entries and a total size of $|R|$ bytes. The header cost depends on the number of responding peers. Recall that λ BubbleStorm peers respond for each tuple, but only one of them will transfer the payload. The expected number of responders is asymptotically $1 - e^{-\lambda r/m}$ percent of the m peers, making the bandwidth cost to both the originator and the network $hm(1 - e^{-\lambda r/m}) + |R|$ traffic. The total cost is therefore,

$$(\mathscr{L} + \mathscr{N})[2(h+q) + hm(1 - e^{-\lambda r/m}) + |R|] + \mathscr{N}2m(h+q) \qquad (1)$$

In some cases, we may have an index available, allowing us to find tuples without a full scan of the table. BubbleStorm has its own indexing mechanism costing e hops on average (DHTs can do the same in $\log n$ hops). If an index is available, the download cost and query forwarding costs remains unchanged. However, $m \approx e$ instead of $\approx \sqrt{\lambda n}$, a potentially significant savings whenever an index is available.

5.2   Post Processing

After receiving matching tuples, the query originator might need to aggregate and sort/filter the result. The user may have specified an SQL aggregation operation like, "SELECT owner, SUM(balance) FROM account GROUP BY owner HAVING SUM(balance) < 0;". He may also have requested the output in sorted order, possibly with distinct results. We perform all of this post processing locally on the originator where standard database techniques apply.

Performing aggregation is relatively inexpensive so long as the result set fits in main memory. Form a hash-table using the GROUP BY expression as the key. Then as results arrive, aggregate them in-place. All of the standard SQL aggregates can be implemented this way; AVG (average) can be implemented using SUM and COUNT. In our scenario, with a slow Internet connection and desktop-class peers, this work can be pipelined with receiving the incoming tuples. If the aggregated result does not fit in main memory, there are standard algorithms to perform aggregation very efficiently. Their cost can be estimated from the estimated size of the result set.

Similarly, sorting the result set can be achieved by storing the incoming tuples in a balanced search tree as they arrive. If the group-by columns appear only as a prefix of the order-by columns, sorting can be combined with aggregation by replacing the hash-table with a balanced search tree. Otherwise sorting must occur after aggregation. If main memory is insufficient and/or sorting cannot be combined with aggregation, the cost of an external sort can be estimated from the size of the result set.

One interesting enhancement is to move the aggregation into the network. A query like "SELECT COUNT(*) FROM account;" can clearly be further optimized. Some of the previous work on peer-to-peer search result retrieval [1] builds a tree, where the aggregation proceeds up the tree. This increases the total traffic, since the leaf peers still send the same results and now intermediate peers must also transmit. However, it does lighten the burden of the originator and parallelizes the load. As a more fruitful approach, one could move the aggregation operator into the leaf peers themselves. Then, each peer reports only its locally aggregated result.

Unfortunately, the result sets from each peer in BubbleStorm are not disjoint. This leads to double-counting. Leaf peer aggregation can be applied to rendezvous systems which guarantee exactly one copy of each result, like [11,10,2]. Eliminating double-counting in a more failure-tolerant scenario like BubbleStorm would be an interesting direction for future work.

5.3   (Block) Nested Loop Join

In a traditional DBMS, a nested loop join is used when one table (S) is small. For each tuple in the smaller table, the larger table (L) is scanned for matching tuples. The block nested optimization simply loads a block of S at a time instead of a tuple. During the scan of L, tuples are matched against the loaded block S.

In some sense, a nested loop join writes a subquery like,

$$\text{SELECT * from } L \text{ WHERE joinColumn=}x; \tag{2}$$

for each tuple $x \in S$. The block nested variant reads like,

$$\text{SELECT * from } L \text{ WHERE joinColumn in } X; \tag{3}$$

for each block $X \subseteq S$. We use this analogy to create a BubbleStorm equivalent.

To execute a block nested loop join in BubbleStorm, first query the network to load the result table S as in Section 5.2. Now there are two options. If an index is available for the join columns in L, we can use query 2 to lookup the join results one at a time. Alternatively, divide S up into 'blocks' that fit inside a query bubble. For each block B, run the query 3 with $X = B$. This select operation can be executed as described in Section 5.1 using rendezvous techniques.

Now we compute the costs. Let $\pi(S)$ be the projection of the columns necessary to perform the join and s the total number of tuples in S. When there is an index, we replace m with e and q with $|\pi(S)|$ in Equation 1 and run it s times,

$$(\mathscr{L} + \mathscr{N})[2sh + 2|\pi(S)| + she + |R|] + \mathscr{N}2e(sh + |\pi(S)|) \tag{4}$$

Similarly, performing a block-nested loop join costs,

$$(\mathscr{L} + \mathscr{N})[2h + 2|\pi(S)| + hm(1 - e^{-\lambda r/m}) + |R|] + \mathscr{N}2m(h + |\pi(S)|) \quad (5)$$

Whenever an index is available and $s < m \approx \sqrt{\lambda n}$, using an index-nested loop join is beneficial. However, if $s > m$ things start to swing the other way. In some sense, this transition captures the selectivity of the query, analogous to a traditional DBMS. As S grows, you need to execute more and more subqueries and batching them together in a scan become cheaper.

5.4   Sort-Merge and Hash Join

In a traditional DBMS, nested loop joins are not ideal for similarly sized, large tables. This is also true for BubbleStorm due to the factors he for index-nexted loop joins and m for block-nested loop joins. For the case where both tables are large, DBMSs use either a sort-merge or hash join.

Ignoring the details, both sort-merge and hash join walk both tables once in their entirety. Sort-merge works well when the tables are already sorted and hash join partitions the tables while it walks them. When an index is present, a nested loop join may be faster since each tuple in the outer table O can find matching inner tuples without walking the entire inner table I. However, there is a cost to this lookup, and once a significant portion of the inner table is retrieved, it becomes faster to simply walk the inner table in its entirety.

The situation in BubbleStorm is more-or-less analogous. The rendezvous system provides an index for any select criteria. Nevertheless, it has a cost m to use per outer tuple. Once $|O|m > |I|$, it becomes cheaper to walk the entire I.

In the setting of BubbleStorm, walking both tables in their entirety simply means to retrieve both tables (after applying any selection and projection operators). This can be done as in Section 5.1. Since a block nested loop join must already retrieve the smaller table, it is quite intuitive that retrieving both is a good plan when they have similar size. After both tables have been retrieved, they can be joined locally using a traditional hash join. Hash join is preferred since the tuples do not arrive in sorted order, and partitioning can be easily pipelined with reception.

6   Query Plan Generation and the Catalog

Armed with equations to estimate the cost of given query plan, we can now pick a good one. The considerations are identical to those in a traditional DBMS; we choose the best left-deep tree using a dynamic programming algorithm [7]. Just as in a traditional DBMS, we push the projection and selection operations as far toward the leaves in the query plan as we can. If a table has an index on the join columns, we also consider a plan which does not push selection to the base table (which would prevent use of the index). The query plan generation for a

BubbleStorm search system is thus completely standard. The only difference is the particular costs for the operators and how we obtain the size estimates for resulting relations.

To compute the cost of our operators, we need to know the size of the result. A traditional DBMS estimates these sizes using the database catalog. The catalog contains, at the least, the database schema, the number of rows in each table, the average bit length of each attribute, the number of distinct values for each attribute, and the maximum/minimum for each attribute. This information can be used to estimate result sizes. For example, if a table Teachers is joined by EmployeeID with another table which has 20 distinct EmployeeIDs, the catalog can be used to estimate the number of matching tuples in Teachers. Take the ratio of the distinct EmployeeIDs to the total number of tuples in the Teachers table (in our example this ratio is probably 1). Now multiply this by 20 to determine that we expect 20 tuples in the result. Sum the average column sizes for the projected columns and multiply by 20 to find the resulting table size.

In a peer-to-peer database like BubbleStorm, the schema is a global piece of metadata. In order to facilitate future development, new, signed versions of the schema can be flooded to all participating peers. Care must be taken between subsequent versions of the software to ensure that the schema is kept backwards compatible with the program logic. Nevertheless, this part of the catalog is relatively straight-forward to access.

BubbleStorm already includes a mechanism for computing sums, averages, minimums and maximums. This measurement protocol can be used to find the average size of each column, the total number of tuples in the table, and the minimum/maximum for each attribute. The global schema tells peers which attributes and tables to gossip about using the measurement protocol.

The only piece of information that is hard to come by in a peer-to-peer setting is the number of distinct values in an attribute. The heart of the problem is that we have no locality and there are duplicate entries. A peer with one value has no way of knowing how many other peers have the same value. However, there is a way to calculate the number of distinct values using statistics.

It is a well-known property of k independent exponential random variables X_i with rate γ that their minimum $Y := \min_i X_i$ is also exponentially distributed with rate $k\gamma$. This can be exploited, as in [8], to calculate sums by finding k. While this technique is inferior to the distributed sum algorithm used in BubbleStorm [6,13], it can be tweaked to calculate the number of distinct objects (a variation we have not seen published yet).

To count the distinct values in a table's attribute, hash each value to obtain a seed for a random number generator. Use this seed to compute an exponential random variable with $\gamma = 1$. Find the minimum of the exponential random variables computed locally. Use BubbleStorm's built-in measurement protocol to find the global minimum Y. Take $1/Y \approx k$ as the number of distinct objects.

This algorithm works because two copies of the same object result in the same seed. Therefore, there are only as many dice rolled as there are distinct objects. Unfortunately, an exponential random variable has standard deviation equal to its mean. However, by averaging several of these minimums, the estimate may be improved. If we average j minimums, the standard deviation falls to $k/\sqrt{j}$. In a practical system where measurements are continuously generated, we can take an exponentially moving average of the minimums. If the weight given to the newest estimate is $1/16$, then the standard deviation is better than $\pm\,25\%$, good enough for our cost estimates.

7 Materialized Views

When a join is executed many times, one way to improve performance is to cache/store the joined table. While traditional DBMS systems do not create materialized views on their own, given a view created by the administrator, most query optimizers will recognize when the view can be used. In this way, materialized views can be used to improve system performance.

Updating a materialized view is quite complicated. When the base tables change, a subquery must be triggered which updates the view. These subqueries may themselves be using auxiliary tables to speedup execution. We believe that most of these trigger-based approaches could be applied one-to-one in a BubbleStorm DBMS.

However, peer-to-peer rendezvous gives us another possibility. We can create a materialized cross-product of two tables at a cost which, while still expensive, is much cheaper than in a traditional DBMS. The core idea is to form a three-party rendezvous instead of the more common two-party scenario. Local to each peer the cross-product need not be materialized; it can execute the join operator directly or perhaps materialize the join instead.

If a query is interested in a join of tables A and B, then a three-way rendezvous will ensure that every pair of tuples $(a,b) \in A \times B$ will rendezvous with the query. The idea is that if there are enough copies of a and b, then many peers will have both of them. When the query is executed, some peer who has both will also receive the query. This allows that peer to execute the join operation completely locally and still produce the resulting tuple.

While we never actually store the cross-product on disk, the increased replication of tables A and B is obviously expensive. Normally, if the query had q replicas and table A a replicas, these must roughly obey $qa = \lambda n$ which leads to $q, a \in O(\sqrt{\lambda n})$. With the materialized cross-product, the relationship is $qab = \lambda n^2$, so $q, a, b \in O(\sqrt[3]{\lambda n^2})$. If one of the relations is small or infrequently changed, replicating it to every node may be less expensive than executing the join repeatedly. Conversely, if the join query is rarely executed, the cost to nearly flood it might be acceptable.

We leave as future work the problem of gauging when/if a three-way rendezvous is cheaper than a trigger-based update for materialized views.

8 Conclusion

In this paper we described how to build a complete SQL query processor for the BubbleStorm peer-to-peer network. The main thrust of our work is how to execute selection, aggregation, index and block nested loop joins, and hash joins. For each operator we provided a cost estimator compatible with a traditional DBMS query optimizer. The cost estimator relies on the system catalog. We designed a distributed version of the system catalog which we show can be done with just BubbleStorm's gossip protocol.

We believe traditional DBMS architecture remains a good fit in the peer-to-peer environment. In particular BubbleStorm provides everything needed to arrive at a simple and natural design. Table scans map to bubblecast, indexes map to key-value lookups, and the system catalog maps to the gossip protocol. Overall it is surprisingly easy to execute SQL queries with BubbleStorm.

References

1. Balke, W.-T., Nejdl, W., Siberski, W., Thaden, U.: Progressive distributed top-k retrieval in peer-to-peer networks. In: Proceedings of ICDE 2005, Washington, DC, USA, 2005, pp. 174–185. IEEE Computer Society Press, Los Alamitos (2005)
2. Barroso, L.A., Dean, J., Hölzle, U.: Web search for a planet: The google cluster architecture. IEEE Micro. 23(2), 22–28 (2003)
3. Bender, M., Michel, S., Triantafillou, P., Weikum, G., Zimmer, C.: Minerva: collaborative p2p search. In: Proceedings of VLDB 2005, Trondheim, Norway, pp. 1263–1266. VLDB Endowment (2005)
4. Coffman, K.G., Odlyzko, A.M.: Internet growth: is there a "moore's law" for data traffic? In: Handbook of massive data sets, pp. 47–93. Kluwer Academic Publishers, Norwell (2002)
5. Dabek, F., Zhao, B., Druschel, P., Kubiatowicz, J., Stoica, I.: Towards a common api for structured peer-to-peer overlays. In: Kaashoek, M.F., Stoica, I. (eds.) IPTPS 2003. LNCS, vol. 2735, Springer, Heidelberg (2003)
6. Kempe, D., Dobra, A., Gehrke, J.: Gossip-Based Computation of Aggregate Information. In: Proceedings of FOCS 2003, Washington, DC, USA, p. 482. IEEE Computer Society Press, Los Alamitos (2003)
7. Kifer, M., Bernstein, A., Lewis, P.M.: Database Systems: An Application Oriented Approach, Compete Version. Addison-Wesley, Reading (2006)
8. Mosk-Aoyama, D., Shah, D.: Computing separable functions via gossip. In: PODC 2006: Proceedings of the Twenty-Fifth Annual ACM Symposium on Principles of Distributed Computing, pp. 113–122. ACM, New York (2006)
9. Ng, W.S., Ooi, B.C., Tan, K.-L., Zhou, A.: PeerDB: A P2P-based system for distributed data sharing. In: Proceedings of ICDE 2003 (2003)
10. Raiciu, C., Huici, F., Handley, M., Rosenblum, D.S.: Roar: increasing the flexibility and performance of distributed search. In: Proceedings of SIGCOMM 2009, pp. 291–302. ACM, New York (2009)
11. Terpstra, W.W., Behnel, S., Fiege, L., Kangasharju, J., Buchmann, A.: Bit Zipper Rendezvous—Optimal Data Placement for General P2P Queries. In: Lindner, W., Mesiti, M., Türker, C., Tzitzikas, Y., Vakali, A.I. (eds.) EDBT 2004. LNCS, vol. 3268, pp. 466–475. Springer, Heidelberg (2004) (received best paper award)

12. Terpstra, W.W., Kangasharju, J., Leng, C., Buchmann, A.P.: Bubblestorm: resilient, probabilistic, and exhaustive peer-to-peer search. In: Proceedings of SIGCOMM 2007, pp. 49–60. ACM Press, New York (2007)
13. Terpstra, W.W., Leng, C., Buchmann, A.P.: Brief announcement: Practical summation via gossip. In: Twenty-Sixth Annual ACM SIGACT-SIGOPS Symposium on Principles of Distributed Computing (PODC 2007), pp. 390–391. ACM Press, New York (August 2007)
14. Van Renesse, R., Birman, K.P., Vogels, W.: Astrolabe: A robust and scalable technology for distributed system monitoring, management, and data mining. ACM Transactions on Computer Systems (TOCS) 21(2), 164–206 (2003)

From the Internet of Computers
to the Internet of Things

Friedemann Mattern and Christian Floerkemeier

Distributed Systems Group, Institute for Pervasive Computing, ETH Zurich
{mattern,floerkem}@inf.ethz.ch

Abstract. This paper[1] discusses the vision, the challenges, possible usage scenarios and technological building blocks of the "Internet of Things". In particular, we consider RFID and other important technological developments such as IP stacks and web servers for smart everyday objects. The paper concludes with a discussion of social and governance issues that are likely to arise as the vision of the Internet of Things becomes a reality.

Keywords: Internet of Things, RFID, smart objects, wireless sensor networks.

> *In a few decades time, computers will be interwoven into almost every industrial product.*
>
> Karl Steinbuch, German computer science pioneer, 1966

1 The Vision

The Internet of Things represents a vision in which the Internet extends into the real world embracing everyday objects. Physical items are no longer disconnected from the virtual world, but can be controlled remotely and can act as physical access points to Internet services. An Internet of Things makes computing truly ubiquitous – a concept initially put forward by Mark Weiser in the early 1990s [29]. This development is opening up huge opportunities for both the economy and individuals. However, it also involves risks and undoubtedly represents an immense technical and social challenge.

The Internet of Things vision is grounded in the belief that the steady advances in microelectronics, communications and information technology we have witnessed in recent years will continue into the foreseeable future. In fact – due to their diminishing size, constantly falling price and declining energy consumption – processors, communications modules and other electronic components are being increasingly integrated into everyday objects today.

"Smart" objects play a key role in the Internet of Things vision, since embedded communication and information technology would have the potential to revolutionize the utility of these objects. Using sensors, they are able to perceive their context, and via built-in networking capabilities they would be able to communicate with each

---

[1] This paper is an updated translation of [19].

K. Sachs, I. Petrov, and P. Guerrero (Eds.): Buchmann Festschrift, LNCS 6462, pp. 242–259, 2010.

other, access Internet services and interact with people. "Digitally upgrading" conventional object in this way enhances their physical function by adding the capabilities of digital objects, thus generating substantial added value. Forerunners of this development are already apparent today – more and more devices such as sewing machines, exercise bikes, electric toothbrushes, washing machines, electricity meters and photocopiers are being "computerized" and equipped with network interfaces.

In other application domains, Internet connectivity of everyday objects can be used to remotely determine their state so that information systems can collect up-to-date information on physical objects and processes. This enables many aspects of the real world to be "observed" at a previously unattained level of detail and at negligible cost. This would not only allow for a better understanding of the underlying processes, but also for more efficient control and management [7]. The ability to react to events in the physical world in an automatic, rapid and informed manner not only opens up new opportunities for dealing with complex or critical situations, but also enables a wide variety of business processes to be optimized. The real-time interpretation of data from the physical world will most likely lead to the introduction of various novel business services and may deliver substantial economic and social benefits.

The vision outlined above is often referred to as the "Internet of Things". In that context, the word "Internet" can be seen as either simply a metaphor – in the same way that people use the Web today, things will soon also communicate with each other, use services, provide data and thus generate added value – or it can be interpreted in a stricter technical sense, postulating that an IP protocol stack will be used by smart things (or at least by the "proxies", their representatives on the network).

The term "Internet of Things" was popularized by the work of the Auto-ID Center at the Massachusetts Institute of Technology (MIT), which in 1999 started to design and propagate a cross-company RFID infrastructure.[2] In 2002, its co-founder and former head Kevin Ashton was quoted in Forbes Magazine as saying, "We need an internet for things, a standardized way for computers to understand the real world" [23]. This article was entitled "The Internet of Things", and was the first documented use of the term in a literal sense[3]. However, already in 1999 essentially the same notion was used by Neil Gershenfeld from the MIT Media Lab in his popular book "When Things Start to Think" [11] when he wrote "in retrospect it looks like the rapid growth of the World Wide Web may have been just the trigger charge that is now setting off the real explosion, as things start to use the Net."

In recent years, the term "Internet of Things" has spread rapidly – in 2005 it could already be found in book titles [6, 15], and in 2008 the first scientific conference was held in this research area [9]. European politicians initially only used the term in the context of RFID technology, but the titles of the RFID conferences "From RFID to the Internet of Things" (2006) and "RFID: Towards the Internet of Things" (2007) held by the EU Commission already allude to a broader interpretation. Finally, in 2009, a dedicated EU Commission action plan ultimately saw the Internet of Things

---

[2] The Auto-ID Center's first white paper [22] already suggested a vision that extended beyond RFID: "The Center is creating the infrastructure […] for a networked physical world. […] A well known parallel to our networked physical world vision is the Internet."

[3] Kevin Ashton commented in June 2009: "I'm fairly sure the phrase Internet of Things started life as the title of a presentation I made at Procter & Gamble in 1999" [2].

as a general evolution of the Internet "from a network of interconnected computers to a network of interconnected objects" [5].

2 Basics

From a technical point of view, the Internet of Things is not the result of a single novel technology; instead, several complementary technical developments provide capabilities that taken together help to bridge the gap between the virtual and physical world. These capabilities include:

- *Communication and cooperation:* Objects have the ability to network with Internet resources or even with each other, to make use of data and services and update their state. Wireless technologies such as GSM and UMTS, Wi-Fi, Bluetooth, ZigBee and various other wireless networking standards currently under development, particularly those relating to Wireless Personal Area Networks (WPANs), are of primary relevance here.
- *Addressability:* Within an Internet of Things, objects can be located and addressed via discovery, look-up or name services, and hence remotely interrogated or configured.
- *Identification:* Objects are uniquely identifiable. RFID, NFC (Near Field Communication) and optically readable bar codes are examples of technologies with which even passive objects which do not have built-in energy resources can be identified (with the aid of a "mediator" such as an RFID reader or mobile phone). Identification enables objects to be linked to information associated with the particular object and that can be retrieved from a server, provided the mediator is connected to the network (see Figure 1).
- *Sensing:* Objects collect information about their surroundings with sensors, record it, forward it or react directly to it.
- *Actuation:* Objects contain actuators to manipulate their environment (for example by converting electrical signals into mechanical movement). Such actuators can be used to remotely control real-world processes via the Internet.
- *Embedded information processing:* Smart objects feature a processor or micro-controller, plus storage capacity. These resources can be used, for example, to process and interpret sensor information, or to give products a "memory" of how they have been used.
- *Localization:* Smart things are aware of their physical location, or can be located. GPS or the mobile phone network are suitable technologies to achieve this, as well as ultrasound time-of-flight measurements, UWB (Ultra-Wide Band), radio beacons (e.g. neighboring WLAN base stations or RFID readers with known coordinates) and optical technologies.
- *User interfaces:* Smart objects can communicate with people in an appropriate manner (either directly or indirectly, for example via a smartphone). Innovative interaction paradigms are relevant here, such as tangible user interfaces, flexible polymer-based displays and voice, image or gesture recognition methods.

Most specific applications only need a subset of these capabilities, particularly since implementing all of them is often expensive and requires significant technical effort.

Logistics applications, for example, are currently concentrating on the approximate localization (i.e. the position of the last read point) and relatively low-cost identification of objects using RFID or bar codes. Sensor data (e.g. to monitor cold chains) or embedded processors are limited to those logistics applications where such information is essential such as the temperature-controlled transport of vaccines.

Forerunners of communicating everyday objects are already apparent, particularly in connection with RFID – for example the short-range communication of key cards with the doors of hotel rooms, or ski passes that talk to lift turnstiles. More futuristic scenarios include a smart playing card table, where the course of play is monitored using RFID-equipped playing cards [8]. However, all of these applications still involve dedicated systems in a local deployment; we are not talking about an "Internet" in the sense of an open, scalable and standardized system.

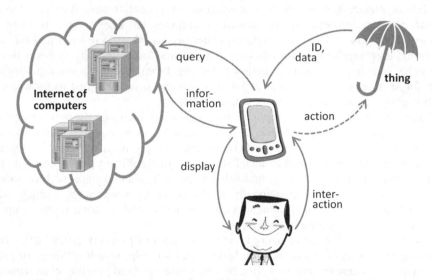

Fig. 1. The smartphone as a mediator between people, things and the Internet

But these days wireless communications modules are becoming smaller and cheaper, IPv6 is increasingly being used, the capacity of flash memory chips is growing, the per-instruction energy requirements of processors continues to fall and mobile phones have built-in bar code recognition, NFC and touch screens – and can take on the role of intermediaries between people, everyday items and the Internet (see Figure 1). All this contributes to the evolution of the Internet of Things paradigm: From the remote identification of objects and an Internet "with" things, we are moving towards a system where (more or less) smart objects actually communicate with users, Internet services and even among each other. These new capabilities that things offer opens up fascinating prospects and interesting application possibilities; but they are also accompanied by substantial requirements relating to the underlying technology and infrastructure. In fact, the infrastructure for an Internet of Things must not only be efficient, scalable, reliable, secure and trustworthy, but it must also conform with general social and political expectations, be widely applicable and must take economic considerations into account.

3 Drivers and Expectations

What is driving the development of an Internet of Things? One important factor is the mere evolutionary progress of information and communications technology which is enabling continuous product improvements. Examples of this include navigation devices that receive remote road traffic messages, cameras that connect to a nearby netbook to exchange photos, tire pressure sensors that send their readings to the car's dashboard, and electronic photo frames that communicate with household electricity meters and display not only family photos but also illustrative graphs showing the power being generated by domestic solar panels.

Instead of giving devices conventional operating controls and displays, it can soon be more cost-effective to fit them with an "invisible" wireless interface such as NFC, WLAN or ZigBee and export their interaction components to the Web or a mobile phone. This development will also benefit smart things that were previously unable to disclose their state to their surroundings, either because they were too small for conventional user interfaces or for other reasons (such as inaccessibility or aesthetics) – examples include pacemakers or items of clothing. From here it is a small but logical step for smart objects to connect to Internet services instead of just to browsers or mobile phones, and even to network with each other.

Larger and more visionary application scenarios are increasingly moving into the realm of what is possible. Although they require a more complex infrastructure, greater investment and cooperation between multiple partners, they can be socially desirable or offer the prospect of novel services with significant profit potential. The first category includes cars communicating with each other to improve road safety, ways of using energy more rationally in the home by cooperating energy-aware household devices [20], and "ambient assisted living" aimed at unobtrusively supporting elderly people in their everyday lives.

Examples of the second category include a virtual lost-property office [10], where a mobile infrastructure would pick up feeble cries for help from lost things, or property insurance where the risk can often be better assessed (and possibly even reduced) if the insured item is "smart". This might be a dynamic car insurance that makes your premium dependent not only on how far you drive ("pay as you drive"), but also on the individual risk. Speeding, dangerous overtaking and driving in hazardous conditions would then have a direct impact on the insurance costs [3].

In general, we can expect the Internet of Things to give rise to increasing numbers of hybrid products that provide both, a conventional physical function and information services. If objects become access points for relevant services, products will be able to provide recommendations for use and maintenance instructions, supply warranty information or highlight complementary products. Furthermore, the digital added value of a company's products can be used not only to differentiate them from physically similar competing products and tie customers to the company's additional services and compatible follow-on products, but can also be used to protect against counterfeit products. Completely new opportunities would arise if products independently cooperated with other objects in their proximity. For example, a smart fridge might reduce its temperature when the smart electricity meter indicates that cheap power is available, thus avoiding the need to consume energy at a later stage when electricity is more expensive.

Another driver for the Internet of Things is the real-world awareness provided to information systems. By reacting promptly to relevant physical events, companies can optimize their processes, as typically illustrated by the use of RFID in logistics applications. Or to put it another way, by increasing the "visual acuity" of information systems, it is possible to manage processes better, typically increasing efficiency and reducing costs [7].

Although such telemetry applications are nothing new in principle, they have previously been restricted to special cases due to the costly technology involved (such as inductive loops in roads that transmit traffic conditions to a central computer in order to optimize the sequencing of traffic lights). Due to diminishing cost and technical progress, many other application areas can now benefit from an increased awareness of real-world processes. For example, it is now becoming worthwhile for suppliers of heating oil to remotely check how full customers' oil tanks are (to optimize the routes of individual fuel tankers), and for operators of drinks and cigarette machines to establish the state of their vending machines (how full they are, any malfunctions, etc.) via a wireless modem.

If a smart object possesses a suitable wireless interface (e.g. NFC), the user can interact with the object via a mobile phone. As mentioned above, when only information about the object is to be displayed, it is often sufficient simply to identify the object in question (Figure 1). For example, if the bar code on a supermarket item can be read using a smartphone, additional data can automatically be retrieved from the Internet and displayed on the phone [1]. The "augmented reality" achieved in this way can be used to display helpful additional information on the product from independent sources, for example a personally tailored allergy warning or nutritional "traffic lights". Political shopping would also be possible (displaying an item's country of origin, seal of approval or CO_2 footprint), as would self-checkouts in supermarkets.

Smartphones can thus provide displays for physical objects and act as browsers for the Internet of Things – with the added benefit that the phone knows something about the current situation (such as the current location or the user's profile). "Pointing" at the object in question also removes the need to manually input an Internet address or search term, making the process extremely quick and easy. It appears conceivable that in the future the ability to obtain information about nearby things will be considered just as important as the "worldwide" Web is today, or that this ability will even become part of the Web.

In summary, the following expectations can be associated with the Internet of Things: from a *commercial point of view*, increased efficiency of business processes and reduced costs in warehouse logistics and in service industries (by automating and outsourcing to the customer), improved customer retention and more targeted selling, and new business models involving smart things and associated services. Of interest from a *social and political point of view* is a general increase in the quality of life due to consumers and citizens being able to obtain more comprehensive information, due to improved care for people in need of help thanks to smart assistance systems, and also due to increased safety, for example on roads. From a *personal point of view*, what matters above all are new services enabled by an Internet of Things which would make life more pleasant, entertaining, independent and also safer, for example by locating things that are lost, such as pets or even other people.

4 Technological Challenges

While the possible applications and scenarios outlined above may be very interesting, the demands placed on the underlying technology are substantial. Progressing from the Internet of computers to the remote and somewhat fuzzy goal of an Internet of Things is something that must therefore be done one step at a time. In addition to the expectation that the technology must be available at low cost if a large number of objects are actually to be equipped, we are also faced with many other challenges, such as:

- *Scalability:* An Internet of Things potentially has a larger overall scope than the conventional Internet of computers. But then again, things cooperate mainly within a local environment. Basic functionality such as communication and service discovery therefore need to function equally efficiently in both small-scale and large-scale environments.
- *"Arrive and operate":* Smart everyday objects should not be perceived as computers that require their users to configure and adapt them to particular situations. Mobile things, which are often only sporadically used, need to establish connections spontaneously, and organize and configure themselves to suit their particular environment.
- *Interoperability:* Since the world of physical things is extremely diverse, in an Internet of Things each type of smart object is likely to have different information, processing and communication capabilities. Different smart objects would also be subjected to very different conditions such as the energy available and the communications bandwidth required. However, to facilitate communication and cooperation, common practices and standards are required. This is particularly important with regard to object addresses. These should comply with a standardized schema if at all possible, along the lines of the IP standard used in the conventional Internet domain.
- *Discovery:* In dynamic environments, suitable services for things must be automatically identified, which requires appropriate semantic means of describing their functionality. Users will want to receive product-related information, and will want to use search engines that can find things or provide information about an object's state.
- *Software complexity:* Although the software systems in smart objects will have to function with minimal resources, as in conventional embedded systems, a more extensive software infrastructure will be needed on the network and on background servers in order to manage the smart objects and provide services to support them.
- *Data volumes:* While some application scenarios will involve brief, infrequent communication, others, such as sensor networks, logistics and large-scale "real-world awareness" scenarios, will entail huge volumes of data on central network nodes or servers.
- *Data interpretation:* To support the users of smart things, we would want to interpret the local context determined by sensors as accurately as possible. For service providers to profit from the disparate data that will be generated, we would need to be able to draw some generalizable conclusions from the

interpreted sensor data. However, generating useful information from raw sensor data that can trigger further action is by no means a trivial undertaking.

- *Security and personal privacy:* In addition to the security and protection aspects of the Internet with which we are all familiar (such as communications confidentiality, the authenticity and trustworthiness of communication partners, and message integrity), other requirements would also be important in an Internet of Things. We might want to give things only selective access to certain services, or prevent them from communicating with other things at certain times or in an uncontrolled manner; and business transactions involving smart objects would need to be protected from competitors' prying eyes.

- *Fault tolerance:* The world of things is much more dynamic and mobile than the world of computers, with contexts changing rapidly and in unexpected ways. But we would still want to rely on things functioning properly. Structuring an Internet of Things in a robust and trustworthy manner would require redundancy on several levels and an ability to automatically adapt to changed conditions.

- *Power supply:* Things typically move around and are not connected to a power supply, so their smartness needs to be powered from a self-sufficient energy source. Although passive RFID transponders do not need their own energy source, their functionality and communications range are very limited. In many scenarios, batteries and power packs are problematic due to their size and weight, and especially because of their maintenance requirements. Unfortunately, battery technology is making relatively slow progress, and "energy harvesting", i.e. generating electricity from the environment (using temperature differences, vibrations, air currents, light, etc.), is not yet powerful enough to meet the energy requirements of current electronic systems in many application scenarios.

  Hopes are pinned on future low-power processors and communications units for embedded systems that can function with significantly less energy. Energy saving is a factor not only in hardware and system architecture, but also in software, for example the implementation of protocol stacks, where every single transmission byte will have to justify its existence. There are already some battery-free wireless sensors that can transmit their readings a distance of a few meters. Like RFID systems, they obtain the power they require either remotely or from the measuring process itself, for example by using piezoelectric or pyroelectric materials for pressure and temperature measurements.

- *Interaction and short-range communications:* Wireless communication over distances of a few centimeters will suffice, for example, if an object is touched by another object or a user holds their mobile against it. Where such short distances are involved, very little power is required, addressing is simplified (as there is often only one possible destination) and there is typically no risk of being overheard by others. NFC is one example of this type of communication. Like RFID, it uses inductive coupling. During communication, one partner is in active mode and the other can be in passive mode. Active NFC units are small enough to be used in mobile phones; passive units are similar to RFID transponders and are significantly smaller, cheaper and do not need their own power source.

- *Wireless communications:* From an energy point of view, established wireless technologies such as GSM, UMTS, Wi-Fi and Bluetooth are far less suitable; more recent WPAN standards such as ZigBee and others still under development may have a narrower bandwidth, but they do use significantly less power.

5   RFID and the EPC Network

RFID (Radio Frequency Identification) is primarily used to identify objects from a distance of a few meters, with a stationary reader typically communicating wirelessly with small battery-free transponders (tags) attached to objects. As well as providing two important basic functions for an Internet of Things – identification and communication – RFID can also be used to determine the approximate location of objects provided the position of the reader is known.

At the end of the 1990s, RFID technology was restricted to niche applications such as animal identification, access control and vehicle immobilizers. High transponder prices and a lack of standards constituted an obstacle to the wider use of the technology. Since then, however, its field of application has broadened significantly, mainly thanks to MIT's Auto-ID Center, which was founded in 1999. The Auto-ID Center and its successor organization EPCglobal have systematically pursued a vision of cheap, standardized transponders identifying billions of everyday objects, and they have developed the necessary technology jointly with commercial partners. The use of RFID technology in the supply chains of retail giants such as Wal-Mart and Metro is the result of these efforts. While the adoption by major retailers represents a remarkable success, the evolution of RFID and its associated infrastructure technologies in recent years also highlights challenges involved in realizing an Internet of Things in the broader sense of the term.

The development of RFID over recent years is reflected not only in technical progress but also in cost reductions and standardization. For example, the power consumption of the latest generation of transponders is less than 30 µW, with reading distances of up to ten meters possible under favorable conditions. Increasing miniaturization has also led to a unit price of close to five cents for bulk orders of simple RFID transponders. Major progress has also been made in the field of standardization, with the ISO 18000-6C RFID protocol – also referred to as EPCglobal Gen2 – being supported by several manufacturers, dominating the market and guaranteeing interoperability.

High cost pressure and the absence of batteries in transponders means that RFID communications protocols cannot be based on established Internet protocols due to a scarcity of resources. For example, a typical RFID microchip merely consists of a few hundred thousand transistors, contains no microcontroller and has minimal storage capacity – usually just a few bytes. Instead of using a battery, passive RFID microchips are supplied with power remotely from a reading device. Since the power supply can frequently be interrupted due to "field nulls", the transmission of large data packets is avoided – at 128 bits, these are typically much shorter than IP packets. Everyday objects that are to be addressed in an Internet of Things using RFID technology will therefore not behave in exactly the same way as Internet nodes. Instead, it is likely that a highly optimized wireless protocol will be used over the last

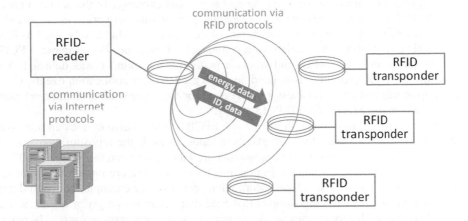

Fig. 2. RFID communication

few meters due to scarce resources and the adverse conditions encountered in the physical world. The RFID reader would act as a gateway between the two different protocols. TCP and HTTP-based protocols have been developed for use in RFID environments, where they are used to configure readers and distribute the data captured via the Internet.

One key application area for RFID is logistics. Whereas previously information systems had to be "hand-fed" with data via a keyboard or bar code reader, data relating to logistics units can now be captured automatically, without delay and at a fraction of the cost using RFID technology. The systematic development of RFID technology now means it is used not only in the commercial supply chain, but also in numerous other application areas. For example, RFID is used to manage books and media in libraries, to locate tools and other portable inventory items in factories, and even in the apparel industry, where RFID systems ensure that the retail store shelves are regularly replenished with the appropriate clothing items.

Most of the RFID applications deployed are closed-loop applications. When RFID systems are introduced in open-loop applications such as supply chains involving many different partners with different commercial interests, the resulting organizational complexity can rapidly become a problem. It is therefore advisable to use RFID initially within a single organization, and perhaps even within a limited geographical area. In such closed-loop applications, costs can be directly offset against added value and gains in efficiency, and technological challenges are often easier to overcome. Transferred to the general Internet of Things vision, this means that we are unlikely to see "global" applications requiring cooperation between many different partners any time soon. It is thus important to use standardized interfaces to implement local applications, which can then be combined at a later point in time.

In the long term, infrastructure such as the EPC network will play an important role [28]. The EPC network takes its name from the "Electronic Product Code" – a structured identifier that uniquely identifies each individual product-related RFID transponder. The aim of the EPC network is not only to enable RFID technology to identify objects, but also to simplify the processing and exchange of the data captured. The EPCIS standard represents a fundamental part of this network, and is already supported by many software manufacturers. It defines events that can be used to link the RFID data captured by readers with contextual information. For example, EPCIS events cannot only tell when and where a particular transponder was detected, but also provide information on associated business processes or application events. Custom, application-specific business logic is used for the contextual data interpretation that results in the generation of EPCIS events.

In addition to defining EPCIS events, the EPCIS standard also defines an interface that can be used to search for such events in repositories. If the repositories that hold information on a particular RFID transponder are known, one can follow the "trail" of the object to which it is attached. In practice, however, there are numerous problems associated with this type of global information scenario. For example, one would not normally know all of the repositories that held data relating to a given object, and a global search of all repositories would be unrealistic as their numbers grow. In many cases, the data would be commercially confidential and not generally accessible – even the fact that a company possesses information relating to a particular object may itself be confidential. These difficulties show that there are still many challenges relating to applicability, scalability and security that need to be overcome before we can achieve an Internet of Things that supports such global queries.

6 IP for Things

If, in a future Internet of Things, everyday objects are to be addressed and controlled via the Internet, then we should ideally not be resorting to special communications protocols as it is currently the case with RFID. Instead, things should behave just like normal Internet nodes. In other words, they should have an IP address and use the Internet Protocol (IP) for communicating with other smart objects and network nodes. And due to the large number of addresses required, they should use the new IPv6 version with 128-bit addresses.

The benefits of having IP-enabled things are obvious, even if the objects in question are not going to be made globally accessible but instead used in a controlled intranet environment. This approach enables us to build directly on existing functionality such as global interoperability, network-wide data packet delivery (forwarding and routing), data transport across different physical media, naming services (URL, DNS) and network management. The use of IP enables smart objects to use existing Internet services and applications and, conversely, these smart objects can be addressed from anywhere since they are proper Internet participants. Last but not least, it will be easy to use important application layer protocols such as HTTP. IPv6 also provides the interesting capability of automatic address configuration, enabling smart objects to assign their own addresses.

Until recently, however, the prospect of full IP support for simple things appeared illusory due to the resources required (such as processor capacity and energy) and thus the costs involved. Instead, it was suggested to connect smart objects to the Internet indirectly via proxies or gateways. But the disadvantage of such non-standardized solutions is that end-to-end functionality is lost because standardized

Internet protocols would be converted to proprietary protocols over the last few meters. Gateways would also generate added complexity, making installation, operation and maintenance time-consuming and costly.

However, there are now not only 16-bit microcontrollers with sufficient storage that require less than 400 µW/MIPS, but also TCP/IPv6 stacks that can operate with 4 kB RAM and 24 kB flash memory [13]. Equally important are wireless communications standards such as IEEE 802.15.4 that cover the layers below IP and consume relatively little power – ZigBee implementations require approximately 20 to 60 mW (for 1 mW transmission power, a range of 10 to 100 meters and a data transmission rate of 250 kbit/s). Whenever possible, the wireless unit is being used for short periods of time only in order to save energy. This approach enables AA batteries to provide a modest level of computing power and wireless communication that is nevertheless sufficient for many purposes over many months.

The opportunities that this opens up have recently led to companies and standards committees adopting various measures. At the end of 2008, Atmel, Cisco, Intel, SAP, Sun Microsystems and other companies founded the "IP for Smart Objects" (IPSO) corporate alliance to promote the implementation and use of IP for low-powered devices such as radio sensors, electricity meters and other smart objects. More specifically, the "IPv6 over Low Power Wireless Area Networks" (6LoWPAN) working group set up by the Internet Engineering Task Force (IETF) is addressing the problem of supporting IPv6 using the 802.15.4 wireless communication standard [14]. This is a technical challenge because the maximum length of 802.15.4 data frames is only 127 bytes due to lower data rate, higher susceptibility to failure and bit error rate of wireless communications. The IPv6 packet header alone is 40 bytes long (primarily due to the source and target addresses each being 16 bytes long), and unfragmented IPv6 packets can be up to 1280 bytes long.

To make IPv6 communications function efficiently in wireless networks, a protocol modification layer has been defined that essentially deals with four issues – embedding IPv6 packets in 802.15.4 frames, fragmenting long packets to fit these frames, statelessly compressing packet headers (typically to just 6 bytes), and forwarding IPv6 packets via multihop wireless routes. It is possible to compress the IPv6 header so drastically because 802.15.4 nodes communicate mainly within their own wireless network, and therefore most of the information can be reconstructed from the general context or the surrounding 802.15.4 frames and considerably shorter local addresses can be used.

The working group's proposal has now been published as proposed Internet standard RFC 4944, and an implementation based on this is described in [13]. In 2009, the ZigBee Alliance announced it would be incorporating this "native IP support" into future ZigBee specifications, "allowing seamless integration of Internet connectivity into each product".

7 The Web of Things

One logical development of the Internet of Things is to leverage the World Wide Web and its many technologies as an infrastructure for smart objects. Several years ago, Kindberg et al. put forward the idea of marking physical objects with URLs that could, for example, be read using an infrared interface and cross-reference Web pages containing information and services on the objects in question [16]. Another fundamental way of using the Web is to incorporate smart objects into a standardized Web service architecture (using standards such as SOAP and WSDL), although in practice this might be too expensive and complex for simple objects.

Instead of conventional Web service technology, the recently established "Web of Things" initiative [12] uses simple embedded HTTP servers and Web 2.0 technology. Modern Web servers with a sufficient feature set (support for several simultaneous connections, an ability to transmit dynamically generated content, and "server push" event reporting) can make do with 8 kB memory and no operating system support thanks to clever cross-layer TCP/HTTP optimization. These web server implementations are therefore suitable for even tiny embedded systems such as smart cards, where they provide a high level API to a low power device [4]. Since embedded Web servers in an Internet of Things generally possess fewer resources than Web clients such as browsers on personal computers or mobile phones, AJAX technology (Asynchronous JavaScript and XML) has proved to be a good way of transferring some of the server workload to the client.

In the Web of Things, smart objects and their services are typically addressed via URLs and controlled via a simple interface using a few well-defined HTTP operations such as GET and PUT. The data that objects transmit to the Web usually takes the form of a structured XML document or a JSON object that is machine-readable (using JavaScript). These formats can be understood not only by machines but also by people, provided meaningful markup elements and variable names are used. They can also be supplemented with semantic information using microformats.

In this way, smart objects can not only communicate on the Web but also create a user-friendly representation of themselves, making it possible to interact with them via normal Web browsers and explore the world of smart things with its many relationships (via links to other related things). Dynamically generated real-world data on smart objects can be displayed on such "representative" Web pages, and can then be processed using the extensive functionality of widely available Web 2.0 tools. For example things could, via their digital representations, be indexed like Web pages, users could "google" their properties, or they could be passed on as references. The physical objects themselves could become active and keep blogs or update each other using social networking tools like Twitter. Although this may sound like an odd humanizing of inanimate objects, it is of practical significance. The Web and its services are being used as ubiquitous middleware – facilitating the implementation of new functionality and innovative applications for smart things. So if, for example, your washing machine is in the basement and you want to monitor its progress, you could subscribe to its atom feed on a Web client and get information on major state changes, or follow its tweets on Twitter.

In a more generalized way, a mashup editor can be used to link event and data streams from physical objects with each other (and with Web services). Here is an example to illustrate this: most planes are equipped with radio beacons ("ADS-B") that transmit a short data packet once or twice per second at 1090 MHz, which can be received within a range of a few hundred kilometers. In addition to the plane's

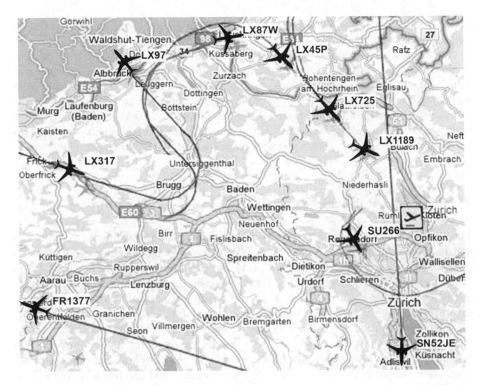

Fig. 3. A mashup displaying flight paths around Zurich [18]

identifier, this packet contains its current position, height, speed and rate of climb or descent. At http://radar.zhaw.ch one can find a mashup that uses Google maps to display the real-time flight paths of planes around Zurich in Switzerland (see Figure 3; the size of the shadow and its proximity to the plane symbol indicates altitude). This mashup is enriched with additional data from various sources such as www.flightstats.com. Clicking on the plane symbol now also results in a display of details such as the airline, departure and destination airports, expected arrival time, etc.

Although planes are not small "everyday objects" as envisaged in an ultimate Internet of Things, this example convincingly illustrates the potential for connecting the physical world with cyberspace. A more "down-to-earth" physical mashup is described in [12] which displays the energy consumption of appliances such as fridges, kettles and PC screens on Web browsers by using smart power sockets and Web technology.

Regardless of the long-term vision of an Internet of Things, cheap embedded Web interfaces could soon open up a wide variety of application opportunities. Take the example of household automation, for instance. To save energy and reduce costs or – particularly in private homes, to increase comfort and security – temperature sensors, motion detectors and other types of sensors will control many different aspects of buildings such as lighting, heating, ventilation, shutters and locking systems. To do so, these units need to be able to communicate. In the past, a variety of standards were developed, such as the European Installation Bus (EIB), but installation was still a rather costly business; and configuring, parameterizing and assigning addresses to the units had to be done in situ by experts using special software.

Since it is cheap, standardized and widely available, Web and Internet technology could be the answer here. Such an approach would allow for the use of tried-and-tested network concepts (such as auto-configuration and network management tools), and remote maintenance would be possible using standard Web browsers and interfaces. With smart household devices ("Web 2.0-ready"), WLAN-enabled electricity meters and other wirelessly communicating and self-integrating gadgets, it might then be possible to gradually realize the old dream (or perhaps nightmare?) of the "smart home"...

8 Social and Political Issues

The Internet has long since changed from being a purely informational system to one that is socio-technological and has a social, creative and political dimension. But the importance of its non-technological aspects is becoming even more apparent in the development of an Internet of Things, since it adds an entirely new quality to these non-technological aspects. So in addition to the positive expectations mentioned above, several critical questions need to be asked with regard to possible consequences.

Much of the public debate on whether to accept or reject the Internet of Things involves the conventional dualisms of "security versus freedom" and "comfort versus data privacy". In this respect, the discussion is not very different from the notorious altercations concerning store cards, video surveillance and electronic passports. As with RFID [27], the unease centers primarily on personal data that is automatically collected and that could be used by third parties without people's agreement or knowledge for unknown and potentially damaging purposes.

And personal privacy is indeed coming under pressure. Smart objects can accumulate a massive amount of data, simply to serve us in the best possible way. Since this typically takes place unobtrusively in the background, we can never be entirely sure whether we are being "observed" when transactions take place. Individual instances of observation might seem harmless enough, but if several such instances were to be amalgamated and forwarded elsewhere, this could under certain circumstances result in a serious violation of privacy.

Irrespective of the data protection issues, there is also the question of who would own the masses of automatically captured and interpreted real-world data, which could be of significant commercial or social value, and who would be entitled to use it and within what ethical and legal framework.

Another critical aspect is that of dependence on technology. In business and also in society generally we have already become very dependent on the general availability of electricity – infrequent blackouts have fortunately not yet had any serious consequences. But if everyday objects only worked properly with an Internet connection in the future, this would lead to an even greater dependence on the underlying technology. If the technology infrastructure failed for whatever reason – design faults, material defects, sabotage, overloading, natural disasters or crises – it could have a disastrous effect on the economy and society. Even a virus programmed by some high-spirited teenagers that played global havoc with selected everyday objects and thus provoked a safety-critical, life-threatening or even politically explosive situation could have catastrophic consequences.

Remotely controlled things could also cause us to become dependent and lose our supremacy on a personal level. And even with no ill intent, our own smart objects might not behave as we would wish, but rather as they "believe" is best for us – presaging a subtle type of technological paternalism [24]. The prompt feedback that smart things can give us about themselves or that helpful tools such as smartphones and augmented reality spectacles can give us about our environment is also a mixed blessing. While it can encourage us to do good, useful things (such as an animated smiley in a smart bathroom mirror that praises us for brushing our teeth properly with the electric toothbrush), it can also seduce us into making unnecessary impulse purchases.

The Internet of Things has now arrived in politics. A study for the "Global Trends 2025" [21] project carried out by the US National Intelligence Council states that "foreign manufacturers could become both the single source and single point of failure for mission-critical Internet-enabled things" [25], warning not only of the nation becoming critically dependent on them, but also highlighting the national security aspect of extending cyberwars into the real world: "U.S. law enforcement and military organizations could seek to monitor and control the assets of opponents, while opponents could seek to exploit the United States" [26].

The European Commission is reflecting vocally but somewhat vaguely on the problem of governance for a future Internet of Things. The issue here is how to safeguard the general public interest and how to prevent excessively powerful centralized structures coming into being or the regulatory power of the Internet of Things falling exclusively into the hands of what they describe as a single "specific authority".

The European Commission's action plan on the Internet of Things [5] mentioned above has also provoked a huge emotional backlash, as critically noted in the German "Telepolis" [17] online magazine with its lead story entitled "A brief route to collective incapacitation" (the tone of the article is that the Internet of Things would cost a lot of money, that consumers would have to pay for it, and that its benefits would be small). Readers' comments on the article describe the Internet of Things as a "world of enforced networking" and a "gigantic funny farm"; it would make us "totally dependent on technology and those in power" and would mean "surrendering all freedom". It was even called a perversion of the Internet and its alleged political mission: "a medium that was developed to free mankind and that should be used for this purpose could hence be misused in order to establish total control".

Although these extreme opinions are not representative, it must be said that for an Internet of Things to be truly beneficial requires more than just everyday objects equipped with microelectronics that can cooperate with each other. Just as essential are secure, reliable infrastructures, appropriate economic and legal conditions and a social consensus on how the new technical opportunities should be used. This represents a substantial task for the future.

Acknowledgements. Our thanks go to Christof Roduner and Kay Römer for their constructive criticism, and to Elgar Fleisch for many interesting discussions and fascinating joint projects on the Internet of Things.

References

1. Adelmann, R., Langheinrich, M., Floerkemeier, C.: A Toolkit for Bar Code Recognition and Resolving on Camera Phones – Jump-Starting the Internet of Things. In: Hochberger, C., Liskowsky, R. (eds.) Proc. Workshop Mobile and Embedded Interactive Systems. Informatik 2006 – GI Lecture Notes in Informatics (LNI) 94, pp. 366–373 (2006)
2. Ashton, K.: That Internet of Things Thing. RFID Journal (2009),
   http://www.rfidjournal.com/article/print/4986
3. Coroama, V.: The Smart Tachograph – Individual Accounting of Traffic Costs and its Implications. In: Fishkin, K.P., Schiele, B., Nixon, P., Quigley, A. (eds.) PERVASIVE 2006. LNCS, vol. 3968, pp. 135–152. Springer, Heidelberg (2006)
4. Duquennoy, S., Grimaud, G., Vandewalle, J.-J.: Smews: Smart and Mobile Embedded Web Server. In: Proc. Int. Conf. on Complex, Intelligent and Software Intensive Systems, pp. 571–576 (2009)
5. European Commission: Internet of Things – An action plan for Europe. COM (2009) 278 (2009),   http://eur-lex.europa.eu/LexUriServ/site/en/com/2009/com2009_0278en01.pdf
6. Fleisch, E., Mattern, F.: Das Internet der Dinge. Springer, Heidelberg (2005)
7. Fleisch, E.: What is the Internet of Things? When Things Add Value. In: Auto-ID Labs White Paper WP-BIZAPP-053, Auto-ID Lab, St. Gallen, Switzerland (2010)
8. Floerkemeier, C., Mattern, F.: Smart Playing Cards – Enhancing the Gaming Experience with RFID. In: Magerkurth, C., Chalmers, M., Björk, S., Schäfer, L. (eds.) Proc. 3rd Int. Workshop on Pervasive Gaming Applications – PerGames 2006, pp. 27–36 (2006)
9. Floerkemeier, C., Langheinrich, M., Fleisch, E., Mattern, F., Sarma, S.E. (eds.): IOT 2008. LNCS, vol. 4952. Springer, Heidelberg (2008)
10. Frank, C., Bolliger, P., Mattern, F., Kellerer, W.: The Sensor Internet at Work: Locating Everyday Items Using Mobile Phones. Pervasive and Mobile Computing 4(3), 421–447 (2008)
11. Gershenfeld, N.: When Things Start to Think. Henry Holt and Company (1999)
12. Guinard, D., Trifa, V., Wilde, E.: Architecting a Mashable Open World Wide Web of Things. TR CS-663 ETH Zürich (2010),
    http://www.vs.inf.ethz.ch/publ/papers/WoT.pdf
13. Hui, J., Culler, D.: IP is Dead, Long Live IP for Wireless Sensor Networks. In: Proc. 6th Int. Conf. on Embedded Networked Sensor Systems (SenSys), pp. 15–28 (2008)
14. Hui, J., Culler, D., Chakrabarti, S.: 6LoWPAN – Incorporating IEEE 802.15.4 into the IP architecture. In: Internet Protocol for Smart Objects Alliance, white paper #3 (2009)
15. International Telecommunication Union: The Internet of Things. ITU (2005)
16. Kindberg, T., Barton, J., Morgan, J., Becker, G., Caswell, D., Debaty, P., Gopal, G., Frid, M., Krishnan, V., Morris, H., Schettino, J., Serra, B., Spasojevic, M.: People, Places, Things: Web Presence for the Real World. Mobile Networks and Applications 7(5), 365–376 (2002)
17. Kollmann, K.: Das "Internet of Things" – Der kurze Weg zur kollektiven Zwangsentmündigung. Telepolis (2009),
    http://www.heise.de/tp/r4/artikel/30/30805/1.html
18. Kramarz, D., Loeber, A.: Visualisierung von Transponder-Daten mittels Mashup. Diplom-arbeit, Zürcher Hochschule für Angewandte Wissenschaften (2007)
19. Mattern, F., Floerkemeier, C.: Vom Internet der Computer zum Internet der Dinge. Informatik-Spektrum 33(2),107–121 (2010)

20. Mattern, F., Staake, T., Weiss, M.: ICT for Green – How Computers Can Help Us to Conserve Energy. In: Proc. e-Energy 2010, pp. 1–10. ACM, New York (2010)
21. National Intelligence Council Global Trends 2025: A Transformed World (2008), http://www.dni.gov/nic/NIC_2025_project.html
22. Sarma, S., Brock, D.L., Ashton, K.: The Networked Physical World. TR MIT-AUTOID-WH-001, MIT Auto-ID Center (2000)
23. Schoenberger, C.R.: The internet of things. Forbes Magazine, March 18 (2002)
24. Spiekermann, S., Pallas, F.: Technology paternalism – wider implications of ubiquitous computing. Poiesis & Praxis 4(1), 6–18 (2006)
25. SRI Consulting Business Intelligence: Disruptive Civil Technologies – Six Technologies with Potential Impacts on US Interests out to 2025 (2008), http://www.fas.org//nic/.pdf
26. SRI Consulting Business Intelligence: Disruptive Civil Technologies, Appendix F: The Internet of Things, Background (2008), http://www.dni.gov/nic/PDF_GIF_confreports//_F.pdf
27. Thiesse, F.: RFID, Privacy and the Perception of Risk: A Strategic Framework. The Journal of Strategic Information Systems 16(2), 214–232 (2007)
28. Thiesse, F., Floerkemeier, C., Harrison, M., Michahelles, F., Roduner, C.: Technology, Standards, and Real-World Deployments of the EPC Network. IEEE Internet Computing 13(2), 36–43 (2009)
29. Weiser, M.: The Computer for the 21st Century. Scientific American 265(9), 66–75 (1991)

Distributed Group Communication System for Mobile Devices Based on SMS⋆

Bettina Kemme[1] and Christian Seeger[2]

[1] McGill University, School of Computer Science,
3480 University Street, Room 318, Montreal, Canada
kemme@cs.mcgill.ca
[2] Technische Universität Darmstadt, Department of Computer Science,
Databases and Distributed Systems Group,
Hochschulstraße 10, 64289 Darmstadt, Germany
cseeger@dvs.tu-darmstadt.de

Abstract. This paper presents a group communication system for mobile devices, called DistributedGCS. Mobile communication is slow, expensive and suffers from occasional disconnections, especially when users are moving. DistributedGCS is based on SMS and enables group communication despite these restrictions. It provides all primitives needed for a chat application and handles process failures. As mobile communication is expensive, DistributedGCS is designed for small message overhead and, additionally, exploits SMS based message relaying to handle short-term disconnections. In this work, we present the group maintenance service and the multicast service of DistributedGCS. In order to distribute the overhead of failure discovery over all processes we introduce the concept of a circle of responsibility for failure detection. We discuss informally that DistributedGCS can handle the most common failures properly while keeping the message overhead very low.

1 Introduction

Mobile phones have not only become a standard commodity for telephony but we also use them for online shopping, to find the nearest restaurants, and to chat with our friends. Text-messaging has become particularly popular, especially in Europe. Nevertheless, basically all interaction we currently do is between two mobile phones or between the mobile phone and a central service. While a central service might disseminate information (e.g., flight information) to many interested phones, a phone usually does not send messages to many recipients. Nevertheless, there are plenty of applications that would benefit from a communication middleware that would allow mobile phones to participate in group communication. Two obvious applications are chat among a group of friends or

---

⋆ The work in this paper is based on an earlier work by Christian Seeger, Bettina Kemme and Huaigu Wu: SMS based Group Communication System for Mobile Devices, that appeared in the Proceedings of the ACM Workshop on Data Engineering for Wireless and Mobile Access, (c) ACM, 2010.

K. Sachs, I. Petrov, and P. Guerrero (Eds.): Buchmann Festschrift, LNCS 6462, pp. 260–280, 2010.

business partners, or information dissemination among a group of people with similar interest (e.g., a common research project).

In this paper, we propose such a group communication system (GCS) providing both the primitives to manage a group of mobile phones as well as offering multicast to group members. A very special feature of our system is that it completely relies on SMS (the GSM Short Message Service) as underlying communication medium. SMS allows short messages to be sent from one mobile device to another without the need of a centrally maintained service that would charge extra service fees. Routing is done through the network carrier. Our decision on this communication medium has two main reasons. Firstly, not all mobile users subscribe to a data plan that would allow Internet connectivity, and access to the Internet through wireless access points is usually very sporadic. In contrast, SMS is basically always provided and continuously available. Secondly, even if a data plan or other wireless access exists, phones cannot be directly accessed by other phones through TCP or UDP as they do not own a permanent IP address. And even if they have for intermittent time, it is usually not possible to connect to them. Thus, any solution based on Internet communication would likely need to rely on a server on the Internet to which the phones connect. The server would be responsible for relaying messages to all phones. However, our goal was to design a truly distributed, server-less solution that is easier to deploy and run. Our GCS solution only relies on a network carrier that supports SMS and a Java-enabled phone. Compared to an ad hoc network solution, users do not need to be in the same communication area.

The solution that we present is a pragmatic one. Mobile communication is expensive and slow. Every message counts. Furthermore, mobile devices have low computing power and restricted memory. Thus, our solution provides much weaker properties than traditional group communication systems. For instance, we consider the communication overhead to maintain virtual synchrony [4,16] too high. Similarly, providing reliable message delivery [4] requires considerable communication and storage overhead that we are not willing to pay. Nevertheless, our system needs to be able to handle the fragile connectivity of mobile phones as phones can quickly disconnect for short, medium and long time periods. Thus, our approach includes extensive failure handling. However, it attempts to keep the overhead as small as possible. As a trade-off, it does not handle all failure combinations correctly. We believe this to be a compromise that users are readily going to accept.

Our solution was influenced by the requirements of the application that we believe will be the first one to adopt group communication technology, and that is chatting. Nevertheless, we believe that other applications can also benefit from our tool. Our GCS offers the chat application to create, join, leave and destroy a chat room and to send FIFO multicast messages. All message exchange is done via SMS and only among the phones.

Failed phones are detected and removed from the group. The system handles short disconnections gracefully. In order to keep the message overhead for group maintenance small and distribute it over all phones, we introduce the concept of *circle of responsibility* as our failure detection system. Group membership changes can be handled and propagated by every group member which automatically distributes the group maintenance overhead.

2 Background

This section depicts different aspects of GCSs and the network environment of mobile devices which we rely on. Additionally, we introduce the GCS requirements of a chat application and close this section with related work.

2.1 Group Communication Systems

GCSs are implemented as a layer between the application and the network layer and provide two types of services [4]: *group maintenance service* and *multicast service*. Group maintenance manages a list of all active members, called *view V*. At any given point in time a view describes the current set of members of a group. Processes can join or leave, and failed processes will be excluded. Members are informed about a view change through the delivery of a *view change* message containing the members of the new view. The big challenge is to find a consensus between member processes about the current view. View proposal algorithms usually involve complex coordination protocols, requiring several rounds of message exchange among all members in order to guarantee that all members agree on the same view. Even more advanced, certain services provide a logical order between view change messages and application messages delivered in each view, such as *virtual synchrony* [16]. In this case, the view change protocol also has to agree on the set of application messages to be delivered at each process.

The *multicast service* propagates application messages submitted by the application layer to all group members. In our notation, we say that the application layer of a member receives a message that the GCS layer delivers to it. There are two main demands on a multicast service: *ordering* and *reliability*. *FIFO ordering* requires that if the application layer of a process sends two messages, then these messages are delivered in the order in which they were sent. *Causal ordering* requires that if an application first receives a message m and then sends a message m', then all members should deliver m before m'. And *total ordering* requires for every two messages m and m' and two processes, if both deliver m and m' they deliver them in the same order. Message delivery can be *unreliable*, *reliable* or *uniform reliable*. Reliable delivery (uniform reliable delivery) guarantees that if a message is delivered to an available member (to any member – available or one that crashes shortly afterwards) then it will be delivered to all available members. The higher the degree of ordering and/or reliability, the more expensive and complex is the message exchange between the members in term of additional messages and message delay.

2.2 Network Environment of Mobile Devices

Mobile devices, especially mobile phones, usually connect to stationary *base stations* provided by network carriers which provide mobile devices with different speech and data services. The most common data services for mobile devices are *SMS, MMS, GPRS* and *UMTS*. SMS and MMS are services designed for direct data communication among mobile phones. Messages are addressed to the receiver's phone number and can be sent even if the receiver is disconnected from the network. The network carriers store the messages and relay them when the receiver is connected again although the number of messages and the time messages are stored are limited. GPRS and UTMS enable mobile phones to establish an Internet connection. The base station allocates an IP address to the device and acts as a router enabling message delivery but only as long as the phone is connected to the Internet. Furthermore, IP addresses can change quickly due to two reasons. Phones automatically disconnect after a certain idle time. When the phone reconnects, the phone's base station might allocate another IP address. Furthermore, if a mobile phone moves from one cell to another, the base stations change and, hence, the allocated IP address changes, too. In addition to this, for propagating a phone's current IP address an additional server is needed and this we want to avoid. Phones could also connect to the Internet through wireless access points. However, such connectivity is very sporadic and not available everywhere. Therefore, we decided to use SMS as underlying communication layer due to its universal, bidirectional and fairly reliable services. MMS would be equally possible and we will look into this in future work. Disadvantages of SMS (and MMS) are an often higher message delay than for IP packets and a payment per message independently of the size of the message.

2.3   Application

We decided for a chat application as our example application and developed our GCS with regard to the primitives a chat application requires. In our opinion, chatting is a feasible scenario for a mobile application, because almost every mobile device fulfills the hardware requirements for a chat application. Additionally, we assume that friends or colleagues have their phone numbers already stored in their mobile phones. Hence, the users do not need additional information from a server as long as the membership consists of known people. Since there is no need for a name server in a chat application with known members, we decided to design a completely decentralized group communication system without an expensive server. However, a server-based naming service could be easily integrated into our GCS architecture. In a chat application typically all members multicast relatively short messages. While causal order would be desirable, FIFO order should be acceptable for most situations. Similarly, while reliability is important, the emphasis is probably more on fast message delivery. We assume that a chat application on a mobile phone is not feasible with more than 20 users, as the message delay would be too high for propagating information to more than 20 users in acceptable time. For applications beyond 20 users, SMS and server-less communication will likely be problematic due to the high message costs and delay. With twenty users, view change messages can be easily propagated within one message assuming phone numbers are process identifiers.

2.4   Related Work

Group communication systems are available for many different network types. The first generation of GCS has been mainly developed for local area networks (LANs) such as Totem [12], Isis [2], Horus [8] and Spread [1]. They provide basically all virtual synchrony and strong ordering and reliability guarantees.

There are also approaches for mobile networks. The authors of [14] propose an algorithm for consistent group membership in ad hoc networks. This algorithm allows hosts within communication range to maintain a consistent view of the group membership despite movement and frequent disconnections. Processes can be included or excluded with regard to their distance from the group. Different groups can be merged when they move into a common geographical area and the partition of one group can be handled as multiple disjoint groups. Another further approach [13] uses not only the ad-hoc network, but also the cellular network and a *Virtual Cellular Network* (VCN). A *Proximity Layer* protocol monitors all network nodes within a certain area and forwards changes to the *Group Membership Layer*. Based on this information a three-round group membership protocol builds a group of mobile nodes.

Closest to the approach presented in this paper is SMS GupShup Chat [18]. SMS GupShup Chat is a commercial group chat application based on SMS and managed by a central server. Users are able to create a group by sending a SMS message to the special phone number of the server. Also invitation messages containing up to four phone numbers are possible. Once a group is created, users can join or leave the group. Users can post a message to the group by sending a simple SMS message to the special phone number. The message forwarding to all group members is done by the server.

Not all existing systems provide strong guarantees. Epidemic approaches only provide guarantees with a certain probability and will only achieve that messages are "eventually" delivered (such [3,6]) or views "eventually" converge (e.g, [7]). The idea is to let nodes regularly exchange their past history of received messages. Given the low memory capacity and the high costs of communication, we do not consider epidemic protocols applicable for mobile phones. Also, in our application context of chatting, we require much lower delivery delays than the ones provided by epidemic protocols.

The work presented in this paper, DistributedGCS, is based on MobileGCS [17]. Message dissemination and failure detection are very similar in both systems but in MobileGCS the group maintenance relies on one specific phone, called master phone. Since the master phone is responsible for distributing group changes, it suffers from a higher message overhead. Therefore, we introduced a *master move* operation for switching these responsibilities from one phone to another. Still, a master move costs additional messages that we want to save. Furthermore, if several membership changes occur the master phone could easily get overloaded. In DistributedGCS, every member can propagate membership changes and every member manages its own list of group members. This makes a master phone and a master move operation unnecessary. On average, membership changes cost the same number of messages in DistributedGCS as in MobileGCS, but DistributedGCS inherently distributes the overhead over all group members and saves the messages for master moves.

3 System Overview

Our GCS layer provides the typical primitives to the application: create, join, leave and destroy a group. The application receives a view change in form of an SMS message every time the group configuration changes. The application can write an SMS and submit it to the GCS layer. The GCS layer will deliver this messages to all group members.

3.1 Multicast

We do not provide reliable message delivery to all available nodes. This would require a node to store messages that it receives from other nodes in order to be able to relay them in case of the failure of the sender. We consider this unfeasible for mobile environments. However, as mentioned above, we can assume each individual SMS message to be delivered reliably, even when short periods of disconnection occur. Therefore, we implement multicast by simply sending the message via SMS to each phone that is currently in the view of the sending phone. This achieves what we call *sender reliability*. A message sent by a node that does not fail during the sending process is delivered to all available members that are in the view of the sending process. If the sender fails during the sending process, some members might not receive the message. If a phone disconnects before the message is received, it will very likely receive it upon reconnection. Furthermore, as SMS offers FIFO delivery, we automatically also provide FIFO delivery.

3.2 Group Membership Guarantees

Considering a chat application, we think that virtual synchrony, although desirable, is not absolutely needed. Thus, view membership is decoupled from the delivery of application messages.

Ideally, we would like to have an eventual agreement, that is, all available members of a group will have eventually the same view of the group if there is a sufficiently long time without membership changes. We achieve this if we assume a strong failure detector that allows for the correct detection of a failure by choosing a sufficiently large timeout interval. In most cases, wrongly suspecting a non-failed node, simply leads to the exclusion of an available node from the group, something that we consider acceptable. However, in some rare cases, a wrong suspicion or short-term disconnections might lead to partitioned, and thus, incorrect views. Nevertheless, we tolerate many forms of concurrent failures, and we believe that our properties are acceptable for chat applications. As a result, we do not offer more than best-effort membership that will handle the most common errors but might not converge in some cases.

The remainder of this paper is dedicated to the discussion of the membership protocols.

4   DistributedGCS without Failures

DistributedGCS provides a totally distributed group maintenance service. All group members are equal and allowed to handle group operations such as join and leave requests. In contrast to the predecessor of DistributedGCS, MobileGCS [17], where group maintenance was coordinated by a master phone, the additional overhead for group maintenance messages is distributed over all processes. This makes costly operations for changing the group master unnecessary. On the other hand, having a master process simplifies the group maintenance. In MobileGCS, when a mobile phone wants to join or leave a group, or if a failure occurs, the corresponding request is sent to the group master, which decides on a new view configuration and sends the new view to all affected phones. As a result, every process that receives the view change has a consistent view with the group master. As long as every message sent by the master is received by all members and the master does not fail, all members install the same sequence of views. In contrast, DistributedGCS allows every process to handle membership operations and to change the view. This prevents overloading a single phone, but makes it more difficult to find a consensus if two or more processes change the view simultaneously. Nevertheless, DistributedGCS eventually achieves the same view among all members after a feasible amount of time.

With regard to a chat application, we assume that it is more important to keep all active processes in the view than excluding left or failed processes. Thus, the view management of DistributedGCS has a higher priority for keeping processes than for excluding them.

4.1   Group Maintenance Service

In DistributedGCS, every process has to maintain the group membership on its own. Although not every process necessarily receives the same messages in the same order, the views of all processes should eventually converge if there are no further configuration changes. This is the main challenge DistributedGCS has to deal with. For this, we first describe the basic communication schemes in the case of only one event at a time. After that, in *View Management*, we explain the processing of more complex events.

In order to identify a process' status change, DistributedGCS uses additional flags behind process identifiers / phone numbers. A flag represents the status a process p_i has stored about a foreign process p_j. It might be that two processes have different flags stored for one process p_j. We distinguish between three different flags.

- "u" - up: process is in the group and has not changed its status recently
- "j" - join: process has recently joined the group
- "l" - leave: process has recently left the group

Figure 1 shows how flags are changed in DistributedGCS. A view change message consisting of a set of processes indicates that a process (e.g., D) has joined by

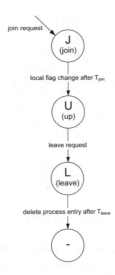

Fig. 1. Flag changes in DistributedGCS

tagging it with a join flag (e.g., D_j). When a process p that is already group member receives the view change message it first keeps this flag for the newly joined process. After a local timeout T_{join} exceeds, p sets the new process' flag set from join to up (e.g., from D_j to D_u). This is done individually at every process. As long as a process has an up or join status, it is considered a member of the group. If a process leaves the group, a new view change message is distributed marking the leaving process with a leave flag (e.g., D_l). When process p receives this message, it changes the leaving process' flag to leaving (e.g., D_l) but it does not immediately remove the process from its view. It is important to keep track of an already left process for a while in order to avoid that it is mistakenly added again. After T_{leave} time passes at process p, it finally removes the leaving process from the view. For simplification in the following figures, a process without a flag has always an up flag.

Create/Destroy. Since we avoid the usage of a central server the existence of a new group has to be propagated. The idea is that when a user wants to create a group, it invites other phones to be members of the group. This means group creation is combined with group invitations. This is useful for chatting as it allows the creation of a new chat room and to invite other people to join it. Figure 2 shows how the creation and invitation is done. In time step T0, the user of the upper phone creates a new group. The create method requires a group name and a list of other phones that are invited to become group members. The phone numbers to be invited must be provided by the user. The group name only needs to be unique over its lifetime across the phones that might want to participate. Given that it is unlikely that a given user will create many chat rooms concurrently, a group name containing the creator's identifier and a sequence number suffice. For a chat application, group creation will open a chat room and invite others to join the

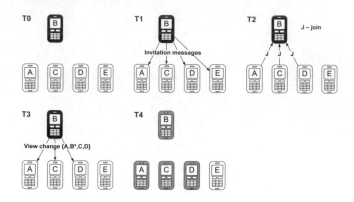

Fig. 2. Create

group. A phone that calls the create method automatically becomes a temporary group master (black color) and the group creation is completed only including the calling phone as group member. The next step involves sending invitations to contacts that are chosen by the user. The chosen phones receive invitation messages including the group name from the temporary master in T1. The GCS layer of these phones relay the message to the application which can now indicate whether it wants to accept the invitation. If it does accept the invitation, the GCS sends a join request to the initiating phone. In the given example, each phone, except for the phone E, sends a join request in step T2. In T3, the black phone adds all joining processes to the view and sends a view change message to all members of the new group. After that, the black phone stops acting as a master. The temporary master only waits a limited time to send the view change as described in the following section. If a further join request is received later, it simply sends a further view change message. At T4 phones A-D are all members of the group and have the same view.

For a chat application, we think, it makes sense that a group can only be destroyed when there is only one process left which is automatically done after/once the last processes leaves the group. Therefore, DistributedGCS does not provide a special destroy operation.

Join. If a phone wants to join after the initial creation has completed, it has to send a join request to one of the group members. Our GCS processes join requests in a completely distributed manner. Figure 3 depicts a simple join request from process D. Time step T0 shows an already existing group of three processes A, B, C that have the same view $\{A, B, C\}$ ($\{A_u, B_u, C_u\}$ including status flags) installed. At T1, process D sends a join request to process C. As all processes are equal, D can send a join request to any group member. In this case, process C is requested and adds the new process D to its view and sets its flag to *join*: $\{A, B, C, D_j\}$. In the next time step process C sends the new view first to the old view members and then to the joining process. At T4, all group members that have received the view update send an acknowledge message to D and D checks whether the join succeeded or not.

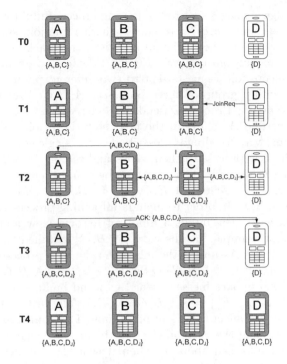

Fig. 3. Join

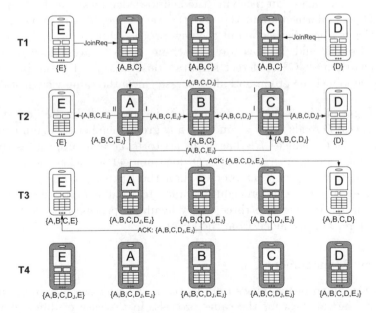

Fig. 4. Two Joins

The acknowledge messages sent to the joining process fulfill two requirements. First, they allow a joining process to check whether the join succeeded or not. And second, by attaching their originator's view, these acknowledge messages allow to capture further join requests. Figure 4 depicts an example that shows how two simultaneous join requests sent to two different phones are processed. Again, we start with a group of three processes A, B, C. Processes D and E want to join the group. Process D sends a join request to C and process E sends a join request to A at T1. In the next step, both join requests are processed in the same way as already described for a single join. The requested processes add the new process to their views and set the *join* flag. Then, they send the resulting views first to the old members and then to the joining processes. Hence, process C sends $\{A, B, C, D_j\}$ to B, C, D and process A sends $\{A, B, C, E_j\}$ to A, B, E. In order to include all joining processes, every process that receives a foreign view builds a union of its own view and the incoming view. Process B, for example, has the view $\{A, B, C\}$ installed and receives both update messages in T2. Assuming the message from C is processed first, it calculates the following view: $\{A, B, C\} \cup \{A, B, C, D_j\} = \{A, B, C, D_j\}$. Then, it processes the second update message sent by A and builds the following view: $\{A, B, C, D_j\} \cup \{A, B, C, E_j\} = \{A, B, C, D_j, E_j\}$. The order of incoming update messages does not affect the result of a union. T3 in our example highlights the reason for attaching the current view to the acknowledge message. At T2, process C was not informed about E when it sent the update message to D. Hence, the update message to D does not include process E. However, at T3 the processes A and B already added E to their views and attached them to their acknowledge messages. On receiving the acknowledge messages from A and B, process D gets informed about the new process E and adds it to its view. And process E gets also informed about the new process D by receiving acknowledge messages from B and C. This way, attaching views to acknowledge messages enables DistributedGCS to detect simultaneous joins. At T4, the processes D and E have joined the group and all processes have the same view installed.

Leave. Figure 5 shows how a leave request is processed. In the first step, the leaving process D sends a leave request to any group member (C in our example). At T2, process C changes D's flag from *up* to *leave* and propagates the view change among all members. Process D does not get an acknowledge message for its request. We let another process than the leaving process propagate the leave request to make this procedure similar to what is done when nodes fail (cp. Section 5). At time step three, every available process has set D to *leave* and, therefore, D is excluded from the group.

4.2   View Management

Building the union of two views only works as long as two incoming views do not carry different flags for the same process. In the case of different flags, a consensus among all processes has to be found. DistributedGCS does not have a group master for conflict resolution and we also want to avoid expensive view

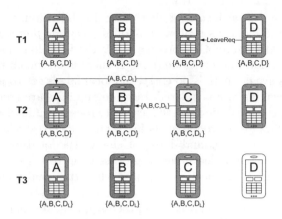

Fig. 5. Leave

proposal algorithms. Therefore, we will present a *view management* scheme that eventually finds a common view with local decisions and with a minimum of message exchanges among processes. It does not use any kind of voting algorithm that guarantees that every member installs the same view. Our goal is to find a common view with local decisions and without sending any additional message. Incoming views are processed sequentially. A foreign view can be received as a *view change* message, an acknowledge message after a join request or as a *safety* message. A safety message is the view from a process to which the process' own view was sent before. It is the response to a strong inconsistency between two views. For example, an up message about a process which has already left the group. Safety messages are not necessary, but they accelerate finding a common status.

local flag	incoming flag			timeout	
	J	U	L	T_{leave}	T_{join}
J	J	J	J		U
U	U	U	L		
L	J	L	L	-	
-	J	U	-		

Fig. 6. View change table of p_i for process p_j

As said before, each process can have one of three different flags (*up, join, leave*) in both the current view of another process and in an incoming message. Figure 6 shows how a process p_i changes the local flag of another process p_j triggered by an incoming view or triggered by one of the timeouts T_{join} and T_{leave}. The first entry in each row is the local flag of p_i for the process p_j ("-" stands for no entry). The following columns show how p_i changes p_j's flag upon receiving a foreign view or when a timeout exceeds.

First, we take a look at incoming views. For simplification, we say a *local flag* is the locally stored flag for a process p_j and an *incoming flag* is the flag for this process p_j received from another process p_u. If the local flag and the incoming flag are the same, nothing has to be done. If there is an incoming join flag and the local flag is leave or there is no entry, the local flag is set to join. If the local flag is up, the incoming join is ignored. Incoming up flags are ignored unless this process is not in the local view. In this case, a process is added with an up flag set. If the local flag for a process p_j is join and p_i receives a leave from p_u, p_i sends a safety message to p_u and does not change the local flag. In the case of a local up and an incoming leave flag, a process is set to leave. A second reason for a safety message is an incoming up flag when the local view has the leave flag set.

Upon receiving an incoming leave of a process p_j a local timer t_{leave} is started. As soon as t_{leave} exceeds T_{leave} process p_j is finally deleted from the local view and incoming leave flags for p_j are ignored. If a process deleted p_j immediately upon receiving the leave message, an incoming view that still contains an up flag for p_j would add the already left process p_j to view again. Therefore, p_j stays in view for T_{leave}. Upon receiving the incoming join of a process p_j a local timer t_{join} is started. As soon as t_{join} exceeds timeout T_{join} the local flag for p_j is changed from join to up. Keeping a local join flag for a while is not necessary but helpful in order to inform simultaneous joining process (cp. Figure 4) about the other recently joined process(es). Assuming that processes can fail, this timeout becomes more important and will be discussed in the next section.

5   Failure Detection

SMS does not establish a connection to other phones nor does it provide a method to check whether a phone is available or not. Hence, the GCS has to detect failures on its own. Failure detectors are a standard component of GCS. They typically require members to send heartbeat messages to each other. Once heartbeat messages are not received for a certain period of time, the member is suspected to have failed. Then, an agreement protocol is run to remove the suspected node. As we mentioned before, we do not want to have a complex protocol requiring many messages, neither heartbeat nor agreement messages. Thus, we use a very pragmatic approach where each member only sends heartbeat messages to one other node, and this node makes a solitary decision to remove the node if it does not receive the heartbeat messages anymore.

The authors in [9] and [15] introduce distributed failure detectors that distribute the workload for failure detection to more than one failure detection module. Each module monitors a subset of nodes and, thus, has a reduced workload compared to a central approach. We use the same idea by introducing a circle of responsibility among all processes. The GCS runs on mobile phones and every phone has a unique phone number. Since we use phone numbers as process identifiers, every process knows all phone numbers in the current view. By sorting the phone numbers and connecting the first number with the last

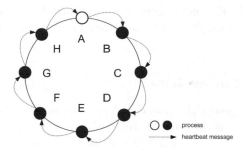

Fig. 7. Circle of Responsibility

number, we get a unique circle of phone numbers which is known by every process. As a result, every process knows its successors and predecessors. Figure 7 illustrates such a circle of responsibility. For simplification, we use again letters instead of phone numbers. The white process A is monitored by the successor process on its right side and, therefore, it sends heartbeat messages to B every time period t. Every successor process also knows its predecessor process and expects heartbeat messages from it.

5.1 Failure of a Process

If an expected heartbeat message is missing for a period T (T is significantly larger than t in order to handle message delay variations), the failure procedure is started. The monitoring process performs a self test, and if it succeeds it sends a *process failure* message to the group. This means that it marks the suspected process as *down* in its view and distributes the new view among all group members of the new group. It also sends the new view excluding the suspected process to the suspected process. In principle, when node B does not receive the heartbeat from A, A could have failed or be disconnected, in which case it should be excluded from the group. Alternatively, B itself could be temporarily disconnected from the network. If the latter is the case, B should not send the process failure message to the group. The self-test allows B to detect whether it is currently connected and is described in Section 5.4.

5.2 Adapting to Process Leaves/Failures

For the circle of responsibility, it makes no difference whether a process leaves the group or has failed. In both cases, the process will be excluded from the circle of responsibility which has to be adapted. The adaption is done as follows: the successor process of a leaving process has to change the process it monitors and the predecessor process has to change its heartbeat receiver. Assume process p_i leaves or fails. Then the successor of p_i, i.e., p_{i+1} must now monitor the predecessor of p_i, i.e., p_{i-1}. That is, p_{i-1} has now to send its heartbeat messages to p_{i+1} instead of p_i. If the leaving process p_i has a temporary status (temporary processes are described in next section), p_{i-1} only deletes p_i as a heartbeat receiver and p_{i+1} stops monitoring it. No other process needs to adjust its monitoring activity.

5.3   Adapting to Process Joins

If a process joins the group, the responsibilities change and the circle of responsibility has to adapt to it. In order to avoid a gap in the circle of responsibility, a joining process p_i is only then completely included into the circle when p_{i+1} actually knows that the join was successful and p_i becomes a permanent member of the circle. For this, a joining process gets a temporary status first. Upon receiving the first heartbeat message from this process, it is assured that the join succeeded. Only the processes p_{i-1}, p_i and p_{i+1} have to adjust their monitoring activity upon receiving the view change message including p_i: (i) p_{i-1} marks p_i as temporary and starts sending heartbeat messages to both p_i and p_{i+1}, (ii) p_i starts sending heartbeat messages to p_{i+1} and monitoring p_{i-1} and (iii) p_{i+1} marks p_i as temporary and starts monitoring p_i (it still monitors also p_{i-1}). Upon receiving p_i's first heartbeat message, p_{i+1} stops monitoring its former predecessor p_{i-1} and deletes p_i's temporary status. In addition to this, p_i sends a *stop heartbeats* message to p_{i-1}. Process p_{i-1}, upon receiving p_{i+1}'s stop heartbeats message, deletes p_i's temporary status and stops sending heartbeat messages to p_{i+1}.

If there are two or more joining processes in a row, they are all first monitored as temporary processes.

5.4   Self Test Message

With a self test, a mobile phone checks whether it is connected to the network. A phone does so by sending a self test SMS to itself. SMS does not distinguish between a message sent to a foreign phone number or the own phone number. It will always use the network carrier to send the message. Thus, we can use SMS to test our own network status. As long as a phone is able to send and receive a self test message, it is also able to receive foreign messages. If a phone does not receive its own self test message (identified by a random number), we can assume that this phone is currently disconnected from the network and, hence, we can avoid wrong failure assumptions. Thus, after not receiving its own self-test message, it suppresses all process down and heartbeat messages until connectivity is re-established and the self test message is received.

5.5   Down Status

Mobile phones can be frequently disconnected for short time periods, for instance, while its user takes the metro for two stops. The network carrier forwards messages sent to a disconnected phone after reconnection. We do not want that short disconnections completely expel a phone from the group. Therefore, we take a two-step approach for removing phones from group activity. When the failure detection mechanism is triggered for a process p_i from which no heartbeat messages are received anymore, p_i is removed from the circle of responsibility. This leads to a view change message excluding p_i. However, the remaining processes keep p_i's phone number and set a *down* flag. They continue sending the application messages to p_i. If p_i does not reconnect within a certain time period, p_i's phone number will be completely deleted and no more messages sent to it. The *down* flag is similar to the *leave* flag with the exception that processes with the leave flag will not receive any application messages anymore as they left the group voluntarily and explicitly.

At the same time, p_i itself detects that it is disconnected as it does not receive any heartbeat messages from its predecessor and performs a self-test which fails. It sets itself to down status and queues all messages that the application wants to send. It also informs the application that there is a disconnection. If p_i does not become connected within a certain time period, it drops all queued messages and informs the application about being removed from the view. When p_i becomes connected it receives all messages sent to it, including the view change excluding itself. It delivers all received application messages. These might not be all messages sent within the view during the downtime because each process handles down flags individually, but the application is aware of this best effort, since it receives the temporary disconnection message. From there, p_i joins again and then sends any message it might have locally queued.

6   Reasoning for Correctness

In this section we argue about the correctness of DistributedGCS. For this, we show that many common join requests, leave requests and failure cases are handled correctly by our approach. But we also show that some cases in DistributedGCS are not handled as well as they were in MobileGCS that we presented in [17]. We will illustrate some of these failure cases by assuming a group of six processes A, B, C, D, E, F. In each of the situations below, we assume there are no further joins, leaves and failures than the ones explicitly mentioned.

One Failure. Assume only one process p_i fails. Then p_i's successor p_{i+1} will detect the failure by not receiving heartbeat messages from p_i. As a result, p_{i+1} will set p_i to down and send a view change message. As no further process fails, all these actions will succeed, and everybody adjusts the circle of responsibility guaranteeing that process p_{i-1} monitored by p_i will receive as new monitor p_{i+1}. Although all nodes will still send application messages to the failed node for a time period after exclusion (as long as the down flag is set), the failed process is removed from the view.

Several Failures. Assume some processes fail. If the failures are not consecutive corresponding to the circle of responsibility, they will be detected concurrently. Every monitor process detects the failure of its predecessor and sends a view change message. For example, if processes B and D fail, C detects B's failure and E detects D's failure. C sends a view change message setting B to down and E sends a view change message setting D to down. Theses view change messages are sent to every member and as no consecutive processes fail, the adjustments to the circle of responsibility are independent of each other. If there are consecutive failures (for e.g., p_i and p_{i+1}), the last process in row (p_{i+1}) will be detected first (by p_{i+2}). After a new view was sent and the responsibilities were adapted, the next process (p_i) will be detected (again, by p_{i+2}) and so on. For our example, if B and C fail, D first detects C's failure. After C is excluded, D becomes monitor of B. But as B has also failed, it does not receive the view change and does not send heartbeats. Thus, D detects B's failure. Additional non-consecutive process failures are detected concurrently.

Concurrent Joins and Leaves. Concurrent joins and leaves are not a problem. As shown in Figure 4, concurrent joins are handled simultaneously. The same applies for one or more simultaneous leave requests. Since a joining process waits for acknowledge messages of members, the missing acknowledge message of a leaving process could be a problem. There are three cases we have to analyze. Assume a group of five processes A, C, D, E, F which have the view $V_i = \{A, C, D, E, F\}$ (with identifier i) installed. Process D sends a leave request to C and process B wants to join the group. Let's take a look at three cases. First, process B requests the leaving process D to join the group and D does not react. Process B will timeout receiving the view change and send the join request to another process. Second, B requests process A and A distributes the new view $V_{i+1} = \{A, B, C, D, E, F\}$. Process D sends a leave request to C. If C receives V_{i+1} after the leave request, C's acknowledge message to B already contains the leave request of D and, hence, B does not wait for D's acknowledge message. Third, if C receives V_{i+1} before the leave request, C automatically forwards D's leave request as it has V_{i+1} already installed. Therefore, concurrent joins and leaves are handled properly.

Concurrent Join and Failure. Assume a view $V_i = \{A, B, C, E, F\}$ and process D joins the group. If D sends the join request to a process that does not fail, this process sends a new view including D. At the same time, the monitor of the failed process sends a view excluding the failed process. Similar to a concurrent leave request as explained in the previous paragraph, D gets informed about the failure and does not expect an acknowledge message from the failed process. The join request and the failure detection will succeed.

If the successor p_{i+1} of a joining process p_i fails, p_{i+2} will detect p_{i+1}'s failure. After excluding p_{i+1}, the circle of responsibility adapts. Hence, p_i monitors p_{i-1} and p_{i+2} monitors p_i.

If the predecessor p_{i-1} of a joining process p_i fails and p_i has not sent its first heartbeat message, then p_{i+1} will detect the failure and p_i might detect it. Both processes send the same resulting view. If p_i has already sent its first heartbeat message, only p_i excludes p_{i-1} from view and sends a view change message. In both cases, p_{i-1} will be correctly excluded from the view.

In fact, processes might fail in any combination concurrently to the join, and as long as the process that processes the join request does not fail, every process might combine view changes. All failed processes are detected and removed and at the end the circle of responsibility is set correctly at all the remaining processes.

Let's have a look at an interesting case. If D requests a process, e.g., A, that fails while it sends the view change message V_{i+1} including D, D will timeout receiving the view change and send the join request to another process. Within the failure of A and the second join request of D exists a period of time with different installed views. Some processes have already installed V_{i+1} and some have V_i installed. If D's successor E has already installed the view V_{i+1}, it detects that D is not in group and send V_{i+2} excluding D. If E and C have still V_i installed, the unsuccessful join of D is not detected. If D does not try to join the group again, there will be two different views installed until a new view change message is sent. In the current version of the system, we do not handle this problem properly. Since heartbeat messages contain the originator's view, a view including D will be propagated slowly and D isexcluded when E is receiving this view. This might take some time.

Failure while Sending View Change Message. The previous example depicts a general problem of DistributedGCS. The distributed approach works fine unless a process fails during view change transmission. In MobileGCS, if the master process fails, a new master is elected and sends a new view to all members. The previously installed views are dropped and, thus, it is not important which view a non-master member had installed before. In DistributedGCS, a new view is the union of the previous view and the incoming view. Therefore, it is important which view was installed before. If a process fails while sending a view change message containing V_i, some processes have more actual information than others. If a further view change V_{i+1} does not contain the information sent before because its originator has not received V_i, group members have still different views installed. Exchanging view information by sending heartbeat messages helps finding a consensus, but since they are only sent to a process' successor, the information flow is very slow.

In particular, there are two cases of missing events: a mistakenly included (join) or a mistakenly excluded (leave, down) process which is only installed at a subset of group members. Let's start with the mistakenly included process. Assume a process p_i likes to join the group and process p_j which processes the join request fails while transmitting the view change and, thus, the view change is not distributed among all group members. If p_i retries to join the group and the new requested process does not fail while transmitting, the join will succeed. If p_i does not retry to join, there could be two situations. First, p_{i+1} already received the view change from p_j and detects a failure of p_i. Process p_{i+1} will send a new view excluding p_i and p_i is completely excluded from the group. Second, p_{i+1} has not received the view change from p_j but at least from one other group member. In this situation, p_{i+1} does not monitor p_i and, hence, it does not recognize the failure of p_i, but other processes which have received the view including p_i assume that the join succeeded. In this case, p_i is mistakenly included in some views. By adding the current view to each heartbeat message and treating inclusions of each incoming heartbeat message like a view change, the group members that have received p_i's join will propagate its inclusion to their successors along the circle of responsibility. With every set of heartbeat messages sent among the group the mistaken inclusion of p_i is forwarded towards p_{i+1}. In worst case, if n denotes the total number of processes in the group and p_{i+2} is the only process that has received the join of p_i, it takes $n-2$ steps until p_{i+1} is informed about the mistaken inclusion of p_i and, thus, it will exclude p_i because it does not receive heartbeat messages from it. In summary, if no further view changes occur, a mistakenly added process is eventually detected after $n-2$ heartbeat steps in the worst case.

A mistaken exclusion could occur when a process p_i suspects its not-failed predecessor p_{i-1} to have failed and fails while transmitting the view change. As a result of p_i's failure, p_{i+1} will send a view change message excluding p_i. If p_{i+1} received the view change from p_i before it failed, the failure assumption of p_{i-1} will also be propagated within the group and p_{i-1} will be excluded. If p_{i+1} has not received the view change before, it will propagate a view including p_{i-1}. Processes which have received the previous exclusion of p_{i-1} will ignore the *up* information until $T_{leave/down}$ exceeded and they have completely deleted p_{i-1} from their view. Once p_{i-1} is deleted, an incoming heartbeat message including this process will add it again. In worst case, a mistakenly added process will be eventually detected after $n-2$ heartbeat steps as soon as $T_{leave/down}$ is exceeded. We would like to mention here that exclusion information carried by a heartbeat message are discarded which emphasizes our assumption to focus more on the inclusion than on the exclusion of processes.

7   Performance Analysis

We only want to provide a rough overhead analysis for simple multicast messages, and single joins and leaves. We consider both the number of messages as well as the communication steps needed to finish the operation. The overhead of heartbeat messages is ignored. In our analysis, we would like to make an assumption that we have a group of n phones. Each **multicast** takes n-1 messages as each group member receives its own copy of a message. As messages can be sent concurrently, there is only one time step. For a **join**, the joining process contacts a group member by sending a join request (1 message and 1 step). Upon receiving this request, a view change message is sent to all group members including the new process except the sending process itself (n messages in 1 step). All group members, except for the requested process, send an acknowledge message to the joining process ($n-1$ messages and 1 step). Once the successor of the joining process p receives the first heartbeat from p (1 step) it sends a stop heartbeat message to p's predecessor (1 message and 1 step). Thus, we have a total of $2n$ messages in 3 steps until the joining process is included and 5 steps until the circle of responsibility is completely adjusted. A **leave** request takes $n-1$ messages and two time steps. One message for the request itself and $n-2$ view change messages to all group members except the requested process. For processing a **failure**, DistributedGCS takes one process down message and $n-1$

messages for the view change to all group members including the failed process. Thus, we have a total of n messages and 2 steps. These two time steps, however, do not contain the delay until a failure is detected.

8   Implementation

Our GCS layer and a corresponding chat application layer have been fully implemented based on Java ME [10]. We decided for Java ME as it is a very common environment for applications running on mobile devices. It allows us to test our GCS on many different devices. Additional toolkits [11,5] for Java ME supported our analysis. Java ME is divided into two base configurations: *Connected Limited Device Configuration (CLDC)* and *Connected Device Configuration (CDC)*. We use CLDC as it is designed for devices with limited capabilities like mobile phones and best fits our purpose. For incoming messages, we utilize a synchronous message listener that listens at SMS port 2000. Thus, messages are redirected to the GCS layer and do not end up in the mailbox of the user. We have thoroughly tested scenarios on a testbed consisting of up to four phones.

9   Conclusions

This paper presents a novel, completely decentralized group communication architecture for mobile devices that uses SMS-based message passing. Compared to our MobileGCS, DistributedGCS inherently distributes the management overhead and does not need special master move operations. It's main target application is chatting but we believe that it can be used for other applications with similar reliability requirements. The system has a thorough failure detection mechanism that keeps the overhead for failure handling very low, while at the same time handling the most common failure scenarios. Our approach handles short disconnections, as this is a common phenomenon in mobile environments. Furthermore, failure handling is equally distributed over all nodes. For future work we will focus on integrating additional communication channels and, hence, supporting a wider spectrum of applications.

References

1. Amir, Y., Stanton, J.: The Spread Wide Area Group Communication System. The Johns Hopkins University, Baltimore (1998)
2. Birman, K., Cooper, R.: The ISIS project: real experience with a fault tolerant programming system. In: EW 4: Proceedings of the 4th Workshop on ACM SIGOPS European Workshop, pp. 1–5. ACM Press, New York (1990)
3. Birman, K.P., Hayden, M., Ozkasap, O., Xiao, Z., Budiu, M., Minsky, Y.: Bimodal multicast. ACM Trans. Comput. Syst. 17(2), 41–88 (1999)
4. Chockler, G.V., Keidar, I., Vitenberg, R.: Group communication specifications: a comprehensive study. ACM Comput. Surv. 33(4), 427–469 (2001)

5. Ericsson, S.: SDK 2.5.0.3 for the Java ME Platform (2010),
   http://developer.sonyericsson.com/wportal/devworld/article/java-
   sdk-versionhistory (Online; accessed October 28, 2009)
6. Eugster, P.T., Guerraoui, R., Handurukande, S.B., Kouznetsov, P., Kermarrec, A.-
   M.: Lightweight probabilistic broadcast. ACM Trans. Comput. Syst. 21(4), 341–374
   (2003)
7. Golding, R.A.: Weak-Consistency Group Communication and Membership. PhD
   thesis, Santa Cruz, CA, USA (1992)
8. Horus. The Horus Project (2009),
   http://www.cs.cornell.edu/Info/Projects/HORUS/index.html
9. Larrea, M., Arevalo, S., Fernandez, A.: Efficient algorithms to implement unreliable
   failure detectors in partially synchronous systems. In: Jayanti, P. (ed.) DISC 1999.
   LNCS, vol. 1693, pp. 34–48. Springer, Heidelberg (1999)
10. Microsystems, S.: Java ME (2009), http://java.sun.com/javame/index.jsp
11. Microsystems, S.: Java Wireless Toolkit (2009),
    http://java.sun.com/products/sjwtoolkit/
12. Moser, L., Melliar-Smith, P., Agarwal, D.A., Budhia, R.K., Lingley-papadopoulos,
    C.A.: Totem: A Fault-Tolerant Multicast Group Communication System. Commu-
    nications of the ACM 39, 54–63 (1996)
13. Prakash, R., Baldoni, R.: Architecture for Group Communication in Mobile Sys-
    tems. In: SRDS 1998: Proceedings of the The 17th IEEE Symposium on Reliable
    Distributed Systems, Washington, DC, USA. IEEE Computer Society Press, Los
    Alamitos (1998)
14. Roman, G.-C., Huang, Q., Hazemi, A.: Consistent group membership in ad hoc
    networks. In: ICSE 2001: Proceedings of the 23rd International Conference on Soft-
    ware Engineering, Washington, DC, USA, pp. 381–388. IEEE Computer Society
    Press, Los Alamitos (2001)
15. Schiper, A.: Early consensus in an asynchronous system with a weak failure detec-
    tor. Distrib. Comput. 10(3), 149–157 (1997)
16. Schiper, A., Birman, K., Stephenson, P.: Lightweight causal and atomic group
    multicast. ACM Trans. Comput. Syst. 9(3), 272–314 (1991)
17. Seeger, C., Kemme, B., Wu, H.: SMS based Group Communication System for
    Mobile Devices. In: ACM Workshop on Data Engineering for Wireless and Mobile
    Access, vol. 9 (2010)
18. SMSGupShup. SMS Gup Shup Chat (2009),
    http://www.smsgupshup.com/apps_chat

Towards Declarative Query Scoping
in Sensor Networks

Daniel Jacobi[1], Pablo E. Guerrero[1], Khalid Nawaz[1],
Christian Seeger[1,*], Arthur Herzog[1,*], Kristof Van Laerhoven[2], and Ilia Petrov[1]

[1] Databases and Distributed Systems Group
[2] Embedded Sensing Systems,
Dept. of Computer Science, Technische Universität Darmstadt, Germany

Abstract. In the last decade, several large-scale wireless sensor networks
have been deployed to monitor a variety of environments. The declarative nature of the database approach for accessing sensor data has gained
great popularity because of both its simplicity and its energy-efficient implementation. At the same time another declarative abstraction made its
way into mainstream sensor network deployments: user-defined groups of
nodes. By restricting the set of nodes that participate in a task to such a
group, the overall network lifetime can be prolonged. It is straightforward
to see that integrating these two approaches, that is, restricting a query's
scope to a group of sensor nodes, is beneficial. In this work we explore
the integration of two such database and scoping technologies: TikiDB, a
modern reincarnation of a sensor network query processor, and Scopes, a
network-wide grouping mechanism.

1 Introduction

Wireless Sensor Networks (WSNs) have been suggested as a potent solution to
monitor large areas with sensing hardware, distributed over hundreds of nodes
that jointly form an ad-hoc multi-hop network. Each node in such a WSN is
equipped with a limited amount of processing and battery resources, communication capabilities to transmit its information to neighboring nodes in the
network, and a set of sensors, which can observe the local environment.

Operating a sensor network originally implied writing code in a procedural
programming language like C (or variants of it) for TinyOS [9]. This code has
to deal with low-level issues such as interrupts, network unreliability and power
consumption. In contrast, declarative operation is simpler than writing procedural code: it allows the user to focus on what needs to be done, without thinking
how to achieve it, and thereby reduces the system complexity.

* Supported by the German Research Foundation (DFG) within the research training group 1362 *Cooperative, Adaptive, and Responsive Monitoring in Mixed Mode
Environments*, and the *Center for Advanced Security Research Darmstadt* (CASED).

K. Sachs, I. Petrov, and P. Guerrero (Eds.): Buchmann Festschrift, LNCS 6462, pp. 281–292, 2010.
© Springer-Verlag Berlin Heidelberg 2010

In sensor networks, declarative data access was investigated by Gehrke [1,19] and Madden [11,12]. Their systems offer a query processor-like interface to the sensor network. The vast amount of work in this context shows general consensus that sensor data access should be declarative.

Another abstraction that has made its way into mainstream sensor network deployments is node grouping[1]. Having its origin in event-based systems [6], the idea of scoping a WSN was published in [16], and related implementations appeared in [18,13,15]. Most of these systems do acknowledge the importance of a declarative operation by providing a simple syntax to define the node groups.

The intuitiveness of the database and scoping approaches makes their combination an ideal integrated solution for query management in sensor networks. To the best of our knowledge no work has explored this intersection. This paper presents a number of extensions that this integration enables, their implementation and evaluation.

The rest of the paper is structured as follows. In the next section we review related sensor network research with distinct attention to declarative query processing and management of node groups, describing specific components of the two approaches and their relevant implementation details. In Section 3, a number of extensions are presented that naturally emerge when using both systems together. An initial evaluation is provided in Section 4 studying the behavior of the system. We summarize our main findings in Section 5, together with future directions of research.

2   Related Work

A significant amount of work has been carried out in the last decade to address the topics of query processing and node group management. In the following two subsections we review these topics. We then describe techniques to constrain a query's span in the network which are, to a certain extent, comparable to the approach presented in this paper.

2.1   From Cougar to TikiDB

The earliest systems to provide a declarative interface for accessing sensor data were Cougar [1,19] and TinyDB [11,12]. In TinyDB, the sensor nodes compose a global, virtual table called **sensors**, which has sensor types as columns (e.g., temperature, humidity), and nodes as rows. Each record is virtually updated by each node at a frequency specified by the user, effectively forming a virtual data cube over time, as illustrated in Fig. 1.

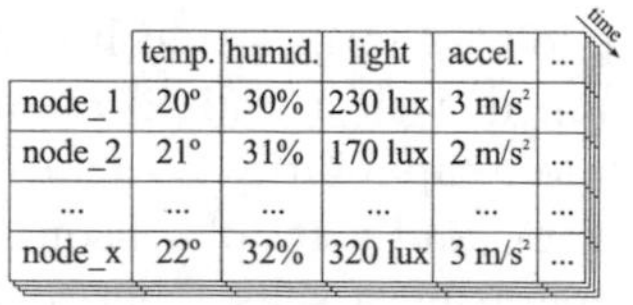

	temp.	humid.	light	accel.	...
node_1	20°	30%	230 lux	3 m/s²	...
node_2	21°	31%	170 lux	2 m/s²	...
...	...	...	...	...	...
node_x	22°	32%	320 lux	3 m/s²	...

Fig. 1. TinyDB's **sensors** virtual data cube

---

[1] Should not be confused with node clustering, a technique to subordinate nodes to a master according to their physical proximity.

Users, in turn, specify a SQL-like query to
extract sensor data from the network. Consider for example a sensor network equipped
with environmental monitoring nodes. A user,
e.g., interested in determining whether air humidity exceeds a threshold of 20%, provides

```
SELECT humidity
   FROM sensors
   WHERE humidity > 20%
   SAMPLE PERIOD 30s
   FOR 3d
```

the query to the right. The `SELECT` clause defines a projection on `humidity`, i.e.,
the result set consists of a table with one column and one row per network node.
The `WHERE` clause reduces the set of results by filtering temperature tuples that
don't fulfill the specified condition. The results are delivered to the base station
at a 30-second sample rate (as specified with the `SAMPLE PERIOD` clause), and
the query lifetime is 3 days.

When users are interested in aggregated
values instead of collecting all individual rows,
the query can include the desired aggregation
and the system performs the computation, as

```
SELECT AVG(temperature)
   FROM sensors
   SAMPLE PERIOD 30s
```

shown in the query to the right. The result of this query is a single row per sample period, based on the non-aggregated rows, with the average temperature.
Performing the aggregation inside the network has the benefit of lowering the
communication costs. TinyDB's data aggregation framework [11] implements
this mechanism, and can be extended with customized functions beyond the
traditional average, max and min functions.

This style of declarative interaction, i.e. issuing queries through the network
via one of its nodes, makes the system flexible to be used and reconfigured without requiring any changes to the individual node's code. TinyDB, alas, has not
been kept up-to-date with the evolution of neither sensor hardware platforms nor
TinyOS, the operating system on which it worked. Therefore we developed our
own system, called TikiDB, which works on Contiki's Rime protocol stack [4,5].
TikiDB behaves just as TinyDB: it exhibits a tree establishment protocol over
which query dissemination, data collection and aggregation functions operate.

2.2   Management of Node Groups

Initial sensor network architectures assumed that all sensor nodes participate in
a single global task. It soon became evident that in many scenarios, a sensor
network could be used for multiple purposes [17]. The idea of creating groups of
nodes evolved naturally [16]: by restricting the set of nodes that participate in
each task, communication costs are reduced, which translates into a prolonged
overall network lifetime. Variations of this idea emerged almost concurrently,
e.g., for groups of physically nearby nodes [18], logical groups [13], and also
under the name of roles [15].

In our group we have built Scopes [10], a framework in which a group of nodes
(called *scope*) can be declaratively defined by specifying a membership condition
that nodes must satisfy.

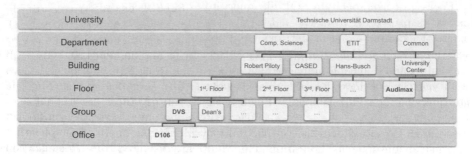

Fig. 2. A hierarchy of scopes for facility management applications at TUD

```
CREATE SCOPE Office_D106
  AS ( ROOM = 'D106' )
  SUBSCOPE OF DVS;
```

Fig. 3. Scope definition for
office D106

```
CREATE SCOPE Temp_Office_D106
  AS ( EXISTS SENSOR 'TEMPERATURE'
       AND TEMPERATURE < 20C )
  SUBSCOPE OF Office_D106;
```

Fig. 4. Specialization for temperature nodes

An important feature of the framework is the possibility to relate scopes to each other in a hierarchy. A scope's definition specializes that of its parent scope: member nodes will be a subset of its parents'. As an example, consider the development of facility management applications at the Technische Universität Darmstadt. Fig. 2 presents one such simple scope hierarchy. The topmost scope, representing the entire university, is split into departments, which in turn are split geographically into buildings, then floors, and so on, until fine granularity scopes are achieved, e.g. D106 being Prof. Buchmann's office. The statements below show how to declaratively express scope Office_D106 as subscope of DVS (Fig. 3), as well as Temp_Office_D106, which picks temperature nodes in the given office (Fig. 4).

A node's membership to a scope might change over time, hence a timely reevaluation at each node is required. The Scopes framework implements mechanisms to correctly deal with the membership, and provides automatic maintenance against network dynamics (nodes leaving and joining and unreliable communication).

In addition to reliably notifying nodes about their membership, Scopes enables a bidirectional communication channel between a scope's creator (called *scope root*) and the scope *members*. The framework resorts to specific routing algorithms that can be chosen to better fulfill the application needs. A naïve implementation simply floods messages throughout the network. An energy-efficient protocol was presented in [10], which uses controlled flooding to disseminate top level scope definitions through the network, and a converge-cast routing tree for relaying data back to the sink. The used tree topology makes this protocol a good candidate for implementing query processing functions, therefore we concentrate on it in this work.

2.3 Node Set Reduction

Semantically, a query is answered by extracting data from the `sensors` table as specified by the `FROM` clause, effectively addressing all nodes. Internally, however, queries do not always necessarily need to be spread across the entire network. Consider a query which requires temperature readings greater than or equal to a certain threshold 'x'. Clearly, nodes with values lower than 'x' can abstain from participating in the query other than for forwarding purposes. TinyDB reduces the set of nodes that participate in answering such queries by using a semantic routing tree (or SRT for short). SRTs are overlays on traditional routing trees that, similar to database indices, are used to locate nodes that have data relevant to the query. An SRT is created over constant values, e.g. temperature and humidity, with the statement:

```
CREATE SRT th_index ON sensors (temperature,humidity) ROOT 1
```

The statement creates an SRT named `th_index` rooted at node 1; nodes then discover the range of temperature and humidity values their children have. That information is used later to determine whether a query must be forwarded downwards or not. To a minor extent, the definition of an SRT resembles those of scopes. The flexibility of scope definitions, as shown in the previous subsection, goes far beyond such indices.

Other techniques exist that reduce the set of nodes participating in a query. Dubois-Ferrière and Estrin investigated a multi-sink scenario, and proposed to partition the network using Voronoi scopes [2]. Gupta et al. [8] investigated an approach to suppress nodes that are in close enough proximity such that they might contribute the same or similar data, effectively assuming node redundancy. These techniques complement the approach presented in this paper, and can be applied a posteriori. When resource constraints are not an issue, the approach for mobile phones and smart objects from Frank et al. [7] can be also used.

In the next section we present and exemplify a number of extensions that emerge from the integration of declarative query processing and network scoping.

3 Integrating Queries with Scopes

As introduced earlier, the declarative approach to querying a sensor network employs a `SELECT-FROM-WHERE-GROUP BY` statement. The user is normally bound to refer to the whole network in these queries: the `FROM` clause is used with the `sensors` table[2]. Scoping a sensor network, on the other hand, enables the definition of dynamic data sources.

---

[2] Other tables can be used, called *materialization points*, but these can't be used to specify node sets.

Therefore, it results natural to extend the query semantics by adding the possibility to use these scopes as sources instead of the entire `sensors` table. This section describes TikiDB's extensions to the query processing data model by resorting to example queries for illustration purposes.

3.1 Data Model Extensions

The simplest way to restrict the set of nodes that participate in a query is by replacing the `sensors` keyword with the name of the scope to be used. Consider the query to the right, where the scope

```
SELECT temperature, humidity
    FROM Office_D106
    WHERE humidity > 20%
    SAMPLE PERIOD 30s
```

Office_D106 is defined as in Fig. 3. In this case, the result set consists of tuples generated at nodes which are members of the specified scope (and which meet the `WHERE` clause).

When multiple scopes are to be used as sources, they can be listed separated from each other by commas as in the query to the right. Here, a user is interested in light sensor values from nodes in both offices.

```
SELECT light
    FROM Office_D106, Office_D108
    WHERE light > 200 lux
    SAMPLE PERIOD 30s
```

It is easy to observe that the notation stands for union between node groups, instead of an implicit cross join between these.

Data aggregation also matches very well with scopes. Aggregating data from a scope's nodes over an epoch is possible by specifying the desired attribute and the aggregation function, as exemplified

```
SELECT AVG(temperature)
    FROM Office_D106
    WHERE humidity > 20%
    SAMPLE PERIOD 30s
```

to the right. The temperature values of all nodes being member of Office_D106 are then averaged and presented to the user at the base station.

Results can also be grouped by common attributes such as node type or room. In this case, the root node will deliver a result set with one row for each unique value of the grouping attribute (e.g. node type) together with the aggregated value.

```
SELECT node_type,
        MIN(battery_voltage)
    FROM ComputerScience
    GROUP BY node_type
    SAMPLE PERIOD 30s
```

The query to the right assumes an attribute node_type, which takes values according to the node's properties such as processor and sensors available. It illustrates how to find the lowest battery level for each node type at a large scope, `ComputerScience`.

Lastly, a more powerful aggregation operation exploits the hierarchical relation between a scope and its subscopes. When a user is interested in an aggregated value for each of the subscopes of a particular scope, he can use the clause SUBSCOPE OF.

```
SELECT SUBSCOPE OF DVS,
        AVG(light)
    FROM DVS
    GROUP BY SUBSCOPES OF DVS
    SAMPLE PERIOD 30s
```

With this, the result set includes one row for each subscope of the specified scope, together with the aggregated value. Consider the query to the right: the grouping element are those subscopes of DVS, that is, each of the offices that belong to it (cf. Fig. 2). Note that the user might not know a priori what the subscopes of a scope are, or if there exist any at all. The system takes care of looking them up and managing the aggregated values independently from each other.

3.2 Design Considerations

Each of the introduced queries require a corresponding mapping to the operations offered by the network scoping interface. We now describe the design considerations and implementation details of the aforementioned operations, as well as modifications to the underlying scoping layers to correctly support these query processing operations.

Architecture. The system follows a layered architecture, as depicted in Fig. 5. Users write and submit queries to TikiDB through a connected node. TikiDB is in charge of parsing the query and allocating the necessary timers and other resources for its execution. Scopes is used for creating the node groups and maintaining them against network dynamics, as well as for disseminating the queries towards scope members and transporting data flowing back to the scope root. We have implemented this stack entirely using Contiki [4], an operating system running threads on a C-based event-driven kernel.

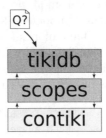

Fig. 5. System layers

Query Dissemination. TikiDB's procedure for query injection uses the communication channel offered by Scopes to disseminate the query specification. In this way, indeed, only nodes that are members of the scope are notified (e.g., nodes circled in green in Fig. 6). The strict layering employed by the Scopes framework avoids notifying intermediate nodes, which only forward data messages to their destination (cf. node 2). This feature is necessary in scenarios where security and privacy are of utmost importance, since the network

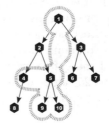

Fig. 6. Query dissemination

may contain multiple scopes from different users and/or companies. The drawback of this approach, however, is that such nodes cannot be used to perform aggregation: when data flows from producer nodes towards the root. In this work we have extended the Scopes framework to enable the user to specify whether this behavior is desired or not.

4 Preliminary Evaluation

In this section we describe a preliminary evaluation of our approach regarding reliability and power efficiency.

4.1 Simulation Setup

We have evaluated the integration of Scopes with TikiDB through simulations. For this purpose we use Contiki's COOJA/MSPSim, which is a simulator providing a very accurate emulation of the node's hardware [14]. This enables the usage of exactly the same binary for simulations as for real hardware. While COOJA offers emulation for several hardware platforms, we chose to use Telos nodes since we plan to evaluate the system in our Tmote Sky testbed.

The energy consumed by the nodes was measured using the power profiling mechanism [3] provided by Contiki. The execution times were measured for different components (e.g., radio and processor) on the nodes while they were awake. This information, along with the current energy consumption obtained from the Tmote Sky datasheet, was used to compute the energy consumed by the nodes. In our experiments, initial energy assigned to all nodes was equal, unless otherwise stated.

```
SELECT INTERNAL_VOLTAGE
   FROM scope_x
   SAMPLE PERIOD 128s
```

```
SELECT ROOM, AVG(TEMPERATURE)
   FROM scope_x
   SAMPLE PERIOD 128s
```

Fig. 7. Query Q_1 **Fig. 8.** Query Q_2

The used network topology was a uniform, 100-node grid of 10 nodes by side. Transmission range was adjusted so that each node can communicate with its four direct neighbors. Despite having used transmission success rates of 100%, radio communication is subject to collisions (we discuss this issue later). We tested the system with two different scopes, which covered 25% of the network (hence 25 nodes were members of it). The first scope, S_1, covered nodes distributed uniformly throughout the network, while for the second scopes, S_2, we chose those in the upper left corner. These scope definitions were used in combination with two queries (presented in Fig. 7 and 8) by replacing scope_x with the respective scope name (S_1 or S_2). Query Q_1 simply requests the internal voltage reading. Despite its simplicity, this query puts the network protocols under stress given the network size (and the respective tree height). Query Q_2 is slightly more complex in that it requires aggregation over an epoch. Radio messages are smaller, however more processing delay is present.

4.2 Simulation Results

In Fig. 9 we present the reliability results for the aforementioned combination of scope definitions and queries. The x axis represents elapsed time. The plain

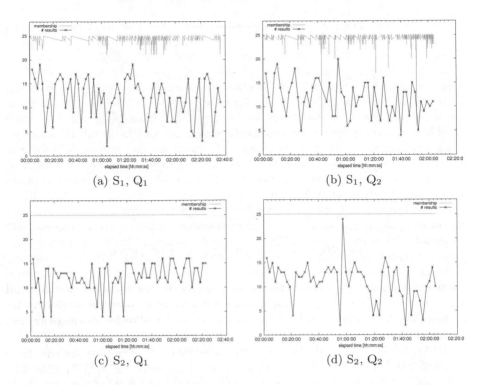

Fig. 9. Result delivery reliability for S_1, S_2 combined with Q_1, Q_2

(green) curve shows node membership, while the line with crosses (blue) represents the number of received results at the scope root (the positions of the crosses indicate the start of a new epoch). The plots show results for the first 60 epochs ($\sim$2.5 hours).

The first aspect to consider is the scope membership (green curve), since nodes that do not become scope members will not generate tuples to contribute to the result. Both scope definitions cover 25 nodes; we observe that while S_2 remains stable over time from the beginning of the test run till the end, S_1 shows a slight variability. This is expected, since S_1 spans the whole network, while S_2 covers a concentrated, smaller fraction of it. In general, however, scope membership remained high, which is to be attributed to the reliability with which *administrative* messages are sent by the Scopes framework.

Given this almost ideal node membership, we consider the amount of received results at the scope root. At first sight, it seems surprising that only around 50% of the results arrive at the root. This suboptimal outcome, however, is due to a number of issues. With query Q_1, messages get longer as nodes are closer to the root. This triggers the message fragmentation function; the Scopes framework, in turn, sends *data* messages without requesting acknowledgements. Occupying the broadcast medium for longer periods of time clearly increases the probability of message collisions. A packet loss near the root implies losing a big part of the

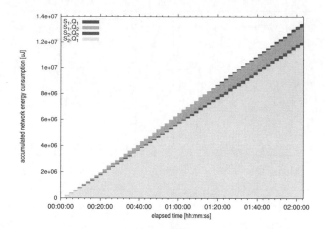

Fig. 10. Power efficiency for the tested queries

results. With query Q_2, on the other side, in-network processing keeps individual nodes busier for longer times. This causes results to sometimes arrive out of order at their next hop, which eventually discards them (out-of-order messages arrived 3% of the time).

In Fig. 10, we present the results for power efficiency. The plot presents time on the x axis, and accumulated network energy consumption on the y axis. The plot contains energy consumption measurements for the first ∼55 epochs. Here it is observed that the queries involving scope S_1 consume 14% more energy than the queries involving S_2. This was expected because nodes in S_1 are spread through the network, which requires spending more energy to collect results. Also, it is noted that the two queries executed on the same scope do not vary drastically (the observed absolute difference was < 2%). As expected, S_1,Q_1 has required more energy than S_1,Q_2, since the latter performs in-network aggregation, therefore minimizing message size. However, the lower energy consumption shown by S_2,Q_1 compared to S_2,Q_2 is contradictory to our expectations: the query executing aggregation requires more energy than the query without it. We speculate that a possible explanation could be that the savings in communication costs are lower than the extra costs for computing aggregates, since in S_2, member nodes are closer to the scope root, thus requiring less communication. A detailed investigation of this issue is a matter of future work.

5   Conclusions and Future Work

In this paper we have proposed an approach to declaratively specify the set of nodes that participate in a query. While, in sensor networks, declarative interfaces to query processing as well as for node group management had already been investigated, the integration of these two is a promising approach which can further improve the usability of sensor networks for non-experts.

We have shown the benefits of this approach by integrating two of such systems. On one side, TikiDB, which is a modern reincarnation of a distributed query processor developed on the Contiki operating system. TikiDB manages query aspects such as query parsing, data acquisition, data aggregation and filtering. On the other side, Scopes, which is a distributed node grouping system that efficiently handles network dynamics and enables a bidirectional communication channel between a scope's root node and its members.

We have proposed four extensions to TinyDB's original data model that make use of scopes to specify or reduce the set of nodes that participate in the query. The easiness in describing its syntax suggests that the constructs are applicable to many situations. Our preliminary evaluation results show a non-ideal result delivery reliability, leaving space for optimizations. Clearly, around the scope root, messages get large enough such that fragments have high probability of collision. Since data messages in Scopes are not acknowledged, data loss becomes an issue.

In the future we plan to enhance our implementation to improve reliability, reduce energy consumption, and also optimize the program size. These activities will be surrounded by extensive test runs on a real deployment to characterize and evaluate our framework in more detail.

References

1. Bonnet, P., Gehrke, J., Seshadri, P.: Towards Sensor Database Systems. In: Proceedings of the Second International Conference on Mobile Data Management, Hong Kong (January 2001)
2. Dubois-Ferriere, H., Estrin, D.: Efficient and Practical Query Scoping in Sensor Networks. In: Procs. of the 1st IEEE International Conference on Mobile Ad-hoc and Sensor Systems, pp. 564–566 (October 2004)
3. Dunkels, A., Österlind, F., Tsiftes, N., He, Z.: Software-based Online Energy Estimation for Sensor Nodes. In: 4th IEEE Workshop on Embedded Netwoked Sensors (Emnets-IV), Cork, Ireland (June 2007)
4. Dunkels, A., Gronvall, B., Voigt, T.: Contiki - a Lightweight and Flexible Operating System for Tiny Networked Sensors. In: 29th Annual IEEE International Conference on Local Computer Networks, pp. 455–462 (November 2004)
5. Dunkels, A., Österlind, F., He, Z.: An Adaptive Communication Architecture for Wireless Sensor Networks. In: Proceedings of Conference on Embedded Networked Sensor Systems (Sensys 2007). ACM Press, New York (November 2007)
6. Fiege, L., Mezini, M., Muehl, G., Buchmann, A.: Engineering Event-based Systems with Scopes. In: European Conference on Object-Oriented Programming 2002, pp. 257–268 (2002)
7. Frank, C., Roduner, C., Noda, C., Kellerer, W.: Query scoping for the sensor internet. In: Proceedings of the 2006 ACS/IEEE International Conference on Pervasive Services, PERSER 2006, Washington, DC, USA, pp. 239–242. IEEE Computer Society Press, Los Alamitos (2006)
8. Gupta, H., Zhou, Z., Das, S.R., Gu, Q.: Connected sensor cover: self-organization of sensor networks for efficient query execution. IEEE/ACM Trans. Netw. 14(1), 55–67 (2006)

9. Hill, J., Szewczyk, R., Woo, A., Hollar, S., Culler, D.E., Pister, K.: System Architecture Directions for Networked Sensors. SIGOPS Oper. Syst. Rev. 34(5), 93–104 (2000)
10. Jacobi, D., Guerrero, P.E., Petrov, I., Buchmann, A.P.: Structuring Sensor Networks with Scopes. In: 3rd IEEE European Conference on Smart Sensing and Context (EuroSSC), Zurich, Switzerland, pp. 40–42. IEEE Computer Society, Los Alamitos (2008)
11. Madden, S., Franklin, M.J., Hellerstein, J.M., Hong, W.: TAG: a Tiny AGgregation Service for Ad-hoc Sensor Networks. In: 5th Symposium on Operating Systems Design and Implementation, vol. 36(SI), pp. 131–146 (2002)
12. Madden, S., Franklin, M.J., Hellerstein, J.M., Hong, W.: TinyDB: an Acquisitional Query Processing System for Sensor Networks. ACM Trans. Database Syst. 30(1), 122–173 (2005)
13. Mottola, L., Picco, G.P.: Logical Neighborhoods: A Programming Abstraction for Wireless Sensor Networks. In: Gibbons, P.B., Abdelzaher, T., Aspnes, J., Rao, R. (eds.) DCOSS 2006. LNCS, vol. 4026, pp. 150–168. Springer, Heidelberg (2006)
14. Österlind, F., Dunkels, A., Eriksson, J., Finne, N., Voigt, T.: Cross-level simulation in cooja. In: European Conference on Wireless Sensor Networks (EWSN), Poster/Demo session, Delft, The Netherlands (January 2007)
15. Römer, K., Frank, C., Marrón, P.J., Becker, C.: Generic Role Assignment for Wireless Sensor Networks. In: Proceedings of the 11th ACM SIGOPS European Workshop, Leuven, Belgium, pp. 7–12 (September 2004)
16. Steffan, J., Fiege, L., Cilia, M., Buchmann, A.: Scoping in Wireless Sensor Networks: A Position Paper. In: Proceedings of the 2nd Workshop on Middleware for Pervasive and Ad-hoc Computing, pp. 167–171. ACM, New York (2004)
17. Steffan, J., Fiege, L., Cilia, M., Buchmann, A.P.: Towards Multi-Purpose Wireless Sensor Networks. In: Systems Communications, Montreal, Canada, pp. 336–341. IEEE Computer Society, Los Alamitos (2005)
18. Whitehouse, K., Sharp, C., Brewer, E., Culler, D.E.: Hood: A Neighborhood Abstraction for Sensor Networks. In: MobiSYS 2004: Proceedings of the 2nd International Conference on Mobile Systems, Applications and Services, Boston, Massachusetts, USA, pp. 99–110. ACM Press, New York (2004)
19. Yao, Y., Gehrke, J.: The Cougar Approach to In-network Query Processing in Sensor Networks. SIGMOD record 31(3), 9–18 (2002)

QPME 2.0 - A Tool for Stochastic Modeling and Analysis Using Queueing Petri Nets

Samuel Kounev, Simon Spinner, and Philipp Meier

Karlsruhe Institute of Technology, 76131 Karlsruhe, Germany
kounev@kit.edu, simon.spinner@gmail.com

Abstract. Queueing Petri nets are a powerful formalism that can be exploited for modeling distributed systems and analyzing their performance and scalability. By combining the modeling power and expressiveness of queueing networks and stochastic Petri nets, queueing Petri nets provide a number of advantages. In this paper, we present Version 2.0 of our tool QPME (Queueing Petri net Modeling Environment) for modeling and analysis of systems using queueing Petri nets. The development of the tool was initiated by Samuel Kounev in 2003 at the Technische Universität Darmstadt in the group of Prof. Alejandro Buchmann. Since then the tool has been distributed to more than 100 organizations worldwide. QPME provides an Eclipse-based editor for building queueing Petri net models and a powerful simulation engine for analyzing the models. After presenting the tool, we discuss ongoing work on the QPME project and the planned future enhancements of the tool.

1 Introduction

QPME (Queueing Petri net Modeling Environment) [20] is a modeling and analysis tool based on the Queueing Petri Net (QPN) modeling formalism. The tool is developed and maintained by the Descartes Research Group [7] at Karlsruhe Institute of Technology (KIT). Introduced in 1993 by Falko Bause [1], the QPN formalism has a number of advantages over conventional modeling formalisms such as queueing networks and stochastic Petri nets. By combining the modeling power and expressiveness of queueing networks and stochastic Petri nets, QPNs enable the integration of hardware and software aspects of system behavior into the same model. In addition to hardware contention and scheduling strategies, QPNs make it easy to model simultaneous resource possession, synchronization, asynchronous processing and software contention. These aspects have significant impact on the performance of modern enterprise systems.

Another advantage of QPNs is that they can be used to combine qualitative and quantitative system analysis. A number of efficient techniques from Petri net theory can be exploited to verify some important qualitative properties of QPNs. The latter not only help to gain insight into the behavior of the system, but are also essential preconditions for a successful quantitative analysis [3]. Last but not least, QPN models have an intuitive graphical representation that facilitates model development. In [11], we showed how QPNs can be used for modeling

K. Sachs, I. Petrov, and P. Guerrero (Eds.): Buchmann Festschrift, LNCS 6462, pp. 293–311, 2010.

distributed e-business applications. Building on this work, we have developed a methodology for performance modeling of distributed component-based systems using QPNs [9]. The methodology has been applied to model a number of systems ranging from simple systems to systems of realistic size and complexity. It can be used as a powerful tool for performance and scalability analysis. Some examples of modeling studies based on QPNs can be found in [14, 15, 18, 21]. These studies consider different types of systems including distributed component-based systems, event-based systems and Grid computing environments.

In this paper, we present QPME 2.0 (Queueing Petri net Modeling Environment) - a tool for stochastic modeling and analysis of systems using queueing Petri nets. The paper is an updated and extended version of [13] where we presented version 1.0 of the tool. QPME is made of two major components, a QPN Editor (QPE) and a Simulator for QPNs (SimQPN). In this paper, we present an overview of these components. Further details on their internal architecture and implementation can be found in [8, 10, 12, 24]. QPME is available free-of-charge for non-profit use (see [7]) and has been distributed to more than 100 universities and research organizations worldwide. The current license is closed-source, however, there are plans to make the tool open-source in the near future.

The most important new features introduced in Version 2.0 of the tool are the following:

- Central queue management and support for having multiple queueing places that share the same underlying physical queue.
- Advanced query engine for processing and visualization of simulation results.
- Support for simulating hierarchical QPNs using SimQPN.
- Support for defining probes that specify metrics of interest for which data should be collected.
- Support for two additional simulation output data analysis techniques: spectral analysis and standardized time series.
- Support for empirical and deterministic distributions.
- Improved performance and scalability of the simulation engine (SimQPN).
- Automatic detection of infinitely growing queues (model instability).
- A number of features improving user friendliness (e.g., simulation progress bar and "stop simulation" button).

The rest of this paper is organized as follows: We start with a brief introduction to QPNs in Section 2. Sections 3 and 4 provide an overview of the QPN editor and the simulation engine, respectively. Section 5 presents the framework for processing and visualization of the simulation results. Finally, Section 6 summarizes the ongoing and future work on QPME and the paper is wrapped up with some concluding remarks in Section 7.

2   Queueing Petri Nets

The main idea behind the QPN formalism was to add queueing and timing aspects to the places of Colored Generalized Stochastic Petri Nets (CGSPNs) [1].

This is done by allowing queues (service stations) to be integrated into places of CGSPNs. A place of a CGSPN that has an integrated queue is called a *queueing place* and consists of two components, the *queue* and a *depository* for tokens which have completed their service at the queue. The behavior of the net is as follows: tokens, when fired into a queueing place by any of its input transitions, are inserted into the queue according to the queue's scheduling strategy. Tokens in the queue are not available for output transitions of the place. After completion of its service, a token is immediately moved to the depository, where it becomes available for output transitions of the place. This type of queueing place is called *timed* queueing place. In addition to timed queueing places, QPNs also introduce *immediate* queueing places, which allow pure scheduling aspects to be described. Tokens in immediate queueing places can be viewed as being served immediately. Scheduling in such places has priority over scheduling/service in timed queueing places and firing of timed transitions. The rest of the net behaves like a normal CGSPN. A formal definition of a QPN follows [1]:

Definition 1. *A QPN is an 8-tuple*
$$QPN = (P, T, C, I^-, I^+, M_0, Q, W) \text{ where:}$$

1. $P = \{p_1, p_2, ..., p_n\}$ *is a finite and non-empty set of* places,
2. $T = \{t_1, t_2, ..., t_m\}$ *is a finite and non-empty set of* transitions, $P \cap T = \emptyset$,
3. C *is a* color function *that assigns a finite and non-empty set of* colors *to each place and a finite and non-empty set of* modes *to each transition.*
4. I^- *and* I^+ *are the backward and forward* incidence functions *defined on* $P \times T$, *such that*
   $$I^-(p, t), I^+(p, t) \in [C(t) \rightarrow C(p)_{MS}], \forall (p, t) \in P \times T^1$$
5. M_0 *is a function defined on* P *describing the* initial marking *such that* $M_0(p) \in C(p)_{MS}$.
6. $Q = (\tilde{Q}_1, \tilde{Q}_2, (q_1, ..., q_{|P|}))$ *where*
   - $\tilde{Q}_1 \subseteq P$ *is the set of timed queueing places,*
   - $\tilde{Q}_2 \subseteq P$ *is the set of immediate queueing places,* $\tilde{Q}_1 \cap \tilde{Q}_2 = \emptyset$ *and*
   - q_i *denotes the description of a queue*[2] *taking all colors of* $C(p_i)$ *into consideration, if* p_i *is a queueing place* or *equals the keyword 'null', if* p_i *is an ordinary place.*
7. $W = (\tilde{W}_1, \tilde{W}_2, (w_1, ..., w_{|T|}))$ *where*
   - $\tilde{W}_1 \subseteq T$ *is the set of timed transitions,*
   - $\tilde{W}_2 \subseteq T$ *is the set of immediate transitions,* $\tilde{W}_1 \cap \tilde{W}_2 = \emptyset$, $\tilde{W}_1 \cup \tilde{W}_2 = T$ *and*
   - $w_i \in [C(t_i) \longmapsto \mathbb{R}^+]$ *such that* $\forall c \in C(t_i)$:

---

[1] The subscript MS denotes multisets. $C(p)_{MS}$ denotes the set of all finite multisets of $C(p)$.

[2] In the most general definition of QPNs, queues are defined in a very generic way allowing the specification of arbitrarily complex scheduling strategies taking into account the state of both the queue and the depository of the queueing place [1]. In QPME, we use conventional queues as defined in queueing network theory.

$w_i(c) \in \mathbb{R}^+$ *is interpreted as a rate of a negative exponential distribution specifying the firing delay due to color c, if* $t_i \in \tilde{W}_1$ *or a firing weight specifying the relative firing frequency due to color c, if* $t_i \in \tilde{W}_2$.

For a more detailed introduction to the QPN modeling formalism, the reader is referred to [1,3]. To illustrate the above definition, we present an example QPN model of a simple Java EE system. The model was taken from [11] and is shown in Figure 1.

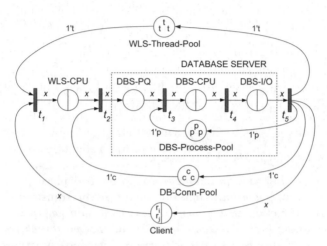

Fig. 1. QPN Model of a Java EE System [11]

The system modeled is an e-business application running in a Java EE environment consisting of a WebLogic Server (Java EE application server) hosting the application components and a backend database server used for persisting business data. In the following, we describe the places of the model:

Client Queueing place with IS scheduling strategy used to represent clients sending requests to the system. Time spent at the queue of this place corresponds to the client think time, i.e., the service time of the queue is equal to the average client think time.

WLS-CPU Queueing place with PS scheduling strategy used to represent the CPU of the *WebLogic Server (WLS)*.

DBS-CPU Queueing place with PS scheduling strategy used to represent the CPU of the *database server (DBS)*.

DBS-I/O Queueing place with FCFS scheduling strategy used to represent the disk subsystem of the DBS.

WLS-Thread-Pool Ordinary place used to represent the thread pool of the WLS. Each token in this place represents a WLS thread.

DB-Conn-Pool Ordinary place used to represent the database connection pool of the WLS. Tokens in this place represent database connections to the DBS.

DBS-Process-Pool Ordinary place used to represent the process pool of the DBS. Tokens in this place represent database processes.

DBS-PQ Ordinary place used to hold incoming requests at the DBS while they
wait for a server process to be allocated to them.

The following types of tokens (token colors) are used in the model:

Token $'r_i'$ represents a request sent by a client for execution of a transaction
of class i. For each request class a separate token color is used (e.g., $'r_1'$,
$'r_2'$, $'r_3'$,...). Tokens of these colors can be contained only in places Client,
WLS-CPU, DBS-PQ, DBS-CPU and DBS-I/O.

Token 't' represents a WLS thread. Tokens of this color can be contained only
in place WLS-Thread-Pool.

Token 'p' represents a DBS process. Tokens of this color can be contained only
in place DBS-Process-Pool.

Token 'c' represents a database connection to the DBS. Tokens of this color
can be contained only in place DB-Conn-Pool.

We now take a look at the life-cycle of a client request in our system model. Every
request (modeled by a token of color $'r_i'$ for some i) is initially at the queue of
place Client where it waits for a user-specified think time. After the think time
elapses, the request moves to the Client depository where it waits for a WLS
thread to be allocated to it before its processing can begin. Once a thread is
allocated (modeled by taking a token of color 't' from place WLS-Thread-Pool),
the request moves to the queue of place WLS-CPU, where it receives service from
the CPU of the WLS. It then moves to the depository of the place and waits for
a database connection to be allocated to it. The database connection (modeled
by token 'c') is used to connect to the database and make any updates required
by the respective transaction. A request sent to the database server arrives at
place DBS-PQ (DBS Process Queue) where it waits for a server process (modeled
by token 'p') to be allocated to it. Once this is done, the request receives service
first at the CPU and then at the disk subsystem of the database server. This
completes the processing of the request, which is then sent back to place Client
releasing the held DBS process, database connection and WLS thread.

3   QPE - Queueing Petri Net Editor

QPE (Queueing Petri net Editor), the first major component of QPME, provides
a graphical tool for building QPN models [8]. It offers a user-friendly interface
enabling the user to quickly and easily construct QPN models. QPE is based
on the Eclipse Rich Content Platform (RCP) and the Graphical Editing Framework (GEF) [23]. The latter is an open source framework dedicated to providing
a rich, consistent graphical editing environment for applications on the Eclipse
platform. As a GEF application, QPE is written in pure Java and runs as a
standalone RCP application on all operating systems officially supported by the
Eclipse platform. This includes Windows, Linux, Solaris, HP-UX, IBM AIX and
Apple Mac OS among others, making QPE widely accessible. The only thing

required is a Java Runtime Environment (JRE) 6.0. It is recommended to run QPE on Windows since this is the platform it has been tested on.

Being a GEF application, QPE is based on the model-view-controller (MVC) architecture. The model in our case is the QPN being defined, the views provide graphical representations of the QPN, and finally the controller connects the model with the views, managing the interactions among them. QPN models created with QPE can be stored on disk as XML documents. QPE uses its own XML schema based on the Petri Net Markup Language (PNML) [4] with some changes and extensions to support the additional constructs available in QPN models. Figure 2 shows the QPE main window which is comprised of four views: Main Editor View, Outline View, Properties View and Console View. The Main Editor View contains a Net Editor, Palette and Color Editor. The Net Editor displays the graphical representation of the currently edited QPN, the Palette displays the set of QPN elements that are used to build QPN models and the Color Editor, shown in Figure 3, is used to define the token colors available for use in the places of the QPN. The Properties View enables the user to edit the properties of the currently selected element in the Net Editor. Finally, the Console View is used to display output from QPE extensions and plug-ins.

A characterizing feature of QPE is that it allows token colors to be defined globally for the whole QPN instead of on a per place basis. This feature was motivated by the fact that in QPNs typically the same token color (type) is

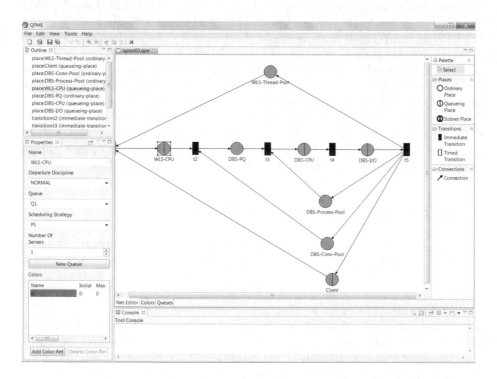

Fig. 2. QPE Main Window

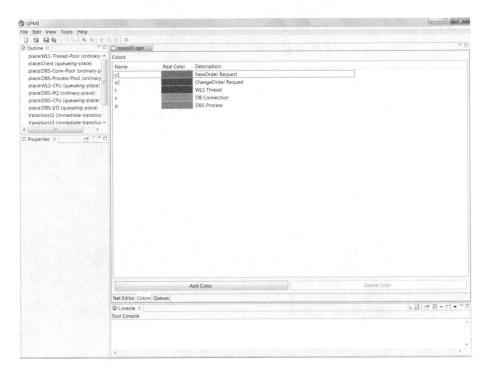

Fig. 3. QPE Color Editor

used in multiple places. Instead of having to define the color multiple times, the user can define it one time and then reference it in all places where it is used. This saves time, makes the model definition more compact, and last but not least, it makes the modeling process less error-prone since references to the same token color are specified explicitly.

Another characterizing feature of QPE, not supported in standard QPN models [21], is the ability to have multiple queueing places configured to share the same underlying physical queue[3]. In QPE, queues are defined centrally (similar to token colors) and once defined they can be referenced from inside multiple queueing places. This allows to use queueing places to represent software entities, e.g., software components, which can then be mapped to different hardware resources modeled as queues [21]. This feature of QPE, combined with the support for hierarchical QPNs, allows to build multi-layered models of software architectures similar to the way this is done in layered queueing networks, however, with the advantage that QPNs enjoy all the benefits of Petri nets for modeling synchronization aspects.

Figure 4 shows the Incidence Function Editor. The incidence function specifies the behavior of the transition for each of its firing modes in terms of tokens

---

[3] While the same effect can be achieved by using multiple subnet places mapped to a nested QPN containing a single queueing place, this would require expanding tokens that enter the nested QPN with a *tag* to keep track of their origin as explained in [2].

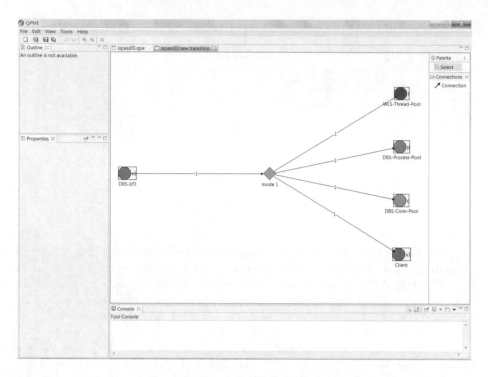

Fig. 4. QPE Incidence Function Editor

destroyed and/or created in the places of the QPN. Once opened the Incidence Function Editor displays the transition input places on the left, the transition modes in the middle and the transition output places on the right. Each place (input or output) is displayed as a rectangle containing a separate circle for each token color allowed in the place. The user can create connections from token colors of input places to modes or from modes to token colors of output places. If a connection is created between a token color of a place and a mode, this means that when the transition fires in this mode, tokens of the respective color are removed from the place. Similarly, if a connection is created between a mode and a token color of an output place, this means that when the transition fires in this mode, tokens of the respective color are deposited in the place. Each connection can be assigned a weight interpreted as the number of tokens removed/deposited in the place when the transition fires in the respective mode.

Further details on the implementation of QPE can be found in [8, 24].

4   SimQPN - Simulator for Queueing Petri Nets

The second major component of QPME is SimQPN - a discrete-event simulation engine specialized for QPNs. It is very light-weight and has been implemented 100% in Java to ensure portability and platform-independence. SimQPN can be run either as Eclipse plugin in QPE or as a standalone Java application. Thus, even though QPE is limited to Eclipse-supported platforms, SimQPN can be run on any platform on which Java SE 5.0 is available. This makes it possible to design a model on one platform (e.g., Windows) using QPE and then analyze it on another platform (e.g., Linux) using SimQPN. SimQPN configuration parameters are stored as metadata inside the XML file containing the QPN model.

SimQPN simulates QPNs using a sequential algorithm based on the event-scheduling approach for simulation modeling. Being specialized for QPNs, it simulates QPN models directly and has been designed to exploit the knowledge of the structure and behavior of QPNs to improve the efficiency of the simulation. Therefore, SimQPN provides much better performance than a general purpose simulator would provide, both in terms of the speed of simulation and the quality of output data provided.

SimQPN currently supports most, but not all of the QPN features that are supported in QPE. The reason for not limiting QPE to only those features supported by SimQPN is that QPE is meant as a general purpose QPN editor and as such the QPN features it offers should not be limited to any particular analysis method. SimQPN currently supports three different scheduling strategies for queues inside queueing places: Processor-Sharing (PS), Infinite Server (IS) and First-Come-First-Served (FCFS). A wide range of service time distributions are supported including Beta, BreitWigner, ChiSquare, Gamma, Hyperbolic, Exponential, ExponentialPower, Logarithmic, Normal, StudentT, Uniform and VonMises as well as deterministic and empirical distributions. Empirical distributions are supported in the following way. The user is expected to provide a probability distribution function (PDF), specified as an array of positive real numbers (histogram) read from an external text file. A cumulative distribution function (CDF) is constructed from the PDF and inverted using a binary search for the nearest bin boundary and a linear interpolation within the bin (resulting in a constant density within each bin).

Timed transitions are currently not supported, however, in most cases a timed transition can be approximated by a serial network consisting of an immediate transition, a queueing place and a second immediate transition. The spectrum of scheduling strategies and service time distributions supported by SimQPN will be extended. Support for timed transitions and immediate queueing places is also planned and will be included in a future release.

4.1   Probes and Data Collection Modes

SimQPN offers the ability to configure what data exactly to collect during the simulation and what statistics to provide at the end of the run. This can be specified on a per *location* basis where location is defined to have one of the following five types:

1. Ordinary place.
2. Queue of a queueing place (considered from the perspective of the place).
3. Depository of a queueing place.
4. Queue (considered from the perspective of all places it is part of).
5. Probe.

A probe is a tool to specify a region of interest for which data should be collected during simulation. The region of a probe includes one or more places and is defined by one start and one end place. The goal is to evaluate the time tokens spend in the region when moving between its begin and end place. The probe starts its measurements for each token entering its region at the start place and updates the statistics when the token leaves at the end place. It can be specified whether the measurements start when the token enters the start place or when the token leaves it. The same can be specified for the end place. Each probe references a subset of the colors defined in the QPN. A probe only collects data for tokens of the referenced colors.

Currently, probes allow to gather statistics for the residence time of a token in a region of interest. For example, in the model shown in Figure 1, a probe can be used to measure the time spent at the database server, which consists of places DBS-PQ, DBS-CPU and DBS-I/O. In this case, the probe starts at place DBS-PQ (on entry) and ends at place DBS-I/O (on exit). For each transaction of type i for which data should be collected, a reference to color 'r_i' is defined in the probe. As a result, the user is provided with the mean residence time of requests in the database server including the associated confidence interval and distribution.

The probes are realized by attaching timestamps to individual tokens. In the start place a probe adds the current simulation time as a timestamp to all tokens of colors it is interested in. A token can carry timestamps from different probes. Thus intersecting regions of several probes in a QPN are supported. Firing transitions collect all timestamps from input tokens and copy the timestamps to the output tokens. For each output token only the timestamps of probes interested in the token color are passed on. In some models, e.g. with a synchronous fork/join, it is possible that a transition gets tokens with different timestamps from the same probe. In this case, a warning is issued and only the minimal timestamp is passed on. The other timestamps are discarded. In the end place of a probe, its timestamp is removed and its statistics are updated.

For each location the user can choose between six modes of data collection (called stats-levels). The higher the mode, the more information is collected and the more statistics are provided. Since collecting data costs CPU time, the more data is collected, the slower the simulation would progress. Therefore, by configuring data collection modes, the user can speed up the simulation by making sure that no time is wasted collecting unnecessary data. The six data collection modes (stats-levels) are defined as follows:

Mode 0. In this mode no statistics are collected.

Mode 1. This mode considers only token throughput data, i.e., for each location the token arrival and departure rates are estimated for each color.

Mode 2. This mode adds token population, token occupancy and queue utilization data, i.e., for each location the following data is provided:
  - Token occupancy (for locations of type 1 or 3): fraction of time in which there is a token inside the location.
  - Queue utilization (for locations of type 2 or 4): proportion of the queue's server resources used by tokens arriving through the respective location.

- For each token color of the respective location:
  - Minimum/maximum number of tokens observed in the location.
  - Average number of tokens in the location.
  - Token color occupancy: fraction of time in which there is a token of the respective color inside the location.

Mode 3. This mode adds token residence time data, i.e., for each location the following additional data is provided on a per-color basis:

- Minimum/maximum observed token residence time.
- Mean and standard deviation of observed token residence times.
- Estimated steady state mean token residence time.
- Confidence interval (c.i.) for the steady state mean token residence time at a user-specified significance level.

Mode 4. This mode adds a histogram of observed token residence times.
Mode 5. This mode additionally dumps token residence times to a file for further analysis.

Since probes currently only support residence time statistics, mode 1 and 2 do not apply to them.

4.2 Steady State Analysis

SimQPN supports the following four methods for estimation of the steady state mean residence times of tokens inside the various locations of the QPN:

1. Method of independent replications (replication/deletion approach).
2. Method of non-overlapping batch means (NOMB).
3. Spectral analysis.
4. Standardized time series.

We refer the reader to [16, 19] for an introduction to these methods. All of them can be used to provide point and interval estimates of the steady state mean token residence time. Details on the way these methods were implemented in SimQPN can be found in [12]. For users that would like to use different methods for steady state analysis (for example ASAP [22]), SimQPN can be configured to output observed token residence times to files (mode 5), which can then be used as input to external analysis tools. SimQPN utilizes the *Colt* open source library for high performance scientific and technical computing in Java, developed at CERN [6]. In SimQPN, Colt is primarily used for random number generation and, in particular, its implementation of the Mersenne Twister random number generator is employed [17].

We have validated the analysis algorithms implemented in SimQPN by subjecting them to a rigorous experimental analysis and evaluating the quality of point and interval estimates [12]. In particular, the variability of point estimates provided by SimQPN and the coverage of confidence intervals reported were quantified. A number of different models of realistic size and complexity were considered. Our analysis showed that data reported by SimQPN is very accurate and stable. Even for residence time, the metric with highest variation, the standard deviation of point estimates did not exceed 2.5% of the mean value. In all cases, the estimated coverage of confidence intervals was less than 2% below the nominal value (higher than 88% for 90% confidence intervals and higher than 93% for 95% confidence intervals). For FCFS queues, SimQPN also supports *indirect estimation* of the steady state token residence times according to the variance-reduction technique in [5].

SimQPN includes an implementation of the method of Welch for determining the length of the initial transient (warm-up period). We have followed the rules in [16] for choosing the number of replications, their length and the window size. SimQPN allows the user to configure the first two parameters and then automatically plots the moving averages for different window sizes. Simulation experiments with SimQPN usually comprise two stages: stage 1 during which the length of the initial transient is determined, and stage 2 during which the steady-state behavior of the system is simulated and analyzed. Again, if the user prefers to use another method for elimination of the initialization bias, this can be achieved by dumping collected data to files (mode 4) and feeding it into respective analysis tools.

4.3   Departure Disciplines

A novel feature of SimQPN is the introduction of the so-called *departure disciplines*. This is an extension of the QPN modeling formalism introduced to address a common drawback of QPN models (and of Petri nets in general), i.e., tokens inside ordinary places and depositories are not distinguished in terms of their order of arrival. Departure disciplines are defined for ordinary places or depositories and determine the order in which arriving tokens become available for output transitions. We define two departure disciplines, Normal (used by default) and First-In-First-Out (FIFO). The former implies that tokens become available for output transitions immediately upon arrival just like in conventional QPN models. The latter implies that tokens become available for output transitions in the order of their arrival, i.e., a token can leave the place/depository only after all tokens that have arrived before it have left, hence the term FIFO. For an example of how this feature can be exploited and the benefits it provides we refer the reader to [9]. An alternative approach to introduce token ordering in an ordinary place is to replace the place with an immediate queueing place containing a FCFS queue. The generalized queue definition from [1] can be exploited to define the scheduling strategy of the queue in such a way that tokens are served immediately according to FCFS, but only if the depository is empty [3]. If there is a token in the depository, all tokens are blocked in their current position until the depository becomes free. However, the generalized queue definition from [1], while theoretically powerful, is impractical to implement, so, in practice, it is rarely used and queues in QPNs are usually treated as conventional queues from queueing network theory.

5   Processing and Visualization of Simulation Results

After a successful simulation run, SimQPN saves the results from the simulation in an XML file with a `.simqpn` extension which is stored in the configured output directory. In addition, a summary of the results in text format is printed on the console and stored in a separate file with a `.log` extension.

QPE provides an advanced query engine for processing and visualization of the simulation results. The query engine allows to define queries on the simulation results in order to filter, aggregate and visualize performance data for multiple places, queues and colors of the QPN. The results from the queries can be displayed in textual or graphical form. QPE provides two editors that can be used as a front-end to the query engine: "Simple Query Editor" and "Advanced Query Editor".

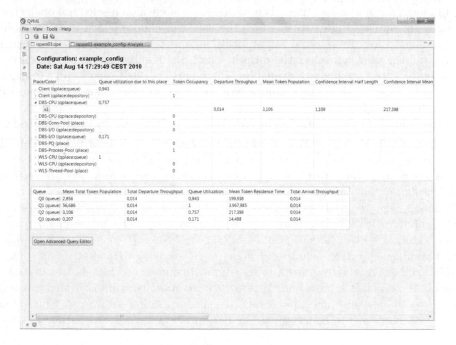

Fig. 5. Basic Query Editor

5.1   Simple Query Editor

The "Simple Query Editor", shown in Figure 5, is displayed when opening the `.simqpn` file containing the results from the simulation. The editor displays the collected statistics for the various places and queues of the QPN. Statistics are reported on a per *location* basis where location is defined as in Sect. 4.1). The five location types are denoted as follows:

1. "place" - ordinary place.
2. "qplace:queue" - queue of a queueing place considered from the perspective of the place.
3. "qplace:depository" - depository of a queueing place.
4. "queue" - queue considered from the perspective of all places it is part of.
5. "probe".

The statistics for the various locations are presented in two tables. The first table contains the statistics for locations of type "place", "qplace:queue", "qplace:depository" and "probe", while the second one contains the statistics for locations of type "queue". Depending on the configured data collection modes (see Sect. 4.1), the set of available performance metrics for the various locations may vary.

By clicking on multiple locations while holding "Ctrl", the user can select a set of locations and respective token colors. A right click on a selection opens the context menu (see Figure 6) in which the user can choose which metric should be visualized for the selected set of locations and token colors. After choosing a metric, the user can select the form in which the results should be presented. Currently, three options are available: "Pie Chart", "Bar Chart" and "Console Output". Figure 7 shows an example of a pie chart and bar chart for the metric mean token residence time.

The "Simple Query Editor" is intended for simple filtering and visualization of the simulation results and does not provide any means to aggregate metrics over

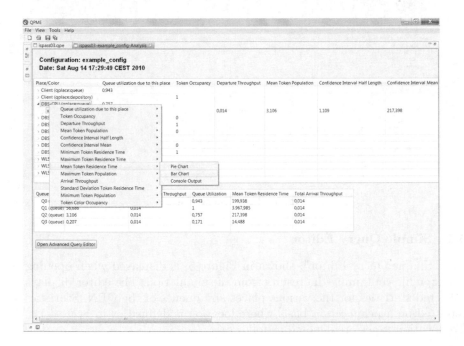

Fig. 6. Context Menu in Basic Query Editor

multiple locations and token colors. Queries involving aggregation are supported by the "Advanced Query Editor".

5.2 Advanced Query Editor

The "Advanced Query Editor" is opened by clicking on the respective button at the bottom of the "Simple Query Editor". Using this editor the user can define complex queries on the simulation results involving both filtering and aggregation of performance metrics from multiple places, probes and queues of the QPN. An example of such a query is shown in Figure 8.

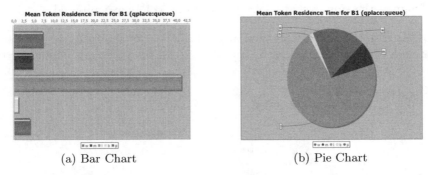

(a) Bar Chart   (b) Pie Chart

Fig. 7. Example Diagrams

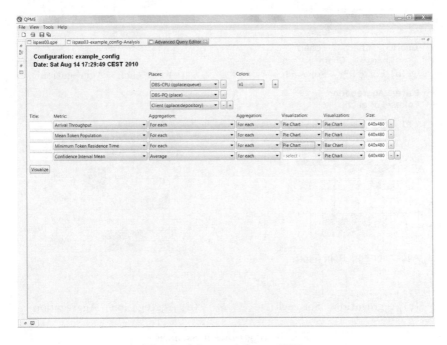

Fig. 8. Advanced Query Editor

A query is defined by first selecting a set of locations and a set of colors using the combo boxes and the +/- buttons at the top of the editor. The selected locations and colors specify a filter on the data that should be considered as part of the query. Using the table at the bottom of the editor, the user can select the specific performance metrics of interest and how data should be aggregated with respect to the considered locations and colors. Three options for aggregating data are available:

- "For each" - no aggregation is applied and performance metrics are considered separately for each location/color.
- "Average" - the average over the selected locations/colors is computed.
- "Sum" - the sum over the selected locations/colors is computed.

Two "Aggregation" fields are available, the left one is applied to the set of locations, while the right one is applied to the set of colors. Similarly, two

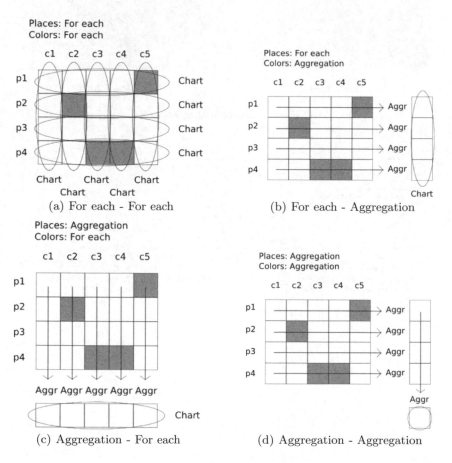

Fig. 9. Aggregation Scenarios

"Visualization" fields are available, one applied to the set of locations, the other one to the set of colors. QPE currently offers three visualization options: "Bar Chart", "Pie Chart" and "Console Output".

Depending on the selected aggregation options, there are four possible scenarios: a) no aggregation, b) aggregation over colors, c) aggregation over locations, d) aggregation over both colors and locations. The four scenarios are depicted in Figure 9 illustrating how performance metrics are aggregated and used to produce a set of charts capturing the results from the respective query. Assuming that the user has selected a set of locations $p_1, p_2, ..., p_m$ and a set of colors $c_1, c_2, ..., c_n$, a matrix is generated that contains the values of the selected performance metric for each combination of location and color. Some of the cells of the matrix could be empty (denoted in grey in Figure 9). This could happen if the metric is not available in the configured data collection mode or if the considered color is not defined for the respective location. The number of charts generated depends on the selected aggregation options. In case no aggregation is selected, $m + n$ charts are generated. In the case of aggregation over the set of colors or locations, one chart is generated. Finally, in the case of aggregation over both colors and locations, the result of the query is a single value.

6 Ongoing and Future Work

As part of our ongoing and future work on QPME, enhancements along three different dimensions are envisioned: i) user friendliness, ii) model expressiveness and iii) model analysis methods. In the following, we outline the major enhancements that have been planned.

Improve User Friendliness. Support for the following features will be added:
  o Introduce modeling templates (e.g., for modeling common types of resources and workloads) to facilitate model reuse.
  o Introduce automated support for sensitivity analysis.

Improve Model Expressiveness. Support for the following features will be added:
  o Load-dependent service times (resource demands).
  o Further scheduling strategies for queues, e.g., GPS, priority scheduling.
  o Timed transitions.
  o Transition priorities and inhibitor arcs.

Improve Model Analysis Methods. Support for the following features will be added:
  o Support for parallel/distributed simulation to take advantage of multi-core processors.
  o Support for analytical model solution techniques (structured analysis techniques, product-form solution techniques, approximation techniques).
  o Further methods for determining the length of the simulation warm-up period.

7   Summary

In this paper, we presented QPME 2.0, our tool for modeling and analysis using queueing Petri nets. QPME provides a user-friendly graphical interface enabling the user to quickly and easily construct QPN models. It offers a highly optimized simulation engine that can be used to analyze models of realistically-sized systems. In addition, being implemented in Java, QPME runs on all major platforms and is widely accessible. QPME provides a robust and powerful tool for performance analysis making it possible to exploit the modeling power and expressiveness of queueing Petri nets to their full potential. The tool is available free-of-charge for non-profit use and there are plans to make it open-source in the near future. Further information can be found at the QPME homepage [20].

Acknowledgements

This work was funded by the German Research Foundation (DFG) under grant No. KO 3445/6-1. We acknowledge the support of Frederik Zipp and Ana Aleksieva from KIT.

References

1. Bause, F.: Queueing Petri Nets - A formalism for the combined qualitative and quantitative analysis of systems. In: Proc. of 5th Intl. Workshop on Petri Nets and Perf. Models, Toulouse, France, October 19-22 (1993)
2. Bause, F., Buchholz, P., Kemper, P.: Integrating Software and Hardware Performance Models Using Hierarchical Queueing Petri Nets. In: Proc. of the 9. ITG / GI - Fachtagung Messung, Modellierung und Bewertung von Rechen- und Kommunikationssystemen, Freiberg, Germany (1997)
3. Bause, F., Kritzinger, F.: Stochastic Petri Nets - An Introduction to the Theory. Vieweg Verlag (2002)
4. Billington, J., Christensen, S., van Hee, K., Kindler, E., Kummer, O., Petrucci, L., Post, R., Stehno, C., Weber, M.: The Petri Net Markup Language: Concepts, Technology, and Tools. In: Proc. of 24th Intl. Conf. on Application and Theory of Petri Nets, June 23-27, Eindhoven, Holland (2003)
5. Carson, J., Law, A.: Conservation Equations and Variance Reduction in Queueing Simulations. Operations Research 28 (1980)
6. CERN - European Organisation for Nuclear Research. The Colt Distribution - Open Source Libraries for High Performance Scientific and Technical Computing in Java (2004), http://dsd.lbl.gov/~hoschek/colt/
7. Descartes Research Group (August 2010), http://www.descartes-research.net
8. Dutz, C.: QPE - A Graphical Editor for Modeling using Queueing Petri Nets. Master thesis, Technische Universität Darmstadt (April 2006)
9. Kounev, S.: Performance Modeling and Evaluation of Distributed Component-Based Systems using Queueing Petri Nets. IEEE Transactions on Software Engineering 32(7), 486–502 (2006)
10. Kounev, S.: QPME 2.0 User's Guide. Descartes Research Group, Karlsruhe Institute of Technology (KIT) (August 2010)

11. Kounev, S., Buchmann, A.: Performance Modelling of Distributed E-Business Applications using Queuing Petri Nets. In: Proc. of the 2003 IEEE Intl. Symposium on Performance Analysis of Systems and Software, Austin, USA, March 20-22 (2003)
12. Kounev, S., Buchmann, A.: SimQPN - a tool and methodology for analyzing queueing Petri net models by means of simulation. Performance Evaluation 63(4-5), 364–394 (2006)
13. Kounev, S., Dutz, C.: QPME - A Performance Modeling Tool Based on Queueing Petri Nets. ACM SIGMETRICS Performance Evaluation Review (PER), Special Issue on Tools for Computer Performance Modeling and Reliability Analysis 36(4), 46–51 (2009)
14. Kounev, S., Nou, R., Torres, J.: Autonomic QoS-Aware Resource Management in Grid Computing using Online Performance Models. In: Proc. of 2nd Intl. Conf. on Perf. Evaluation Methodologies and Tools - VALUETOOLS, Nantes, France, October 23-25 (2007)
15. Kounev, S., Sachs, K., Bacon, J., Buchmann, A.: A Methodology for Performance Modeling of Distributed Event-Based Systems. In: Proc. of 11th IEEE Intl. Symp. on Object/Comp./Service-oriented Real-time Distr. Computing (ISORC), Orlando, USA (May 2008)
16. Law, A., Kelton, D.W.: Simulation Modeling and Analysis, 3rd edn. Mc Graw Hill Companies, New York (2000)
17. Matsumoto, M., Nishimura, T.: Mersenne Twister: A 623-Dimensionally Equidistributed Uniform Pseudo-Random Number Generator. ACM Trans. on Modeling and Comp. Simulation 8(1), 3–30 (1998)
18. Nou, R., Kounev, S., Julia, F., Torres, J.: Autonomic QoS control in enterprise Grid environments using online simulation. Journal of Systems and Software 82(3), 486–502 (2009)
19. Pawlikowski, K.: Steady-State Simulation of Queueing Processes: A Survey of Problems and Solutions. ACM Computing Surveys 22(2), 123–170 (1990)
20. QPME Homepage (August 2010), http://descartes.ipd.kit.edu/projects/qpme/
21. Sachs, K.: Performance Modeling and Benchmarking of Event-based Systems. PhD thesis, TU Darmstadt (2010)
22. Steiger, N., Lada, E., Wilson, J., Joines, J., Alexopoulos, C., Goldsman, D.: ASAP3: a batch means procedure for steady-state simulation analysis. ACM Transactions on Modeling and Computer Simulation 15(1), 39–73 (2005)
23. The Eclipse Foundation. Graphical Editing Framework (GEF) (2006), http://www.eclipse.org/gef/
24. Zipp, F.: Study Thesis : Filterung, Aggregation und Visualisierung von QPN-Analyseergebnissen. Descartes Research Group, Karlsruhe Institute of Technology (KIT) (May 2009) (in German)

A Logistics Workload for
Event Notification Middleware

Stefan Appel and Kai Sachs

TU Darmstadt, Germany
lastname@dvs.tu-darmstadt.de

Abstract. The event-based paradigm plays an important role to reflect logistics processes in modern IT infrastructures. Events occur at many stages, e.g., when goods tagged with RFID chips are scanned, when transportation vehicles move or when sensors report environmental observations. These events have to be delivered to interested consumers by a reliable notification middleware, which is crucial for a successful implementation of event-based applications. Specified service levels have to be fulfilled and to guarantee them, an exhaustive evaluation and analysis of the underlying event notification middleware is required. This can be achieved by applying well-defined test scenarios that allow us to analyze different aspects of the middleware in an independent and representative way.

In this paper we present a realistic workload originating from a real world scenario in the logistics domain. Our workload is suited to test event notification middleware under realistic conditions; it stresses different aspects of the middleware while being scalable.

1 Introduction

Designing systems that follow the event-based paradigm are necessary to develop new types of applications [6,3]. These application have to handle large amounts of data originating from, e.g., sensor networks or the Internet of Things. The devices collect a variety of data that is potentially interesting for different applications. For example, nowadays mobile phones are equipped with GPS sensors and accelerometers allowing applications for monitoring the environment [9,15]. All these events, or more precisely, their representations, the event notifications, need to be transported from the event producers to event consumers [6]. To reach a high amount of flexibility throughout this communication process, event producers and consumers need to be decoupled physically and logically. Therefore, event notifications are routed from event producers to event consumers by a notification middleware (also called notification service, see Figure 1). This underlying notification middleware allows us to decouple producers and consumers and is responsible for a reliable message transportation [10].

Driven by the research in *ADiWa*[1] we identified the need for testing and analyzing event notification middleware. Within ADiWa business processes adapt and react dynamically to events.

---

[1] Alliance Digital Product Flow (ADiWa). Funded by the German Federal Ministry of Education and Research under grant 01IA08006.

K. Sachs, I. Petrov, and P. Guerrero (Eds.): Buchmann Festschrift, LNCS 6462, pp. 312–324, 2010.

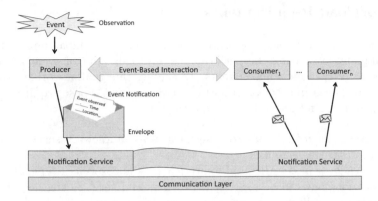

Fig. 1. Event-based System - Schematic Overview

In this paper, we present a novel workload based on a logistics scenario. Our goal is to support exhaustive testing and analysis of a notification middleware by stressing the system in different ways. The remainder of this paper is structured as follows: we first present related work in the area of quality of service (QoS) and workload characterization of event-based systems (EBS). In the next section we discuss requirements a workload has to fullfil with a focus on the logistics domain. We then introduce a logistics workload which models three interactions among different entities and derive variable message rates to describe the workload. The paper concludes with a short summary of our results and an outlook on future research.

2   Related Work

Several test harnesses and benchmarks for different EBS were published, e.g., [8,5,7]. However, previous work in the area of benchmarking mostly focuses on the design and development of test frameworks, but not on the definition of workloads. An example for a well-defined workload scenario used for the industry standard benchmark SPECjms2007 can be found in [13]. The application scenario models seven business interactions of a supermarket's supply chain where RFID technology is used to track the flow of goods. SPECjms2007 includes some limited publish/subscribe communication as part of the workload, but mainly focusing on point-to-point communication. The setup of consumer, producer and subscriptions is static and does not change at runtime. A benchmark for publish/subscribe systems built on top of the SPECjms2007 workload is jms2009-PS [12]. However, the implemented topology is static and subscriptions do not change at runtime. For a comprehensive overview of existing benchmarks and test harnesses we refer to [11]. An overview of relevant QoS metrics in the context of distributed and decentralized publish-subscribe systems is provided in [2]. Further, QoS of EBS is discussed in [1].

3   Workload Requirements

The major goal of this paper is to provide a standard workload and metrics for measuring and evaluating the performance and scalability of event notification middleware in dynamic environments. To achieve this goal, a workload must be designed to meet a number of important requirements. These requirements can be grouped in the following five categories [11]:

1. *Representativeness:* It has to reflect the way middleware services are exercised in real-life systems.
2. *Comprehensiveness:* All middleware features and services typically used in applications have to be exercised. Features and services stressed should be weighted according to their usage in real-life systems.
3. *Focus:* The emphasis has to be on the event notification middleware and the impact of other components and services has to be minimized.
4. *Configurability:* The workload should be configurable to provide a base for exhaustive system analysis.
5. *Scalability:* The workload must not have any inherent scalability limitations and provide ways to scale the workload in a flexible manner.

Based on these categories, we specified a set of requirements, which differ in major points from previous work. For example:

1. *Independent Participants:* Event producers and consumers should be logically decoupled.
2. *Communication Plattform:* An event service bus [4] should be used for communication.
3. *Dynamic Environment:* Subscriptions, subscribers and message producers should not be static and change frequently.

Keeping these requirements in mind we specified a novel workload for performance analysis of event notification middleware based on a real-world scenario.

4   Logistics Workload

In this section we present a logistics workload to evaluate event notification middleware. The workload models three different interactions in a company. Figure 2 gives a schematic overview and shows the information flow as well as the flow of goods. A logistics workload stresses different aspects of the middleware; especially high fluctuation rates of event producers and consumers are characteristic.

In the following sections we first introduce event notification producers and and interacting entities involved in our scenario. Three different interactions between the entities are simulated to evaluate the event notification middleware. For this we derive interaction rates and publish/subscribe parameters.

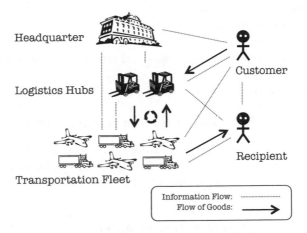

Fig. 2. Flow of Information and Goods

4.1 Event Notification Producers

In our scenario the event notifications are generated by different entities. Either humans or three different types of devices, RFID Readers, On-board Units or Environment Sensors, are involved in the event detection and notification generation process:

Humans (H). To initiate a shipment process an order has to be triggered by humans. The addresses of sender and recipient are submitted to and verified by the company. Afterwards, the order is acknowledged and the transportation process starts.

RFID Reader (RFID). We assume a scenario where RFID tags are attached to all transported goods. These tags are read when goods enter and leave hubs as well as when they are delivered.

On-board Units (OBU). Modern trucks are equipped with on-board units including GPS receivers so that the vehicle position can be tracked. The update interval is a tradeoff between accuracy and system utilization in terms of bandwidth, CPU utilization and network traffic. For our scenario we assume an update interval of three minutes.

Environment Sensors (ENV). To ensure that goods are transported appropriately, environment sensor can be installed to monitor, e.g., the temperature. Customers are interested in whether the conditions were met throughout the transportation process.

4.2 Interacting Entities

The above listed notification producers act in the context of entities. The following parties participate in interactions modeling the message flow:

1. *Company Headquarters* (HQ):
   Messages generated by humans.
2. *Logistics Hubs* (LH):
   Messages generated by RFID readers and environment sensors.
3. *Customers* (C):
   Messages generated by humans.
4. *Transportation Vehicles* (V):
   Messages generated by on-board units and environment sensors.

We consider that customers are performing monitoring and tracking of goods. For better usability, we specified a fixed ratio between different entities based upon data from a real-world company [14]. The base value for scaling the entities is the number of hubs $BASE_L$.

$$|Logistics\ Hubs| := BASE_L$$
$$|Headquarters| := 1$$
$$|Vehicles| := 53 \cdot BASE_L$$
$$\left|\frac{Customers}{day}\right| := 1000 \cdot BASE_L$$
$$\left|\frac{Shipments}{day}\right| := 8384 \cdot BASE_L$$

4.3   Interaction Patterns

Throughout the delivery process different interactions between the entities take place. Each interaction involves messages, subscriptions and quality of service requirements. We identify three interaction patterns for which we derive the message rates depending on the number of hubs:

Interaction 1 (I1): Shipment Order and Proof of Delivery
Interaction 2 (I2): Real-time Shipment Tracking
Interaction 3 (I3): Freight Monitoring

While I1 is a common interaction in logistics companies, I2 and I3 are currently popular trends, but are still in the early adopter phase. We expect the widespread deployment of real-time tracking and freight monitoring in the future.

I1 - Shipment Order and Proof of Delivery. The most important interaction is receiving shipment orders from customers and providing a proof of delivery (PoD) once the shipment is successfully delivered. The first event in this interactions is a message originating from a customer requesting pick up of goods (ShipmentOrder). Afterwards, shipment IDs are generated and the goods are tagged with RFID labels. The order confirmation message containing shipment IDs is then sent to the customer (OrderConfirmation). A hub close to the customer is selected and a pickup order is sent (PickupOrder). As soon as the goods leave the customer, the headquarters is responsible for tracking

Table 1. Interactions

(a) *Interaction 1* - Shipment Order and Proof of Delivery

Message Publisher	Message Subscriber	Type	QoS
Customer	Headquarters	ShipmentOrder	Reliable
Headquarters	Customer	OrderConfirmation	Reliable
Headquarters	Logistics Hub	PickupOrder	Reliable
Logistics Hub	Headquarters	ShipmentScan	Reliable
⋮	⋮	⋮	⋮
Recipient	Headquarters	ProofOfDelivery	Reliable

(b) *Interaction 2* - Real-time Shipment Tracking

Message Publisher	Message Subscriber	Type	QoS
Logistics Hub	Customer	ShipmentScan	Reliable
Vehicle	Customer	PositionData	Unreliable

(c) *Interaction 3* - Freight Monitoring

Message Publisher	Message Subscriber	Type	QoS
Vehicle	Customer	EnvironmentData	Reliable
Logistics Hub	Customer	EnvironmentData	Reliable

the goods and thus it receives messages whenever a shipment enters or leaves a hub (`ShipmentScan`). Finally, a proof of delivery message is generated once the shipment receives its final destination (`ProofOfDelivery`). With this message the interaction ends. Table 1(a) shows the message exchanges within I1; during the shipment process, the goods enter and leave several hubs. Thus multiple `ShipmentScan` messages occur within this interaction.

In terms of QoS, I1 has to be reliable. This means that the delivery of all messages has to be ensured in case of failures. This requires persistence mechanisms and recovery strategies integrated in the middleware.

I2 - Real-time Shipment Tracking. Real-time shipment tracking is an interaction pattern involving multiple entities and advanced application logic. It requires the knowledge of shipment IDs; based upon those IDs, it is possible to track the flow of goods. For tracking, the first step is subscribing to `ShipmentScan` messages matching the IDs of the shipments to track to receive messages originating from RFID readers. These events indicate whenever a shipment leaves or enters a hub. As soon as the shipment enters a transportation vehicle an additional subscription has to be issued to receive position events from the respective transportation vehicle.

Table 1(b) shows the messages within I2. Besides `ShipmentScan` messages, which need to be delivered reliably, `PositionData` messages are generated. The latter do not require reliable delivery since positions updates are generated regularly and only the last position is of major interest.

I3 - Freight Monitoring. Some goods require special treatment throughout the transportation process. For example, fresh products have to be kept below a

Table 2. Messages per Shipment

Message Type	Messages per Shipment
ShipmentOrder	1
OrderConfirmation	1
PickupOrder	1
ShipmentScan	4
ProofOfDelivery	1
PositionData	720
EnvironmentData	1440

certain temperature, other goods can only be transported in an upright position. Thus, it is essential to monitor goods and to identify improper treatment. An early detection is desirable to inform customers as fast as possible. This gives the opportunity to react quickly while the goods are still on their way. Real-time monitoring stresses the middleware and thus it is included in this workload. We choose temperature monitoring since it is one characteristic application of freight monitoring.

Table 1(c) shows the message exchange within I3. Opposed to PositionData messages in I2, EnvironmentData messages require reliable transportation since a violation of environmental conditions has to be reported.

4.4   Workload Generation

To simulate the message flow within a company, we derive rates at which messages enter the system. These rates are determined by the scenario design and scale with the number of hubs, $BASE_L$. Based upon the number of shipments per day (cp. Section 4.2) the rates can be calculated. We further make the following assumptions:

1. Time from pickup of goods to delivery is 3 days.
2. The goods are in transit 1.5 days (real transportation time), the goods are processed at hubs the other 1.5 days.
3. Vehicles and environment sensors submit messages every 3 minutes.
4. The goods pass 2 hubs until the recipient is reached.
5. Shipment scans and transportation are uniformly distributed over time.
6. All shipments are tracked in real-time.
7. The environmental conditions of 30% of the shipments are monitored.

This results in multiple messages for each shipment as shown in Table 2. Position and environment data messages are relevant for multiple shipments, thus the use of publish/subscribe mechanisms is the delivery paradigm of choice.

To generate the workload, five components are necessary, one for each message type. Each message driver component produces messages with certain rates, consumes them and simulates join and leave of producers and consumers at certain rates. Therefore, the message driver components have to ensure that published messages are consumed according to the scenario specification.

For describing the behavior of workload generating components (drivers) we use the following terms:

- *Active Entity:* Producer/consumer which publishes/subscribes to messages.
- *Messages min^{-1}:* Total number of published messages per minute.
- *Parallel Subscriptions:* Number of subscriptions in parallel.
- *Parallel Publishers:* Number of parallel message publishers.
- *Subscription join/leave min^{-1}:* Rate at which subscribers leave, respectively join the system.
- *Publisher join/leave min^{-1}:* Rate at which publishers leave, respectively join the system.
- *Pub/Sub Factor:* The number of recipients for each published message.

Table 3 lists all the message driver components along with the derived service rates.

ShipmentOrder Driver. Shipment orders are generated by customers, the destination is always the headquarters. Multiple customers issue shipment orders in parallel and customers enter, respectively leave, the system constantly. Each costumer only sends one shipment order. The pub/sub factor of one indicates that each messages is delivered to one destination, the headquarters.

OrderConfirmation Driver. As for the shipment orders, order confirmations are a one-to-one communication between headquarters and customers. Each customer receives one order confirmation.

PickupOrder Driver. Pickup orders are messages from the headquarters to hubs; each hub is supposed to receive the same number of messages. Since hubs and the headquarters are static parts of the infrastructure, a change rate of zero is assumed.

ShipmentScan Driver. Goods are scanned whenever they enter or leave hubs. The resulting messages are part of I1 and I2 and thus consumed by the headquarters as well as by customers. Many customers are subscribed simultaneously since transportation of goods lasts three days. Each message is consumed by the headquarters and by one customer.

ProofOfDelivery Driver. The proof of delivery (PoD) denotes the arrival of the shipment at the designated recipient. The final delivery is performed by vehicles, whereas the driver triggers the generation of the PoD message. PoD messages are consumed by customers as well as by the headquarters.

PositionData Driver. Position data is sent by all vehicles. Multiple shipments are transported within one vehicle, this motivates the high pub/sub factor; each position data message has to be received by around 474 customers. We assume that all shipments within a vehicle belong to different customers. The total number of subscriptions is determined by the goods being in move in parallel.

EnvironmentData Driver. We assume that 30 percent of all shipments require monitoring, e.g., of temperature. The monitoring is either performed within the trucks or the hubs which then generate the environment data messages; the messages are consumed by multiple customers.

Table 3. Event Driver and their Characteristics

Type	Characteristic	Rate	Active Entity
ShipmentOrder	Messages min^{-1}	$5.82 \cdot BASE_L$	C
	Parallel Subscriptions	1	HQ
	Parallel Publishers	$8.43 \cdot BASE_L$	C
	Subscription join/leave min^{-1}	0	HQ
	Publisher join/leave min^{-1}	$0.69 \cdot BASE_L$	C
	Pub/Sub Factor	1	HQ
OrderConfirmation	Messages min^{-1}	$5.82 \cdot BASE_L$	HQ
	Parallel Subscriptions	$8.43 \cdot BASE_L$	C
	Parallel Publishers	1	HQ
	Subscription join/leave min^{-1}	$0.69 \cdot BASE_L$	C
	Publisher join/leave min^{-1}	0	HQ
	Pub/Sub Factor	1	C
PickupOrder	Messages min^{-1}	$5.82 \cdot BASE_L$	HQ
	Parallel Subscriptions	$BASE_L$	LH
	Parallel Publishers	1	HQ
	Subscription join/leave min^{-1}	0	C
	Publisher join/leave min^{-1}	0	HQ
	Pub/Sub Factor	1	LH
ShipmentScan	Messages min^{-1}	$7.76 \cdot BASE_L$	LH
	Parallel Subscriptions	$25152 \cdot BASE_L$	C
	Parallel Subscriptions	1	HQ
	Parallel Publishers	$BASE_L$	LH
	Subscription join/leave min^{-1}	$5.82 \cdot BASE_L$	C
	Subscription join/leave min^{-1}	0	HQ
	Publisher join/leave min^{-1}	0	LH
	Pub/Sub Factor	1 / 1	HQ / C
ProofOfDelivery	Messages min^{-1}	$5.82 \cdot BASE_L$	V
	Parallel Subscriptions	1	HQ
	Parallel Subscriptions	$25152 \cdot BASE_L$	C
	Parallel Publishers	$53 \cdot BASE_L$	V
	Subscription join/leave min^{-1}	$5.82 \cdot BASE_L$	C
	Subscription join/leave min^{-1}	0	HQ
	Publisher join/leave min^{-1}	0	LH
	Pub/Sub Factor	1 / 1	HQ / C
PositionData	Messages min^{-1}	$8.83 \cdot BASE_L$	V
	Parallel Subscriptions	$25152 \cdot BASE_L$	C
	Parallel Publishers	$53 \cdot BASE_L$	V
	Subscription join/leave min^{-1}	$5.82 \cdot BASE_L$	C
	Publisher join/leave min^{-1}	0	V
	Pub/Sub Factor	474.74	C
EnvironmentData	Messages min^{-1}	$2.91 \cdot BASE_L$	LH
	Messages min^{-1}	$2.91 \cdot BASE_L$	V
	Parallel Subscriptions	$7546 \cdot BASE_L$	C
	Parallel Publisher	$BASE_L$	LH
	Parallel Publisher	$53 \cdot BASE_L$	V
	Subscription join/leave min^{-1}	$1.75 \cdot BASE_L$	C
	Publisher join/leave min^{-1}	$1.75 \cdot BASE_L$	V
	Pub/Sub Factor	142.36	C

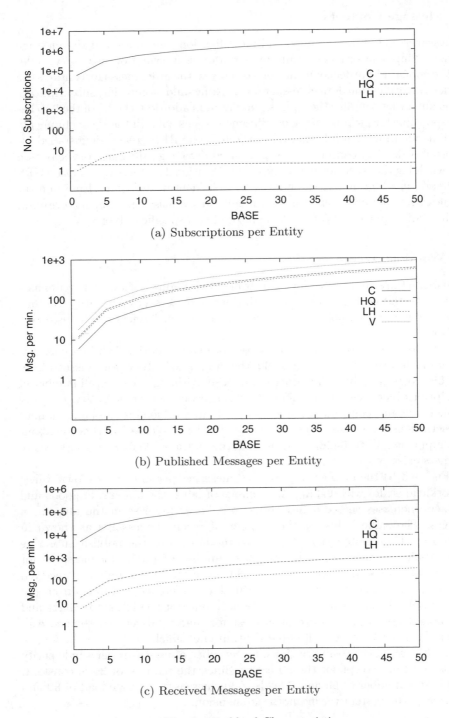

(a) Subscriptions per Entity

(b) Published Messages per Entity

(c) Received Messages per Entity

Fig. 3. Workload Characteristics

4.5 Message Contents

All messages include timestamps and identification information of the message producer. Shipment orders contain further address information necessary to deliver the goods. The order confirmation, as reply to the order message, contains the shipment identification data necessary for tracking- and monitoring-subscriptions. The pickup order contains the address data and, in addition, the ID of the hub being responsible for picking up goods. Shipment scans contain the ID of shipments as well as identification information of the hub the RFID reader is installed at. The proof of delivery contains recipient related data, e.g., the name of the person acknowledging the reception of the shipment. Position data messages contain GPS coordinates in addition to the mandatory vehicle identification data. Environment data messages contain the environment monitoring values, e.g., temperature data, as well as all shipment IDs of goods monitored at a specific hub or vehicle.

4.6 Workload Characeristics

To illustrate the scaling behavior of our workload, Figure 3 shows different characteristics in terms of number of subscriptions and messages per entity. At this, entities are seen as a whole, e.g., LH refers to all hubs, C refers to all customers together.

Figure 3(a) shows the number of subscriptions per entity. While a constant number of subscriptions is issued by HQ, the number of subscriptions issued from C and LH grows linearly with an increasing base. Although the overall number of subscriptions increases, the number of subscriptions per single entity, e.g., per customer, remains constant. Characteristic of our workload is the large number of subscriptions; many customers subscribe in order to receive information about their shipments. With $BASE_L = 10$ already more than 500.000 subscriptions of customers exist.

In Figure 3(b) the number of published messages per minute is shown. Since our workload scales with $BASE_L$, the number of hubs, the amount of goods and customers increases accordingly leading to a linear increase in the number of messages. The same holds for the number of received messages as shown in Figure 3(c). The combination of both figures illustrates the publish/subscribe characteristics of our workload; while the number of published messages for $BASE_L = 10$ ranges from around 60 to 180 per entity, the number of received messages for customers goes up to 50.000. This difference originates from the nature of publish/subscribe communication. In our workload PositionData and EnvironmentData messages are of interest for many different customers, e.g., position data is relevant for all parcels within one vehicle.

As for the number of subscriptions, the number of messages per single entity remains constant except for the HQ entity. Since the number of HQ is constant, an increasing number of LH and C leads to an increased message load of HQ and thus stresses the system yet in another dimension.

5   Conclusion and Outlook

In the ADiWa project we identified the middleware as a key component for a successful adoption of event-based architecture in business environments. In particular, a reliable event transportation mechanism is needed that is highly scalable and performs according to the business needs. To ensure that a notification middleware provides the QoS specified in the service level agreements, a detailed analysis and evaluation has to be performed. This can be achieved by applying comprehensive workloads to compare various setups with respect to different system dimensions in a realistic and independent way.

In this paper we introduced a novel workload for event notification services in highly dynamic environments. We specified three realistic business interactions (including event types and communication patterns) covering several processes of the logistics domain. Characteristic of the logistics domain is a large number of subscribers (e.g., customers) whereas each subscriber receives only a small amount of messages (e.g., tracking information of specific shipments). Further, subscribers and publishers join and leave the system constantly, i.e., the event notification middleware has to orchestrate a highly dynamical environment. In contrast to synthetic workloads often used to demonstrate the capabilities of systems, our workload is specified independently from a particular event notification middleware or standards and allows us to evaluate different features of a middleware in a realistic way. Furthermore, previous realistic workload definitions targeting event-based systems assumed that publishers and consumers stay connected to the middleware. While this assumption is true for many scenarios, in this paper we considered scenarios with a dynamic changing environment with event producers and consumers joining and leaving the system. With each join or leave the event notification routing has to be adapted and potentially calculated subscription aggregates have to be revised. Handling this task efficiently is a key point in providing a high level of service quality. Our workload is the first considering these dynamic environments and allows evaluating system quality in highly dynamic environments.

As part of the ADiWa project, we are working on a prototype implementation of our workload and plan to analyze the service quality of the event notification middleware.

References

1. Appel, S., Sachs, K., Buchmann, A.: Quality of service in event-based systems. In: Proceedings of the 22. GI-Workshop on Foundations of Databases, GvD (2010)
2. Behnel, S., Fiege, L., Mühl, G.: On Quality-of-Service and Publish/Subscribe. In: Proceedings of the 26th IEEE International Conference on Distributed Computing Systems Workshops: Fifth International Workshop on Distributed Event-based Systems (DEBS 2006). IEEE Computer Society, Los Alamitos (2006)
3. Chandy, K.M., Schulte, W.: Event Processing: Designing IT Systems for Agile Companies. Mcgraw-Hill Professional, New York (2009)
4. Chappell, D.: Enterprise Service Bus. O'Reilly, Sebastopol (2004)

5. Geppert, A., Gatziu, S., Dittrich, K.R.: A Designer's Benchmark for Active Database Management Systems: oo7 Meets the BEAST. In: Sellis, T.K. (ed.) RIDS 1995. LNCS, vol. 985, Springer, Heidelberg (1995)
6. Hinze, A., Sachs, K., Buchmann, A.: Event-Based Applications and Enabling Technologies. In: Proceedings of the International Conference on Distributed Event-Based Systems (DEBS 2009). ACM, New York (2009)
7. McCormick, B., Madden, L.: Open architecture publish subscribe benchmarking. In: Proceedings of the OMG Real-Time and Embedded Systems Workshop (2005)
8. Mendes, M.R.N., Bizarro, P., Marques, P.: A framework for performance evaluation of complex event processing systems. In: Proceedings of the Second International Conference on Distributed Event-based Systems (DEBS 2008): Demonstration Session. ACM, New York (2008)
9. Moore, J., Collins, T., Shrestha, S.: An open architecture for detecting earthquakes using mobile devices, vol. 1, pp. 437–441 (April 2010)
10. Mühl, G., Fiege, L., Pietzuch, P.: Distributed Event-Based Systems. Springer-Verlag New York, Inc., Secaucus (2006)
11. Sachs, K.: Performance Modeling and Benchmarking of Event-Based Systems. PhD thesis, TU Darmstadt (2010)
12. Sachs, K., Appel, S., Kounev, S., Buchmann, A.: Benchmarking Publish/Subscribe-based Messaging Systems. In: Yoshikawa, M., Meng, X., Yumoto, T., Ma, Q., Sun, L., Watanabe, C. (eds.) DASFAA 2010. LNCS, vol. 6193, pp. 203–214. Springer, Heidelberg (2010)
13. Sachs, K., Kounev, S., Bacon, J., Buchmann, A.: Performance evaluation of message-oriented middleware using the SPECjms2007 benchmark. Performance Evaluation 66(8), 410–434 (2009)
14. United Parcel Service of America, Inc. UPS facts website (August 2010), http://www.ups.com/content/us/en/about/facts/worldwide.html
15. Varshney, U.: Pervasive healthcare and wireless health monitoring. Mob. Netw. Appl. 12(2-3), 113–127 (2007)

Live Business Intelligence for the Real-Time Enterprise

Malu Castellanos, Umeshwar Dayal, and Meichun Hsu

Hewlett Packard Laboratories
Palo Alto, USA
{malu.castellanos,umeshwar.dayal,meichun.hsu}@hp.com

Abstract. We present our vision of a *unified data management and analytics platform*, which we call "Live Business Intelligence" (LiveBI) that transforms business intelligence from the traditional back-office, report-oriented platform, to an enabler for delivering data-intensive, real-time analytics that transform business operations in the modern enterprise. The LiveBI Platform leverages data management technology and fuses it with new paradigms for analytics and application development. We present the architecture of the platform and illustrate its value in a couple of applications.

1 Introduction

Many emerging application scenarios motivate the creation of a new business intelligence (BI) platform and BI solutions that deliver quality insights and predictive analytics within actionable time windows (i.e., "at the speed of business"). Examples of such scenarios include: situational awareness, sentiment analysis, environmental sensing, and smart meters and smart appliances. These BI solutions will need to integrate information of diverse data types from an increasing number of sources, handle explosive growth in data volumes, and deliver shorter cycle times to quality decisions as well as a higher degree of automation that, on the one hand, will require sophisticated aggregated analysis, and on the other hand, must be personalized or individually targeted.

We envision the existence of a *unified data management and analytics platform*, which we call "Live Business Intelligence" (LiveBI), and which transforms BI from the traditional back-office, report-oriented platform, to an enabler for delivering data-intensive analytics that transform operational business processes. LiveBI platform enables 3 business loops, strategic (targeted by traditional BI platforms), operational (targeted by operational data store (ODS) platforms), and automation loops (targeted by complex event processing (CEP) and main memory database platforms), to operate from a unified framework. In doing so, it is capable of delivering complex analytics over large volumes of data while reducing the latency to quality analytics results.

The LiveBI Platform leverages data management technology and fuses it with new paradigms for analytics and application development. The platform supports declarative models for computation and data management conducive to massively parallel processing. It integrates multiple types of analytics that currently are supported by separately managed technologies: information extraction, information transformation, analytics over static data, analytics over streaming data, and computation

K. Sachs, I. Petrov, and P. Guerrero (Eds.): Buchmann Festschrift, LNCS 6462, pp. 325–336, 2010.

for visualization. Our approach to the LiveBI platform breaks down the stove-piped barriers that have contributed to significant latency and cost.

In the BI software platform arena, LiveBI is closest to existing categories of ETL, BI reporting, stream databases, rule or CEP engines, data flow engines, and data warehouses, appliances, and accelerators. Our goal, however, is to create a unified platform supporting an advanced model of analytic applications that enables automation in parallel deployment and data management. Table 1 summarizes LiveBI's position against a number of representative existing and emerging product categories.

Table 1. LiveBI positioning against representative product categories

	Data mgmt - scale		Analytics - scale		Analytics– event/data flow		Live Analytics + Data Mgmt
	SMP	MPP	SMP	MPP	pull	push	
DBMS	x	x					
Analytics Engine			x		x		
ETL			x		x		
CEP							
Stream Processing Engines				x		x	
Live BI		x		x	x	x	x

In a nutshell, the vision of LiveBI is one of a unified system that removes barriers across different dimensions:

1. Latency dimension: process both streaming and stored data.

2. Data dimension: process both structured and unstructured data.

3. Architectural dimension: data management and analytics are integrated in the same platform; data is not pulled out of the database into an external analytics engine.

In this paper we outline the architectural components of the LiveBI platform and some of the main research problems that need to be addressed to enable the realization of these components (section 2). We also describe some compelling applications of LiveBI that clearly demonstrate its value and benefits over existing solutions (section 3).

2   LiveBI Architecture

The overall system architecture of the LiveBI Platform is shown in figure 1. The system is layered on top of a massively parallel, shared nothing (cluster, Grid, or Cloud) Infrastructure layer. Data from many different sources (streaming and batch-oriented, structured and unstructured) is ingested into the system through the Information Capture and Access layer. Depending on the latency requirements, fast moving data streams can be piped directly to the Analytics Execution layer without loading it first into a data warehouse, or the data can be captured in a repository for later processing, or both. The Analytics Execution layer provides highly parallel execution of query operations and analytic computations drawn from a library of smart operators. Applications are developed as data flow graphs, whose nodes are these smart operators. The Optimization and Automation layer takes as input a specification of the data flow graph representing the processing required by the application, and a set of performance and other quality objectives, and produces an optimal plan that can be executed by the Analytics Execution layer. The results of the processing are delivered through the Interaction and Service Integration layer, which also provides multi-modal interfaces for user interaction.

The rest of this section describes the functionality of these layers and some of the research challenges we are addressing to realize this architecture.

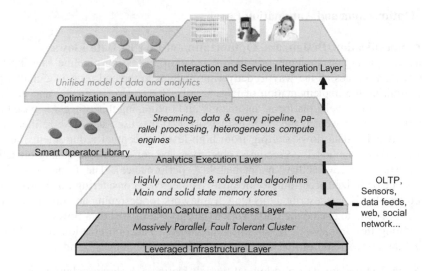

Fig. 1. LiveBI Platform

2.1 Interaction and Service Integration Layer

This layer consists of components and tools that enable the Live BI Platform to easily capture, deliver, visualize, analyze, and act on information in multiple domains.

Visual analytics is an important mechanism for delivery of analytic results, especially in the context of Live BI. The challenges here are to enable real-time interactive exploration and analysis of high dimensionality data streams, including unstructured information. Research to solve these challenges addresses the following issues: (1) Mechanisms for visualizing and interacting with streaming data. (2) Techniques for integrating text analytics with visual methods. (3) Automation of the selection of parameters for visualization, avoiding clutter and focusing the user's attention on the most interesting patterns through smart analytics (e.g., motif pattern detection, neighborhood marking, alerts). (4) Tight integration of automated analytics (e.g., correlation, similarity, clustering, and classification) with visual methods. (5) Incorporation of users' expert domain knowledge to enable interactive and collaborative exploration, discovery, and analysis.

Our approach is to deal with user interactions in the context of tasks that the user is trying to accomplish, which may span locations (e.g. home, store, work etc.), multiple touch points (e.g. online, discussions with friends and family, mobile etc.) and tools (e.g. to-do lists, email, SMS, social networking websites, reminders etc.). Mobile devices play an important role in determining the context associated with user interactions. These devices can be used to obtain indicators of the current context or environment in which the user is interacting with the service.

From an architectural point of view, this layer has a SOA based unifying architecture that exposes the visual analytics and user interaction management capabilities as composable services, deployed on the 'cloud' [1]. In addition, the visual analytics techniques become "smart operators" to be included in the Smart Operator Library.

2.2   Optimization and Automation Layer

2.2.1   Specification, Design, and Optimization of Live BI Data Flows

Today, designing and implementing the information processing pipeline, starting from the raw data sources all the way to delivering insights to the end user, is a challenging task, requiring the implementation of ETL scripts, SQL queries, reports, and analytics programs. In the LiveBI platform, automating and optimizing this process is based on a framework (which we call the QoX framework [2]) that uses step-wise refinement to produce detailed data flows starting from high-level conceptual requirements, and incorporates both functional (correctness) objectives and non-functional quality objectives (e.g. freshness, recoverability, maintainability, performance). The framework allows flows to be optimized according to the quality objectives, considering trade-offs among objectives. In [3], we described this QoX framework for designing and optimizing ETL flows. We intend to extend the framework to end-to-end LiveBI data flows.

Enabling this framework to automate the design and optimization of end-to-end LiveBI data flows requires that the following research challenges be addressed:

1. Specification language and logical model: Define a declarative language for specifying the functional and quality objectives of the end-to-end flows, and define a logical data flow model into which the business-level specifications can be translated and which serves as the input to the optimizer.
2. Design methodology and tools: Create tools that map from the high-level specifications to the logical model, preserving the functional and quality objectives.
3. QoX-driven optimization: The quality objectives define a multi-objective optimization problem, where trade-offs may need to be made among different objectives. This requires to formulate cost models and optimization techniques that enable these trade-offs to be made automatically, and result in optimized execution plans that can be passed to the Execution layer. In [4], we showed how to optimize ETL flows for fault tolerance, latency, and performance.
4. Information extraction operators: Define a set of operators for extracting structured information from less-structured data sources, so that this information can be integrated into the end-to-end data flows. These operators will also be included in the Smart Operator Library and can be incorporated into the design and optimization of data flows.

2.2.2 Physical Design Tuning and Workload Management

One big challenge in LiveBI is to dramatically reduce the cost of ownership by making its components easy to manage and tune. This requires tools to simplify or automate the many management tasks that today require highly skilled administrators to set and tune thousands of configuration parameters. To this end, two aspects of the problem need to be addressed:

The first one is to develop a physical design tool with the capability to handle LiveBI mixed workloads and perform on-line tuning so as to dynamically adapt the physical database design to continuously changing workloads. In addition, this tool should consider new data structures and access methods (e.g., new kinds of indexes) and new layouts (e.g., column stores) which are part of the execution layer of the LiveBI stack. Finally, the impact of the QoX qualities of the dataflows of the specification and optimization layer on physical design and tuning needs to be considered as well.

The workload management capabilities of the layer should go beyond management of traditional data warehouses. First, it needs to manage more complex mixed workloads consisting of ETL jobs, queries, reports, analytics and stream processing tasks (since these will all be running on the LiveBI platform). Second, it needs to manage workloads that might be distributed over multiple engines (for purposes of load balancing, fault tolerance, or customer preference). Third, it should manage LiveBI workloads running over virtual resources (deployed in the Cloud, for instance).

Managing a workload that consists of a diverse set of queries against large amounts of complex data is an expensive, labor-intensive task. The scale, complexity and loose coupling of a Live BI system add tremendous uncertainty to this picture. Workload management thus becomes substantially difficult in the context of Live BI for exactly the same reasons that it also becomes critically important. Automating policy management to provide a feedback-based mechanism that will automatically adjust workload management admission control, scheduling, and execution control policies in response to dynamic changes to a running workload is of utmost importance [5].

2.3 Analytics Execution and Operator Library Layer

2.3.1 Data-Intensive Analytics Engine

LiveBI is a data-intensive and knowledge-rich *computation pipeline* from data streams to high-level analytics results, in which the dynamically collected data and the statically stored data are used in combination. The existing database query processing and user-defined function (UDF) technologies have several limitations in handling unbounded stream data, applying a query to data chunks divided by time-windows and supporting general graph-structured dataflow. These problems have been gradually addressed by related work with the common characteristics of building a stream processing system from scratch or providing a middleware layer on top of the query engine, rather than extending the query engine directly.

The unified LiveBI engine extends the query engine while achieving high performance. A parallel database engine constitutes a suitable foundation to develop a massively-parallel, scale-out LiveBI infrastructure. Two major issues need to be tackled [need reference: Qiming and Mei's papers]:

(1) Enabling query engine for stream processing. The general goal is to allow the query engine to execute a single, long-standing, truly continuous query on the unbounded streaming data often divided by time-windows.

(2) Extending SQL to functional form-SQL (FF-SQL) based on a calculus of queries, to *declaratively* express general graph-structured dataflows, and extend the query engine to support the execution of FF-SQL queries. This includes: (a) developing a query algebra by introducing functional forms on queries to express graph-structured dataflow, and (b) developing a super query container to interact with the query executer for carrying out data intensive computations in a query network.

2.3.2 High-Performance Analytic Operators

Not only does the LiveBI platform need to achieve effective integration of analytics with data management, it also needs to exploit emerging parallel architecture to reduce time to solution. Parallel architectures consisting of commodity components promise to provide high performance at a much lower cost. For example, Google's MapReduce is built on the principle of large-scale low-cost cluster computing. Parallel co-processors, such as Intel's Larrabee processors and the OpenCL effort, and Nvidia's CUDA-enabled general purpose graphics processors (GPGPUs), also have great potential. The goal here is to develop *high-performance implementations* of core analytic operators in the context of emerging parallel architecture.

We argue that memory utilization is a crucial factor in data intensive analytics. We propose to refine memory utilization across multiple levels - cache, memory, disks, and distributed memory, and use it to devise data movement algorithms that optimize performance of very large (both in terms of data set size and in non-linear time computation) analytical computations. Research should address the following: (1) Definition of the new concept of memory utilization. (2) Selection of a suite of operators. (3) Design of algorithms for the suite of operators to achieve high performance and memory utilization. (4) Application of the principle to high performance implementation of core analytic operators.

2.3.3 Multi-dimensional and Multi-level Streaming Analytic Operators

Enterprises are starting to actively monitor data streams and need to react quickly to unfolding events. For example, detecting the cause of a power outage in a smart grid can be implemented as a continuously running OLAP aggregation of the power consumption at all different levels of the grid. Examples of the problems that are important to these new applications include: (a) continuous OLAP queries (Skyline, Iceberg, Pivot, Top k, etc); (b) multi-level, multi-dimensional sequence and pattern detection; and (c) multi-level, multi-dimensional learning (outlier detection, clustering, association rules, etc).

The *Smart Operator* layer in the LiveBI includes new operators that are impossible or extremely expensive to realize today. These operators will, in turn, enable a whole new class of applications. In the context of LiveBI applications, it is crucial to have *streaming versions* of the operators and analytic tasks, where availability of data is a function of time, and the analytic results are refined continuously over time. These operators should be parallelizable and should scale up (and out) along with the LiveBI environment, and they should support seamless time windows over streaming and historical data [6, 7].

2.4   Information Capture and Access Layer

2.4.1   High-Bandwidth Information Capture and Robust Query Processing

Some streaming applications require that input data, intermediate data, or output items be captured in a persistent store yet be made available for query & analysis with minimal or no delay. This problem is very similar to the old tension in data warehouses between *high load bandwidth* and *query processing performance* – for high load bandwidth, one must avoid indexes and other auxiliary data structures; for high performance query processing, a database must provide indexes, histograms (or equivalent synopsis information), materialized views, etc.

Multiple traditional indexes permit optimal query performance at the expense of rather poor load performance. Heaps without indexes permit load at hardware write bandwidth but lead to poor query performance, in particular for highly selective queries. Partitioned B-trees combine high load bandwidth and high query performance but only at the expense of intermediate operations that reorganize and optimize the B-tree indexes. Thus, the load bandwidth that can be sustained over a long period is less than the ideal load bandwidth by a small factor.

LiveBI requires a technique that combines high information capture bandwidth with high query processing performance immediately after new information is committed to the data store. This technique will enable the following: a) capture and index new information at a small fraction of hardware bandwidth (e.g., ¼ of disk write bandwidth), b) perform insertions and deletions (roll-in and roll-out) at this high bandwidth, c) proceed with information capture and query processing concurrently, each at half of their maximal (stand-alone) bandwidth, and d) sustain such high bandwidths indefinitely as long as storage space remains.

Information capture should pair with *robust* query and analytics processing. Robust processing reduces total cost of ownership and the risk of poor performance, system overload, and associated costs. The goal is to enhance robustness of complex analytics processing in addition to query processing. The research involves developing algorithms that measurably improve robustness of the system.

2.4.2   Column Store

The main advantages of a columnar data layout are: (a) reading just the subset of columns relevant to any given query, (b) higher compression rates for any given column, as the values of a single column exhibit less entropy than a set of values from different columns, and (c) the ability to implement several code optimizations given that operators operate on a vector of packed values belonging to the same column [8].

All current column-stores have opted for developing database software from scratch, instead of modifying existing row-store systems. While the performance of a column-store is highly desirable in a Live BI platform, where a large fraction of analytic tasks are powered by selecting columns in data sets, the rich feature set of traditional row-store database systems is indispensable for the rest of the tasks supported by the Live BI platform. Therefore, our BI platform would benefit the most by incorporating a row-store database system that can also reap the performance benefits of columnar data orientation. To this end, research aims at developing a set of techniques and algorithms to support column-store functionality inside a row-store with a minimal set of changes in the row-store code base.

3 Applications

In this section, we describe two representative LiveBI applications that we are developing. These applications exercise different aspects of the LiveBI architecture shown in Figure 1. The first application, Situational Awareness, illustrates the integration of insights gleaned from unstructured and structured data, and deals with both streaming and stored data. The second application, Live Operational Intelligence, illustrates the application of scalable analytics to a combination of time-series and event steam data and stored historical data to derive insights for improving business operations.

3.1 Situational Awareness

In today's fast paced and competitive economy, it is increasingly important for companies to become aware of events occurring in the world that can affect their business. We call this *situational awareness* and correspond to what [9] calls situational business intelligence. It is an application of LiveBI where the goal is to provide real-time (or better said, right-time) actionable insight to support decision making in business operations. For instance, when a natural disaster occurs in some part of the world, it is important for a manufacturing company to know which contracts exist with suppliers located in the affected region so that it can take appropriate actions to minimize the effect on its business operations [10, 11]. As another example, for the same manufacturing company, it is important to know what customers are saying (i.e., what is their sentiment) about its new products or its competitors' products so that it can intervene in blog discussions or provide immediate feedback to the development or support teams. An important requirement of situational aware applications is to provide timely insight into these situations so that appropriate actions can be taken.

In general terms, situational awareness consists of two phases. In the first phase (Extraction) facts are extracted from different data sources [12]; and in the second phase (Correlation) these facts are correlated to detect potentially relevant situations. Then, queries from the end users (ad-hoc queries) and from BI applications (predefined queries) can be formulated over the extracted and correlated information to get insight into these situations. A simple example of a situational awareness query could be: "*give me the names of the products in product line Laptops that are receiving greater than 2:1 ratio of negative to positive comments on social media web sites*". A BI application could include this kind of query to alert the marketing manager for this product line, together with links to the actual reviews. A more sophisticated query could be "give *me the aggregated value of the contracts on deals greater than 1 million dollars that exist with suppliers in any region affected by a natural disaster*". A BI application including such a query could alert a business executive with the information of the natural disaster, together with the contract IDs and contact information of the suppliers in the affected region.

In the extraction phase, relevant information can come from any kind of data source: stored or streaming, structured or unstructured data, and internal or external to the organization. In general, stored data sources are updated over time, and for our purposes, they can be viewed as slow data streams. In the contracts example, the slow stream would be the internal contracts collection (where new contracts come in at a relatively slow pace) and the fast stream would be news feeds like the New York

Times RSS feeds that contain news about world events. In the sentiment analysis example, the slow stream would be the IT news on new products and the fast stream could be tweets and blogs.

Once relevant information has been extracted from the data sources, correlations are detected to identify relevant situations. One data stream (e.g., New York Times RSS feeds) contains interesting events, and the other contains information about business entities (e.g., suppliers, products) that can be affected by the events. By correlating them, we can identify which entities are potentially affected by the events. Notice that doing this task manually is infeasible since there is so much information in both streams that it would be impossible to keep track of all the potentially relevant events and all the entities that can be affected by them. LiveBI addresses this problem and reduces the time and effort to develop situational awareness applications (where data flows integrate structured, unstructured, slow and fast streams) and execute them (extracting, transforming and correlating the streams) while satisfying different quality and performance objectives. Four of the main components of the LiveBI platform are essential here:

a) An application development interface which allows situational aware applications to be expressed declaratively as data flow graphs. Figure 2 illustrates a simple data flow for sentiment analysis to illustrate this concept.

b) A set of smart operators to perform different functions required to detect potentially relevant situations. These functions include: text mining operations (for extracting structured data such as events and entities from text [12], cleansing extracted data, mining customer opinions, classifying documents, and so on); and streaming correlation operations to identify which events affect which business entities. Any of these operations, together with SQL query operations, can be included in the data flow graphs to create a situational awareness application.

c) A QoX-driven optimizer.that takes the data flow graph specification of the application and generates an optimal execution plan that satisfies different quality objectives specified by the user. These quality objectives may include: performance (e.g., minimum number of situations detected per minute), freshness (e.g., time elapsed from an event being reported to the time it is detected as a relevant situation), accuracy (e.g., at least 80% of true relevant situations detected).

d) An execution engine that executes the plan produced by the optimizer.

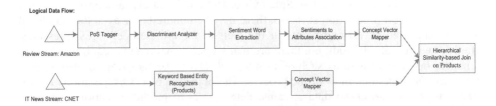

Fig. 2. Sentiment Analysis Data Flow

For situational-aware applications, the main data flow can be separated into two primary components: information extraction (IE) where the structured or unstructured data sources are transformed into concept vectors, and hybrid query processing where these vectors are correlated. The analysis challenge in situational awareness is to query both stored and streaming data. These queries could involve standard SPJ (Select, Project, Join), roll-ups and correlations. Computing correlations is a critical operation for situational awareness. Although correlations can be expressed in terms of joins, performing correlation via exact keyword matching or via equi-joins is overly restrictive in the context of situational awareness. A new operator, the hierarchical-based similarity join (or correlation) has been defined for this purpose [10, 13]. The basic idea is that of using the extracted information as features and extending them along predefined hierarchies. The similarity is computed in terms of hierarchical neighbors using fast streaming data structures called Hierarchical Neighborhood Trees (HNT). Based on HNT, a scale based neighborhood relationship can be specified which measures the level in the HNT tree of the closest common ancestor. The hierarchical neighborhoods are critical to finding correlations between the two streams (e.g., the contracts and the news items) [10, 13]. For example, assume a contract doesn't mention Mexico by name but is negotiated in Mexican pesos, and a news article talks about a hurricane in the Gulf of Mexico. The peso belongs to a hierarchy where one of its ancestors is Mexico, and similarly Gulf of Mexico belongs to a hierarchy that also contains Mexico as an ancestor. In this case, the contract and the news article are neighbors at the level of Mexico. As a result we not only learn that these are neighbors but also that they are related through "Mexico".

3.2 Live Operations Intelligence

Business process complexity is growing at an exponential rate. A breakdown in the operational management of these complex business processes can have catastrophic results. As sensor technology develops, enterprises are now increasingly able to place sensors and measure different aspects of their business processes. Managing and analyzing all this sensor and event data is a big challenge for human operators. The use of live BI for operations intelligence (we call this *Live Operations Intelligence*) can result in high efficiency and in being able to use business operations data for true competitive advantage.

Examples of domains that can benefit from operations intelligence solutions include: Oil and Gas Drilling and Production, IT Operations Management, Healthcare Operations, Smart Transportation, Smart Grid, and Public Safety, amongst others. For instance, in an oil production scenario, there may be hundreds (or even thousands) of sensors deployed at various points in the well to monitor temperatures, pressures, fluid flow rates, etc. In addition, there are many operational events (equipment maintenance, operational actions such as turning on valves, weather related events, etc.) that can affect the outcomes of the process. The objective of Live Operations Intelligence is to monitor these data streams, detect or even predict situations that may cause operational problems (e.g., production losses), diagnose such situations, and recommend corrective or preventive actions that help to avert or minimize the impact of problems on the operational process.

Figure 3 shows a general data flow for such Live Operations Intelligence applications. Streaming time-series data from sensors or event sequence data from operational logs is analyzed in real-time to detect patterns or events of interest. These might be anomalies in operational parameters, sudden changes in value of some variable, rapid fluctuations in value, or some other domain-dependent patterns. This phase of processing converts raw time-series data or low level event sequence data into streams of patterns or meaningful events. These higher level events are then subject to further analysis to detect complex events, discover correlations, perform diagnostics and root cause analyses, and predict events that are likely to occur in the future. The models that drive these analytic operations are typically learnt from historical data. For instance, we might mine historical event data to identify frequently occurring patterns (or *motifs*) and learn rules for detecting such patterns. These rules are then installed in the stream processing path of the data flow shown in Figure N to detect occurrences of the patterns in real time. Analogously, we build diagnostic and prediction models by mining historical data, and apply these models in real-time to the event streams. Finally, since the operational processes being monitored and analyzed typically exist in physical environments that change over time, we have to apply continuous learning techniques to adapt the models as the process changes.

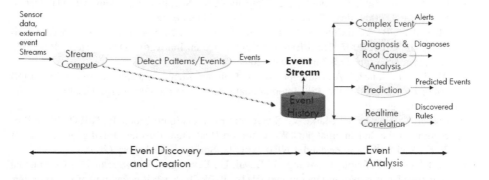

Fig. 3. Live Operations Intelligence Data Flow

4   Conclusions

We have presented our vision of Live BI, a unified data and analytics platform that aims to deliver quality insights and predictive analytics within actionable time windows (i.e., "at the speed of business"). It integrates data-flow and streaming analytics with large scale data management, exploits massively parallel processing, and promises to significantly reduce latency and cost in large scale business intelligence. The value of such a platform has been illustrated with two concrete applications.

Acknowledgement. The authors wish to thank the researchers who have contributed to the Live BI research: Qiming Chen, Mohamed Dekhil, Goetz Graefe, Chetan Gupta, Ming Hao, Jhilmil Jain, Harumi Kuno, Choudur Lakshminarayan, Abhay Mehta, Alkis Simitsis, Krishna Viswanathan, Janet Wiener, Song Wang, Kevin Wilkinson, Ren Wu, and Bin Zhang.

References

1. Eidt, E., Salle, M., Wallikci, J.: Cloud Ecosystems: Architectural Principles and Preferences. Whitepaper (June 2009)
2. Dayal, U., Castellanos, M., Simitsis, A., Wilkinson, K.: Data integration flows for business intelligence. In: EDBT 2009: Proceedings of the 12th International Conference on Extending Database Technology: Advances in Database Technology, Saint Petersburg, Russia, vol. 360, pp. 1–11 (March 2009)
3. Simitsis, A., Wilkinson, K., Castellanos, M., Dayal, U.: QoX-driven ETL design: reducing the cost of ETL consulting engagements. In: SIGMOD 2009: Proceedings of the 35th SIGMOD International Conference on Management of Data, Providence, Rhode Island, USA, pp. 953–960 (June 2009)
4. Simitsis, A., Wilkinson, K., Dayal, U., Castellanos, M.: Optimizing ETL Work-flows for Fault-Tolerance. In: ICDE 2010: Proceedings of the 26th IEEE International Conference on Data Engineering, Los Angeles, USA (March 2010)
5. Stefan Krompass, S., Dayal, U., Kuno, H., Kemper, A.: Dynamic Workload Management for Very Large Data Warehouses: Juggling Feathers and Bowling Balls. In: VLDB 2007: Proceedings of the 33rd International Conference on Very Large Databases, Vienna, Austria, pp. 1105–1115 (September 2007)
6. Golab, L., Johnson, T., Seidel, J.S., Shkapenyuk, V.: Stream warehousing with DataDepot. In: SIGMOD 2009, Providence, USA, pp. 847–854 (June 2009)
7. Magdalena, B., YongChul, K., Nathan, K., Dennis, L.: Moirae: History-Enhanced Monitoring. In: CIDR 2007: Third Biennial Conference on Innovative Data Systems Research, Asilomar, USA, pp. 375–386 (January 2007)
8. Abadi, D.J., Boncz, P.A., Harizopoulos, S.: Column-oriented Database Systems. In: VLDB 2009: Proceedings of the 35th International Conference on Very Large Databases, Lyon, France (August 2009)
9. Loeser, A., Hueske, F., Markl, V.: Situational Business Intelligence. In: BIRTE 2009: Proceeding of the 2nd International Workshop on Real-Time Business Intelligence at VLDB 2009, Auckland, New Zealand. LNBIP, vol. 27, Springer, Heidelberg (2008)
10. Castellanos, M., Gupta, C., Wang, S., Dayal, U.: Leveraging Web Streams for Contractual Situational Awareness in Operational BI. In: BEWEB 2010: Proceedings of the 1st International Workshop on Business Intelligence for the Web at EDBT 2010, Lausanne, Switzerland (March 2010)
11. Castellanos, M., Dayal, U.: FACTS: An Approach to Unearth Legacy Contracts. In: WEB 2004: Proceedings of the 1st International Workshop on Electronic Contracting, San Diego, USA (July 2004)
12. Sarawagi, S.: Information Extraction. Foundations and Trends in Databases 1(3), 261–377 (2008)
13. Castellanos, M., Wang, S., Dayal, U., Gupta, C.: SIE-OBI: A Streaming Information Extraction Platform for Operational Business Intelligence. In: SIGMOD 2010, Indianapolis, USA (June 2010)

Author Index

Printing: Mercedes-Druck, Berlin
Binding: Stein+Lehmann, Berlin